Taking
SIDES

Clashing Views on
Controversial Issues in
**Business Ethics
and Society**

Third Edition

Taking SIDES

Clashing Views on Controversial Issues in
Business Ethics and Society
Third Edition

Edited, Selected, and with Introductions by

Lisa H. Newton
Fairfield University
and
Maureen M. Ford
Fairfield University

The Dushkin Publishing Group, Inc.

To our husbands—Victor J. Newton, Jr., and James H. L. Ford, Jr.

Photo Acknowledgments

Part 1   UN PHOTO 150,094 by Yutaka Nagaza
Part 2   United Motor Manufacturing
Part 3   Pamela Carley/DPG
Part 4   UNITED NATIONS/WHO/Almasy
Part 5   UNHCR Photo No. 12130 by Y. Müller

Cover Art Acknowledgment

Charles Vitelli

Library of Congress Cataloging-in-Publication Data

Main entry under title:
  Taking sides: clashing views on controversial issues in business ethics and society/edited,
  selected, and with introductions by Lisa H. Newton and Maureen M. Ford.—3rd ed.
  Includes bibliographical references and index.
  1. Business ethics—United States. 2. Industry—Social aspects—United States. 3. Social
  responsibility of business—United States. I. Newton, Lisa H., *comp.* II. Ford, Maureen
  M., *comp.*
    HF5387.T36   658.4'08—dc20
    ISBN: 1-56134-247-5   93-50063

Printed on Recycled Paper

DPG

The Dushkin Publishing Group, Inc.

PREFACE

> From the very beginning of critical thought, we find the distinction between topics susceptible of certain knowledge and topics about which uncertain opinions are available. The dawn of this distinction, explicitly entertained, is the dawn of modern mentality. It introduces criticism.
>
> —Alfred North Whitehead
> *Adventures of Ideas* (1933)

This volume contains 36 selections, presented in a pro and con format, that debate a total of 18 different controversial issues in business ethics. In this book we ask you, the reader, to examine the accepted practices of business in light of justice, right, and human dignity. We ask you to consider what moral imperatives and values should be at work in the conduct of business.

This method of presenting opposing views on an issue grows out of the ancient learning method of *dialogue*. Two presumptions lead us to seek the truth in a dialogue between opposed positions: The first presumption is that the truth is really out there and that it is important to find it. The second is that no one of us has all of it (the truth). The way then to reach the truth is to form our initial opinions on a subject and give voice to them in public. Then we let others with differing opinions reply, and while they are doing so, we listen carefully. The truth that comes into being in the public space of the dialogue becomes part of your opinion—now a more informed opinion, and now based on the reasoning that emerged in the course of the airing of opposing views.

Each issue in this volume has an issue *introduction*, which sets the stage for the debate as it is argued in the YES and NO selections. Each issue concludes with a *postscript* that makes some final observations and points the way to other questions related to the issue. The introductions and postscripts do not preempt what is the reader's own task: to achieve a critical and informed view of the issue at stake. In reading an issue and forming your own opinion, you should not feel confined to adopt one or the other of the positions presented. There are positions in between the given views, or totally outside of them, and the *suggestions for further reading* that appear in each issue postscript should help you find resources to continue your study of the subject. At the back of the book is a listing of all the *contributors to this volume*, which will give you information on the philosophers, business professors, businesspeople, and business commentators whose views are debated here.

Changes to this edition There are 11 completely new issues: *Should the United States Have a National Industrial Policy?* (Issue 1); *Are Business and*

i

Medicine Ethically Incompatible? (Issue 3); *Are Leveraged Buyouts Bad for the Bottom Line?* (Issue 4); *Are Corporate Codes of Ethics Just for Show?* (Issue 5); *Should Women Have the Same Right to Work as Men?* (Issue 6); *Does Blowing the Whistle Violate Company Loyalty?* (Issue 8); *Should Concern for Drug Abuse Overrule Concerns for Employee Privacy?* (Issue 9); *Are Pharmaceutical Price Controls Justifiable?* (Issue 10); *Should Property Rights Prevail Over Environmental Protection?* (Issue 14); *Is Incineration a Cost-Efficient Way to Dispose of Solid Waste?* (Issue 15); and *Should the Less Developed Countries Be Encouraged to Develop High Technology?* (Issue 18). In addition, the YES article has been changed in the issue on product liability (Issue 12) in order to bring a different perspective to the debate. In all, there are 22 new readings. Wherever appropriate, new introductions and postscripts have been provided.

A word to the instructor An *Instructor's Manual With Test Questions* (multiple-choice and essay) is available through the publisher for the instructor using *Taking Sides* in the classroom. And a general guidebook, *Using Taking Sides in the Classroom*, which discusses methods and techniques for integrating the pro-con approach into any classroom setting, is also available.

Acknowledgments We were greatly assisted in this enterprise by Mimi Egan, publisher for the Taking Sides series, who was unstinting with her time, effort, and insight. Praise and thanks are also due to our families, without whose patience and support this volume would never have been completed. Special thanks go to those who responded to the questionnaire with specific suggestions for the second edition:

Daniel A. Augsburger
Andrews University

Karen S. Burn
Fort Lewis College

Hugh M. Curtler
Southwest State University

Gerard P. Downey
La Salle University

Ronald Duska
Rosemont College

Francis Foley
Berry College

Timothy C. Fout
University of Louisville

Ronald R. Gauch
Marist College

Susan Helf
University of Washington

Alec Hill
Seattle Pacific University

Frank L. Kahl
Ohlone College

Leon Levitt
Madonna University

Dean C. Ludwig
University of Toledo

Ronald L. Massanari
Alma College

Corinne Nicholson
Saint Andrews Presbyterian
    College

John Pogue
Lebanon Valley College

Robert D. Waldo
University of Puget Sound

George E. Weber
Whitworth College

Lisa H. Newton
Fairfield University

Maureen M. Ford
Fairfield University

CONTENTS IN BRIEF

CONTENTS

Management professor Lester Thurow argues that in order to achieve global
business success, the United States should adopt a national industrial policy.
Cynthia A. Beltz, a technology policy analyst, argues that a system in which
government targets specific industries for promotion is no substitute for the
workings of the free market.

News reporter Carolyn Lochhead asserts that agribusiness cartels—who,
through federal "marketing orders," determine the amount of produce that
independent fruit growers may sell—have frozen the market. The Farmers
for an Orderly Market, a coalition of citrus growers formed to defend flow-
to-market regulation, support federal marketing orders as the only way to
ensure a 12-month supply of high-quality fruit.

Fredrick R. Abrams, director of the Clinical Ethics Consultation Group, argues that there is an essential difference between the ethic of the physician and the ethic of the businessperson. Associate professor David R. Larson argues that in any business, including medicine, conscientious attention to the customer is essential for long-term profits.

Frank A. Olson, chief executive officer of the Hertz Corporation, argues that the unprecedented level of debt contracted by major U.S. corporations in the 1980s could lead to economic disaster. Michael T. Tucker, an associate professor of finance, argues that the increased indebtedness in the United States is simply an example of efficient markets at work.

LaRue Tone Hosmer, a professor of corporate strategies, argues that codes of ethics are ineffective in bringing about more ethical behavior on the part of employees. Professor of philosophy Lisa H. Newton holds that the formation and adoption of corporate codes are valuable processes.

George J. Annas, a professor of law and medicine, argues that women may not
be legally excluded from traditionally male jobs without some real relation of
gender to job performance. Hugh M. Finneran, former senior labor counsel for
PPG Industries, Inc., holds that women should be excluded from industries
involving substances that can deform or destroy a growing embryo.

Professor of philosophy Lisa H. Newton argues that programs of preferential
treatment represent reverse discrimination and are therefore unjust. Professor
of philosophy Richard Wasserstrom argues that there is no inconsistency in
objecting to discrimination while favoring preferential treatment.

Philosopher Sissela Bok asserts that blowing the whistle involves a breach of
loyalty to the employer. Philosopher Robert A. Larmer argues that attempting
to stop unethical company activities exemplifies company loyalty.

Michael A. Verespej, a writer for *Industry Week,* argues that a majority of employees are tolerant of drug testing. Jennifer Moore, a researcher of business
ethics and business law, asserts that employers' concerns about drug abuse
should not override employees' right to dignity and privacy.

Mark Green, the commissioner of Consumer Affairs in New York City, attacks
a popular cigarette advertising campaign that seems to be aimed directly
at children. Professor of philosophy John Luik argues that restricting the
freedom of speech cannot be justified unless it is shown to be absolutely
necessary to avoid certain harm, which has not been done in this case.

Professor of law Richard Epstein argues that if a law is passed that robs an
individual's property of all value, he or she should be compensated for it.
John Echeverria, a legal counsel to the National Audubon Society, argues that
environmental regulations do not violate a right to one's property.

Incineration industry executives John Shortsleeve and Robert Roche argue
that an integrated system that includes incineration is the best disposal option.
Neil Seldman, a waste disposal consultant, claims that intensive recycling and
composting alone can do the job.

Doug Clement, formerly the coordinator of the National Infant Formula Action (INFACT) coalition, argues that Nestlé has caused the deaths of countless infants by marketing infant formula to the Third World. Maggie McComas et al. present Nestlé's response and the company's view of its present and future role in protecting infant nutrition in the Third World.

Professor of philosophy Michael Philips argues that there may be no *prima facie* reason to refuse the offer of a bribe. Professor of philosophy Thomas L. Carson argues that every acceptance of a bribe involves the violation of an implicit or explicit promise or understanding connected with one's office.

Social commentator Alvin Toffler argues that the less developed countries (LDCs) should be prompted to catch up with the Western nations in the development of high technology. Economist E. F. Schumacher argues that the current level of technology in the LDCs is appropriate for them.

INTRODUCTION

The Study of Business Ethics: Ethics, Economics, Law, and the Corporation

Lisa H. Newton
Maureen M. Ford

This book is aimed at an audience of students who expect to be in business, who know that there are knotty ethical problems out there, and who want a chance to confront them ahead of time. The method of confronting them is an invitation to join in a debate, a contest of contrary facts and conflicting values in many of the major issues of the decade. This introductory essay should make it easier to join in the arguments. Managing ethical policy problems in a company requires a wide background—in ethics, economics, law, and the social sciences—which this book cannot hope to provide. But since some background assumptions in these fields are relevant to several of the problems we examine in this volume, we will sketch out very briefly the major understandings that control them. There is ultimately no substitute for thorough study of the rules of the game and years of experience and practice; but an overview of the playing field may at least make it easier for you to understand the object and limitations of the standard plays.

ETHICS

"Business ethics" is sometimes considered to be an oxymoron (a term that contradicts itself). Business and ethics have often been treated as mutually exclusive. But ethics is an issue of growing concern and importance to businesses, and we believe that many share our conviction that value questions are never absent from business decisions, that moral responsibility is the first characteristic demanded of a manager in any business, and that a thorough grounding in ethical reasoning is the best preparation for a career in business. The first imperative of business ethics is that it be taken seriously.

This book will not supply the substance of a course in ethics. For that you are directed to any of several excellent texts in business ethics or to any general text in ethics. (See Suggested Readings at the end of this introduction.) *Taking Sides: Clashing Views on Controversial Issues in Business Ethics and Society* teaches ethics from the issue upward, rather than from the principle downward. You

Table 1

Fundamental Duties

	Beneficence—promoting human welfare	Justice—acknowledging human equality	Respect for Persons—honoring individual freedom
Basic fact about human nature that grounds the duty	Humans are animals, with vulnerable bodies and urgent physical needs, capable of suffering.	Humans are social animals who must live in communities and therefore must adopt social structures to maintain communities.	Humans are rational, free—able to make their own choices, foresee the consequences, and take responsibility.
Value realized in performance of the duty	Human welfare; happiness.	Human equality.	Human dignity; autonomy.
Working out of the duty in ethical theory	Best modern example is utilitarianism, from Jeremy Bentham and John Stuart Mill, who saw morality as that which produced the greatest happiness for the greatest number. Reasoning is consequential, aimed at results.	Best modern example is John Rawls's theory of justice as "fairness"; maintaining equality unless inequality helps everyone. Reasoning is deontological: morality derived from duty, not consequences.	Best modern example is Immanuel Kant's formalism, where morality is seen as the working out of the categorical imperative. Reasoning is deontological.
Samples of implementation of the duty in business	Protecting safety of employees; maintaining pleasant working conditions; contributing funds to the local community.	Obedience to law; enforcing fair rules; nondiscrimination; no favoritism; giving credit where credit is due.	Respect for employee rights; treating employees as persons, not just as tools; respecting differences of opinion.

© 1988 Lisa Newton

will, however, come upon much of the terminology of ethical reasoning in the course of considering these cases. For your reference, a brief summary of the ethical principles and forms of reasoning most used in this book is found in Table 1.

ECONOMICS

Adam Smith

Capitalism as we know it is the product of the thought of Adam Smith (1723–1790), a Scottish philosopher and economist, and a small number of his European contemporaries. The fundamental capitalist act is the *voluntary exchange:* two adults, of sound mind and clear purposes, meet in the marketplace, to which each repairs in order to satisfy some felt need. They discover that each has that which will satisfy the other's need—the housewife needs flour, the miller needs cash—and they exchange at a price such that the exchange furthers the interest of each. To the participant in the free market, the *marginal utility* of the thing acquired must exceed that of the thing traded, or else why make the deal? So each party to the voluntary exchange walks away from it richer.

Adding to the value of the exchange is the *competition* of dealers and buyers; because there are many purveyors of each good in the marketplace, the customer is not forced to pay exorbitant prices for things needed. (It is a sad fact of economics that to the starving man, the marginal value of a loaf of bread is very large, and a single merchant could become unjustly rich). Conversely, competition among the customers (typified by an auction) makes sure that the available goods end up in the hands of those to whom they are worth the most. So at the end of the market day, everyone goes home not only richer (in real terms) than when they came—the voluntariness of the exchange ensures that—but also as rich as they could possibly be, since each had available all possible options of goods or services to buy and all possible purchasers of the goods or services brought to the marketplace for sale.

Sellers and buyers win the competition through *efficiency;* that is, through producing the best quality goods at the lowest possible price or through allotting their scarce resources toward the most valuable of the choices presented to them. It is to the advantage of all participants in the market, then, to strive for efficiency (i.e., to keep the cost of goods for sale as low as possible while keeping the quality as high as possible). Adam Smith's most memorable accomplishment was to recognize that the general effect of all this self-interested scrambling would be to make the most possible goods of the best possible quality available at the least possible price. Meanwhile, sellers and buyers alike must keep an eye on the market as a whole, adjusting production and purchasing to take advantage of fluctuations in *supply and demand.* Short supply will make goods more valuable, raising the price, and that will bring more suppliers into the market, whose competition will lower the price to just above the cost of manufacture for the most efficient producers. Increased demand for any reason will have the same effect. Should supply exceed demand, the price will fall to a point where the goods will be bought. Putting this all together, Smith realized that in a system of free enterprise, you have demonstrably the best possible chance of finding for sale what you want, in good quantity and quality and at a reasonable price. Forget benevolent monarchs ordering things for our own good, Smith suggested; in this system, we are led as by an *invisible hand* of enlightened self-interest to achieve the common good, even as we think we are being most selfish.

Adam Smith's theory of economic enterprise emerged in the natural law tradition of the eighteenth century. As was the fashion for that period, Smith presented his conclusions as a series of laws: the law of supply and demand, which links supply, demand, and price; the law that links efficiency with success; and, ultimately, the laws that link the absolute freedom of the market with the absolute growth of the wealth of the free market country.

To these laws were added others, specifying the conditions under which business enterprise would be conducted in capitalist countries. The laws of *population* formulated by English clergyman and economist Thomas Malthus (1766–1834) concluded that population would always outstrip food production, ensuring that the bulk of humanity would always live at the subsistence level. Since Smith had already postulated that employers would purchase labor at the lowest possible price, it was a one-step derivation for English economist David Ricardo (1772–1823) to conclude that workers' *wages* would never exceed the subsistence level, no matter how prosperous industrial enterprise should become. From these capitalist theorists proceeded the nineteenth-century assumption that society would inevitably divide into two classes, a minority of fabulous wealth and a majority of subsistence level workers.

These laws, like the laws of physics advanced at that time by Sir Isaac Newton (1642–1727), and laws of psychology and government advanced at that time by John Locke (1632–1704), were held to be immutable facts of nature, true forever and not subject to change. No concept of progress, or of the historical fitness of a system to society at a point in time, was contemplated.

Karl Marx

Only within the last century and a half have we learned to think "historically." The notion of progress, the vision of a better future, and even the very idea that we might modify that future, in part by the discernment of historical trends, were unknown to the ancients and of no interest to medieval chroniclers. For Western political philosophy, history emerged as a factor in our understanding only with the work of the nineteenth-century German philosopher G. W. F. Hegel (1770–1831), who traced the history of the Western world as an ordered series of ideal forms, evolving one from another in logical sequence toward an ideal future. A young German student of Hegel's, Karl Marx (1818–1883), concluded from his study of philosophy and economics that Hegel had to be wrong: the phases of history were ruled not by ideas but by the *material conditions* of life, and their evolution one from another came about as the ruling class of each age generated its own revolutionary overthrow.

Marx's theory, especially as it applies to the evolution of capitalism, is enormously complex; for the purposes of this unit, it can be summarized simply. According to Marx, the *ruling class* in every age is the group that *owns the means of production* of the age's product. Throughout the seventeenth century, the product was almost exclusively agricultural, and the means of production was almost exclusively agricultural land: landowners were the aristocrats and rulers. With the coming of commerce and industry, the owners of the factories joined the ruling class and eventually dominated it. It was in the nature of such capital-intensive industry to concentrate within itself more capital: as Adam Smith had proved, its greater efficiency would drive all smaller labor-intensive industry out of business, and its enormous income would be put to work as more capital, expanding the domain of the factory and the machine indefinitely (at the expense of the cottage and the human being). Thus would the wealth of society concentrate in fewer and fewer hands, as the owners of the factories expanded their enterprises without limit into mighty industrial empires, dominated by machines and by the greed of their owners.

Meanwhile, all this wealth was being produced by a new class of workers, the unskilled factory workers. Taken from the ranks of the obsolete peasantry, artisans, and craftsmen, this new working class, the *proletariat*, expanded in numbers with the gigantic mills, whose "hands" they were. Work on the assembly line demanded no education or skills, so the workers could never make themselves valuable enough to command a living wage on the open market. They survived as a vast underclass, interchangeable with the unemployed workers (recently displaced by more machines) who gathered around the factory gates looking for jobs—*their* jobs. As Ricardo had demonstrated, they could never bargain for any wage above the subsistence level—just enough to keep them alive. As capitalism and its factories expanded, the entire population, excepting only the wealthy capitalist families, sank into this hopeless, pauperized class.

So Marx saw Western society under capitalism as one that ultimately would be divided into a small group of fabulously wealthy capitalists and a mass of paupers, mostly factory workers. The minority would keep the majority in strict control through its hired thugs (the state—the army and the police), control rendered easier by thought control (the schools and the churches). The purpose of the ideology taught by the schools and the churches—the value structure of capitalism—was to show both classes that the capitalists had a right to their wealth (through the sham of liberty, free enterprise, and the utilitarian benefits of the free market) and a perfect right to govern everyone else. Thus, the capitalists could enjoy their wealth in good conscience and the poor would understand their moral obligation to accept the oppression of the ruling class with good cheer.

Marx foresaw, and in his writings attempted to help bring about, the disillusionment of the workers: there would come a point when the workers would suddenly ask, *Why* should we accept oppression all our lives? Their search for answers to this question would show them the history of their situation, expose the falsehood of the ideology and the false consciousness of those who believe it, show them their own strength, and lead them directly to the solution that would usher in the new age of socialism—the revolutionary overthrow of the capitalist regime. Why, after all, should they not undertake such a revolution? People are restrained from violence against oppression only by the prospect of losing something valuable, and, as Marx concluded, the industrialized workers of the world had nothing to lose but their chains.

As feudalism had been swept away, then, by the "iron broom" of the French Revolution, so capitalism would be swept away by the revolt of the masses, the irresistible uprising of the vast majority of the people against the minority of industrial overlords and their terrified minions—the armed forces, the state, and the church. After the first rebellions, Marx foresaw no lengthy problem of divided loyalties in the industrialized countries of the world. Once the scales had fallen from their eyes, the working class hirelings of the army and police would quickly turn their guns on their masters and join their natural allies in the proletariat to create the new world.

After the revolution, Marx predicted, there would be a temporary "dictatorship of the proletariat," during which the last vestiges of capitalism would be eradicated and the authority to run the industrial establishment would be returned to the workers of each industry. Once the economy had been decentralized, to turn each factory into an industrial commune run by its own workers and each landed estate into an agricultural commune run by its farmers, the state as such would simply wither away. Some central authority would certainly continue to exist, to coordinate and facilitate the exchange of goods within the country (one imagines a giant computer, taking note of where goods are demanded, where goods are available, and where the railroad cars to take the goods from one place to the other are). But with no ruling class to serve and no oppression to carry out, there will be no need of the state to rule *people*; what is left will be confined to the administration of *things*.

Even as he wrote, just in time for the revolutions in Europe of 1848, Marx expected the end of capitalism as a system. Not that capitalism was evil in itself; Marx did not presume to make moral judgments on history. Indeed, capitalism was necessary as an economic system to concentrate the wealth of the country into the industries of the modern age. So, in Marx's judgment, capitalism had a respectable past and would still be necessary for awhile in the developing countries to launch their industries. But that task completed, it had no further role in history, and the longer it stayed around, the more the workers would suffer and the more violent the revolution would be when it came. The sooner the revolution, the better; the future belonged to communism.

As the collapse of the communist governments in Eastern Europe demonstrates (if demonstration were needed), the course of history has not proceeded quite as Marx predicted in 1848. In fairness, it might be pointed out that no other prophets of the time had any more luck with prognostications about the twentieth century. In any case, since Marx wrote, all participants in the debate on the nature and future of capitalism have had to respond to his judgments and predictions.

LAW: RECOVERING FOR DAMAGES SUSTAINED

Life is full of misfortune. Ordinarily, if you suffer misfortune, you must put up with it and find the resources to deal with it. If your misfortune is my fault, however, the law may step in and make me pay for those damages, one way or another.

Through *criminal law,* the public steps in and demands punishment for an offense that is serious enough to outrage public feeling and endanger public welfare. If I knock you on the head and take your wallet, the police will find me, restore your wallet to you, and imprison or otherwise punish me for the crime.

Through *civil law,* if I do you damage through some action of mine, you may take me to civil court and ask a judge (and jury) to determine whether or not I have damaged you, if so by how much, and how I should pay you back for that damage. There are a number of forms of action under which you may make your claim; the most common for business purposes are *contract* and *torts.* If you and I agree to (or "contract for") some undertaking, and I back out of it after you have relied on our agreement to commit your resources to the undertaking, you have a right to recover what you have lost. In torts, if I simply injure you in some way, hurting you in health, life, or limb, or destroying your property, I have done you a wrong (*tort,* in French), and I must pay for the damage I have done. How much I will have to pay will depend (as the jury will determine) on (1) the amount of the damage that has been caused, (2) the extent to which I knew or should have known that my action or neglect to act would cause damage (my *culpability*), and (3) the extent to which *you* contributed to the damage, beyond whatever I did (*contributory negligence*).

In the debates that follow, one of them (on the Pinto automobile) has to do with a suit at law alleging *negligence,* a tort, on the part of a company, in that it made and put up for sale a product known to be defective and that the defect injured its users. To establish negligence, civil or criminal, four elements must be demonstrated: First, there must have been a *duty*—the party accused of negligence must have had a preexisting duty to the plaintiff. Second, there must have been a *breach of,* or failure to fulfill, that duty. Third, the plaintiff must have suffered an *injury.* And fourth, the breach of the duty must have been the *proximate cause* of the injury, or the thing that actually brought the injury about. Where negligence is alleged in a product liability case, it must be established that the manufacturer had a duty to make a product that could not do certain sorts of harm, that the duty was breached and the harm was caused, that nothing else was to blame, and that the manufacturer therefore must compensate the victim for the damage done.

Two other topics (cigarette advertising and Nestlé infant formula) contain very similar allegations—although no lawsuit is at issue at this point. (Tobacco manufacturers have already been sued for negligence in deaths from lung cancer; the results are uncertain.) In all of these cases, one set of claims amounts to an accusation of deliberately damaging innocent consumers, placing them in harm's way for the sake of profit; the other set counters that the company did not know and could not have known that the product was dangerous and/or that the freely chosen behavior of the consumers contributed in some way to the damage that was done, so the company cannot be held totally responsible. In all cases, *risk* and *responsibility* are the central issues: when a small car explodes and burns when hit by a much larger van, to what extent is the company responsible for the flimsiness of the car and to what extent did the consumer assume the risk of that happening when she bought a small, economical car? When infants sicken and die because their mothers misuse an infant formula, to what extent are the mothers at fault for failing to read and follow the directions, and to what extent should the company have foreseen that the directions would be unreadable and unworkable in the contexts of the product's sale and use?

Should companies ultimately be responsible for any harm that comes from the use of the products they so profitably marketed and sold? Or should consumers be content to bear the responsibility for risks they have freely accepted? Our ambivalence on this question as a society mirrors, and proceeds from, the ambivalence of the individual at the two poles of materialization of risk: when we are in a hurry, short of cash, or in need of a cigarette, then risky behavior looks to us to be our right, and we are resentful of the busybodies who would always have us play it safe. But when the risk materializes—when the accident or the disease happens—the perception of that risk (and the direction of that resentment) changes drastically. From the perspective of the hospital bed, it is crystal clear that the behavior was not worth the risk, that we never realized the behavior was risky, that we should have been warned, and that it was someone's duty to warn us. In that instantaneous change of perspective, three elements of negligence come into view: duty, breach, and injury. No wonder product liability suits are so common.

Yet, the suit is a relatively recent phenomenon because of a peculiarity in the law. Until the twentieth century, a judge faced with a consumer who had been injured by a product (physically or financially) applied the principle of *caveat emptor*—"let the buyer beware"—and could ask the seller to pay damages only to the original buyer, and only if the exact defect in the product could be proven. For example, a defective kerosene lamp might explode and burn five people, but the exact defect (broken seam or shoddy wick) had to be brought into court or the case would be thrown out. In addition, the buyer could sue only the seller, not the manufacturer or designer, because the right to collect damages rested on the law of *contract*, not torts, and on the warrant of merchantability implied in the contractual relationship between buyer and seller. The cause of the action was understood to be a breach in that contract.

There matters stood until 1916, when an American judge allowed a buyer to sue the manufacturer of a product. A Mr. MacPherson had been injured when his car collapsed under him due to a defect in the wood used to build one of the wheels, and MacPherson went to court against the Buick Motor Company. The judge reasoned that the action was in torts, specifically "negligence," and not in contract, for a manufacturer is under a duty to make carefully any product that could be expected to endanger life, and this duty existed irrespective of any contract. So if MacPherson, or any future user of the product, was injured because the product was badly made, he could collect damages even if he had never dealt with the manufacturer in any way.

In the 1960s the automobile was still center stage in the arguments over the duties of manufacturers. Consumer advocate Ralph Nader's book *Unsafe at Any Speed* (1966) spearheaded the consumer rights movement with its scathing attack on General Motors and its exposé of the dangerous design of the Corvair. In response to the consumer activism resulting from that movement, Congress passed the Consumer Product Safety Act in 1972 and empowered the Consumer Product Safety Commission, an independent federal agency, to set safety standards, require warning labels, and order recalls of hazardous products. When three girls died in a Ford Pinto in 1978, the foundations of consumer rights against careless manufacturers were well established. What was new in the Ford Motor Company case was the allegation of *criminal* negligence—in effect, criminal homicide.

At present, product liability suits are major uncharted reefs in the navigational plans of American business. If a number of people die in a fire in a hotel, for instance, their families will often sue not only the hotel, for culpable negligence, but the manufacturers of the furniture that burned, alleging that it should have been fire-retardant; the manufacturers of the cushions on the furniture, alleging that they gave off toxic fumes in the fire; and the manufacturers of the chemicals that went into those cushions, alleging that there was no warning to the consumers on the toxicity of those chemicals in fire conditions. The settlements that can be obtained are used to finance the suit and the law firm that is managing it for the years that it will take to exhaust all the appeals. This phenomenon of unlimited litigation is relatively new on the American scene, and we are not quite sure how to respond to it.

THE CORPORATION

The human being is a social animal. We exist in the herd and depend for our lives on the cooperation of those around us. Who are they? Anthropologists tell us that originally we traveled in extended families, then settled down into villages of intensely interlocked groups of families. With the advent of the modern era, we have found our identities in family, village, church, and nation. Yet, in the great transformation of the obligations of the Western world (see Henry Maine [1822–1888], *From Status to Contract*), we have abandoned the old family-oriented care systems and thrown ourselves upon the mercy of secondary organizations: club, corporation, and state. The French sociologist Emile Durkheim (1858–1917) suggested (in his classic work *Suicide*) that following the collapse of the family and the church, the corporation would be the association in the future that would supply the social support that every individual needs to maintain a moral life.

Can the corporation do that? Or is the corporation merely the organization that implements Adam Smith's self-interested pursuit of the dollar, with no purpose but to maximize return on investment to the investors while protecting them from unlimited liability?

On the other hand, once formed, and having become a major community figure and employer, does the corporation have a right to exist that transcends at least the immediate pursuit of money? The issue of so-called hostile takeovers sends us back to the purpose and foundation of business enterprise in America. Let us review: When an entrepreneur gets a bright idea for how to make money, he or she secures the capital necessary to run the business from investors (venture capitalists), uses that capital to buy the land, buildings, and machinery needed to see the project through, hires the labor needed to do the work, and goes into production. As the income from the enterprise comes in, the entrepreneur pays the suppliers of raw materials, pays the workers, pays the taxes, rent, mortgages and utility bills, keeps some of the money for him- or herself (salary), and then divides up the rest of the income (profit) among the investors (probably including him- or herself) in proportion to the capital they invested. Motives of all parties are presupposed: the entrepreneur wants money, the laborers and the landlords want money, and the investors, who are the shareholders in the company, want money. The investors thought that this enterprise would yield them a higher return on their capital than any other investment available to them at the time; that is why they invested. However, this is a free country, and people can move around. If the workers see better jobs, they will take them; if a landlord can rent for more, the lease will be terminated; and if the investors see a better place to put their capital, they will move it. The determiner of the flow of capital is the rate of return, no more and no less. Loyalty to the company, faithfulness to the corporation for the sake of the association itself, is not on anyone's agenda—not on the worker's, certainly not on the landlord's, and *most* certainly not on the shareholder's.

The shareholders are represented by a board of directors elected by them to see that the company is run efficiently; that is, that costs are kept down and income up, to yield the highest possible return. The board of directors hires management—the cadre of corporate officers headed by the president and/or chief executive officer to do the actual running of the company. The corporate officers thus stand in a *fiduciary* relationship to the shareholders; that is, they are forbidden by the understandings on which the corporation is founded to do anything at all except that which will protect and enhance the interests of the shareholders. That goes for all the normal business decisions made by the management; even the decision not to break the law can be seen as a prudent estimate of the financial costs of lawbreaking.

Yet, our dealings with the business world, as citizens and as consumers, have always turned on recognition and support of the huge reliable corporations in established industries: not just coal and steel, which had certain natural limitations built into their consumption of natural resources, but the automobile companies, the airlines, the consumer products companies, and even the banks. Companies had "reputations," "integrity," cultivated (and bought and sold) "good will." Consumers cooperated with the companies that catered to them in developing "brand loyalty." And, most importantly, those working in business cooperated with their employers in developing "company loyalty," which became a part of their lives as loyalty to one's tribe or nation was part of the lives of their ancestors. Is the company that sought our loyalty—and got it—just a scrap of paper, to disappear as soon as return on investment falls below the nearest competition? What part do we want corporations to play in our associative lives? If we want them to be any more than profit maximizers for the investors, what sorts of protections would we have to offer them, and what sorts of limitations should we put on their extra-profit-making activities?

CURRENT ISSUES

Business ethics ultimately rests on a base of political philosophy, economics, and philosophical ethics. As these underlying fields change, new topics and approaches will surface in business ethics. For example, hostile takeovers did not take place very often in the regulatory climate that existed prior to the Reagan administration. The change in political philosophy introduced by his administration resulted in new business practices, which resulted in new ethical problems. Also, the work of John Rawls, a professor of philosophy at Harvard University, profoundly influenced our understanding of distributive justice and, therefore, our understanding of acceptable economic distribution in the society. The work currently being done in postmodern philosophy will change the way we see human beings generally and, hence, the activity of business.

No single work can cover all the issues of ethical practice in business in all their range and particularity, especially since, as above, we are dealing with a moving target. Our task here is much more limited. The purpose of this book is to allow you to grapple with some of the ethical issues of current business practice in the safety of the classroom, before they come up on the job where human rights and careers are at stake and legal action looms outside the boardroom or factory door. We think that rational consideration of these issues now will help you prepare for a lifetime of the types of problems that naturally arise in a complex and pluralistic society. You will find here no dogmas, no settled solutions to memorize. These problems do not have preset answers but require that you use your mind to balance the values in conflict and to work out acceptable policies in each issue. To employ business ethics, you must learn to think critically, to look beyond short-term advantages and traditional ways of doing things, and to become an innovator. The exercise provided by these debates should help you in this learning.

There is no doubt that businesspeople think that ethics is important. Sometimes the reasons why they think ethics is important have to do only with the long-run profitability of business enterprise. There is no doubt that greater employee honesty and diligence would improve the bottom line or that strict attention to environmental and employee health laws is necessary to preserve the company from expensive lawsuits and fines. But ethics goes well beyond profitability, to the lives that we live and the persons we want to be. What the bottom line has taught us is that the working day is not apart from life. We must bring the same integrity and care to the contexts of factory and office that we are used to showing at home and among our friends. An imperative of business ethics is to make of your business life an opportunity to become, and remain, the person that you know you ought to be—and as far as it is within your capability, to extend that opportunity to others.

We attempt, in this book, to present in good debatable form some of the issues that raise the big questions—of justice, of rights, of the common good—in order to build bridges between the workaday world of employment and the ageless world of morality. If you will enter into these dialogues with an open mind, a willingness to have it changed, and a determination to master the skills of critical thinking that will enable you to make responsible decisions in difficult situations, you may be able to help build the bridges for the new ethical issues that will emerge in the next century. At the least, that is our hope

SUGGESTED READINGS FOR ETHICS BACKGROUND

Tom L. Beauchamp and Norman E. Bowie, *Ethical Theory and Business*, 3rd ed. (Prentice Hall, 1988).

John Matthews, Kenneth Goodpaster, and Laura Nash, *Policies and Persons: A Casebook in Business Ethics*, 2d ed. (McGraw-Hill, 1991).

Manuel Velasquez, *Business Ethics: Concepts and Cases*, 2d ed. (Prentice Hall, 1987)

PART 1

Capitalism and Corporations in Theory and Practice

The nations of the Western European tradition tend to regard business as central to their citizens' lives and the meaning of their national life. But does business always represent what we want our countries to be about? This first section initially explores business theory. Would a national industrial policy improve our international performance? Is America's prized free enterprise system always more efficient than alternatives? This section also explores three relatively new enterprises for business: the rapidly expanding medical field, the corporate world of buyouts and takeovers, and the efforts of business to develop codes of ethics to handle rapidly growing problems.

- Should the United States Have a National Industrial Policy?

- Is Free Enterprise Always More Efficient?

- Are Business and Medicine Ethically Incompatible?

- Are Leveraged Buyouts Bad for the Bottom Line?

- Are Corporate Codes of Ethics Just for Show?

1

ISSUE 1

Should the United States Have a National Industrial Policy?

YES: Lester Thurow, from *Head to Head: The Coming Economic Battle Among Japan, Europe, and America* (William Morrow, 1992)

NO: Cynthia A. Beltz, from *High-Tech Maneuvers: Industrial Policy Lessons of HDTV* (AEI Press, 1991)

ISSUE SUMMARY

YES: Management professor Lester Thurow argues that the United States may soon be the only nation in the world in which attempts to achieve global business success are allowed to be obstructed by short-term economic interests. To amend this situation, he maintains that a national industrial policy should be adopted.

NO: Cynthia A. Beltz, a technology policy analyst, argues that a system in which government targets specific industries for promotion, which is currently being promoted in Washington, D.C., is no substitute for the workings of the free market. Government, she asserts, is no better than the market at picking the "winners" of the next century's high-technology competitions, and, in fact, it may be considerably worse.

We live in a global society with a global economy. The United States, however, is currently having a difficult time competing in some global markets and seems, on occasion, to be taking on the role of a less developed nation; that is, it supplies food and lumber to the manufacturing economies that supply the United States with VCRs and automobiles.

Japanese industry has consistently been able to put good products on America's shelves more cheaply than domestic industries can. This has resulted in national humiliation (especially in the automobile industry), loss of jobs (primary and secondary), and a serious trade deficit. Japan established preeminence in manufacturing by maintaining close partnerships between industry and government, accepting enough regulation and structure to protect the industry while it was growing and preserve it when mature. American responses to such international economic threats has historically been to raise tariffs, restrict imports, or wage "buy American" advertising campaigns. The kind of genuine cross-industry partnerships found in Japan, including government authorizations and advisors' putting their heads together to make an industry work properly, are very rare among U.S. businesses. Only now is America beginning to see computer manufacturers taking up partnerships for more effective competition. Should businesses be doing more of that?

The question is, Does free enterprise (and the free market) work to increase the national wealth, or should America turn to some contemporary form of socialism to improve the efficiency and effectiveness of its industries? The question goes to the very heart of the capitalist system. If free enterprise is nationally beneficial, then America has nothing to fear from competitors with national industrial policies. For although government encouragement may propel their infant industries for awhile, ultimately they will find that such subsidy creates inefficiencies—inefficiencies in the form of complacent, overstaffed bureaucracies in the favored industries and opportunity costs in the industries not picked for encouragement—and America will best them at the competitive game. However, if free enterprise works solely to the individual's advantage, then America will likely lose the trade war against more organized competition.

For defenders of industrial policy, the issue is plain: competitors who have bested the United States in world trade have done so by dynamic partnerships of business and government that make sure investment money is at the right place at the right time (rather than leaving it up to the entrepreneur to sell his or her ideas to a hesitant group of investors).

For skeptics, the issue is much more complicated. First, in cases of successful industrial policy partnership, to what extent was government the initiator (as opposed to a follower) of the policy? Second, what other factors enter into successful international competition? Is it true, for example, that Japanese workers put in longer hours, concentrate harder, pay more attention to details, and generally make fewer mistakes than American workers? If two competitors are operating with different workforces, they will likely come out with different results. And third, are there any industries backed by governments that did not succeed and that the governments have kept secret? Where there are no controls, or where the whole universe of relevant cases is not taken into account, the anecdotal positive cases, while heartwarming, are fatally inconclusive.

Ask yourself, as you read the following selections, who you trust. Do you trust the market to make the economy eventually come right? Or do you think a more visible process might provide a better chance for success in the world competition?

YES

Lester Thurow

HEAD TO HEAD

Consider the comments of Ichiro Fujiwara, former vice-minister of the Japanese Ministry of International Trade and Industry (MITI), on national strategies.

> Let's take the case of the mainframe computer as an example. After the war, Japanese business firms had to start from scratch. To survive, they had to struggle with outmoded technology and meager capital to fend off foreign competitors armed with computerized manufacturing systems and management. No responsible government leaders, faced with such a situation, would have sat on their hands and watched domestic industries crushed under the juggernaut of foreign competition. We had to help the domestic computer industry to get on its feet. Government leaders of other countries had done, and are still doing, the same thing.

A wide variety of techniques were used to develop the Japanese mainframe computer industry. To set up a wholly owned subsidiary in 1960, IBM had to make its basic patents available to Japanese manufacturers. A government-financed computer-leasing company made it cheaper and less risky to buy Japanese computers. Directly and indirectly, large government investments were made in establishing a successful computer industry in Japan.

The Japanese government has never picked winners and losers. Their strategies have always been bottom-up, industry-led strategies, where government was a participant but never a dictator. Companies could, and do, reject government initiatives. The auto manufacturers rejection of a consolidation plan in the 1960s is only the most dramatic of many such examples.

In developing national strategies, the Japanese goal is to focus on those industries with high income elasticities of demand, high rates of growth in productivity, and high value added per employee. High value added means that high wages can be paid. When productivity has a high rate of growth, wages can go up rapidly even as product prices are going down. With falling prices and a high income elasticity of demand, markets will be expanding rapidly as consumer incomes grow, and labor won't need to be fired. Those trained and added to the work force can remain as permanent employees. In the 1990s there are believed to be seven industries that meet these criteria—microelectronics, the new materials-science industries, biotechnology, telecommunications, civilian aircraft manufacturing, robots plus machine tools, computers plus software.

Business firms are believed to be too risk-averse when it comes to projects that require large investments. Rationally, private firms see a riskless project with a payout of $1 billion as much better than a project with a $2.4 billion expected payoff but a 50 percent risk of failure. What is rational for business firms is, however, irrational for nations. Nations can average out their risks across many such projects. Government support encourages private industries to make the *right* market choices—like getting into aircraft manufacturing in the 1990s.

Similarly, private time horizons are believed to be too short. Private hurdle rates used in business-investment calculations are always far above the economy's long-term rate of return on assets. In the United States the private hurdle rate is 15 to 20 percent, while the historical rate of return on business assets is 7 percent. Banks such as the Japanese Development Bank or the Long-Term Credit Bank are designed to finance the long-term investments that normal banks and firms avoid.

Private firms invest too little in research and development (R&D) and don't want to diffuse the fruits of such activities fast enough. All empirical studies show that the social rate of return on R&D is far above the private rate of return. This occurs because new technologies often prove to be of most use to a company other than the one that paid to develop them. As a result, firms invest too little in R&D.

Those who invest in private R&D also want a monopoly on their ideas, so that they can earn the largest possible rate of return on their investments. To encourage R&D investment, monopolistic patent rights are given. Yet any society is much better off if the ideas developed within its jurisdictions are diffused to every producer as fast as possible. What is needed to stimulate R&D investments (patents) reduces their payoff (diffusion). Joint, partly government financed, cooperative R&D projects such as those found in the Japanese Key Technologies Center are one way to simultaneously get more investment and more diffusion. The former head of R&D at Nippon Electric Corporation notes that "R&D resources in the world are scarce; even big companies scream for these resources. If we don't collaborate, we can't advance. It's too expensive even for NEC. MITI is the third party needed to coordinate industry."

Certain industries are seen as key industries with linkages (externalities) affecting other industries. Strengthen them, and other industries get stronger. Machine tools and key component suppliers, such as semiconductor chip manufacturers, are seen as linkage industries. A stronger machine-tool industry and a stronger semiconductor industry allows Japan to be more competitive in automobiles and consumer electronics. As a result, the total return to these investments is higher than the returns that show up in machine tools or semiconductor manufacturing alone.

Above all, government has an important role to play in accelerating economic growth. This means raising investments in plant and equipment, skills, infrastructure, and R&D above the levels that would occur in unfettered markets. Market participants are believed to have too much interest in the present. Government essentially represents the interest of the future in the present. It works to speed up markets and to encourage firms to go down their learning curves faster than they would if they were on their own.

As an illustration, the Japanese Development Bank provided funds for the Japanese semiconductor firms to continue building production facilities during recessions when their American competitors would stop construction. This gave the Japanese the capacity to service demands that could not be met by the Americans during the next cyclical boom. A government-financed short-term robot-leasing company persuaded firms to use robots faster than they otherwise would have. As a result, the market for robots grew far faster and became far larger in Japan than elsewhere in the industrial world. With larger and faster-growing markets, Japan's robotic firms could go down their learning curves faster and get a cost advantage over the rest of the world.

If Japanese firms are not yet prepared to compete, foreign firms are held at bay. Satellite television is such an industry at the moment. To give the domestic industry time to get organized, the Ministry of Post and Telecommunications prohibits Japanese citizens from having the dishes necessary to receive satellite signals from foreign broadcasters.

Over time the instruments used to implement national strategies have changed. The foreign-exchange controls of the 1950s were replaced with capital allocation in the income-doubling decade of the 1960s. Today the focus is on research support, as in the case of the Japanese Key Technologies Center, where government and private funds are commingled to lower private risk.

MITI's vision for the 1990s calls for securing the foundations for long-term economic growth. A flexible industrial infrastructure is to be combined with a better public infrastructure and improved capital and human resources. Despite the shift to services, manufacturing continues to be seen as crucial to technological innovation and growth. Basic science is to be strengthened, and the country is to make whatever efforts are necessary to stay at the forefront of the information revolution.

These strategies create a problem for nations that do not believe in national strategies. How are countries without national strategies to compete? Japan recently announced a national strategy for capturing 10 percent of civilian aircraft manufacturing by the year 2000. A 10 percent market share must be dislodged from one of three competitors—Airbus Industries in Europe, Boeing in the United States, or McDonnell Douglas in the United States. Since McDonnell Douglas is the weakest of the three, its market share will probably go to the Japanese.

Historically, Americans have never had comprehensive civilian economic strategies. Only in wartime have such efforts occurred. Until recently, Anglo-Saxon economics denied the validity of national strategies. Economies of scale were exhausted, and diseconomies of scale set in long before any one supplier could capture an industry. If economies of scale were not exhausted, monopolies emerged, and these had to be broken up with antitrust laws to maintain a competitive market. No industries were believed to have externalities that were important to the existence of other industries. One could always buy one's supplies on the same basis as any other buyer—even if the seller were foreign. Profit-maximizing sellers do not discriminate, since to do so is to fail to maximize profits. Yet according to the U.S. General Accounting Office, American firms seem to find that when supplies are scarce, they don't get their equipment as fast from Japanese suppliers as the Japanese firms who belong to the same business group.

In Anglo-Saxon economics there are no intrinsically high value-added industries. High-wage industries only look like high-wage industries because they use more skills. Higher wages are merely compensation for the costs of creating those skills. Once returns on human capital investments are subtracted, wages—the bribe for sacrificing leisure—are the same in every industry.

Even if national strategies could be made to work theoretically, many Americans argue that they cannot work practically. Sometimes this argument is narrowed still further to state that even if national strategies are shown to work abroad, they could not work in the United States because of its brand of special-interest-group politics.

Others argue that Americans should just accept the below-cost (subsidized) goods that they are getting as a result of these foreign strategies and withdraw from the businesses that are being targeted by others. If foreigners raise their prices when there are no American producers left, Americans will simply get back into those businesses. This argument ignores what happens when an American industry is driven out of business. The Japanese business firm is not in the business of making permanent gifts to Americans. When competition is gone, prices rise. American competitors do not come back into business because of the high transition costs of going in and out of business and because they know that if they were willing to come back

into business, those fat Japanese profit margins would promptly disappear.

WHO WINS?

Abstractly, firms based upon the motivation of value added or market-share maximization and those based upon the motivation of profit maximization would each seem to have advantages. The strategic-conquest firm is willing to work for a lower rate of return and can use this ability to force profit-maximizing firms to drop out of an industry. It simply accepts a rate of return below the minimum thresholds of the profit-maximizing firm.

From the perspective of Anglo-Saxon economics, however, the profit-maximizing firms should win. They should be better cost minimizers. They are both more concerned about lowering costs and more willing to do it (i.e., fire workers), and this advantage should be large enough to allow them to meet their rate of return on investment targets and still sell products at prices equal to, or lower than, that of empire-building firms. Empire-building firms may not have a high demanded rate of return on investment, but they do have a profit constraint. They cannot grow unless their profits are positive. If profit-maximizing firms costs are low enough, they can defeat empire-building firms by forcing consistent losses upon them.

Recent empirical evidence would also seem to favor the long-run success of the empire-building firms. Firms based on the principle of producer economics are clearly on the offensive in international markets, while those based upon profit maximizing are on the defensive. But perhaps this is just the ebb and flow of economic battle. In the 1950s and

1960s the profit-maximizing firms of the United States put their competitors on the defensive.

Which of the two is to triumph will depend in the long run upon the extent to which the problems of growth (economic dynamics) are different from those of competition in a static environment (comparative statics). The theoretical advantages of profit maximization were in fact mathematically derived under the assumptions of what economists call "comparative statics." In comparative statics, a stable no-growth environment, firms prove their effectiveness by becoming efficient (moving from inside the production-possibilities curve to a place on the maximum production-possibilities curve). The cost minimizer wins. In getting onto that maximum production-possibility curve, Japanese lifetime employment and seniority wages should, for example, be a handicap. Labor is not paid in accordance with its individual marginal productivity. It is not laid off when it should be laid off. It is not paid the wages it should be paid.

In economic dynamics the central problem is rapid growth (getting the production-possibility curve to move to the right as rapidly as possible). Being on the curve, being the most efficient at any moment in time, is unimportant.

In reaching this growth goal, many of the cost-cutting advantages of comparative statics may be liabilities. Reducing wages and firing people may allow the firm to cut costs, but it lowers the willingness of the work force to accept new technologies, leads to a less well trained labor force, and eliminates loyalty—the willingness to make short-run self-sacrifices for the good of the firm. Similarly, the Anglo-Saxon willingness to reduce R&D spending, investment, and training in recessions may similarly be a short-run static advantage that turns out to be a long-run dynamic handicap.

By reducing the individual's risks with lifetime employment and seniority wage systems, the Japanese firm handicaps itself in the world of comparative statics. It cannot efficiently cut costs. But if the name of the game is dynamic growth, lifetime employment means that no one will become unemployed if new technologies reduce the demand for labor. Workers will be retrained if new technologies come along and make one's skills obsolete. With seniority wages, whatever happens, one's wages will not be reduced. Producer economics forces investments in skills and creates motivation that may offset its static inefficiencies. It has what Ronald Dore, an MIT Japanologist, calls "flexible rigidities."

The economic risks of change are the same in the two systems, but in one system the risks of economic change are carried by the individual, and in the other, by the group. When the risks are carried by the group, individuals lose their rational incentive to fight technical change. What is good for the group is automatically good for the individual. In contrast, in the American system, what is good for the group—higher productivity from new technologies—is often bad for particular individuals.

In the long run history will tell us which theory is right. An empirical experiment is now under way. The profit-maximizing firms of the United States have faced off against the empire-building firms of Japan. Individualistic capitalism meets communitarian capitalism. Eventually, the winners will be known. In the end the winner will force the losers to change and play by the winner's rules....

* * *

It is the official American position that it does not need to worry about the national strategies of other countries. Foreign national strategies simply won't work. But this is a belief that looks increasingly untenable if one looks at the industries that have been lost, such as robots, or industries under threat, such as aircraft manufacturing. It also confronts a world of man-made comparative advantage where the brainpower industries of the future will exist in those places where institutions organize to capture them.

The rest of the world is not cheating when it employs national strategies. That is just the way those nations play economic football. Americans can respond in one of three ways:

1. True believers in the American way can argue that we Americans have got it right and that the Germans and the Japanese have got it wrong. In the end their national strategies will hurt them more than they help. Keep the faith!

2. The agnostics can argue for changing American laws to permit American firms to get together if they wish. Try a few experiments with national industrial policies. Let a thousand flowers bloom!

3. The converts (heretics?) can argue for an aggressive American effort to counter foreign national strategies with American strategies. Fight fire with fire!

Bench marking reveals a variety of foreign models. The Japanese Ministry of International Trade and Industry... orchestrates the development of a game plan in Japan. In Germany the large industrial banks, among them, the Deutsche Bank, are the conductors of the economic orchestra. Government-owned firms play a key role in France. But none of these foreign systems could easily be grafted onto the U.S. system. America is going to have to find a uniquely American way to develop a game plan.

The nature of the problems are neatly encapsulated in America's experience with amorphous metals—metals made by rapidly quenching alloys of iron, boron, and silicon to give them a glasslike consistency that has exceptional electrical and magnetic properties. Amorphous metals were developed by Allied-Signal, a New Jersey–based firm, in the early 1970s. Much of the market for the products it makes is in Japan. If Japanese engineers had used amorphous metals, they would have saved one billion dollars per year in electricity costs alone. But Japanese officials intervened to delay patent approval for eleven years, which left very little time to use the products before the original patents expired. Japanese companies were also persuaded not to use amorphous metals until the American patents expired. As the end of the patents approached (1993), MITI announced a catch-up program involving thirty-four Japanese companies in an effort to learn how to make amorphous metals themselves so that no time would be lost when the patents expired. What should have been a market of over one hundred million dollars per year has never been a market of more than a few million.

What should Americans do when other nations target an industry where they have a technical lead? Screams and protests do very little good. After intensive negotiations with the American trade representative, the Japanese agreed to buy thirty-two thousand amorphous-metal transformers (0.5 percent of the market) before the patents run out in 1993—essentially nothing. Allied-Signal has been accused by security analysts of having spent too much money on research and development. If it cannot make its R&D pay off by selling its products, it should do no R&D. On one level, the stock-market analysts are right. If products cannot be sold, they should not have been invented.

To be successful, American firms have to be able to build dominant market shares when they have technological leadership. If this is prohibited by foreign industrial policies, others will effectively compete in the U.S. market when they have technical superiority, but American firms will not be able to compete effectively in foreign markets when Americans have technological superiority.

The key difference between the United States and the rest of the industrial world is not the existence of protection. About 25 percent of all U.S. imports, double the amount of two decades ago, are now affected by nontariff trade barriers. International businessmen see Japan as the world's most unfair trading nation, but they see the United States as the third most unfair after Korea and Japan. The European Community has published a book listing hundreds of American violations of free trade.

If industrial policies are defined as trade protection, American industrial policies are as extensive as those in either Germany or Japan. But as the Japanese say, it is a "loser-driven" industrial policy—the product of random political lobbying power to gain protection for dying industries. The rest of the world's industrial policies involve strategic thinking and are "winner-driven." The Japanese protect amorphous metals; the Americans protect low-tech steel. While Americans are afraid to use the term *industrial policy*, the Europeans are proudly designing pan-European industrial policies.

The results show. Although a big decline in the value of the dollar succeeded in reducing the Japanese–U.S. trade deficit, the high-tech, high-wage part of the trade deficit is expanding. America is increasingly depending upon low-wage, low-tech commodity exports to balance its trading accounts. Any country can be competitive as a low-wage country. Any country can reduce its wage level by reducing the value of its currency. The issue is not balancing trading accounts but being competitive while paying high wages.

At some point Washington will have to come to grips with foreign industrial policies. What does one do when other nations target an industry? The American solution to Airbus is to try to stop European funds from going into Airbus Industries by getting GATT [General Agreement on Tariffs and Trade] to rule their activities illegal. As in amorphous metals, America will fail. It does not have the power to force the rest of the world to abandon national strategies. Airbus subsidies won't be ruled illegal by GATT; if ruled illegal, the ruling would simply be ignored by the Europeans.

In 1989 and 1990 the Bush administration was engaged in an internal intellectual debate revolving around high-definition television (HDTV): Should the Defense Department subsidize research on HDTV? Sadly, the debate remained an abstract ideological debate about the merits of government interference in the market rather than a real debate over whether HDTV was the place to jump back into consumer electronics, and if so, how? The ideological crusaders in the White House, a troika composed of John Sununu, Richard Darman and Michael Boskin, beat the advocates of government research subsidies in the Commerce and Defense departments, but it is also clear that their victory was temporary. The issue will continue to reappear.

It is of course possible to argue that the American system is uniquely unsuited to formulating strategic policies. A recent article by Pietro S. Nivola in the *Brookings Review* provides a good example of the argument. In outline, the argument is as follows:

1. America has a "closet industrial policy" hidden in its Defense Department.

2. Target industries in the rest of the world haven't earned high or even normal rates of return.

   a. Scholars argue over whether Japanese industrial policies have helped or hurt.

3. Industry-led industrial policies could become self-serving to the firms that participated.

   a. It is hard to figure out "who is us" when American firms manufacture abroad and foreign firms manufacture in the United States.

   b. Lemon socialism* might result.

4. Americans would not be very good in defensive "tit-for-tat" industrial policies, since American government institutions aren't very flexible.

   a. Random interventions aren't always bad.

Because of our own incompetence, we may be able to do nothing better than do nothing. No one can prove with complete certainty that this argument is wrong. But what we do know for certain is that the American system as it is now formulated isn't working. That is what falling real

---

* [Thurow's term for industrial policy.—Ed.]

wages, stagnant productivity growth, and a growing high-wage trade deficit mean. America may try something new, and it may fail, but nothing will have been lost—the old ways aren't working anyway.

In the real world of the twenty-first century, defensive industrial policies are unavoidable. To have any chance, America's corporations at least need a defensive strategic-trade policy in the United States. Such a policy is not designed to help American corporations (there is the problem of who is us), it is simply part of a general strategic-growth policy designed to help the American people. Public investments made to gain sustainable advantages should be limited to investments that will stay in America, such as investments in skills or domestic infrastructure.

Beyond such home investments, the search for strategic advantage abroad now revolves around process R&D investments. In Japan, MITI has shifted from the foreign-exchange and capital-allocations strategies of earlier decades to a strategy of pushing key technologies. The Europeans have set up an alphabet soup of cooperative R&D projects— Esprit, Jessi, Eureka—designed to do the same for European firms. While the details differ as to how it is done on the other sides of the Atlantic and Pacific oceans, the basic organizational structures are similar.

As George Lodge, a Harvard Business School professor, has described in detail in his recent book, *Perestroika for America*, strategies are industry-led when groups of companies, not government civil servants, propose the technologies that should be pushed. Governments never provide more than 50 percent of the total funding. If companies don't think that projects are worth risking some of their own money, the projects simply aren't done. Companies have to put together consortia, so that the government is not subsidizing a special favorite. More than one company has to think that the technology is important. In Europe the consortia have to come from more than one country. In the United States they could be required to come from more than one region. The idea is to magnify private funds with public funds, not to publicly finance research and development. The projects must have finite lifetimes with clearly stated objectives. No project is publicly funded forever. The purpose of a project must never be to advance knowledge for the sake of advancing knowledge. Other institutions, such as the National Science Foundation, have that task. The bureaucracy that makes the funding decisions can be very small, since business firms are making the basic go–no-go decisions when they decide whether they are willing to risk their own money.

Economic analysis shows that there are gains to be made with strategic trade policies, especially in industries with increasing returns, and this advantage will get bigger in a world of man-made comparative advantage and trading blocks. If government aid drives technology faster, everyone is a winner in the long run. More funds go into important areas that will raise long-run living standards, and no region of the world is going to be able to keep any key technology secret for more than a short period of time. A twenty-first-century civilian R&D race for supremacy among the economic superpowers is far better than the twentieth-century military R&D race for supremacy among the military superpowers.

Ideally, a new GATT for quasi trading blocks would limit government aid to R&D subsidies. But in a world without clearly defined rules that determine what governments can permissibly do to aid their strategic industries, America's game plan has to go beyond an R&D policy. Like American companies that advertise they will not knowingly be undersold, the United States should announce that it will duplicate any policies put in place in the rest of the world. Foreign industrial policies in wealthy countries will be matched dollar for dollar. Any subsidy going to Airbus Industries in Europe will be matched by an equivalent subsidy to the American airframe-manufacturing industry. Any delay in permitting an American telecommunication device to be used abroad, such as the delays Motorola experienced in Japan with its cellular telephones, will be matched with delays for advanced Japanese equipment in the United States. Americans are no longer in a position to force the rest of the world to play the economic game by its rules but Americans can play the game by their rules. If they want to play hardball, we'll play hardball.

Change is blowing in the winds. Listen to the words of two prominent economists that used to argue regularly against industrial policies:

Unlike the United States, both Japan and Europe have had extensive programs aimed at improving commercial performance.... As long as Japan and other nations helped companies that produced goods that the United States imported, such as textiles and steel, the United States was likely to gain. But the United States was hurt as countries started to subsidize products that competed with U.S. exports, such as aircraft, satellites, and computers. Targeting by foreign countries must be taken more seriously as they become competitive with the United States.

—Robert Lawrence,
Brookings economist

My own proposal is that we adopt an explicit, but limited, US industrial policy. That is, the US government should make a decision to frankly subsidize a few sectors, especially in the high technology area, that may plausibly be described as "strategic." ... One of the main purposes of this proposal is precisely to provide an alternative to managed trade.... Viewed from the right perspective, then, limited US industrial policies could be a relatively cheap way to cope with the stresses produced by the relative US decline and the special problem of dealing with Japan.

—Paul Krugman,
MIT economist....

AN EMPIRICAL EXPERIMENT

A decade ago it was possible to argue that instead of experimenting with strategic-growth policies to stimulate investments (physical and human), business groups, and national strategic planning, America could solve its problems by moving to a more vigorous form of traditional Anglo-Saxon capitalism. Both [former prime minister] Mrs. Thatcher in Great Britain and Mr. Reagan in the United States were elected on such platforms. Both advocated a return to "ancient virtues"—that is, they emphasized the role of the individual in economic performance, the stress on the Anglo-Saxon I. Government enterprises were privatized in Great Britain. American personal income taxes were dramatically lowered.

Both experiments are now more than a decade old. Neither succeeded.

In the United Kingdom unemployment is higher than it was when Mrs. Thatcher came into office (7.3 percent versus 5.8 percent), and the UK continues its slow drift down the list of the world's richest countries. In the United States productivity growth was negative in the two years before Reagan took office and in the two years after he left office. What was a small trade surplus became a large trade deficit.

Empirical experimentation revealed that a return to ancient Anglo-Saxon virtues is not the answer.

BOTTOM-LINE BENCHMARKING

Japan and Germany, the countries that are outperforming America in international trade, do not have less government or more motivated individuals. They are countries noted for their careful organization of teams—teams that involve workers and managers, teams that involve suppliers and customers, teams that involve government and business.

There is nothing antithetical in American history, culture, or traditions to teamwork. Teams were important in America's history—wagon trains conquered the West, men working together on the assembly line in American industry conquered the world, a successful national strategy and a lot of teamwork put an American on the moon first (and thus far, last). But American mythology extols only the individual—the Lone Ranger or Rambo. In America halls of fame exist for almost every conceivable activity, but nowhere do Americans raise monuments in praise of teamwork. Only national mythology stands between Americans and the construction of successful economic teams. To say this is not, however, to say that change is easy. History is littered with the wrecks of countries whose mythologies were more important than reality.

Systematic benchmarking reveals that the United States does not have to undergo a period of blood, sweat, and tears to regain its productive edge. Much of what has to be done, such as improving the K–12 education system, would make America a better place to live. With clear goals, schools would be more fun—not less. If spread out over time, even changes that would require a reduction in short-term American standards of living, such as a shift from consumption to investment, would be barely noticeable. Consumption, both public and private, just has to grow more slowly than the GNP [gross national product]. It doesn't have to fall.

While the necessary solutions would impose small burdens on the present, the failure to adopt these small solutions will impose major burdens on the future. We and our children will not have a world-class standard of living, and some of the chances for the good things of life that Americans have come to expect, such as heading major corporations, will diminish. Not doing anything is far worse than doing something.

The American problem does not lie in the severity of the necessary solutions. America's tough problem is realizing that there are problems that must be solved. Without that realization, nothing can be done. Minor problems that remain unsolvable in the present will create major problems that are difficult to solve in the future.

NO
Cynthia A. Beltz

THE STRATEGIC INDUSTRY DEBATE

While there is some agreement that much of trade is not based on perfectly competitive markets, there is little agreement about what the government should or can do about it: can the government act as a distinctively useful agent in markets on behalf of all its constituents, and if so, should it try to do so?

At the risk of oversimplification, the debate breaks down into skeptic and activist positions. The former starts by asking for evidence that a market failure exists, that it is relatively important for the nation, and that it can be corrected by government intervention to stimulate domestic producers in particular industries. The latter shifts the burden of proof and asks for evidence that a market failure does not exist.

On the activist side researchers at the Berkeley Roundtable on International Economy (BRIE) have argued that externalities in high-tech industries are important and should not be ignored by the government. Tyson has commented that the ability to innovate

> is not easily retained within firms or sectors but is much more easily retained within national borders. Thus, an important externality of market promotion policies in high-technology sectors is the creation of a national pool of R&D [research and development] talent and the maintenance and strengthening of the human capital necessary to innovate.

When externalities of this type are used to support the case for industrial policy, skeptics have taken issue with the argument for two reasons. The first challenge concerns the form of support chosen to promote human capital development in the United States. In particular skeptics have argued that industrial policy is a poorly designed policy tool if the intention is to increase the quality and quantity of skilled workers. They also question the extent to which the mix of a nation's output determines the availability and growth of skilled workers, instead of vice versa. They suggest that policies designed to increase investment in education and in worker training have a record of generating national returns and therefore are likely to serve national interests better than reliance on uncertain spillovers from favoring producers in particular industries.

Skeptics have also argued that as agents of global integration and increasing interdependence, multinationals [companies with divisions in more than two countries] have greatly complicated the spillover issue. David Richardson has argued that however large externalities may have been, they are likely getting smaller because of the moves of large multinationals to diversify across sectors and borders to improve their ability to appropriate interindustry spillovers or more formally to internalize externalities. To the extent this occurs, the distinctive role of the government in improving the performance of the market seems to have been at least partially bypassed by the actions of private participants. Additional moves to internalize information flows are suggested by the growth of transnational, corporate alliances in research, production, and marketing.

Economists often attempt to resolve contending policy conclusions through empirical analysis. But it is inherently difficult to quantify the relative importance of technological spillovers without a paper or objective trail of economic transactions. The case studies available also are historical in nature and offer little guidance for policies intended to improve national welfare over time. To what extent is the current commitment of private and public resources to the activity in question inadequate to secure the potential benefits for national welfare? Without clear rules and established procedures to evaluate questions such as these systematically, many economists conclude that it is not possible for the policy process to determine objectively the economic merits of a candidate's case for special attention or to determine the appropriate form and level of assistance. Thus an inherent risk is that

the policy will be ad hoc and prone to lengthy debates on individual claims for assistance.

Moreover, the claim that industrial targeting is welfare-enhancing also cannot be substantiated. The ITC [International Trade Commission] found in the early 1980s that the available evidence could not prove that industrial targeting improved national economic welfare in the home country. The ITC added that the evidence of proponents "usually consists of a selection of successful industries in successful countries, assertions that their success is due to targeting, and conclusions that the country's success is due to the targeting of these industries." Conversely cases such as the commercial failure of the supersonic transport suggest that one can win by not picking. Further, although an industry's success and an economy's success may be correlated with industrial targeting, as in Japan, there is no reason to presume that industrial policy has been the main cause of the nation's growth rate.

It would be useful to hold constant all the other factors that may affect growth rates and to explore why they differ across countries to discern what the growth rate would have been without industrial targeting. This is, however, virtually impossible. Rigorous attempts in this area have found that while targeting can alter the composition of what a nation produces, no one has clear empirical proof that industrial policy is welfare-enhancing even in Japan. Marcus Noland found in a recent econometric study that the Japanese industrial policy tools he could measure had a noticeable impact on its trade pattern and generally shifted resources from competitive to less competitive industries. He concluded that "while in some [manufacturing] cases

Japanese industrial policy may have successfully targeted industries, welfare-enhancing interventions appear to have been the exception, rather than the rule."

A key limitation of the industrial policy prescription is its industry-specific focus: even if the experts can agree about which industries are strategic, how to build strength in the industries remains a subject of dispute. Strategic industrial policy proponents assume that industry-specific promotion plans are the answer. But a nation's strength in the target industries may be based on broader factors such as average worker productivity, the education system, and strength in a wide variety of other industries. If this is the case, then a policy designed to stimulate selected firms and industries would tend to yield disappointing results at the expense of returns from alternative uses of public and private resources. If the long-run policy objective is to maintain an attractive manufacturing environment to capture spillovers generated by domestic production, then general support for factors of production tied to the United States—such as the physical infrastructure and a skilled labor force—may be a better expenditure of public and private resources. An unfortunate side effect of the industrial policy debate is the shift of attention from the need to promote and to maintain general economic strengths such as the ones both sides agree are necessary.

Yet... the central issue—rather than a sideline issue—should be the relative benefits of policies that promote general strengths versus those that promote the success of domestic producers in specific industries. How should the government promote national participation in technologically and economically promising industries wherever and whenever they may emerge? The final policy decision will necessarily rest on the judgments of policy makers and their advisers. But the following questions and issues merit the attention of those leaning toward instituting a policy of strategic industry promotion.

Is industrial policy worth the risk? Most realize that promotion programs are not free but require some budget and administrative costs. Economists warn that indirect costs should also not be overlooked. The strategic industrial policy case must show that the benefit side of the ledger from steering resources toward particular industries covers not only the apparent budget costs but also the costs of diverting domestic resources from alternative public and private uses.

Further, the unyielding process of rising technological and economic interdependence in the global economy dramatically complicates the practical problem of promoting domestic production in one industry without damaging the competitiveness of related industries. The 1986 U.S.–Japan Semiconductor Trade Arrangement, for example, raised the price of Japanese chips to U.S. computer firms, damaging their competitive position. Managing a policy of strategic industry promotion thus requires detailed information not only about the industry under consideration but also about the nature and extent of other resource constraints in the economy both today and over time.

Promotion and protection: linked in practice. As another hazard of the promotion of a strategic industry, the initial policy decision could be poorly designed and the costs imposed on other sectors magnified over time, particularly if for political reasons the strategic label cannot be repossessed. This raises the larger issue of the link in practice between promotion and protection. Once an industry is selected as strategic, is it always strategic? What should the limit of government responsibility be, and what is it likely to be? The... pressures for follow-up promotion are real since industries will return and ask for restrictions on foreign activities in the name of safeguarding earlier public and private investments in the industry.

If a strategic industry is one on which national economic strength and competitiveness depend, then the list of industries should be expected to change over time as the national economy changes. History suggests that the list of potential candidates has changed, or perhaps merely grown: textiles and machinery were considered critically important spillover industries in the early 1800s, followed by iron and steel in the late 1800s, automobiles, chemicals, and electrical equipment in the first part of the twentieth century, and more recently various subindustries in electronics. The twenty-first century also promises its share of candidates.

Although an industry may not always be strategic in economic terms for the nation, the accumulated political power of domestic producers in the industry may make it difficult to deny additional support for the industry. Witness the current problems in agriculture in the European Community or the current debate over continued support for textiles and steel in the United States. Furthermore the policy of strategic industry promotion seems predisposed to calls for follow-up promotion and protection because the nation has by definition taken a long-term stake in the domestic growth of a particular industry.

The international trading system. The dynamics of many nations pursuing policies of strategic industry promotion will also affect the long-term costs of this approach both for an individual nation and for the global trading system. This set of factors is perhaps the most critical, and yet the one most often overlooked in the policy debate.

All else equal, each nation acting alone has an incentive to subsidize domestic production in strategic industry candidates if the expected benefits outweigh the national costs of promotion and any necessary follow-up protective measures. Few variables remain unchanged, however, in the real world. National economic opportunities, risks, and decisions are not independent but increasingly intertwined. Considerable economic and political problems may arise as a result if trading partners simultaneously target the same industries for promotion.

This is not an idle concern. One popular suggestion for picking industries in the United States is the crowd-mentality approach to targeting. "The Japanese realize it [high-definition television (HDTV)] is important and the Europeans realize it too. And all we're doing is playing ball." The nation should wake up, the argument continues, and stop debating the merits of industrial policy or the possibility of identifying strategic industries: if both the Japanese and the Europeans believe HDTV is strategic, then it must be, and the United States should also target it. But does this make sense? If trading partners target the same industry, important niche markets may be overlooked, potential benefits from specialization may be lost, market overcrowding will occur, government will be pressed to respond by managing trade in the industry with protective measures that fragment markets further, the scale economies everyone is seeking will be reduced, and the global pace of technological progress may ultimately be slowed. It is hard to imagine anyone winning in this context.

Some will argue that this scenario is extreme, but it amply illustrates that the strategic industrial policy approach is not just a challenge to American policy makers but a challenge to the international trading system. On this point activists are conspicuously silent, leaving unanswered how problems of excessive duplication of R&D, congestion, and rising trade tensions can be avoided or addressed if—as seems likely—each nation pursues the same list of strategic industries.

Managing Strategic Industry Lists Without Rules

Without firm rules and the risk of costly mistakes considerable for both the nation and the international trading system, few economists are optimistic about whether a U.S.-style strategic industrial policy can be welfare-enhancing. Some, however, remain optimistic and have suggested that the policy gamble be managed by keeping the list of candidates short. But how will the list be kept short in practice? And without detailed policy guidelines how can the nation be sure that the composition of the list will be determined by economic criteria?

The list-making industry is already working overtime. Lists of critical technologies are particularly popular. The stated reason for the lists initially seems straightforward: the social benefits of some technologies are clearly evident but exceed perceived private marginal benefit so the investment that is undertaken today is inadequate to generate the socially optimal result. Several members of BRIE, for example, suggested in 1989 that only those technologies that promise to "radically transform products and production processes of a wide range of sectors" should be chosen as strategic. They emphasized new materials, microelectronics technologies, superconductivity, and biotechnologies. Under the strategic label they suggest that intervention to subsidize the fixed costs of development and to help create initial markets could be justified. More recently the lists of critical technologies circulating through trade associations, the Defense and Commerce Departments, and the administration include ten to thirty critical technologies. Digital imaging technologies, which underlie the HDTV and computer industries, are among the additions to the list.

The list makers these days are, however, extremely vague about the nature and amount of government support they believe is necessary to advance U.S. interests in successful commercialization of the technologies. To avoid the stigma attached to the label of industrial policy, most also explicitly state that picking winners and losers is not part of their policy agenda. They suggest instead that the United States should make the support of critical technologies that cut across industry borders a national priority. Around the corner are more explicit and ambitious industry-specific plans. In the spring of 1990 Rep. Norman Y. Mineta (D, Calif.) called for the secretary of commerce to devise a list of critical American industries that "will provide the bulk of economic opportunity and economic growth" in the future. Deciding which industry to include and exclude, however, sounds suspiciously like picking winners and losers.

Pressure will also undoubtedly continue to build to tilt broad concerns over U.S. technological and commercial capabilities toward preferential treatment for selected industries as competition worldwide continues to increase and perception of unfair foreign trade practices persists. Two issues in this debate merit particular attention.

Advanced technologies and strategic industry claims. In the debate over the nature of U.S. technology policy, the strategic industrial policy case should not be confused with the one for advanced technologies, which may have multiple applications. The case for supporting the development of these technologies in the precompetitive stage is fundamentally different from the one for strategic industry promotion. Support for the former is by definition broad in orientation, while the other is selective. Support for generic technologies should not try to pick a development path, while it is the objective of the latter to steer resources toward particular industries and applications. One defines a limit for government support, while it is in effect left open-ended in the strategic industry case.

Imperfect political markets. The issue of strategic industry promotion is not only a matter of foresight but also inherently one of compatible incentives and institutions. The length and substance of a strategic industry list, for example, are likely to depend more on the nature of [a] nation's political institutions than on the ideas of economists and technology experts about strategic industries.

Some in favor of more activist industrial policies have suggested that the United States should not be deterred by the policy gamble associated with picking strategic industries, especially since the European[s] and Japanese apparently do not have such reservations. Differences in institutions and capabilities across countries preclude, however, this simple comparison. Leaving aside the information requirements and the questionable record of success in Europe, calls for more industrial targeting in the United States need to be evaluated in the context of the special nature of American institutions.

The dynamics of the American policy process, for example, seem likely to be at odds with those of strategic industries. The strategic industrial policy approach requires difficult choices about the distribution of private and public resources, which conflicts with the incentives of elected officials to avoid decisions that give the appearance of favoring one group over another. As a result the politics of building a constituency for industry-specific assistance may spread activities across the United States such that the potential for reaping the technological benefits from the geographic concentration of related industrial activities (local spillovers) is curtailed rather than enhanced by intervention.

The issue is not simply whether the nation can pick industries to promote commercial interests. Clearly it can try to do so. Rather the issue is whether the United States can pick only those candidates that merit selection on the basis of economic criteria and whether assistance can be structured such that national welfare is improved rather than curtailed. Another important factor is whether assistance to the industry can be discontinued if the policy gamble does not pay off for the nation. There is no reason to presume that a strategic industry list could be kept short in practice. Indeed the reverse seems more likely. The preestablished economic conditions for identifying strategic industries are vague, open to interpretation, and therefore likely to encourage strategic industry claims without providing a defensible rationale for resisting pressures to attach the strategic label to a variety of activities. Moreover, since interindustry spillovers are not uncommon, practically any industry could marshal a case for strategic treatment.

Skeptics have argued in this context that the American political process is not well equipped for the task of identifying or determining how to assist potentially strategic industries. Anne Krueger has pointed out that relying on the political process to select strategic industries without a set of clearly defined rules and procedures invites capture by special interest groups. Or, in the words of George Eads, "if care is not taken, 'externalities' will be discovered primarily where it is politically advantageous to discover them."

To heed his advice, it is incumbent upon those who believe that the United States needs to take a more activist stance to explain how policy makers will know in practice which industries or subcomponents should be included on the list and how much assistance they require. Also, how can they exclude those seeking to jump on the bandwagon and push off those that no longer merit preferential treatment? Is it possible to insulate the selection process from political pressures? Activists need to show specifically how the abuse of interindustry spillover arguments for strategic industry promotion will be avoided or minimized. At a minimum, flexibility would have to be designed into list management so that preferential treatment could be discontinued if the policy gamble appears unlikely to pay off for the nation. Otherwise, without mechanisms of this type and without rules, the political-economic cycles engendered by strategic industrial policy seem more likely to be vicious than virtuous.

POLICY IMPLICATIONS FOR THE 1990s

The friction between the concept of a strategic industry and its application can be summarized by four simple statements: If we do not change paths, we may lose (dynamic comparative advantage). Yet we cannot know in advance where we are going (the intricate nature of economic progress). It is unclear how we will get there or how we will know once we have arrived (no simple rules or accepted procedures). And if we follow each other, we may all get lost (crowd mentality).

POSTSCRIPT

Should the United States Have a National Industrial Policy?

"In the long run," Thurow concludes, "history will tell us which theory is right. An empirical experiment is now under way. The profit-maximizing firms of the United States have faced off against the empire-building firms of Japan. Individualistic capitalism meets communitarian capitalism. Eventually, the winners will be known. In the end the winner will force the losers to change and play by the winner's rules."

If the United States were to adopt an industrial policy, the question would still remain of what form it should take. To what degree would the government be a participant? Would government have a direct, controlling role or simply a participatory role, with the industries themselves creating the bulk of the industrial strategies? Would an industrial policy necessarily be forever? That is, can a case be made for adopting a national policy only until the United States is undeniably the industrial superpower of the world and then gradually returning to an absolute free market system?

Many argue that it is not necessary to modify the American industrial system at all in order to remain a competitor in the world market. Even now, the United States threatens to capture the market in machine tools, quite without the benefit of industrial policy. Who would have thought it possible? Proponents of free competition, such as Beltz, support letting the problem of America's decline in international economic competitiveness work itself out, especially in light of the American propensity to favor industries with strong labor unions over industries that tend to rely on legislative resource allocation.

SUGGESTED READINGS

Michael Calingaert, "Government-Business Relations in the European Community," *California Management Review* (Winter 1993).

John Carey, "Industrial Policy, or Industrial Folly?" *Business Week* (May 17, 1993).

Robert Cizik, "It's Time for a New Industrial Revolution," *Industry Week* (February 1, 1993).

L. G. Georghiou and J. S. Metcalfe, "Evaluation of the Impact of European Community Research Programmes Upon Industrial Competitiveness," *R & D Management* (April 1993).

Robert Oxnam, "Asia/Pacific Challenges," *Foreign Affairs* (vol. 72, no. 1, 1993).

Ronald Rotenburg and John Southerst, "Do We Need an Industrial Strategy?" *Canadian Business* (October 10, 1992).

ISSUE 2

Is Free Enterprise Always More Efficient?

YES: Carolyn Lochhead, from "Fruit Fight: Independent Growers Challenge Agribusiness Giants," *Insight* (July 29, 1991)

NO: Farmers for an Orderly Market, from *Democratic Self-Determination: An Alternative to Subsidies* (Sunkist Growers, Inc., 1984; reissued 1991)

ISSUE SUMMARY

YES: News reporter Carolyn Lochhead asserts that agribusiness cartels—who, through federal "marketing orders," determine the amount of produce that independent fruit growers may sell—have frozen the market. She argues that allowing small growers more independence in the marketing of their fruit would result in greater profit for both the companies and the public.

NO: The Farmers for an Orderly Market, a coalition of citrus growers, including Sunkist Growers, Inc., formed to counter the arguments being made by dissident citrus marketers, support the tradition of federal marketing orders as the only way to ensure a 12-month supply of high-quality fruit and solvency for the fruit farmer.

The "marketing orders" of the California fruit growers are an anomaly in the free enterprise system. Free competition among individual suppliers of some fruits has been replaced by an old-fashioned cartel that regulates the picking, packing, shipping, and marketing of the fruit according to a schedule that purports to give each supplier a fair share of the market. The cartel is, by order of Congress in 1937, immune from antitrust action.

The cartel was formed during the Depression. At that time, farms were quickly going out of business, and the Roosevelt administration was interested in saving them. In order to do this, it had to take into account the peculiar nature of farming as a business: the farmer generally has no knowledge of or control over his or her market share for any but the most specialized products, no way to distinguish his or her product from that of many other farmers, little control over production (which mostly depends on the weather and externals such as insect infestation), and, unless he or she is a neighborhood "truck farmer," the farmer has little control over the shipment of his or her goods to the customers. Further, farmers are constantly in crushing debt, borrowing each season for the seed for planting and repaying when the harvest is marketed. A single bad year can put a farmer out of business.

To bring some of the lethal economic variables under control, certain fruit growers were permitted to form an association that would regulate them. A democratically elected panel would decide what markets needed how much fruit, determine the most economic ways of getting that fruit to those markets, assign quantities to the growers of the associations, and check on the quality of the product. Thus, to everyone's advantage, the customers would receive a steady supply of high-quality, fresh fruit, the growers could count on a steady market, reasonable prices would be maintained for all, and all would be spared the stress of guessing yearly on the timing and quantity of product picking, shipping, and buying. Farmers stopped going out of business, and the customers were happy.

This, however, is the type of happiness the free enterprise system was set up to *avoid*, some of the growers now argue. The free enterprise system thrives on uncertainty and on the consequent efforts to develop cost savings, new markets, new products, and new efficiencies. Whatever the costs to the cartel, some independent growers feel they ought to be able to go out on their own and struggle for a higher market share.

Disagreements on cause and consequences plague this issue. *Cui bono* ("to whose advantage?") is one of the classic questions of ethics: For whose good does this cartel function? Who would profit if the cartel were destroyed or its power undermined? First, who are the chief growers and who are the chief complainers? Both sides claim that their side represents small, hardworking family farms and that the other side represents giant corporations. Second, what would happen to the customers if the cartel ceased to function? Would they be able to take advantage of bargains resulting from the discovery of new efficiencies, or would the supply of fresh, high-quality fruit dry up? Third, what would happen to the industry? Would the power of the big growers be curtailed by competition, or would they be the only survivors in a resulting free-for-all and possibly erratic price fluctuations?

Amid these questions stands a classic confrontation. Suppose it can be shown that the customers and the producers of a particular product will both fare much better if a centrally placed association controls the flow of goods to market and dictates the quantity to be produced by all. A moderately profitable life can be enjoyed by all, if only they will forget about their liberty to produce what they want, in any quantity they want, and to sell to anyone they want. Does this ignore the essence of the free enterprise system? Is free enterprise desirable? Can it be mathematically proven that free enterprise makes everyone more prosperous? Do we simply value the liberty to make our own choices in the economic sphere?

Ask yourself, as you read these selections, who are the growers who run the cartel, as described by the Farmers for an Orderly Market, and who are the growers who oppose it, as described by Carolyn Lochhead? What are the fundamental grounds for maintaining each side of the argument?

YES

Carolyn Lochhead

FRUIT FIGHT: INDEPENDENT GROWERS CHALLENGE AGRIBUSINESS GIANTS

In California grove country, a bruising battle pits the small, independent growers and packers against a cartel system backed by the force of the federal government. The farmers pick, pack and sell under their competitors' rule. A recent ruling concurs with their claims of constitutional infringement.

Dan Gerawan sits in the packinghouse of his family farm—a farm started from scratch back in 1938 in California's San Joaquin Valley—and tries to explain the inexplicable. He opens a carton of beautiful nectarines. Their natural aroma wafts into the room.

"You're in the presence of an illegal substance," he says.

The fruit is not poisoned. These nectarines are entirely edible. They pose no threat to consumers; indeed, retail buyers across the country are clamoring for them, and the Gerawan family prides itself on their superior quality. Nonetheless, this fruit must be destroyed, by order of a nectarine cartel composed of Gerawan's chief competitors, backed by the full power of the U.S. government.

In fact, while this valley is one of the richest agricultural regions in the world, it is also consumed by a rot both literal and metaphoric. Here tons of choice fruits and nuts are left to spoil in the fields or are fed to cattle, not because they are unfit for human consumption, but because agribusiness cartels say they must. These cartels operate in a number of major commodities. These include California and Arizona citrus, an industry dominated by the $1 billion-a-year company Sunkist Growers Inc.

Welcome to the world of "marketing orders," which are more aptly termed antimarketing orders. An obscure relic of Franklin Roosevelt's New Deal, these regulations create government-enforced cartels in certain produce markets. Growers of some commodities are allowed to restrict output in order to raise prices—behavior that in other industries would be considered a violation of antitrust laws.

The orders deny farmers the right to sell the product of their labor to Americans who want to buy it. The farmers argue that the orders inhibit innovation—and, more fundamentally, deny them their constitutional rights to due process, free speech and protection against the taking of private property without just compensation.

Norman Freestone owns a 36-acre organic farm where he grows navel oranges. He is ordered to withhold a large portion of his oranges from the market each week by a committee of his competitors dominated by Sunkist. If Freestone disobeys, he faces a federal fine and imprisonment.

"I'm the smallest of the small," he says. "I'm not a threat to anybody. This is the United States of America. This is a free market system, or I thought it was. But you have somebody looking over your shoulder telling you how many oranges you can sell in a given week, and that someone happens to be an entity that's in the same business you are, selling the same things you are. It's grossly unfair."

The basic aim of marketing orders is to raise commodity prices and thereby aid farmers. But while they do indeed hurt consumers, they do not, in the long run, help farmers. Instead, the system has spawned a classic treadmill: Higher prices induce more production, so that quotas must be tightened further to achieve the same effect. The cost to consumers in higher prices and economic waste runs to hundreds of millions of dollars each year. Poorer consumers are entirely denied access to some fresh fruits (small, less attractive and therefore less expensive produce that is held off the market).

* * *

Growers, for their part, must sacrifice millions in lost sales. More than one-third of the entire crop of fresh California navel oranges is held off the market each year and left to rot, dumped into cattle feed or sold at a loss to juice plants.

The U.S. Department of Agriculture, which oversees the orders, has been captured by the cartels; indeed, the department runs what many call a kangaroo court system that effectively shields the orders from legal attack. And according to a recent court decision, federal bureaucrats charged with overseeing the system at times deliberately overlook obvious corruption.

The cartels wield formidable political power; they overcame substantial opposition during the early years of the Reagan administration, partly with the aid of high-ranking California Republicans. Congress, for its part, has prohibited the Federal Trade Commission and other agencies from even studying marketing orders.

Now a full-scale farmer rebellion is under way in the San Joaquin Valley that promises to spill over into the halls of Congress. Dissident growers at war with the cartels say they now represent 35 percent of the industry. The results of a June referendum of growers to decide the fate of navel and Valencia orange orders are pending, following a dissident triumph earlier this year when growers voted out a marketing order for plums. Several other orders are in limbo after contested balloting.

At stake is the enormous power of the Sunkist cooperative, as well as several other cartels. Blue Diamond Growers, the $500 million almond cooperative, is under heavy attack as well.

The fight has been bitter. Sunkist executives paint the dissidents as an annoying but tiny minority, upset primarily because the USDA has accused the farmers of cheating on cartel rules. In a May 31 letter to member growers signed by President Russ Hanlin and Chairman Tom Dungan, Sunkist referred to the leading dissident, Carl "Skip" Pescosolido, and his fellow opponents as "Pescosolido and his stooges."

"Of which I am a proud member," retorts Dennis Johnston of Johnston Farms near Bakersfield. The dissident ranks are growing, led primarily by a younger generation of growers who say they want to join the world of modern, aggressive marketing. They think they are faster and leaner than their large competitors. They believe that they can move more fruit to more people at lower prices than the cartels allow. They want the opportunity to do so.

Stripped of their bureaucratic complexities, marketing orders are quite simple. Enacted in 1937 over the constitutional objections of the pre-Roosevelt Supreme Court, the law allows farmers to form committees for the purpose of controlling the flow of produce to market. (It exempts the committees from antitrust law.)

Compliance with the marketing orders is compulsory. No farmer who grows produce governed by the orders is allowed to operate outside of them—a farmer who does faces federal prosecution.

Most of the 43 marketing orders that currently exist are fairly innocuous, establishing quality categories and joint advertising efforts. Several, however, are openly anticompetitive. The orders governing California and Arizona citrus maintain strict controls on the amount of fruit that can be sold, as do the smaller-volume spearmint and filbert orders. Several others, including the California almond, nectarine and peach orders, manipulate quality standards and advertising programs to inhibit competition.

Committees of a dozen or so industry members administer the orders. Their regulations carry the weight of federal law, and dissidents say that the Agriculture Department simply rubber-stamps committee recommendations, instead of exercising oversight. So, in effect, the committees have the power to make law in their industries.

Large growers and packers dominate these committees. Because the amount of sales usually determines committee membership, cooperatives like Sunkist with their big market shares often exercise total control. The almond marketing order even stipulates that Blue Diamond Growers must have four of the 10 seats on the almond committee, regardless of how many almonds it sells.

Sunkist controls more than half of the California citrus industry. Through its alliance with a few large independents, including a huge limited partnership, it controls the navel committee with six of 11 members. Although there are no cooperatives in tree fruit (also called stone fruit in the industry), large packers also dominate those boards. Says Rep. Richard K. Armey, a Texas Republican, "These are government-created and government-enforced cartels that protect a very few producers invested with enormous power, in the case of citrus most notably Sunkist."

In Cutler, Calif., F. T. "Tokkie" Elliott, a tree fruit and citrus grower and packer, explains how things work in tree fruits. Elliott was forced to dump some 35,000 cartons of nectarines because of rules handed down by the nectarine cartel. When he complained earlier about similar rules promulgated by the plum committee, he says he was told that if he couldn't pack under the committee's regulations, he could pull up his trees.

The committees have argued that Elliott and others are merely trying to ship poor-quality fruit, or "put crap in a box," as some have phrased it. However, according to a May 1991 decision by USDA Administrative Law Judge Dorothea Baker, the nectarine and plum committees deliberately held Elliott's and other growers' fruit off the market so that it would not compete with the varieties sold by committee members.

* * *

They did this, the judge found, by manipulating "quality" standards governing fruit size and maturity. Using color chips—like those found in paint stores and determined by an eminent fruit scientist, Gordon Mitchell of the University of California at Davis, to lack any validity—the committee set a standard that declared Elliott's varieties of fruit to be immature and therefore unshippable.

In fact, Elliott's fruit was often so ripe that it rotted by the time it reached East Coast markets—and yet it still could not meet the maturity standard. The standards clearly had nothing to do with buyer judgments: One gourmet retailer was selling an entire crop of Elliott's Tom Grand nectarines at premium prices, even as the nectarine committee ruled them unfit to eat.

However, Judge Baker ruled, when committee members' own fruit failed the same standards, the committees granted special "variances" from the rules. Other packers could obtain variances only if they sold the same varieties grown by the chairman of the nectarine committee, Leroy Giannini. According to the decision, it was common knowledge that a variance was never granted unless "Leroy gets it." Committee members, the judge found, would sometimes not even bother with the formality of a variance; they would simply order that fruit pass inspection if it was grown by themselves and certain "friends."

"All I want to do is grow my crops, pack them, market them and sell them," says Elliott. "Let my customer determine what product he wants. Not my competitors."

It pays to advertise: The tree fruit committees also levy hefty assessments on growers to fund promotion campaigns. The Gerawans, for instance, are forced to pay $660,000 each year to the tree fruit committees, and Elliott more than $100,000. These huge sums go toward generic advertising, like the California "summer fruits" campaign, that undermines the efforts of individual growers to promote their own branded varieties.

Most packinghouses have their own brands, and there may be vast quality differences from one brand to the next. The Gerawans, for example, pick their Fairlane nectarine trees eight to 10 times a season to ensure a uniform degree of ripeness in each carton. Most growers pick the trees only two or three times, so a carton might contain both immature and overripe fruit.

Forcing growers to fund generic advertising in these commodities has costs for both growers and consumers. If consumers are led to believe that plums are plums, and there is no variation between them, no specific brand can stand out and command a higher price. Growers have little reason to improve quality and are severely constrained from promoting their own brands by being forced to shovel huge assessments into committee coffers.

To top things off, some of the generic advertising is not generic at all, but rather promotes the fruit of committee members, such as the Red Jim nectarine grown by committee member Jimmy Ito.

The orders also place very real limits on innovation. Grand Union supermarkets had asked the Gerawans to pack their Prima brand plums in a 24-pound box rather than the standard 28-pound carton to reduce shrinkage and create a better display. The plum committee prohibited the new container, claiming that it would create "confusion" in the marketplace— even though the *retailer* had asked for it.

Grand Union also wanted to experiment with 21-pound cartons. This time Gerawan decided to play the game. He called the head of the nectarine committee, Mickey George, who called a meeting. "I sat there in front of them and they said, 'We resent having to be here in the middle of the season for this request you've made.' I said, 'I resent having to be here in front of a group of my competitors to ask if I can sell nectarines to a customer who wants them that way.' This is the type of thing we deal with."

George, president of George Bros. in Sultana, confirms Gerawan's account, adding however that such requests are usually made in the fall. "We're all growers of these commodities, serving on these committees without compensation," he says, "and sometimes that takes a lot of our time, so it's volunteer work." For growers to get a proper hearing, he says, the requests should be made when the committee has time to deliberate, "when you're not in the heat of battle, so to speak, with your crop." Inconvenient or not, Gerawan responds, he had a customer who wanted the product at that time, and he was willing to provide it.

The Tree Fruit Reserve: It also turns out that the tree fruit committees have for years been engaged in funneling grower money through a mysterious organization called the Tree Fruit Reserve. Most packers were unaware of its existence before it was uncovered in the proceedings before Judge Baker. According to the court, this shadow entity was used for such illegal activities as hiring attorneys to defend "the industry" in litigation involving the committees' administration of marketing orders.

The Tree Fruit Reserve also hired lawyers to aid committeemen charged by growers with antitrust violations. The court found that Agriculture Department employees, charged with oversight of the marketing orders, knew of and even abetted the illegal scheme.

In her ruling, Judge Baker found the tree fruit committees in violation of federal law. Baker also made note of the constitutional issues posed, including violations of the First Amendment right of free speech, the 14th Amendment right to due process and the Fifth Amendment prohibition against the taking of private property without just compensation.

This is nuts: Cloyd Angle has been battling similar "quality" standards, volume controls and forced advertising in the almond industry for several years. Angle was living in a trailer when he started his almond packinghouse near Modesto. He is now one of the most successful independents in the industry, selling almonds primarily as an ingredient for ice cream, candy and bakery goods.

Until its market share recently dipped below 50 percent, the Blue Diamond cooperative had voting control of the Almond Board. It still retains four votes, enough to block most reforms. Roger Baccigaluppi, president and chief executive officer of Blue Diamond, says the idea that the cooperative ever controlled the board is "totally false"—even though it has usually had a majority of votes and voted as a bloc.

Last year, the board ordered Angle and other packers to dump 7 percent of their crop—42 million pounds of almonds worth an estimated $82 million wholesale—into uneconomic outlets such as cattle feed, even though almonds are so expensive that many Americans cannot afford them. If that 7 percent had reached the market, prices would have fallen.

Surveillance: To make sure packers do in fact dump their almonds, the board operates an extensive compliance operation. Six investigators keep close surveillance on packers. "There's more rules and regulations for this one little almond than if you raised all the dope, marijuana and cocaine in the whole world," says Angle. "And here you've got your own [almond police] out there looking for violators, hiding under bushes, out at night following trucks. I mean, you can't believe all the stuff that's gone on." These are laws, Angle says, "that your competitor puts in to monitor you."

The board also ordered packers to hold 35 percent of last year's almond crop in "reserve" for later sale. It is claimed that these reserves smooth out the market between bumper and small crops and so protect consumers, although no accepted economic theory substantiates this claim. Moreover, Blue Diamond wanted to impose a 10 percent reserve this year, despite a very small crop. Clearly, such action would not "smooth the market" so much as jack up prices.

The real purpose of the reserves, Angle charges, is to restrict the sales of independents that might cut into Blue Diamond's market share. "We can market ours in a heartbeat," he says. "They can't. So what they want to do is make you hold along with them."

The board also imposes huge advertising assessments, some $500,000 a year in Angle's case, and sets out detailed rules on how to advertise and what to say. The rules are constructed in such a way that the bulk of this advertising must be targeted at the retail consumer. Perhaps it is a coincidence that Blue Diamond controls some 90 percent of the retail shelf space, while most independents sell almonds wholesale as ingredients. In fact, Angle exports most of his to Europe.

It's like a foot-race, Angle says. "The great big, old, clumsy, fat guy is trying to run the 100-yard dash, and he knows you're going to beat him. So he wants to put enough weight on you so that he can get there first."

The clumsy, fat guy has until now faced little internal opposition, in part because the Department of Agriculture exercises weak oversight and in part because growers are intimidated by the committees' power to do things like order audits of their compliance with federal regulations.

The audit game: This is the area that frightens growers most—the quasi-police power of the committees and the possibility of its misuse. For example, Elliott spoke up against quotas at a 1984 hearing on the orange quotas in Bakersfield. The next day, orange committee auditors were in his packinghouse.

The man who sent the auditors there is the manager of the orange committee, Billy Peightal. Peightal is a former Sunkist employee whose salary is set by committee vote—the very committee controlled by Sunkist. He insists that all packinghouses are audited equally. Yet the USDA's Office of Inspector General, acting after bitter complaints by dissident packer Pescosolido, discovered that Peightal failed to turn in to the

Department of Agriculture several rule violations by *Sunkist* packinghouses.

Peightal admits he did not do so. "They just weren't forwarded, for whatever reason, and I can't tell you why not," he says. "They were in our compliance group's office in Lindsay, and they simply weren't forwarded. Frankly, I think they were lost."

The explanation doesn't satisfy James Moody, a Washington public interest attorney who works for the dissidents. "When you're in charge of a compliance operation, when your whole reason to be there is to make sure people follow these rules, I would respectfully say that 'Whoops, I forgot' isn't good enough."

The significance of Peightal's laxity is hard to overstate. If selective enforcement does happen on a larger scale, it might indicate that by using its committee control, Sunkist can ship as much as it wants while throttling shipments by competitors. William Quarles, Sunkist's vice president for government relations, says, "We are not aware of any such [cheating]."

From a consumer's standpoint, cartel cheating is to be encouraged: the more oranges shipped, the better. But for a packer who faces steep penalties for overshipments while competitors ship at will, his livelihood could be at stake.

David Roth, manager of Cecilia Packing Corp. in Orange Cove, Calif., describes the choices the independent faces: "It depends on how much you're cornered, how much against the wall you are, what you're losing and what you have to sell to keep packing," he says. "You've got a multimillion-dollar facility out here, and they've stopped you from packing. It's not good for you, it's not good for your workers. If I can't pack, I can't pick. I can't do anything. I'm stopped."

Pressure for change within Sunkist may be mounting. According to the confidential minutes of an April 18 meeting, the board of directors of its largest packinghouse group, the Central California Citrus Exchange, voted unanimously to oppose quotas in the June referendum.

Despite this opposition from a key group of members, Sunkist cast a bloc vote in favor of the controls. Each of its thousands of members counts as a "yes" by proxy. Thus, Sunkist picks up a large apathy vote and turns potential nays to yeas. Given Sunkist's huge market share, the bloc vote is expected to carry the referendum.

Sunkist's Quarles justifies the decision to vote as a bloc by citing the devastation wrought by last December's freeze, which killed nearly the entire California citrus crop. The Sunkist board was concerned that growers whose crops were damaged in the freeze might "have their minds on other things during this voting period, and they just didn't want to take any chances that apathy would be a negative factor," says Quarles.

In other words, Sunkist simply assumed its growers would support its vote. The dissidents say that explanation is disingenuous; Sunkist had to impose the bloc vote or lose the referendum, they assert. Sunkist's own economic interests are exclusively involved in moving oranges to market. Sunkist itself doesn't own an orange tree. It merely markets oranges grown by its members and collects a per-carton fee.

"That's their income," says John Ford, who as a deputy assistant agriculture secretary led the Reagan administration's mostly unsuccessful battles against marketing orders. "They don't care about whether the growers are making any profit on their oranges. They just care about getting those fees."

Sunkist staunchly defends the system, arguing that it benefits both growers and consumers. "Consumers for the most part are more interested in market stability than in wildly fluctuating prices," says Quarles. "And of course, fluctuating prices are attendant to markets that are glutted and starved. Consumers want a continuous supply of high quality produce at reasonable prices, and that's what we provide."

Peightal of the navel orange committee also defends the controls. "Market needs are satisfied," he contends. Some growers may want to ship more oranges than the committee allows, he concedes, "but the objective of the marketing order is to equate the needs of the market with the supplies that the committee thinks should be moved."

* * *

In fact, unregulated produce markets contradict government and cartel claims that without controls markets would be "chaotic" and prone to ruinous "gluts and famines," and consumers would be denied a stable supply. Volume controls were suspended on California Valencias some four years ago, and no "chaos" developed. Florida orange markets are unregulated.

Others insist that it makes little sense to limit the volume of California navel oranges when competing fruits, including imports, are unregulated. If retailers can't get California navels, they can get Washington apples or Chilean grapes. "All we are doing is just giving away shelf space every time we restrict shipments of oranges," says Perry Walker, a former packinghouse executive.

The dissidents have a model to follow. Florida grapefruit growers voted out their controls years ago on the grounds that they were archaic, unfair and disruptive, says Doug Bournique, executive vice president of the Indian River Citrus League, which represents 1,600 growers. He says a younger generation of growers and packers "came on board and said, 'We don't want any constraints. We want to let the free enterprise system work.'"

The results? The Indian River name is renowned for quality, and exports to Europe and Japan are booming. "I haven't heard any conversation here about resurrecting [controls]," says Bournique. "Not one iota."

As for revamping the system, Secretary of Agriculture Edward Madigan could terminate the marketing orders immediately, as every administration and every Congress could have since the 1930s. But none has. Dissident growers are left to seek redress through endless court battles.

These growers despise their peculiar brand of socialist state planning and economic control. They speak often of free enterprise. "In the United States," says Kent Burt, a citrus grower in Exeter, Calif., "you should have the freedom to buy and sell, as you see fit, what you grow and raise. It's so basic. And yet we don't."

"Release it," he urges. "Release the orange."

Farmers for an Orderly Market

DEMOCRATIC SELF-DETERMINATION: AN ALTERNATIVE TO SUBSIDIES

Marketing orders keep citrus flowing to the supermarkets and other outlets in steady supply year-round, and, over the years, have kept prices in a relatively stable range.

Federal marketing orders for fruit and vegetables, enabled under the Agricultural Marketing Agreement Act of 1937, allow farmers to develop and implement self-help programs to regulate the marketing of certain specialty crops.

There are many types of marketing orders because each program is specifically designed to meet the needs of a particular commodity. For example, there are size and grade orders which remove undesirable sizes and qualities of fruit from the marketplace. Marketing orders covering commodities that are harvested once a year and then preserved for use at a later time, such as raisins, almonds and prunes, rely on set-aside or reserve-pool provisions which allow the surplus portion of a crop to be stored for sale later.

The citrus industry utilizes a flow-to-market feature or prorate provision that works like this: An industry committee, nominated by the growers and appointed by the Secretary of Agriculture, determines the amount of fruit that can be absorbed into the domestic market *each week* without glutting or shorting the market. (Fruit for export channels and the juice market is exempt.)

This has the effect of spreading both the harvesting and marketing of the crop in an orderly fashion over its full life cycle. By tying harvesting to market demand, consumers get a continuing supply of fresh fruit each week of the season while warehouse storage of citrus is kept to an absolute minimum. Uncontrolled glutting of the market with a perishable product like oranges would cause consumers to receive unappealing, aged fruit out of storage until the supply returns to normal.

It should be clearly understood that while the marketing order authorizes volume regulations, it does not establish the price. The price of an orange is, for example, established in the overall marketplace on the basis of supply and demand.

The marketing order does not diminish the need for a grower to compete efficiently. Nor does it guarantee a sale. It is still the grower's responsibility to grow a quality product, package it properly and market it aggressively. He will not survive if he produces something that is not acceptable to the consumer.

Under the prorate provisions in 1982, when there was a normal production of navel oranges, the California-Arizona citrus industry was able to move 38 million cartons. Conversely, in 1983, a year with an enormous crop of navels, the industry moved 49 million cartons. The price, however, was $1.13 less per carton than it had been the previous year. So the laws of supply and demand continue to work under the marketing order system.

In no way can the prorate system constitute what one critic has called "a hidden tax on consumers." This would be true only if the effect were to maintain consumer prices consistently higher than the free market. However, in fact and by design, the effect is to cut price troughs relative to price peaks. Thus, the week-by-week determination of market demand ensures stability in the price of citrus and keeps price fluctuations within a narrow range of slightly higher prices during some parts of the season and lower prices at others.

Citrus fruit has the unusual characteristic of storing well on the tree; this natural gift, combined with self-regulation by the growers themselves, accounts for the steady supply of freshly picked, quality fruit consumers enjoy year-round.

Without the mechanisms for the orderly marketing of citrus, the general structure of the fresh food distribution system and, indeed, the dietary pattern of the U.S. consumer would be quite different.

The importance of fresh fruit in the diet is universally accepted and the availability of such products is considered a routine accomplishment. What is ignored is the fact that there are only three fruits that are widely accepted by consumers and available on a daily basis at reasonable prices throughout the year. These fruits are oranges, apples and bananas; all other available fruits are seasonal in nature and subject to a high degree of variability in price, quantity and quality.

Through the influx of South American fruit in the last few years, some fruit has been made available for a longer period of time. However, price and quality still fluctuate greatly.

Of the three basics, bananas are mostly imported and thus supplies are largely dependent on economic and political conditions in those areas.

The second, apples, have become available on a 12-month basis because of technological developments with controlled atmosphere (CA) storage. The use of CA technology has had only limited value with other fresh fruits and vegetables; with citrus it has proven to be completely unworkable.

Oranges, the third of the basic three, have remained important in the diet because of the development of a marketing strategy in California and Arizona that has turned a seasonal fruit into a year-round staple. (Florida oranges are used mostly for processing, whereas Western oranges are largely marketed fresh.) Oranges have a unique characteristic—they can be stored on the tree for up to several months. Unlike other tree crops, which must be picked immediately upon ripening or else rot on the tree, oranges can remain on the tree for a reasonable time until the market demand calls for them to be picked. This is the basis on which the orange marketing orders were established.

The removal of the orderly marketing system could result in the "dependable" orange becoming a seasonal specialty.

Agriculture is the only industry that cannot control its supply of raw material; that fact of nature is the realistic foundation for instituting marketing orders.

Weather occurrences — hail, frost, wind, storms and drought—along with inexplicable vagaries of nature, cause crop harvests to fluctuate tremendously. In the citrus industry, for example, crop sizes can easily vary 50 percent up or down from one year to the next.

Agriculturists have long realized that in order to produce to the point of normal demand, it is necessary to plant deliberately to the point of surplus. This is because in two out of five years, crops are small, causing the supply to be barely enough to satisfy the needs of our domestic and export markets. Had farmers not planted to abundance, however, those years would have seen severe shortages of food. This means that for the other three years, or 60 percent of the time, production will be excessive.

While the years of abundant production protect the consumer, they can force farmers into bankruptcy because production beyond consumer demand forces prices below the farmer's costs. Therefore, a major part of our national agricultural policy is designed to protect our farmers who, in turn, are responsible for protecting our food supply. Some protective measures are in the form of direct subsidies paid for by taxpayers, e.g., target price systems, parity programs and government purchase of surplus. These allow the farmer to continue producing abundant food supplies.

Others—and these include federal marketing orders such as those for citrus—likewise allow the farmer to produce abundant supplies, *but with no subsidy paid by the taxpayer to the grower.*

Volume controls, as permitted under the citrus marketing orders, are not rigid. As mentioned above, there are no limits on the amounts that can be exported or marketed as processed products. In addition, donations to charity, direct sales to consumers and parcel post sales are not regulated by volume restrictions. Further flexibility is provided by the automatic lifting of limits when 85 percent of the crop has been harvested. In addition, each handler is permitted to over-ship his allotment by up to 10 percent each week, subject to repayment in subsequent weeks; the borrowing and lending of prorate within the same district are also permitted.

All in all, even in years of record production, such as the 1980–81 season, virtually the entire crop is used. That year was also characterized by a very large number of undersized and poor quality fruit, which are not highly prized by the consumer. Despite the difficulties in moving such a large crop with a disproportionate number of small fruit, 92 percent of it did reach the consumer as fresh fruit or orange juice in the U.S. and abroad. Included in that amount were donations to charitable organizations of 2.4 million pounds of navel oranges.

When the juice processing plants could not handle the excess amounts available, the overflow of undersized or damaged fruit was marketed to cattle feeding operations where the oranges were dried by solar heat and ground into livestock feed. Agricultural commodities, such as apples, carrots, potatoes and beets, are regularly used as livestock feed when the cost of other uses is higher than the return to the farmer. This provides additional income to the agricultural producer and is an inexpensive feed source for livestock and poultry. This should ultimately benefit the consumer by making meat, poultry and dairy products available at lower prices.

"Large surpluses contribute to the economic turmoil that is driving family farmers out of business and forcing a dramatic restructuring of agriculture, America's largest industry."—Larry Green, Los Angeles Times Staff Writer, in a feature entitled Agriculture in Turmoil, May 13, 1985. The above quote is true—except for California and Arizona citrus.

Thus, at a point when most of the United States farmers' livelihoods are being undercut by spiraling production costs and declining market prices, the California and Arizona citrus farmer is thriving. The Farmers for an Orderly Market group believes the economic stability stems from the implementation of marketing orders.

Many of the opponents of citrus marketing orders are companies whose primary economic interest is in something other than farm income.

For several years now we have heard a small, but vocal minority claim that our federal marketing orders are unfair. Who are these opponents to marketing orders? Most entered the industry only recently. Some are huge conglomerate corporations and large "real estate syndicators" who calculate their yields in terms of tax shelters and asset appreciation rather than in oranges.

We are forced, for example, to wonder how Belridge Farms, an opponent of marketing orders, can make an issue of "fairness." Belridge is wholly owned by the Shell Oil Company of the United States, which is, in turn, controlled by Shell Petroleum N.V. of the Netherlands. Is it fair for a foreign oil company to try to dictate marketing policies for American farmers?

Shell Oil, like the majority of opponents to marketing orders, consists of people who do not rely on regular farm income for economic survival.

On the other hand, Farmers for an Orderly Market, fighting to protect the marketing order system, presents a different profile. Records of a typical marketing organization show that four out of five growers live on or near their farms. They are not absentee owners. They are not in the orange business as a tax shelter. The range of motivations or circumstances under which they became and are orange producers is very wide. For some it represents their entire subsistence. For others—retired couples, business people with small enterprises, farmers with other farming interests nearby—growing oranges serves to supplement their limited incomes and is vital to their well-being. For example, a check of the zip codes of Sunkist's 6,000-member growers confirms the basic fact that 80 percent are family farmers who live on or near their farms.

It is these real farmers, most of whom rely on farming for economic survival, who are represented by Farmers for an Orderly Market. They recognize the responsibility for self-regulation as well as the benefits to society flowing from these programs. The 1981 referendum demonstrated the support of these farmers. Ninety-one percent voted in favor of maintaining the order.

As reason for this support, an economist testifying at a recent hearing stated that without the marketing order, the instability created could result in 20 to 30 percent of the production being forced out of the orange industry. All things being equal, this means the smaller farmers. If these farms go out of business, we could project one of two scenarios (or a mix):

If they were sold to developers, that would severely reduce production and threaten the current system of planting to abundance in order to prevent shortages.

If the farms were gobbled up by large corporate growers, they in turn might develop the land and take it out of production, or if they continued in the business, the industry could tend toward monopoly, with the consequences we have learned to expect from monopolies with respect to maximizing profits at the expense of consumers.

In either case, there is only one conclusion: In the long run, there would be less fruit reaching the consumer and at higher prices.

Despite everything said above, it would be a distortion of the Farmers for an Orderly Market position to interpret it as solely defending small farmers against large. Proponents of marketing orders include both large and small farmers. As is more fully discussed later, marketing orders prevent overconcentration of supply in the hands of a few large farmers and allow both large and small growers to sell their produce on an equal footing.

Many groups benefit from marketing orders because of the interweaving of interests in an advanced economy.

The marketing order system for citrus has proven its value over more than three decades. Today the Western citrus industry is one of the strongest in all agriculture, while much of the rest of U.S. agriculture is depressed. It is obvious that Western citrus has not only avoided the calamities experienced by most of American agriculture, but the economic outlook for the future looks very good. The industry has achieved this by democratic self-determination, not government regulation.

Despite this beneficial result, it is wrong to focus so much attention on the first section of the policy—that is, the establishing and maintaining of orderly market conditions for the benefit of the farmer—to the point of overlooking the second portion of the Congressional intent, " . . . to protect the interest of the consumer . . .". Indeed, this function of protecting the consumer's food supply has been accomplished so well that it has become a basic part of the national food distribution system and is largely taken for granted. If citrus fruit is available in steady supply year-round, it is because of the marketing order and the sensible way it is carried out by the shippers.

With marketing orders, shippers do not sit back and wait for their prices to rise before shipping oranges to market. If they did, they would lose their allotment. The opponents of marketing orders have another point of view. One such packer, in a published interview, said, "Without prorate we can sit back and wait for the market to go up. If the market is there, pick oranges. If it isn't, wait."

Who loses? The consumer who has to wait until the price goes up before he can buy a fresh orange.

That is not the pattern under marketing orders. Both availability—so important to the customer—and reasonable price—even more crucial on a day-to-day basis—are satisfied. In spite of all the difficulties and costs involved in the production and distribution of fresh oranges, oranges are consistently lower priced at retail than other fruit, according to USDA studies, and are often a better retail buy than many other staples.

Stabilizing the flow of food is in the best interest of everyone. The entire distribution chain operates more efficiently. Supermarkets and produce wholesalers can count on a steady supply throughout the season, knowing that when they place an order, it will be filled. Transportation companies can plan when and where to have equipment available. Warehouses can plan for optimum storage space utilization.

The labor force benefits because the marketing order stretches the citrus consuming season, thus assuring longer periods of employment. Steady supply means steady employment. In most instances, farm laborers no longer need to be transient. Surveys have shown that because of these stable working conditions, California and Arizona citrus workers are among the most highly paid and enjoy some of the best benefits in agriculture.

And, finally, the grower benefits from stability of prices and has his proportional opportunity to market his fruit, no matter how small he might be.

Marketing orders are programs of self-regulation adopted by farmers through a democratic process to solve agricultural problems. They are not subsidies. They do not use tax dollars.

Although the Secretary of Agriculture has the authority to administer marketing order programs for various commodities for the purpose of stabilizing the market, these programs are not ordered by the government, but rather are voted into existence by a referendum of growers themselves, and then paid for by the growers. Since the marketing orders were established, they have been amended by growers' votes several times in recognition of changes within the industry.

Some critics of marketing orders have spread confusing information about barriers to entry, suggesting they were applicable to navel and valencia oranges. It is true that some marketing orders, for reasons particular to these industries, do limit the entry of new growers. However, *there are no imposed limits on becoming a navel orange or valencia orange farmer*—all claims to the contrary notwithstanding.

Recently, critics of the orange marketing orders have complained about the composition of the Administrative Committees that implement the orders. As they well know, the composition is provided for in the marketing orders themselves: six growers, four marketers and one consumer. The United States Department of Agriculture is now entertaining suggestions from several sources as to how that composition might be changed.

Marketing orders are supported by grower-paid assessments and are virtually without cost to the U.S. government. Commodities regulated by marketing orders, such as citrus, have not sought or received the costly assistance of government subsidies. Farmers operating under marketing orders believe that a better way to address the problems facing agriculture is to focus on marketing crops, not removing them from production. They continue to support responsible self-regulation rather than expensive subsidy programs.

When marketing orders are suspended, the result can be an adverse effect on orange growers without any benefit to consumers.

Early this year, the Secretary of Agriculture, noting the Florida freeze, also observed that the price of oranges had risen. Apparently, he assumed that the increase in the price of oranges was related to the shortage caused by the freeze. So, without consulting or communicating with the citrus growers, he suspended the flow-to-market provisions of the navel orange marketing order.

However, California/Arizona eating oranges and the juice oranges of Florida are marketed differently. In the case observed by the Secretary of Agriculture, the improved prices for navel oranges were actually the result primarily of a smaller navel orange crop. Because 90 percent of Florida oranges are made into juice products, the freeze may have substantially raised orange juice prices but it had little effect on navel oranges. Navel oranges have excellent fresh eating qualities, and consequently their prices are determined by what is happening in the fresh fruit market, not the processed fruit market.

The suspension of the navel orange marketing order had an immediate negative effect on the market. Produce industry buyers expected—correctly, as it turned out—a temporary oversupply and a consequent drop in the price they would have to pay to farmers. And indeed, the average price to growers decreased from over $6.00 per carton to about $4.30 within five weeks. As of mid-March 1985, the growers had lost over $10 million. While this was occur-

ring, there was little or no change in the consumer's price for navel oranges.

When critics attack marketing orders in the name of buzz words like "deregulation" and "free enterprise," they ignore some basic truths with respect to farming and the free market.

The free enterprise system is based on the premise that the law of supply and demand will keep the economic activities of producers in balance with the needs of consumers—that the former will increase or decrease production as demand increases or decreases. If current producers do not respond quickly enough, thus causing prices to rise inordinately, then new producers will come in to meet the need.

This economic model comes largely from the industrial and service sectors. Agriculture—and tree crops, especially—cannot respond quickly to the need for more produce. The trees, which are the raw material, require, in the case of citrus, some six years to come into production. A manufacturing concern can relatively quickly increase production in response to market demand by ordering more raw material and putting on another shift. So can a professional service firm—only its raw material is people.

Farmers cannot suddenly make more citrus come into existence. So they plant a generous number of trees, six years in advance, knowing that in some years they will have crops that are more than the domestic market can absorb as fresh fruit, but also knowing that in poor years the consumer will not be deprived.

Farmers have no control over production. But the need for a balance between supply and demand remains. Consumers still want a steady supply of fresh fruit at reasonable prices. Marketing orders do what is practical: control the rate at which fruit enters the market; this takes the place of the needed—but impossible—control over production. It replaces something nature does not permit with something that is within the farmer's control—as long as it is applied universally to the total supply. The universal application assures that there will be no discrimination between large and small farmers—shipments are prorated according to crop size and everyone ships his fair share.

This is the justification for limited government intervention: it is the only way to make the program universal, practical and fair. Marketing orders, established by government, free the citrus industry to regulate itself through joint action. The Secretary of Agriculture appoints members of the Administrative Committee from nominees of the industry. The members decide the amount of fruit that should be shipped each week. The USDA holds referenda among farmers as to whether they wish to continue the marketing orders. Farmers rely on self-assessments for the money needed to carry out the work necessitated by the marketing orders, so they are not a burden to the taxpayers. This self-reliance is consonant with their basic position as fiscal conservatives.

The prorate system protects small farmers against monetary losses occurring during times of surplus. Farmers want and need rules—not economic anarchy—so they can stay in business and practice the free enterprise they believe in.

American agriculture is a twentieth-century miracle.

It is indeed a miracle that 3 percent of the people of America produce enough food for all their fellow countrymen plus 150 million others in foreign lands. The American farmer is the most productive human being on earth. While improved technology has contributed greatly to increased production, another major factor is an outstanding national agriculture policy that has been in place for many years.

Federal marketing orders, which permit farmers in democratic elections to use self-control rather than tax dollars to solve their problems, represent an appropriate and efficient part of agriculture in this country.

POSTSCRIPT

Is Free Enterprise Always More Efficient?

As an industry, agribusiness is unique: to an extent that may be astounding in the late twentieth century, farmers are dependent on luck and providence for the quantity, quality, and even existence of their product. Yet we are learning to treat this ancient occupation the same, ethically, as we do other businesses. We are beginning to ask agribusiness to take the same kind of responsibility for its environmental pollution (for instance, in the use of pesticides), its dealings with its human resources (for example, the migrant workers), and the content of its marketing campaigns (like the "organically grown" label) that we ask of any other industry. Farmers are not immune from the strictures of business ethics.

Beyond agribusiness, the dispute among the growers raises the issue of the scope of the principles. The orderly determination of demand in order to regulate the supply in this business leads to the satisfaction of the consumer and the survival of the farmer. But is that not also the case for many other industries? Would some of the solutions adopted by the western fruit growers work as well in some of our troubled industries, such as steel manufacturing, where we have all but given up the hope of reclaiming our dominance on the world market?

Consider the following: The United States is in serious competition with Japanese industry, which has consistently turned out good products more cheaply than domestic industries. This has resulted in national humiliation (especially in the automobile industry), loss of jobs (primary and secondary), and a serious trade deficit in the United States. Japan accomplished its preeminence in manufacturing by maintaining close partnerships between industry and government, accepting regulation and structure to protect the industry while it was growing and to preserve it when it became mature. Our responses to such threats are historically limited: we can raise tariffs, restrict imports, or wage "buy American" advertising campaigns. The kind of genuine partnership among competitors that also includes government authorizations and advisers, formed and maintained to make an industry work properly, is very rare in American business. Only now are computer manufacturers beginning to combine into partnerships for more effective competition. Should businesses be doing more of this? If it works for the growers (and does it?), is it worth testing on other canvases?

SUGGESTED READINGS

Julian Alston and Colin Carter, "Causes and Consequences of Farm Policy," *Contemporary Policy Issues* (January 1991).

Alessandro Bonanno, ed., *Agrarian Policies and Agricultural Systems* (Westview Press, 1990).

James Bovard, "Apologists for the Farm Lobby," *The Wall Street Journal* (July 24, 1990).

Lester R. Brown, "Sustaining World Agriculture," in Lester R. Brown et al., eds., *State of the World, 1987: A Worldwatch Institute Report on Progress Toward a Sustainable Society* (W. W. Norton, 1987).

Thomas M. Burton, "Many Farmers Harvest Government Subsidies in Violation of Law," *The Wall Street Journal* (May 8, 1990).

Edward Carr, "A Survey of Agriculture: Grotesque," *The Economist* (December 12, 1992).

Ralph King, Jr., "Let the Growth Come by Itself," *Forbes* (April 17, 1989).

Claire Poole, "Land and Life!" *Forbes* (April 29, 1991).

Rick Reiff, "They Don't Need Farm Aid Concerts Now," *Forbes* (April 17, 1989).

Philip Revzin, "EC's Farm Subsidies That Imperil Trade Have Deep Roots," *The Wall Street Journal* (May 17, 1991).

Khalil Sesmou, "FAO: An Insider's View," *The Ecologist* (March/April 1991).

Ewen M. Wilson, "Subsidy Cuts Help U.S. Farmers—Why Not Others," *The Wall Street Journal* (January 9, 1990).

ISSUE 3

Are Business and Medicine Ethically Incompatible?

YES: Fredrick R. Abrams, from "Caring for the Sick: An Emerging Industrial By-Product," *Journal of the American Medical Association* (February 21, 1986)

NO: David R. Larson, from "Business and Medicine: Are They Ethically Compatible?" *Update* (September 1991)

ISSUE SUMMARY

YES: Fredrick R. Abrams, director of the Clinical Ethics Consultation Group, argues that there is an essential difference between the ethic of the physician and the ethic of the businessperson and that where physicians are controlled by the "bottom line," the patient's medical care does suffer.

NO: David R. Larson, codirector of the Loma Linda University Center for Christian Bioethics, argues that there are several versions of the "business ethic" and that not all of them demand maximum profits. In any business, he maintains, conscientious attention to the customer is essential for long-term profits.

The heart of this issue may lie with the confusion between the two types of ethics involved: the *professional ethic* and the *market ethic*. The *professional,* or *fiduciary,* ethic, applicable to all professional-client relationships and all commercial fiduciary-beneficiary relationships, requires that the active party (professional or trustee) act *only in the interests of the other.* For example, doctors must act only in the interests of their patients, lawyers for their clients, pastors for their congregations (individually and collectively), and the managers of funds and trusts for those who have entrusted funds to them. By this ethic, boards of directors of publicly owned corporations must act only in the interests of the shareholders in the corporation.

The *market* ethic, on the contrary, requires that each party protect *its own interests,* abstaining only from force and fraud as means to achieving an agreement. This adversarial ethic, best seen in labor negotiations and proceedings in a court of law, underlies the "voluntary transaction" on which the free market is based. The free market assumes a universe of rational free agents, each acting to maximize self-interest within a legal framework designed to protect the rights of all. Not all people fit that assumption—especially the very young, very old, sick, or disabled, or simply those who are very far away from the dealings—which is why there are fiduciary relationships.

The professional ethic of the physician is brief and simple, and it is reflected in the Hippocratic oath that is generally taken by those about to begin a medical practice:

> In whatsoever houses I enter, I will enter to help the sick, and I will abstain from all intentional wrongdoing and harm.... And whatsoever I shall see or hear in the course of my profession in my intercourse with men, if it be what should not be published abroad, I will never divulge, holding such things to be holy secrets. Now if I carry out this oath, and break it not, may I gain forever reputation among all men for my life and for my art.

There is much more to the oath than this, but the essence of the oath is as applicable now as it was 2,500 years ago when Hippocrates first established it; the essence is that the physician acts only for the benefit of the patient, attending to the patient's illnesses, comforting and reassuring him or her, tailoring diets and advice to the patient's particular case, and keeping her or his secrets in absolute confidence.

The relationship between the physician and the patient remained the same in the period between 500 B.C. and A.D. 1900. Sick people sought out healers, trusted their advice, often were helped by their ministrations, and, to the extent the patients were able, paid them for their services. In the twentieth century however, medicine began to be "professionalized": Licensing laws were established to eliminate quacks; legislation was enacted requiring licensed professionals to supervise a required professional education; professional organizations active in advancing the state of the art and protecting the professional image surfaced; and, generally, higher rates of reimbursement were charged by the physicians. Rapid advances in medical technology at mid-century sent medical costs beyond the reach of people with ordinary incomes and savings; third-party reimbursement—first from private insurers and then from the federal government (in the form of Medicare and Medicaid)—was introduced at the third quarter of the century and helped relieve the extraordinary burden on patients, but it also allowed the medical profession to prescribe ever more expensive technological cures, which sent health care costs through the roof.

As the twentieth century draws to a close, the consequences of these costs for the economy as a whole are becoming clear. "Cost-containment" measures that take medical care decisions out of the physician's private office and put them into the hands of corporate boards of Health Maintenance Organizations (HMOs) and hospitals dominate medical progress at this point. But how does this affect the privacy aspect of the patient-physician relationship?

As you read the selections that follow, ask yourself whether or not Fredrick R. Abrams's view of business really is incompatible with the physician's ethic. Do the varying models of business proposed by David R. Larson help?

YES

Fredrick R. Abrams

CARING FOR THE SICK: AN EMERGING INDUSTRIAL BY-PRODUCT

At the critical moment mankind too often forgets precisely what it is trying to accomplish.

—NIETZSCHE

Imprecise use of terminology and a fuzzy focus on basic objectives have led health care provision to a position of conflicting values. "Cost containment" means money is to be saved (implicitly, regardless of consequences). "Cost efficiency" means money is to be allotted to the best advantage (often saving money, but usually over a longer time span).

CONFUSION OF PURPOSE

Professor of Economics Uwe Reinhardt states the *business ethic* is to maximize the return on investment without breaking the law. The *medical ethic* is to relieve suffering, to prolong life (when the patient judges this to be his desire), and to make each individual physically able to pursue happiness in whatever socially acceptable way he desires.

The very thing that makes American business successful in a populous land of consumers—mass production—is essentially incompatible with the aspect of medical care most Americans treasure, viz, competent personal care clearly in the interest of the patient; a fiduciary relationship. It is the unique interaction between doctor and patient that is valued. Countless treatises on the art of medicine point this out as critically important to healing people in contrast to treating disease.

To put it in business terms, health is the capital of the individual, permitting him to apply himself without handicap to pursue his interests. Contrast this with the avowed aim of the corporation—to make profit, to justify its existence to its shareholders. The very success of medicine has been its

From Fredrick R. Abrams, "Caring for the Sick: An Emerging Industrial By-Product," *Journal of the American Medical Association*, vol. 255, no. 7 (February 21, 1986), pp. 937–938. Copyright © 1986 by The American Medical Association. Reprinted by permission.

undoing—coupled with the greed of some of its practitioners who have profited inordinately from its practice. Unfortunately, medicine has caught the eye of those who look to its profitability and not to its purpose, of which profits are only a spin-off. The tail will soon wag the dog.

QUALITY OF PATIENT CARE MUST BE DETERMINED BY PHYSICIANS

Financial incentives of cost-plus hospital payments and fee-for-service physician payments have encouraged excessive diagnostic and therapeutic procedures (not a little stimulated by the legal imperatives to avoid error or the appearance of error, for which an inordinate price is also paid via the tort system). In an attempt to modify these incentives, the prospective payment systems have been devised. Institutions make more money by delivering less care. Certainly money can be saved as a result of undertreatment, resulting from a different set of incentives, but patients will suffer the consequences. How can we distinguish and eliminate treatments and diagnostic procedures with marginal benefits without harming the patient? Patients need a professional shield to ensure that quality of care is not compromised when corporate profit is threatened. There must continue to be a group of physicians *independent of corporate control* to which conflicts can be appealed.

Current economic forces encourage the for-profit corporations to select those treatments (or fads) that spin off the greatest profit, leaving difficult and expensive care to other health care providers in community hospitals or state and municipal hospitals. This will not contain costs, but simply leach profits out of the system completely. "Profits" in nonprofit institutions can be used (in unofficial mini-insurance company style) to provide care for others less able to pay and also to pay for teaching and research and upgrading equipment. In other words, any excess revenues go back into the health care system. For-profit institutions do this also, but dividends must be removed from the system to satisfy shareholders.

Legislatures point to these misleading corporate models as indicators of how efficient private industry can be. They then cut back allocations to the institutions caring for the less wealthy patients, presuming the institutions are inefficient (rather than caring for more difficult hence more expensive types of illnesses). There is a move to eliminate the shield of professional judgment by letting corporations hire and fire doctors. This they would do on the basis of performance. *Not* professional performance, but financial performance; *not* good medical practice, but the ability to make profit for the corporation. A recent article in *Time* magazine (Dec 10, 1984, p 70) anecdotally cites a case in a New Jersey hospital where a thoracic surgeon's privileges were withdrawn because he was compared with another surgeon who "screened his patients carefully, rejecting smokers, overweight people, and other risks." The surgeon who lost privileges "accepted sicker patients," and his patients "had to stay in the hospital an average of five days longer." There is no information about whether the costlier surgeon's patients were less happy to be alive or less worthy contributors to society. Simply, "his work cost the hospital more than insurance carriers were willing to pay."

QUALITY OF PRACTICE AND STAFF PRIVILEGES MUST BE DETERMINED BY PHYSICIANS

The issue is unsettled at this time, but the possibility remains for terminating the privileges of those doctors who deal with more difficult cases and who inevitably have the poorer statistical (not individual) results, ie, doctors who are not profitable for hospitals to keep on staff. And the more a hospital states its purpose as profit from dealing with the sick, in contrast to healing the sick, the more likely it will lose sight of the primary purpose of medical practice. It leads to the paradox that the more care a patient needs, and the more a doctor is recognized by his peers as particularly able and hence is referred complex cases, the less likely he is to retain his privileges. Can we look forward to this reductio ad absurdum [reduction to absurdity] when corporations that are in business to make money restrict staff privileges to the physicians not necessarily efficient, but only careful in selecting patients and illnesses that are profitable to treat? Physicians must be responsible for credentialing their peers and these decisions must be made only on the basis of medical competence. Cost consciousness must be maintained, but not as the basis for withdrawal of hospital privileges.

Let us do what we must in public education, legislatures, staff committees, and professional organizations to be certain that hospital bylaws retain professional supervision over quality of care and staff privileges based on competent medical practice. Let us stop the remolding of a profession whose main thrust is healing the sick into an industry controlled by impersonal bureaucratic forces whose main purpose is to make a profit.

NO

David R. Larson

BUSINESS AND MEDICINE: ARE THEY ETHICALLY COMPATIBLE?

"Yes," says the patient in a recent Frank and Ernest cartoon, "the operation made a new man out of me—The old one had some money in the bank."[1]

This cartoon expresses the tension many feel between medicine as a business and medicine as a service. This tension is by no means unique to our own time and place, as evidenced by the complaint of the 17th-century Chinese sage Chen Shih-kung that "When doctors visit the rich, they are conscientious; when they visit the poor, careless."[2] But because of the growing emphasis upon managed-care medicine in the United States and elsewhere, the tension between medicine as a business and medicine as a service is now felt in especially painful ways.

No less astute an observer of modern medicine than Dr. Arnold S. Relman, a distinguished physician who has served as the editor of the *New England Journal of Medicine*, warns of the dangers of what he and others call "The New Medical-Industrial Complex."[3] Relman's concern, as articulated in more than one of his published statements, is that in some of the newer forms of financing health-care delivery there is a strong temptation to place the financial interests of stockholders before the medical needs of patients.

Few physician ethicists have expressed alarm about this temptation more severely than has Dr. Fredrick R. Abrams[4] of the Center for Applied Biomedical Ethics in Denver, Colorado. Beginning his commentary in the *Journal of the American Medical Association* with Nietzsche's reminder that "at the critical moment mankind too often forgets precisely what it is trying to accomplish," Abrams draws a sharp distinction between the moral purpose of business and the moral purpose of medicine. According to this distinction, "the *business ethic* is to maximize the return on investment without breaking the law. The *medical ethic* is to relieve suffering, to prolong life (when the patient judges this to be his desire), and to make each individual physically able to pursue happiness in whatever socially acceptable way he desires." Abrams does not flinch from the full implications of distinguishing the moral purposes of business and medicine so dramatically. "The very thing that makes American business

From David R. Larson, "Business and Medicine: Are They Ethically Compatible?" *Update*, vol. 7, no. 3 (September 1991). Copyright © 1991 by David R. Larson. Reprinted by permission.

successful in a populous land of consumers—mass production—is," he asserts, *"essentially incompatible* with the aspect of medical care most Americans treasure, viz. competent personal care clearly in the interest of the patient; a fiduciary relationship."[5]

Is it actually the case that mass production accounts for the successes, such as they are, of American business and that this is *essentially incompatible* with the fiduciary relationship between doctors and patients? Perhaps so. But is it also the case, as Abrams implies, that the business ethic is essentially incompatible with the medical ethic? This more sweeping insinuation deserves careful consideration.

Much depends, of course, upon how one defines the moral purpose of business. Abrams did not create his definition of the *business ethic* out of nothing, or *ex nihilo* as theologians might say. He drew it from the formulations of economist Uwe Reinhardt. In addition, it is a definition of the moral purpose of business that is similar to economist Milton Friedman's famous insistence that "there is one and only one social responsibility of business—to use its resources and engage in activities designed to increase its profits so long as it stays within the rules of the game, which is to say, engages in open and free competition without deception or fraud."[6] Still further, Abrams's definition is congruent with significant decisions in American courts, particularly the often cited 1919 case of *Dodge v. Ford Motor Company*, in which a court in Michigan declared that "A business corporation is organized and carried on primarily for the profit of the stockholders. The powers of the directors are to be exercised for that end. The discretion of the directors is to be exercised in the choice of *means* to attain that end and does not extend to a change in *the end itself.*"[7]

So Abrams's definition has much in its favor. Nevertheless, it might be useful to remind ourselves that this "narrow" definition of the moral purpose of business for which Friedman and others of his persuasion are so famous is by no means the only plausible alternative. Some define the moral purpose of business in ways that are more broad, complex and pluralistic, and these more-comprehensive definitions of the *business ethic* leave more room for the *medical ethic*. If Friedman's definition is the "classical" account, there are also "neoclassical" and "maximally broad" accounts that deserve consideration as well. According to one formulation of the "neoclassical" view, "The function of the corporation is to maximize profits consistent with the universal norms of justice and with respect for legitimate individual rights."[8] And according to one expression of the "maximally broad" view, the proper aim of business is "the maximization and harmonization of the interests of all of a business' constituencies."[9]

We therefore have at least three possible definitions of the business ethic that differ from each other in how comprehensively they portray the moral purpose of business. Thus, even if Dr. Abrams is right in his insinuation that the business ethic is essentially incompatible with the medical ethic, his point is pertinent to one, but not necessarily all, depictions of business.

There are also good reasons to wonder if there is an essential incompatibility between the medical ethic and even the narrow or classical view of the business ethic. Some of these considerations are historical in nature. It is difficult to identify a period of human history in which the intention to benefit financially from the practice of medicine was not present in some form and to some degree, even if the institutional arrangements were so very different from our own that we may find it difficult to discern the monetary dimensions of some medical interactions.[10]

Other reasons for doubting an essential incompatibility between the medical ethic and the narrow or classical definition of the business ethic are more political. It would seem inappropriate in a free society to forbid capitalistic transactions between competent, free, and informed adults even if in such an interaction someone trades cash for medical services.[11] Such a barter would seem essentially incompatible with the medical ethic only if certain other claims are also valid, one of which might be that unless medical care is delivered as a gratuity it is not genuinely moral. But this assertion and others like it need to be argued and not merely assumed.

Still other reasons for doubting an essential incompatibility between the business ethic and the medical ethic are more financial. Any business, medical or not, that is perceived as being concerned only with its own profits will not be in business long. The paradox of business is that those who wish to profit must serve actual or felt needs and they must serve those needs well. This is an economic parallel to the New Testament idea that those who would save their lives must lose them.

Even if the narrow or classical definition of the moral purpose of business is correct, even if a firm has only one moral responsibility which is to achieve as much profit for its owners as possible without breaking the law, it can [be] doubted that there is an essential incompatibility between the business ethic and the medical ethic. There is an *essential incompatibility* between the medical ethic and a business ethic that settles for momentary, though possibly large, profits. And there is *a tension*, a very real tension, between the medical ethic and a business ethic that is concerned with achieving significant profits over an extended period of time. But this *tension*, great though it undoubtedly is, is not so intense as to amount to an *essential incompatibility*. Indeed, in some instances it might well be creative rather than destructive.

Miles F. Shore and Harry Levinson of Harvard Medical School helpfully draw a distinction between two business strategies, both of which might be able to accept a narrow or classical view of the purpose of business:

> Reputable businesses are less concerned about short-term profit than about their organizational character and integrity and their perpetuation. Their focus is on long-term continuity and growth, which they seek by establishing a distinct organizational character that sets the corporation and its products apart from the competition. There are characteristic ways of doing things, values that the organization stands for, and expectations between the company and its employees, which are made explicit. The distinct character of the business is understood by the public and is related to the confidence that the public has in its products or services. In leading corporations, that organizational character provides the work place and influences the kinds of people who are recruited and who choose to work there.
>
> Top management is concerned about long-range strategy for corporate longevity rather than short-term returns. Managers attend to the development of their work force as well as to the

Table 1

Purposes and Priorities in Business

	Short-Term Strategies	Long-Term Strategies
Classical Definitions of Business: Profit	1. Business Ethic: Short-Term Profit	2. Business Ethic: Long-Term Profit
Neoclassical Definitions of Business: Profit + Justice + Respect for Rights	3. Business Ethic: Short-Term Profit + Justice + Respect for Rights	4. Business Ethic: Long-Term Profit + Justice + Respect for Rights
Maximally Broad Definitions of Business: Maximization & Harmonization of All Interests	5. Business Ethic: Short-Term Maximization & Harmonization of All Interests	6. Business Ethic: Long-Term Maximization & Harmonization of All Interests

choice and nurturance of their own successors. Service to society, both national and international, is a tangible influence on corporate and executive behavior. This kind of corporation is stable over several generations and is unlikely to be acquired easily by merger or acquisition.

A second, quite different strategy is, of course, possible: to organize a business around short-term profits and expediency. In that case, the measure of success is only the bottom line. Management and the owners are primarily interested in maximal return on capital in minimal time. Employees are recruited by financial inducements and remain only so long as their remuneration is above the going rate. The time span of the business is from one quarterly statement to the next—perpetuation of the organization and its work force is not a goal. The business has little distinctive character, its products exploit the market, and the psychological contract with the work force is primarily in terms of short-term economic gain. The organization is easy prey to merger or acquisition and its life span is short.[12]

In view of these suggestions, before we conclude that there is an essential incompatibility between the business ethic and the medical ethic we need to answer at least two prior questions. First, are we functioning with a "classical," "neoclassical," "maximally broad" or some other definition of the moral purpose of business? Second, do we envision a short-term or long-term business strategy? If we combine these alternatives, we can identify and assess at least six ways of viewing the purposes and priorities of business [see Table 1].

The first alternative, the one that emphasizes profits in the short-term, is the least attractive of the six alternatives, both from an ethical and from a financial point of view. This option is cynical. The fifth and sixth alternatives are so idealistic and vague as to be almost impractical at the present time, though they do possess the value of relevant but impossible ideals. These alternatives are utopian. The second, third, fourth and fifth alternatives; the ones that either emphasize profits in the long run, or considerations in addition to profits in the short run or long run, are the alternatives from which we are now morally free to choose. The important point is that irrespective of which of these "middle" options we select, it will be necessary to function in ways that serve the actual or felt needs of citizens as well as the interests of stockholders.

As Aristotle understood so clearly so long ago, in circumstances like this virtue does not lie in fulfilling one purpose to the exclusion of all others but in finding the "relative mean" between competing factors.[13] If any business strives only to serve with no regard for profits, it will eventually cease to exist. This is obvious. It is also true, if perhaps less obvious, that if any business strives only to profit without also serving, it too will eventually cease to exist.

Where there is no margin, in time there is no mission. And where there is no mission, in time there is no margin.

This is true for all enterprises, whether for-profit or not-for-profit, private or public, secular or religious. The challenge in managed-care medicine, as in all business, is to serve citizens while making a profit, and to make a profit while serving citizens, and to accomplish both of these for the long-term rather than the short-term.

Honorable physicians will shy away from investing in or practicing medicine for managed-care programs that are preoccupied with short-term profits. The corporate character of such enterprises is essentially incompatible with the professional character of medicine, as Dr. Abrams so ably contends.

Conscientious physicians will also function within the managed-care practices in which they have an interest, or in which they practice medicine, in ways that serve the genuine needs of each and every patient to the greatest possible degree, given the priorities and resources of the organization. Some physicians who will serve in such ways will do so merely because they rightly believe this approach makes for good business. Their motivations are prudential. Other physicians who will serve in these ways will do so out of deference for justice and respect for persons, or perhaps even out of a desire to maximize or harmonize the interests of all constituents. Their motivations are moral *as well as* prudential, or perhaps even moral *instead* of prudential. But in many instances it may be difficult to distinguish the two motivations merely by observing the public actions of individuals or institutions.

The priorities, practices, procedures and policies of medicine as a business do not always coincide with those of medicine as a service. But in a significant majority of instances in this nation at this time they do, especially if one takes an extended view of things. If one takes the long view, usually it is not financially good for a business to act in morally wrong ways, and usually it is not financially bad for a business to act in morally right ways. The contrary convictions suffer from myopia, and this short-sidedness is financial as well as moral.

ENDNOTES

1. These remarks were prepared for a conference on managed-care medicine presented by the Department of Family Practice at Loma Linda University Medical Center on April 10, 1991. I am thankful to Doctors Dalton Baldwin and Paul Giem for their written criticisms. I am also grateful to Gayle Foster for her assistance.

2. Albert R. Jonsen, "Ethics Remain at the Heart of Medicine: Physicians and Entrepreneurship," *Western Journal of Medicine*, 144:480 (April, 1986).

3. Arnold S. Relman, "The New Medical-Industrial Complex," *New England Journal of Medicine*, 303:17 (October 23, 1980), pp. 963–970.

4. Fredrick R. Abrams, "Caring for the Sick: An Emerging Industrial By-Product," *Journal of the American Medical Association*, 255:17 (February 21, 1986), p. 937.

5. Ibid.

6. Tom L. Beauchamp and Norman E. Bowie, eds., *Ethical Theory and Business*, 3rd ed. (Englewood Cliffs, New Jersey: Prentice Hall, 1988), p. 91.

7. *Dodge v. Ford Motor Company* (S. Ct. Mich. 1919) 204 Mich. 459, as cited in Norman Bowie, *Business Ethics* (Englewood Cliffs, NJ: Prentice Hall, 1982), pp. 18–19.

8. Bowie, p. 34.

9. Bowie, pp. 37–38.

10. Jonsen, pp. 480–83.

11. H. Tristram Englehardt, Jr. and Michael A. Rie, "Morality for the Medical-Industrial Complex," *New England Journal of Medicine*, 319:16 (October 20, 1988), pp. 1086–1089.

12. Miles F. Shore and Harry Levinson, "On Business and Medicine," *New England Journal of Medicine*, 313:5 (August 1, 1985), pp. 319–320.

13. J. A. K. Thomson, *The Ethics of Aristotle: The Nicomachean Ethics Translated* (Middlesex, England: Penguin Books, 1974), pp. 65–75.

POSTSCRIPT

Are Business and Medicine Ethically Incompatible?

There is no end in sight to the growth of health care costs in the United States: as the population ages and needs more medical care, and as the technology continues to advance, costs will continue to rise. Under the heading of "respect for liberty," or contractual freedom, there is no natural limit on what an individual might medically "need," or, more accurately, what an individual might be permitted to buy in the medical marketplace—and, therefore, what a physician might prescribe for personal patients. Under the heading of "distributive justice," any necessary medical treatment that is available to the rich ought also to be available to the poor, which places an incredibly large demand on the public coffers. Nowhere else in the economy is there this fatal combination of an *essential* service (necessary for life), a strong history of *private* allotment (through physicians and their individual patients), and a *public* responsibility for payment.

It can be argued, and Larson occasionally does argue, that the market ethic will protect the health care consumer because the for-profit hospitals and HMOs want to retain their customer bases. However, as Abrams points out, because the oldest and sickest patients (the ones who need medical care the most) cost the most to treat, the HMOs do not want them as customers. In a hospital or HMO that is a publicly owned corporation, management is responsible to the directors, who are responsible to the shareholders and therefore have a fiduciary responsibility to maximize the financial position of the institution. As a result, the physicians who are the employees of the corporation may very well be held to *financial* standards of performance as well as—or instead of—*medical* standards.

SUGGESTED READINGS

Adrienne C. Locke, "Doctors View Ethics of Cost Control," *Business Insurance* (February 25, 1991).

Chris Messina, "The Heart Attack Business," *High Technology* (March 1989).

Michael Schachner, "On-Site Medical Centers Touts: Employer-Owned Facilities Can Reduce Costs, Improve Quality," *Business Insurance* (May 11, 1992).

Matthew Schwartz, "Self-Referrals Pump Up Health Care Costs," *National Underwriter* (October 26, 1992).

ISSUE 4

Are Leveraged Buyouts Bad for the Bottom Line?

YES: Frank A. Olson, from "Twilight of the LBOs," *Fairfield Business Review* (Spring 1991)

NO: Michael T. Tucker, from "LBOs May Not Be Dead Yet—A Response to Frank Olson," *Fairfield Business Review* (Spring 1991)

ISSUE SUMMARY

YES: Frank A. Olson, chief executive officer of the Hertz Corporation, argues that the unprecedented level of debt contracted by major U.S. corporations in the 1980s could lead to bankruptcies, unemployment, and widespread corporate inflexibility in the face of change.

NO: Michael T. Tucker, an associate professor of finance, argues that the increased indebtedness in the United States is simply an example of efficient markets at work within the rules of the game, satisfying shareholders' desire for a higher return on investment.

The issue of leveraged buyouts (LBOs) centers on the purpose and foundation of business enterprise in America, or at least the legal and financial foundation for the corporation. The directors of the corporation are elected by the stockholders and have no right to do anything except for the greater profit of the investors; to this end, all the business of the corporation is conducted.

But what if the decision to maximize shareholder gain is also a decision to severely weaken or terminate the company? At issue here is not bankruptcy— the condition in which the business simply cannot bring in enough income to cover its costs. At issue here is a decision to liquidate or cripple a company because some individual or investment group—often including managers of the company—offers a price for a controlling portion of the shares that is much higher than any projection of reasonable yield from operation would predict. Why such a price would be offered (by anyone) is one of the topics at issue in the debate that follows.

On one side, Frank A. Olsen claims that the buyout results in large profits to the shareholders of record who tender their shares at the right time and in very large profits for the buyout group. However, the members of the buyout group spend very little of their own money in bringing off this type of deal. Most of the money to buy shares comes from loans, with the company's assets and future operating profits as collateral (which provides the "leverage" for the buyout). Therefore, the executives and deal makers who orchestrate a buyout take little financial risk in the face of tremendous benefits, while the company itself and its employees (as the collateral) risk total collapse. The rest who profit are the lawyers and bankers, leaving nothing of the accumulated investment for later owners.

Michael T. Tucker argues that an extraordinarily high price for shares can be offered only when the company is badly mismanaged and when a better management system could make the same assets yield a much higher return. Tucker's formula says, in effect, that if your objective is to increase present shareholder wealth (and it should be), then, given the current tax structure, your best bet is to reduce equity and get yourself as far into debt as possible while subtracting the costs of possible bankruptcy.

From a consequential perspective, the dispute sets up the ethical evaluation of the leveraged buyout as follows: If it succeeds in producing more efficient and more effective corporate operations, then the buyout is justified; if it succeeds only in increasing the wealth of the buyout engineers and destroying an American enterprise, then it is criminally wrong.

What is the board of directors to do, faced with a tender offer (offer for all shares of stock tendered, or presented, to the buyer) at an unimaginably high price, given the market history of the stock? If the return to the shareholder would be higher than the shareholder would otherwise expect from that stock, does the board have any right to resist the offer? But if a perfectly good company that makes a profit, provides jobs, and pays taxes to the community would be killed by this deal, do they have any right *not* to resist it? One problem with this kind of offer is the number of conflicting interests faced by the board of directors. For example, members of the board are from the company itself; usually at least half the board are also corporate officers. Consequently, they will likely lose their jobs if the deal goes through. Some members of the board are also in management and may be in the group engineering the buyout. Under normal circumstances, all of the directors are also shareholders and stand to improve their personal fortunes substantially if the buyout succeeds.

Under the circumstances, what should the board do? Protect the individuals? Protect the company itself? Is a company valuable in and of itself for the products it makes and for its contribution to the economy? Ask yourself, as you read the following selections, if the purpose of the corporation ever does, or can, or should, go beyond the return on investment for the investor, such as to take on a social role in the nation as a whole. Should the public be concerned about protecting corporations from leveraged buyouts?

YES   Frank A. Olson

TWILIGHT OF THE LBOs

It is a real privilege for me to have this opportunity to participate in the Olin Fellow lectures. I compliment you on the high standards you have set by this lecture series. They present me with quite a challenge today.

I would like to share with you the introduction to a recent article in *Forbes* Magazine by James Grant:

> "Trammell Crow, the king of the surviving Dallas real estate developers and a charter Forbes Four Hundred member, is credited with a number of pithy business sayings. Builders are leveraged and optimistic fellows, and some of Crow's remarks are inspirational, e.g., "The way to wealth is debt." However, recent goings-on in the credit markets may force a revision in that epigram. The updated version may read, less pithily, "The way to oblivion in a bear market is also debt, and nobody rings a bell."

Debt is the original fair-weather friend. It is with you on the upside and against you on the downside. So long has the financial sun been shining that it seems—especially—to the bulls on Wall Street—as though the skies will never darken. But if you can acknowledge the possibility of even one inclement business session, you will want to reflect on the leveraged American condition, and on many of the private American fortunes that constitute the Forbes Four Hundred. You will want to consider that debt may become just as unpopular one day as it now is popular.

Financially speaking, the story of the 20th century has been the mellowing of the American lender. At the turn of the century, it was hard to get a loan. In 1989, if you have a mailbox into which a credit card can be dropped, it is almost impossible not to get one. Consumers, governments and businesses have borrowed as never before. It is the decade of the Five-Year Yugo Loan, the leveraged buyout loan, the unsecured bridge loan, the teaser-rate adjustable-rate mortgage loan, the rescheduled Brazilian or Mexican loan, the Sotheby's Art-Quality Loan and the liposuction and breast-enlargement loan. It is the decade of retractable facsimile bonds, subordinated primary capital perpetual floating rate notes and collateralized fixed-rate multi-tranche tap notes. All in all, the 1980s are to debt what the 1960s were to sex.

Therefore I have chosen as my subject today one of the most controversial economic phenomena of recent times: the madcap LBO binge that has been restructuring corporate America. Most people speaking and writing on this subject have a substantial vested interest in it. I refer of course to the investment bankers and dealers, commercial bankers, legal and financial mergers and acquisitions experts and other buyout players, including many corporate executives. Many of these people have made fortunes by playing this high-stakes game.

My own direct exposure to this subject derives from my experience as a member of the Board of UAL Corporation, parent of United Airlines. As you know, the management and pilots of UAL initially launched a $6.8 billion tender offer for the company, to be paid for mostly by $7.2 billion in loans.

Since this particular buyout case is still in development and has raised some complex, unresolved issues as well as controversy, I shall refrain from commenting upon it today. But my interest in the whole leveraged buyout phenomenon that has swept American industry extends beyond my immediate concerns with UAL.

From my own vantage point, I shall attempt to do four things today:

- give you my views on the nature and magnitude of the LBO phenomenon;

- focus on some of the good and the bad elements in it;

- step back and consider some of the serious dangers developing for our economy as a whole as a result of the torrent of LBO-induced changes that have been flowing through corporate America;

- and, finally, suggest to you some measures I believe must be taken to curb the excesses and potential dangers developing in the most recent wave of leveraged financing.

As most of you know, the leveraged buyout, or LBO as it is called, has been used increasingly in recent years in two ways. It has been used as an aggressive move by corporate managers or financial experts who stand to make enormous profits for themselves. And it has been used as a defensive tactic by managements seeking to protect their companies from takeovers.

In both cases, investors take advantage of the fact that the value put on a company's assets in the public markets is less than the "true value" of those assets if they were better managed or sold to others. LBO investors also take advantage of GAAP accounting, which penalizes public companies, particularly goodwill accounting.

In an LBO, a group of investors that often includes company management buys a publicly-owned company or a division of such a company with mostly borrowed money, taking the company private. Using little of their own funds, the investors borrow against the assets and expected cash flow of the target company. That is how they get their leverage.

Frequently the money is raised through the sale of high-risk, high-yield securities popularly known as junk bonds. The risks of such leveraging fall on the lenders who advance the money and the employees of the company who are asked to make sacrifices, not on the dealmakers and executives. The capital structure of a typical LBO has been senior debt 50–60%, junior debt 20–30% and equity 10%.

Investors repay LBO loans from the company's cash flow or from the sale of its assets, which could be anything from a division or subsidiary to the company's planes or manufacturing facilities or equipment. To increase cash flow and service the heavy debt load, management usually takes an ax to the company's costs, often including its personnel.

The big argument in favor of LBOs has been that they force managements to make more productive use of assets. They are supposed to give managers more incentive to make tough decisions, such as selling off some assets. No one who believes in free markets could argue against that. If a company sells off a mediocre division to a buyout group led by the division's management, the managers become owners with more stake in success than they have ever had before.

The most convincing argument for junk bonds is that they provide financing for entrepreneurs who otherwise might not get it. The ex-king of junk bonds, Michael Milken, recently noted that there are 20,000 to 30,000 U.S. companies that are not investment grade but need and deserve capital to build their businesses. Milken made the case that these companies play a vital role in U.S. economic growth.

Investors who have participated in the leveraged buyout binge have reaped enormous rewards. In the heydays of LBOs, until the last few years, their returns very often were more than 40% a year, sometimes more than 50% or 60% a year, returns that not many of us achieve with our more mundane investments. The quick money earned by short-term players in these games is no small change. Arbitrageurs, the short-term investors who have a major influence on equity prices, encourage buyouts and stir up the equity markets with their speculative activity. Investment and commercial bankers pull down huge financial and advisory fees, typically totaling four percent of a company's purchase price.

The number of LBOs rose from 99 in 1981 to 316 in 1988, an increase of over 300%. The dollar value of these transactions exploded from about $10 billion in 1980 to something between $52 billion and $67 billion in 1988, depending upon which estimate is used. There are about $200 billion or more worth of junk bonds now outstanding.

By the end of 1988, one estimate put total debt of U.S. corporations (excluding financial institutions) at $1.8 trillion, with interest payments of these corporations amounting to an all-time high approaching 30% of their internal cash flow, and roughly half their taxable income, as compared with 25% a decade ago. Corporate borrowing increased at a 15.4% annual rate during the last economic cycle versus an average 8.4% for the previous six cycles, according to economist Henry Kaufman, causing a severe drop in credit ratings. Corporate borrowing amounted to some 43% of gross national product last year, up from 32% five years earlier.

To keep all this in perspective, we must acknowledge that, while banks have been the biggest buyout lenders (and this has been one of their most lucrative businesses in recent times), LBO loans made up only about 10% of total commercial loans by big banks last year, and some 55% at smaller banks. Nevertheless, the growth of this debt should raise anxieties, not least among lenders such as those who are already wrestling with the problems of Latin American loans gone bad. At one New York bank LBO loans accounted for more than 11% of all outstanding loans a year ago and have increased since then.

Naturally the banks and other financial experts who serve as advisers and buyout fund managers earn higher fees when higher prices are paid for LBO targets. This tends to make the LBO phenomenon a fee-driven binge, unrelated, for instance, to the use of debt for greater corporate productivity.

Needless to say, the restructuring and radical surgery precipitated by LBOs can, and does, create a great amount of turmoil and tension in the corporate world. Whether the result of aggregate LBO transactions is good or bad for the American economy is not an easy question to answer. Many academics and others are still trying to answer it.

I believe the answer to this question was more positive in the early days of LBOs than it is today. The first buyout targets were companies with either poor management that simply was not delivering the returns on assets that shareholders had a right to expect, or with cash flows that could not be plowed back into the business because of the dearth of attractive internal investment opportunities. Typically they were companies in relatively non-cyclical industries, companies with fairly steady cash flows that could finance the debt incurred in the buyouts.

For companies that generated a lot of cash, but did not have any exciting opportunities to reinvest in their own operations, LBOs made sense as a way to get cash out without paying it in dividends, which are taxed twice under one of the most misguided provisions of our tax code.

The basic objectives of the "good," old LBOs was to improve management of assets. Another objective was to increase returns on shareholder equity through financial leverage and, in some cases, simply to get rid of unpromising businesses by taking the cash out of them for more productive use. By and large the LBOs occurred in industries that could best afford to support them with strong, assured cash flows.

No one could object to the good intentions reflected by most of these early buyouts. Many of them helped companies operate more efficiently. Often they kindled new entrepreneurial sparks by giving management, and often their employees also, an ownership interest. Just the mere scare of LBOs undoubtedly has caused corporate managements to pay more attention to how they utilize their assets.

However, many buyouts in the recent headlines have less to do with improving management than with financial gymnastics. In my view the buyout craze can lead to unhealthy extremes when the smart-money crowd looks upon businesses simply as cash machines. Focusing on cash generation is fine, but it is not the whole function of management. If management makes decisions solely for short-term cash generation, it is likely to neglect a lot of other things that make for long-term business success.

Perhaps most worrisome of all, the buyout binge has moved into industries and companies that are more volatile or cyclical than early buyout targets. In some cases these latest corporate targets are intimately involved with basic public concerns like transportation and safety.

Take the case of the recent $7.5 billion bid for American Airlines made, and then withdrawn, by real estate investor-promoter Donald Trump. With this attack, American became the third of the nation's major airlines to be engaged in takeover or buyout battles featuring massive borrowing.

Investors jumped at the possibilities for making quick gains in this industry where management may have done many things right but perhaps have not translated the full value of their assets into the price of their stock. The battle for American would have pitted a financial promoter, who has been in and out of other companies before for short-term profits when takeover rumors drove their prices up, against AMR Chairman Robert Crandall, the man who built American into the nation's leading airline. Crandall has an unequaled reputation for topnotch airline management and has argued against leveraging of companies in his industry.

Taking on massive debt in the airline industry is different from doing so in most of the traditional LBO situations. The industry is fiercely competitive and volatile. A heavy debt load could disadvantage an airline when it needs to lower fares or buy new aircraft, and could reduce its flexibility to react to problems such as rising fuel or wage costs, or a drop in traffic.

This kind of situation raises the question of what effect the LBO binge has had across American industry. When CEOs are more preoccupied with short-term takeover strategies than they are with long-range planning to improve performance and service to their customers, there is good cause for alarm.

Perhaps most repugnant is the spectacle of well-heeled investors reaping enormous quick profits just by stock buyups that send takeover rumors flying, and then selling their shares when someone else moves in. That is what happened when Beverly Hills billionaire Marvin Davis made his bid for NWA, the parent of Northwest Airlines, and then walked away with a profit variously estimated at $50 to $100 million by selling his appreciated shares.

Similarly, one has to worry about the public and congressional reaction to a management-led buyout where a corporate officer who stands to make many millions on the sale of his stock asks wage and salary concessions of employees down the line, who are making very modest salaries, to help make the deal go through. One cannot help wondering how much damage such stories have done to the image of business and financial executives in the mind of the American public.

The takeover of NWA and the bid for UAL spread takeover fever through the whole U.S. airline industry and fueled the fires of speculators. This drove up the prices of still-independent Delta Air Lines and USAir, in fact the whole Dow Jones transportation average, and stirred members of Congress into action. When Congress is aroused, the specter rises of new government controls on this industry that has gained so much from deregulation.

The Trump bid for American Airlines was one signal that the LBO era is entering the twilight zone, insofar as the willingness of responsible people to tolerate it is concerned. But this and other airline industry fracases are not the only indications that the buyout binge may have peaked. LBO companies are turning out to be a mixed bag, some good, some bad, including those engineered by the most successful buyout firm, Kohlberg, Kravis, and Roberts [KKR].

We have heard mostly about KKR's success stories. RJR Nabisco paid down its debt easily and has announced new product drives and other initiatives. KKR's studies of its LBOs in general found increases in employment, research and development spending and capital spending by 17 LBOs in which the firm still had an equity stake in January 1989.

However, the number of highly leveraged companies running into trouble in paying their creditors appears to be increasing steadily. Some of KKR's buyouts have gotten into difficulties recently that could result in losses for investors, or even bankruptcies, instead of the big returns that investors expected.

SCI Television of Nashville, for example, formerly part of Storer Broadcasting, failed to make a September debt payment and saw its junk bonds plunge in value. Seaman Furniture ran into trouble meeting interest and principal payments. Rumors of possible troubles also have floated over other KKR buyout companies including Beatrice, Jim Walter and Owens-Illinois.

In retailing, Campeau Corporation, which bought the two biggest department store chains in America, saw its leveraged empire head into a cash-flow crisis that wreaked havoc with such prestigious stores as New York's Bloomingdales and Boston's Jordan Marsh. In the financial services field, Integrated Resources failed to make interest payments on nearly $1 billion of debt, raising fears of bankruptcy among its creditors.

Some companies that undertook management-led buyouts to avert hostile takeovers have been casualties in the buyout game. Trailer-maker Fruehauf Corporation, for instance, was forced to sell most of its businesses to pay for its $1.5 billion LBO to thwart investor Asher Edelman.

All of these situations are signs that the financial extremes of the 1980s, the leveraging of corporate America, are already causing pain in many quarters. Yet despite the clear warning signs, there is still plenty of money around to bankroll LBOs, as recent oversubscribed takeovers such as Warner Communications and NWA have indicated. KKR alone is reported to have access to a $30 billion "war chest," ready for more action, based on $3 to $4 billion subscribed but uncommitted money for equity investments leveraged at 8 to 1.

But if the LBO scares and casualties I have mentioned can occur in the heady atmosphere of our recent bullish markets, what would happen to all the firms leveraged with unprecedented debt in the crunch of a serious recession? You can be sure that the severity of any such recession would be accentuated by the rush of defaults and bankruptcies that could occur.

Federal Reserve Chairman Alan Greenspan noted, in testimony before the House Ways and Means Committee earlier this year, that greater use of debt makes the corporate sector more vulnerable to an economic downturn or a rise in interest rates. Would LBO companies go bankrupt when they lacked the cash flow to service their debt and were unable to restructure their indebtedness? What would be the consequences for many thousands of investors who have put money into junk bonds? What would be the consequences for the banks that hold large quantities of LBO debt in their loan portfolios? What would happen to the workers employed by LBOs that might be forced into bankruptcy? To what extent would the Federal Reserve Board be forced to ease monetary policy to avoid financial calamity, risking renewed inflation?

Defaults of junk bonds in the first half of this year already were double those of the previous year, at some $3.2 billion. Downgrades of corporate debt by at least one major rating service currently are exceeding upgrades two-to-one because of restructurings and takeovers. As

Federal Reserve Vice Chairman Manuel Johnson has pointed out, in the event of recession companies could be forced to sell assets at a time when there was little demand for corporate assets. High debt levels, he warned, could bring a series of bankruptcies that could cause a crisis of confidence.

Instead of focusing on these scary possibilities, however, I want you to think with me today about some of the lessons of the LBO era, lessons that put this whole phenomenon into historical perspective. I think these lessons point the way to some public policy imperatives.

Our great free market system has its excesses, and the LBO craze is one of them. These are among the prices we pay for freedom. They are typically followed by some kind of government regulation that puts limits of one kind or another on our freedoms. Let us be sure this time that any government intervention strengthens the system, rather than weakens it.

Congress, however, has looked at the challenge presented by the LBO binge and reacted in a piecemeal manner rather than focusing on the root causes of the abusive fee-driven deals. They have proposed new rules which could restrict the deductibility of interest incurred in financing acquisitions. This is a mistake. In its efforts to create an appearance of political action, Congress has closed its eyes to the fact that these restrictions could very well have the opposite effect.

The limitations on the interest deduction would impact all financings, whether driven by fees or sound business judgment. In addition, such limits would merely make financings more costly. Finally, they would only serve to lead the buyout brokers to create new, and, depending on your perspective, innovative or junk financing vehicles.

This band-aid approach by Congress is bad public policy. Instead of patchwork restrictions, Congress should encourage what is needed most: the infusion of equity into the financing of America's growth. The excesses of the LBO revolve around its very name, the "leveraged" part of the buyout.

Congress has, in fact, encouraged this leverage up to now by providing powerful incentives for corporate debt as opposed to equity. These incentives are provided through our tax laws. Equity investors have had to pay a tax twice on their return on equity: once through the corporate tax and again on the tax they pay on dividends. Lenders, on the other hand, face no such double tax in that interest is deductible at the corporate level. This has led to junk bonds replacing what would otherwise be equity investment.

Fed Chairman Greenspan has recognized this and warned in recent testimony before Congress that double-taxation of earnings from corporate equity capital has encouraged leveraging, causing debt levels to be higher than they should be. So long as equity securities are handicapped in this way, we will not provide the incentives for the broadest public participation in ownership of our enterprises. The critics who say that abolishing this discrimination against equity financing is unthinkable in these times of big budget deficits simply have not thought this through.

One, the deficit impact of allowing companies to deduct dividends as well as interest payments could be minimized. The goal should be to equalize treatment of dividends and interest, and this need not add to deficits. If the same percentage of each were deductible by corporations, as proposed in June by Congress's Joint Committee on Taxation, equity would have a chance, and the budgetary effect would be neutral.

Second, there has been much recent focus on lowering the tax on capital gains as a means of generating investment in the economy. A far more powerful incentive would result with the phase out of the double tax penalty. Equity capital has many advantages over debt, and as a nation we have every reason to encourage it.

A company weathering hard times can cut dividends on stock instead of laying off workers and closing plants. If it cuts payment on its debt, cutbacks and layoffs and even bankruptcy are much more likely, exacerbating an economic downturn. A company with lower debt and higher equity has more ability to invest in research and development and in more efficient production equipment. This is hardly a new theme for American business. It is a very old theme. But it needs to be played over and over again, until people outside the business world understand it.

If the rules of the game are skewed to favor debt, naturally there will be an accumulation of debt. And naturally there will be people finding ways to use the leverage of debt for their own quick profit. If the rules of the game encourage the public to own, not just loan to, American business, corporate management will act from a longer-term perspective which will be in the best long-term interests of the U.S. economy.

It probably would be helpful also to increase the capital requirements of lending by the banks and others who finance these leveraged deals. Efforts are under way in some areas, such as the savings and loan bailout law, which prohibits thrifts from owning junk bonds.

Another possible solution, recommended by Dr. Albert Wojnilower of First Boston, is to impose mandatory capital standards on large corporations such as those already imposed on banks and savings and loan associations. Small firms would be exempt, since they do not contribute materially to the systemic problem. He has in mind a financial ratio approach similar to that already applied by lenders and bond rating agencies. The equity requirement would be satisfiable only by pure equity.

The required ratios would have to be set at different levels for different firms, depending on their size and industry. It has long been known that debt-equity and other financial ratios differ according to industry and size of firm. A certain arbitrariness is unavoidable, but it would hardly be greater than that already involved in the setting of bond ratings by the private rating agencies.

The twofold penalty for noncompliance would be simple and automatic. The lesser penalty would be the withdrawal of the tax advantage for the excess debt. Interest would be treated as though it were dividends. This would limit the tax incentive for equity retirement without radically revising our tax system. But in many cases this would not be an adequate deterrent. The more potent penalty to be applied would be the compulsory dismissal of senior management, with forfeiture of equity entitlements, golden parachutes and such benefits.

Those of us who cherish and understand our free market economy will not stand by forever and see fortunes made overnight by the buying and selling of our companies instead of the building of our companies. For these times, we need builders more than we need master jugglers of corporate assets. We must not tolerate a system that provides richer rewards for purely financial driven transactions than for efforts to increase manufacturing and marketing productivity and industrial creativity.

We must not tolerate forever an American tax code that penalizes management for seeking public participation in ownership over financial institutions' participation in loading companies with debt. We must not allow American companies to load themselves with so much debt as to make them vulnerable when the economy turns down. These are big imperatives as we head into the 1990s and the fierce global competition that is going to characterize the next decade.

NO

Michael T. Tucker

LBOs MAY NOT BE DEAD YET—
A RESPONSE TO FRANK OLSON

News of the death of LBOs is likely to be as premature as that of the early reported demise of Mark Twain. Mr. Frank A. Olson might wish LBOs would go away because of the problems they cause for corporate management, but the underlying rationale that has driven LBOs has not vanished with the inability of United Airlines to raise sufficient debt capital to consummate the deal to which Mr. Olson is so strongly opposed.

During the 1980s, U.S. companies retired $500 billion in equities while piling up $1 trillion in new debt. Merrill Lynch estimates that meeting the obligations to all those bondholders garners as much as 30% of corporate cash flow, a greater percentage allocated to interest than in either of the two worst postwar recessions.

Yet the merger and acquisition tidal wave of the 1980s characterized by corporations amassing debt while retiring equity has a strong foundation in financial theory. Its philosophical origins can be traced to the 1958 Modigliani and Miller (MM) pioneering work on corporate capital structure published in the *American Economic Review*. At the time of the paper's appearance, corporate America heavily favored equity over debt. The generation that made financing decisions had all too current memories of the Depression. Balance sheets with zero long-term liabilities were not unusual. All-equity companies were deemed prudent instead of ripe for takeover. Fiscal conservatism was the rule rather than the exception.

The premise of MM's paper was that leveraged firms are worth more than firms without debt. An unleveraged firm is defined as having a worth equivalent to the present value of its after tax cash flows in perpetuity:

$$V_u = \frac{\text{EBIT}(1 - t)}{k_c}$$

V_u = value of a firm without debt

k_c = the required rate of return on equity capital

EBIT = earnings before interest and taxes

t = the firm's tax rate.

The above example assumes no growth in the firm's earnings stream. The formula can be easily adjusted to account for growth without impact on its basic implications.

MM define the value of a leveraged firm in terms V_u:

$$V_L = V_u + tD$$
V_L = value of a leveraged firm
tD = tax shield on debt.

Firms with debt have the ability to deduct interest payments. That deductibility protects a proportion of earnings from taxes, resulting in a tax shield. Although there is a cost associated with debt, tax deductibility is a form of government subsidization of debt financing, making it a less costly form of financing than equity.

Dividends, lacking tax deductibility, cost a firm more than debt. In addition, shareholders receiving the dividends pay taxes on them. Equity financing does, however, have advantages. Failure to make an expected dividend payment will not result in the firm being in default. Defaulting on interest or principal payments may cause bankruptcy, with creditors suddenly becoming owners of the firm. Equity holders, as former owners of the firm, lose all value. In the 1980s, with the help of junk bond messiah Mike Milken, the tax advantages of deducting interest payments, together with the threat of others borrowing and buying up the company, convinced financial officers that bonds were the safest route

for financing their growth needs while insuring their employment.

As debt replaced equity, stock prices soared until that fateful day in October 1987. In the halcyon days of early 1987, a $500 million firm could peddle 10% of itself for $50 million. In the winter of 1987–88, 18% of corporate control would have to be surrendered to raise the same $50 million. Further tilting the scales toward debt was the 9% interest-rate on benchmark long-term Treasury bonds.

While debt has inherent bankruptcy risk, failure to have some debt could imply overly cautious management under MM's Proposition I. A firm with no debt is undervalued when compared to a similar firm with leverage. The benefits of the tax shield are lost. Issuance of debt increases firm value and also gives management the opportunity to repurchase shares at a premium from current shareholders. Repurchasing shares offers a better alternative for shareholder gain than dividends. Because share repurchases are not taxed twice like dividends, firms can offer a premium to shareholders. The only tax due is paid by the shareholders based on capital gains.

Management that fails to keep shareholders financially satisfied may find itself prey to takeover attempts by groups offering shareholders the opportunity to sell their shares at prices considerably higher than current valuations. In the early 1980s, companies in noncyclical industries, i.e., businesses unaffected by the business cycle, became the favored targets of leveraged buyout artists. Companies with low debt to equity ratios had large amounts of unused debt capacity. Kohlberg, Kravis and Roberts (KKR), premier takeover artists of the 1980s, employed the purchased companies' own assets to engineer takeovers. By borrowing heavily they were able to buy back all shares of these companies at substantial premiums. Shareholders were happy, and the newly constituted companies paid off handsomely. Creditors received high interest payments on "junk bonds." New equity investors reaped large returns when the company was subsequently broken up and went public as a new entity some years later.

T. Boone Pickens of Mesa Petroleum, a major buyout player, described himself as a champion of neglected shareholders. By borrowing large amounts of money and buying firms, Pickens and his ilk promised full value. They blamed management for squandering the firm's assets. Of course, all those involved in consummating these deals did not labor out of charity.

Agency theory is the philosophical underpinning of Pickens' rhetoric. According to agency theory, management, acting as agents of the shareholders, does not necessarily maximize shareholder utility. Managers are out to maximize their own utility. Rather than take greater investment risks through borrowing and financing new projects in order to give shareholders maximum payouts, management may elect a more conservative course that protects their interests. Debt also tends to restrict free cash flow, channeling it into interest payments. The more fixed payment obligations, e.g., interest, that a firm has to meet, the less spending flexibility management retains. Agency theorists, ever suspicious of management misappropriation of funds, view limiting free cash flow as a way to control management actions. Companies with less cash flow will have to do more with what they do have. This is sometimes described as becoming "lean and mean." The implication is that these aggressive, slimmed-down firms have fewer layers of middle management, and fewer country club memberships and corporate jets.

Cutting costs too much can be bad for business. Mr. Olson argues that firms with too much debt are severely constrained and at risk of bankruptcy. While some debt may be beneficial, overdoing it can be harmful. A corollary to MM Proposition I adds a third term to the formula, taking Mr. Olson's objections into account. The present value of bankruptcy costs serves as a check against balance sheets too heavily weighted in favor of debt:

$$V_L = V_u + tD - \text{PV(Bankruptcy Cost)*(Probability of Bankruptcy)}$$

Bankruptcy, in a perfectly functioning market, would imply a smooth and costless transmission of the corporation's assets from shareholders to creditors. Given our efficient but less than perfect markets, bankruptcy has costs such as litigation, lost operational efficiency, and lost investment opportunities. As the debt of a firm increases, the probability of insolvency also rises. At some point the present value of bankruptcy costs is greater than any gains from further debt. When that level of debt has been attained, the firm can be said to have reached its optimal capital structure.

Corporations in cyclical industries will have a lower optimal debt level than firms in noncyclical industries, because their cash flows are susceptible to greater variability. The airline industry, a very competitive and cyclical segment of the economy, has a lower optimal debt level than the food industry with its noncyclical cash flows. United Airlines, as Mr. Olson pointed out, if subjected to the leveraged buyout terms proposed in October 1989, would entail high debt service levels. Those debt service levels could supersede optimal level of debt, resulting in the restructured firm being worth less than it was prior to restructuring.

While this decline in value would be true if the newly constituted United Airlines were in all ways the same as the former firm, it may not be true if the nature of the firm itself has changed. Agency theory argues that when management and ownership are closely linked, maximizing corporate and managerial goals will imply the same actions. Waste is eliminated through self interest, and the firm functions more efficiently. Firm ownership by employees, as proposed by the United Airlines LBO, would have created such a situation. The deal did not collapse because of feared inability to service excess debt. The demise was reported to be due to an excess of greed on the part of management anxious to reap an immediate payout upon consummation. This does not preclude the success of a differently structured deal to accomplish a similar change in ownership.

The tilt of balance sheets toward more debt and away from equity is simply an example of efficient markets working within the confines of the current rules of the game. Firm valuation is enhanced with more debt, as pointed out by Modigliani and Miller. Management failing to restructure accordingly will be subject to replacement by others willing to use the firm's debt capacity to satisfy shareholder's desire for higher returns on investment.

The form of that restructuring has not been limited to traditional subordinated debenture* debt. Borrowing has undergone some dramatic changes under the creative tutelage of investment bankers eager to package new products. Some of the most original thinking has been done for oil and gas companies. A menagerie of quasi-debt, quasi-equity issues has emerged over the last few years with acronyms that speak more of the jungle than Wall Street. Triton Energy and Maxus were the first to use Liquid Yield Options Notes (LYONS), convertible zero coupon bonds. LYONS investors have the option of either holding the note to term, collecting interest, or converting to equity. This differs from traditional convertible bonds which pay interest until conversion. Triton's seventeen year $314 million debt issue (face value) with 8.25% interest sold at $253.01 per bond and could be converted into 15.6 shares. With the stock selling at $14.50 at time of issue, the $16.25 conversion price was well within range (Triton's high for 1989 was 16 5/8). A straight debt offering would have carried a coupon of 12.5%.

Maxus's LYONS retained some added options for the firm. While the holder could convert the notes into equity, the firm could elect to convert it into cash based on 8.5% interest after five years, or after ten years it could issue new notes at the then prevailing interest rate. The issue was oversubscribed at a conversion price of $8.05 with the stock selling at $7. The stock's high for 1988 was 9 5/8. Vice President and Treasurer of Maxus, Glen Brown, explained why LYONS were the financing of choice: "We chose LYONS because they were zero coupon, meaning no interest is paid out in the first five

---

* [Debentures are bonds that are backed by the general good name of the issuing company in lieu of collateral.—Ed.]

years. That allows us to reduce our cash outflow. And the dollars saved from not having to pay cash interest should, over the life of this issue, add a lot of value to Maxus."

Presidio Oil found a cash rich seam with its $100 million, 13.25% interest offering of gas indexed notes. Each one cent increase in the price of gas above $1.75 per mmbtu will push up the bond's interest rate by $2^1/_2$ basis points. Presidio won't balk at paying that extra interest. If the rate on the note increases by 1%, resulting in an additional $1 million in debt payments, the company would realize more than $7.5 million in added revenues from the hike in the price of gas.

Mr. Olson's suggested possible changes in the tax laws will not end the creativity of investment bankers demonstrated above. However, it may direct their endeavors toward capital structures he would find more efficacious. Any change in the tax law would cause a revision in a firm's optimal capital structure to whatever fits newly created economic constraints. If dividends were made tax deductible, as proposed by Mr. Olson, they would produce a tax shield similar to that of interest on debt. Limiting the amount of interest a firm could deduct according to some debt/equity ratio ceiling would also change the valuation and consequently the optimal capital structure, much as the minimum tax has changed investment decisions.

Mr. Olson can take comfort in knowing that all tides eventually turn, and the rising wave of debt financing is already ebbing as a function of a slowing economy and perhaps the absence of Michael Milken. One of the first signs of the beginning of a new trend was in August 1989, when investors turned their backs on Ohio Mattress's (Sealy) 15% junk bond issue. Many debt-laden companies are now selling divisions at 10% to 30% less than they had planned when they borrowed all those billions, adding a dose of reality to new would-be LBOs. The savings and loan bailout bill has raised another specter over the debt market. The bill gives S&Ls five years to sell off their junk bonds. Those bonds represent 17% of the junk bond market. After growing at 34% per annum since 1981, junk bonds are about to come back down to earth.

Regardless of whether or not Congress tinkers with the tax law, efficient capital markets will vote with dollars on the acceptability of corporate capital structures. While it is true that higher amounts of debt in cyclical industries may lead to severe financial constraints and/or bankruptcies, it is also true that rational investors will reject deals that lower firm values. Of course there will be excesses, bankruptcies and unhappy management. In equilibrium the efficient market shakes out the bad deals and maximizes value. Markets are always getting back to equilibrium, which implies some bumps along the way such as experienced in the October 1989 stock market dive precipitated by the collapse of the United Airlines deal. In the long-term, rough spots, while painful, create far fewer inefficiencies than constant tinkering with the tax laws.

POSTSCRIPT

Are Leveraged Buyouts Bad for the Bottom Line?

The leveraged buyout is a new phenomenon in America. How should we characterize this situation? Do LBOs simply reflect business as usual, in which some people (raiders, bankers, knowledgeable inside executives, lawyers) get rich, while others (employees, bondholders, long-range shareholders of the company) suffer? Or is this an unethical practice, from which businesspeople should abstain?

Interestingly, until very recently, most businesspeople would have abstained. In a sense, the leveraged buyout is made possible by massive changes in American society, which include the dissolution of old guard bonds of faithfulness to class and structure and the legitimization of the pursuit of self-interest across the social levels of society.

For much of America's economic history, people have relied on the banks to keep restraints on the pursuit of gain and the indulgence of greed. The banker was the embodiment of prudence and long-term thinking, the chief conservative of the community, financially and usually in all other respects, too.

Furthermore, the chief executive officers and boards of directors of the major corporations were builders rather than speculators, responsible to a small group of shareholders who believed that economic safety lay in building up the corporations. The destruction of a company for the sake of instant cash would not have occurred to any of them; a single discontented shareholder could always sell out his shares without disturbing the structure of the whole. And between them, the major corporations and the major banks controlled all the cash in the country; the money to make a multibillion-dollar offer for a huge company simply was not available.

Two major changes in the financial world upset this order. First, individual shareholders were replaced by institutional funds. Second, and possibly more important, the whole social order of friendship and class loyalty that bound major banks to major corporations has been toppled by the newly democratic mergers-and-acquisitions divisions of banking houses. While some will see a healthy opening of opportunities, entirely appropriate to a democracy committed to the dream of success for everyone, others will be alarmed by the collapse of the institutions and social practices that succeeded in maintaining a degree of ethical restraint on a runaway economy.

Are LBOs a threat to American enterprise as a whole? Should we call for legislation to prohibit the practice? This seems to be Olson's view when he says, "For these times, we need builders more than we need master jugglers

72

of corporate assets." The jugglers and the liquidators, the people who brought us the LBOs, also brought us the Savings and Loan debacle and the trillion-dollar deficit. It may be time to try a little building again.

SUGGESTED READINGS

Robert Almeder and David Carey, "In Defense of Sharks: Moral Issues in Hostile Liquidating Takeovers," *The Journal of Business Ethics* (vol. 10, 1991).

Douglas Bandow, "Curbing Raiders is Bad for Business," *The New York Times* (February 7, 1988).

Carl C. Icahn, "The Case for Takeovers," *The New York Times Magazine* (January 29, 1989).

Laura Jereski, "Ill Will," *Forbes* (January 23, 1989).

Frank R. Lichtenberg, "Takeovers Slash Corporate Overhead," *The Wall Street Journal* (February 7, 1989).

Martin Lipton, "Paying the Price of Takeover Money," *Manhattan, Inc.* (May 1989).

Michael Lubatkin, "Value-Creating Mergers: Fact or Folklore?" *The Academy of Management Executive* (November 1988).

Lisa H. Newton, "Charting Shark-Infested Waters: Ethical Dimensions of the Hostile Takeover," *Journal of Business Ethics* (January–February 1988).

Robert B. Reich, "America Pays the Price," *The New York Times Magazine* (January 29, 1989).

ISSUE 5

Are Corporate Codes of Ethics Just for Show?

YES: LaRue Tone Hosmer, from *The Ethics of Management* (Irwin Press, 1987)

NO: Lisa H. Newton, from "The Many Faces of the Corporate Code," in *The Corporate Code of Ethics: The Perspective of the Humanities,* proceedings of the Conference on Corporate Visions and Values (Fairfield University, 1992)

ISSUE SUMMARY

YES: LaRue Tone Hosmer, a professor of corporate strategies, argues that codes of ethics are really only for show and that they are ineffective in bringing about more ethical behavior on the part of employees.

NO: Professor of philosophy Lisa H. Newton holds that the formation and adoption of corporate codes are valuable processes because they raise corporate awareness of ethical issues and because they can be a valuable part of the corporate action review process.

Business ethics, as an academic discipline and a corporate concern, is the product of the combination of two unlikely companions. Early in the century, what was called "business ethics" was in reality a set of agreements, created for and by businessmen, concerning the way they did business, and for the most part they were highly *un*ethical. These agreements demanded that you keep your salesman off the other guy's turf; that you refrain from introducing new products in direct competition with other members of the club; that you hire only white males, or at least make sure that only white males made it to the upper echelons of the company; and that you keep secret whatever you might know about your fellow businessmen's adulterated products or fictional tax returns. In short, like the "ethics" of any profession of the period, business ethics were the rules of the in-group—self-protective and self-serving.

Meanwhile, the ethics taught in colleges was linguistic and analytic. Professors taught only terms and their meanings, conversed only with themselves and their students, and were well aware that their teachings were of little use in the real world of business. Business ethics was not seen as a serious discipline.

However, starting in the late 1950s, scandals began to surface: price-fixing, unsafe products, and foreign bribes, for example. In response, the "social responsibility" movement, led primarily by the churches and a few crusading consumer advocates such as Ralph Nader, attempted to make business accountable to the general public for its practices. Business were told to get out of South Africa because of apartheid, to ensure product quality and safety, and to take responsibility for the natural environment. Although the business community's first response was to ignore the activists, some severe legal consequences—such as jail terms for some very respectable corporate officers, demonstrations, and hostile regulatory legislation—made it clear that some attention would have to be paid to ethics, or at least to the *appearance* of ethics.

Businesspeople started thinking seriously about public accountability around the time when the armed conflict in Vietnam brought the ethics professors out of their classrooms and into the public arena. Philosophy developed a new, socially relevant branch of ethics, soon to be called "applied ethics," and by the early 1970s the ethicists of the applied branch were in dialogue with physicians over medical ethics, lawyers on legal ethics, and businesspeople on business ethics. Some familiarity with ethics is now required of most undergraduate business majors.

But does writing and teaching about ethics do any good? LaRue Tone Hosmer says no. He sees a fundamental problem with codes of ethics, in that "ethics in management represents a conflict between the economic and the social performance of an organization." Accordingly, codes of ethics must be exercises in futility, since they direct the corporation away from its primary function. Lisa H. Newton, on the contrary, asserts that the actual code is the least important element in the development of the corporate culture. She argues that the process of code development—principled, comprehensive, and participative—is the most valuable part of the development exercise.

Ask yourself, as you read these selections, if there is a conflict between economic and social performance—that is, between business and ethics. Is *business ethics* an oxymoron?

YES

LaRue Tone Hosmer

ETHICAL CODES

Ethical codes are statements of the norms and beliefs of an organization. These norms and beliefs are generally proposed, discussed, and defined by the senior executives in the firm and then published and distributed to all of the members. Norms, of course, are standards of behavior; they are the ways the senior people in the organization want the others to act when confronted with a given situation. An example of a norm in a code of ethics would be, "Employees of this company will not accept personal gifts with a monetary value over $25 in total from any business friend or associate, and they are expected to pay their full share of the costs for meals or other entertainment (concerts, the theatre, sporting events, etc.) that have a value above $25 per person." The norms in an ethical code are generally expressed as a series of negative statements, for it is easier to list the things a person should not do than to be precise about the things a person should do.

The beliefs in an ethical code are standards of thought; they are the ways that the senior people in the organization want others to think. This is not censorship. Instead, the intent is to encourage ways of thinking and patterns of attitudes that will lead towards the wanted behavior. Consequently, the beliefs in an ethical code are generally expressed in a positive form. "Our first responsibility is to our customer" is an example of a positive belief that commonly appears in codes of ethics; another would be "We wish to be good citizens of every community in which we operate." Some company codes of ethics appear in [the two boxes that follow].

Do ethical codes work? Are they helpful in conveying to all employees the moral standards selected by the board of directors and president? Not really. The problem is that it is not possible to state the norms and beliefs of an organization relative to the various constituent groups—employees, customers, suppliers, distributors, stockholders, and the general public— clearly and explicitly, without offending at least one of those groups. It is not possible to say, for example, that a company considers its employees to be more important to the success of the firm than its stockholders, without putting the stockholders on notice that profits and dividends come second. Stockholders, and their agents at trust departments and mutual funds, tend

THE ETHICS CODE OF BORG-WARNER CORPORATION, "TO REACH BEYOND THE MINIMAL"

Any business is a member of a social system, entitled to the rights and bound by the responsibilities of that membership. Its freedom to pursue economic goals is constrained by law and channeled by the forces of a free market. But these demands are minimal, requiring only that a business provide wanted goods and services, compete fairly, and cause no obvious harm.

For some companies that is enough. It is not enough for Borg-Warner. We impose upon ourselves an obligation to reach beyond the minimal. We do so convinced that by making a larger contribution to the society that sustains us, we best assure not only its future vitality, but our own.

This is what we believe....

We believe in the dignity of the individual. However large and complex a business may be, its work is still done by people dealing with people. Each person involved is a unique human being, with pride, needs, values and innate personal worth. For Borg-Warner to succeed we must operate in a climate of openness and trust, in which each of us freely grants others the same respect, cooperation and decency we seek for ourselves.

We believe in our responsibility to the common good. Because Borg-Warner is both an economic and social force, our responsibilities to the public are large. The spur of competition and the sanctions of the law give strong guidance to our behavior, but alone do not inspire our best. For that we must heed the voice of our natural concern for others. Our challenge is to supply goods and services that are of superior value to those who use them; to create jobs that provide meaning for those who do them; to honor and enhance human life, and to offer our talents and our wealth to help improve the world we share.

We believe in the endless quest for excellence. Though we may be better today than we were yesterday, we are not as good as we must become. Borg-Warner chooses to be a leader—in serving our customers, advancing our technologies, and rewarding all who invest in us their time, money, and trust. None of us can settle for doing less than our best, and we can never stop trying to surpass what already have been achieved.

We believe in continuous renewal. A corporation endures and prospers only by moving forward. The past has given us the present to build on. But to follow our visions to the future, we must see the difference between traditions that give us continuity and strength, and conventions that no longer serve

Box continued on next page.

us—and have the course to act on that knowledge. Most can adapt after change has occurred; we must be among the few who anticipate change, shape it to our purpose, and act as its agents.

We believe in the commonwealth of Borg-Warner and its people. Borg-Warner is both a federation of businesses and a community of people. Our goal is to preserve the freedom each of us needs to find personal satisfaction while building the strength that comes from unity. True unity is more than a melding of self-interests; it results when values and ideals are also shared. Some of ours are spelled out in these statements of belief. Others include faith in our political, economic and spiritual heritage; pride in our work and our company; the knowledge that loyalty must flow in many directions; and a conviction that ownership is strongest when shared. We look to the unifying force of these beliefs as a source of energy to brighten the future of our company and all who depend on it.

Source: Company booklet, published 1982.

to resent that, just as the employees would if the conditions were reversed. Consequently codes of ethics are usually written in general terms, noting obligations to each of the groups but not stating which takes precedence in any given situation.

The basic difficulty with codes of ethics is that they do not establish priorities between the norms and beliefs. The priorities are the true values of a firm, and they are not included. As an example, let us say that one division in a firm is faced with declining sales and profits; the question is whether to reduce middle-management employment and cut overhead costs—the classic downsizing decision—but the code of ethics says in one section that we respect our employees and in another section that we expect "fair" profits. How do we decide? What is "fair" in this instance? The code of ethics does not tell us.

Let us look at two other examples very briefly. Another division in our company is in a market that has grown very rapidly and has now reached such a large size that direct distribution from the factory to the retail outlets would be much more economical. Our code of ethics says that we will "work closely with our suppliers and distributors, for they too deserve a profit," but perhaps we can reduce our prices to our customers, and gain a competitive advantage for ourselves, if we eliminate the wholesalers and ship directly. The code does not tell us how to choose between our distributors, our customers, and ourselves.

As a last example, we are fortunate in having within our company another division that also is growing rapidly; it needs to build a new manufacturing plant, but a town in an adjoining state has offered much more substantial tax concessions than the town in which we have operated for 60 years, and in which, let us assume, there is substantial unemployment and need for additional tax revenues. Our (continued on p. 80)

THE ETHICS CODE OF JOHNSON AND JOHNSON, "OUR CREDO"

We believe our first responsibility is to the doctors, nurses and patients, to mothers and all others who use our products and services.

In meeting their needs everything we do must be of high quality.

We must constantly strive to reduce our costs in order to maintain reasonable prices.

Customers' orders must be serviced promptly and accurately.

Our suppliers and distributors must have an opportunity to make a fair profit.

We are responsible to our employees, the men and women who work with us throughout the world.

Everyone must be considered as an individual.

We must respect their dignity and recognize their merit.

They must have a sense of security in their jobs.

Compensation must be fair and adequate, and working conditions clean, orderly and safe.

Employees must feel free to make suggestions and complaints.

There must be equal opportunity for employment, development and advancement for those qualified.

We must provide competent management, and their actions must be just and ethical.

We are responsible to the communities in which we live and work and to the world community as well.

We must be good citizens—support good works and charities and bear our fair share of taxes.

We must encourage civic improvements and better health and education.

We must maintain in good order the property we are privileged to use, protecting the environment and natural resources.

Our final responsibility is to our stockholders.

Business must make a sound profit.

We must experiment with new ideas.

Research must be carried on, innovative programs developed and mistakes paid for.

New equipment must be purchased, new facilities provided and new products launched.

Reserves must be created to provide for adverse times.

When we operate according to these principles, the stockholders should realize a fair return.

Source: Company annual report for 1982, p. 5.

code of ethics says that we will be "good citizens" in every community in which we operate, but it does not explain how to choose between communities, or what being a "good citizen" really means.

Ethical dilemmas are conflicts between economic performance and social performance, with the social performance being expressed as obligations to employees, customers, suppliers, distributors, and the general public. Ethical codes can express a general sense of the obligation members of senior management feel towards those groups, but the codes cannot help a middle- or lower-level manager choose between the groups, or between economic and social performance. Should we reduce employment and increase our profits? Should we eliminate our wholesalers and cut our prices? Should we build in another city and reduce our taxes? Should we—and this is the reason I have included the code of ethics of Johnson and Johnson, Inc.—spend over $100 million removing Tylenol from the shelves of every store in the country after the nonprescription drug was found to have been delib-

erately poisoned in the Chicago area during 1982, causing the deaths of four individuals. James Burke, chairman of Johnson and Johnson, credits that code with guiding the actions of his company. "This document (the code of ethics) spells out our responsibilities to all our constituencies: consumers, employees, community, and stockholders. It served to guide all of us during the crisis, when hard decisions had to be made in what were often excruciatingly brief periods of time. All of our employees world-wide were able to watch the process of the Tylenol withdrawal and subsequent reintroduction in tamper-resistant packaging, confident of the way in which the decisions would be made. There was a great sense of shared pride in the knowledge that the Credo was being tested... and it worked!" I think that we can agree that the employees of Johnson and Johnson should be proud of the response of their firm, which put consumer safety ahead of company profits, but we also have to agree that that response, and that priority ranking, is not unequivocally indicated in the Credo of the company.

NO   Lisa H. Newton

THE MANY FACES OF THE CORPORATE CODE

We seem to be in another of our code-writing phases. Interest in the development of corporate codes of ethics—by which term we encompass corporate Aspirations, Beliefs, Creeds, Guidelines and so on through the alphabet—has continued to rise since the 1970's, in tandem with the interest in the teaching and taking of ethics, in colleges and workplaces alike. In what follows, I take on some of the dominant themes in the codes of ethics literature, in an attempt to give a partial overview of the state of the art in the formulation of the corporate code.

The attempt turns out to be a study in multiple function. The much-recommended "corporate code of ethics" serves a diversity of functions, and must avoid a similar diversity of pitfalls. Some of these we will survey; to anticipate the end, we will discover that for maximum effectiveness and ethical validity, each code ought to meet three specifications:

1. In its *development and promulgation,* the code must enjoy the maximum participation of the officers and employees of the corporation (the principle of *participation*);

2. In its *content,* the code must be coherent with general ethical principles and the dictates of conscience (the principle of *validity*);

3. In its *implementation,* the code must be, and must be seen to be, coherent with the lived commitments of the company's officers (the principle of *authenticity*).

1. CLEAR AND PRESENT NEED

Businesses ought to have codes of ethics, if for no other reason than to allay real doubts that businessmen are capable of morality at all. Leonard Brooks has recently taken note of the " . . . crisis of confidence about corporate activity. Many corporate representations or claims have low credibility, including those made regarding financial dealings and disclosure, environmental protection, health and safety disclosures related to both employees and customers, and questionable payments." That is quite a list of things to be distrusted about. If we were looking for a blanket indictment of business, that one ought to cover the ballpark.[1] Or as Michael Hoffman and Jennifer Moore put it somewhat more concisely, it is the opinion of many of our wiser heads that "... business faces a true crisis of legitimacy."[2]

We cannot, *pace* Milton Friedman, leave the governance of the corporation to the forces of the market. While the market may bring about economic efficiency, Gerald Cavanagh points out, it cannot guarantee that corporate performance will be ethically and socially sensitive. Here the responsibility lies with the Board of Directors and top management, and it is "essential that board and management step up to the task," ascertain the ethical climate already prevailing and guide policy and decision in ethical directions. He adds as a final qualification that "while codes, structures and monitoring can encourage ethical decisions, it is even more important to have ethical people in the firm who want to make ethical judgments, know how to, and are not afraid to do so."[3] This is surely true: there is no structure or device in the universe, let alone within the capability of the American business community, that will keep people moral if they are determined to be immoral. But most people, at least most businesspeople, it seems are really neither one nor the other; they are prepared to be either, depending on the prevailing culture, and that is where the code can help.

There is nothing new in the aspiration to ethical codes. As early as 1961, Fr. Raymond Baumhart's survey of 2,000 business managers showed two-thirds of them interested in developing codes of ethics, which they thought would improve the ethical level of business

practice.[4] By the seventies, public attention reinforced that view. George Benson traces the current effort on codes to the revelations on foreign and domestic bribery in government investigations 1973–1976, leading to the Foreign Corrupt Practices Act of 1977.[5] In the mid-seventies, W. Michael Blumenthal, then CEO of Bendix, went so far as to propose that the business executives of America organize a professional association to develop a comprehensive code of ethics for business with a review panel to enforce it. The idea died at the time, but might be worth following up at some point.[6] To this day, the most highly placed businessmen support the development of codes of ethics. In a survey conducted by Touche Ross in October, 1987, 1,082 respondents concluded that the most effective way to encourage ethical business behavior was the adoption of a code of ethics—outscoring the adoption of further legislation by 19%.[7] Nor is this support surprising. Ethics pays, not just in public relations but in company work. As the Business Roundtable, an association of Chief Executive Officers of major U.S. companies, concluded in 1988,

> It may come as a surprise to some that... corporate ethics programs are not mounted primarily to improve the reputation of business. Instead, many executives believe that a culture in which ethical concern permeates the whole organization is necessary to the self-interest of the company.... In the view of the top executives represented in this study, there is no conflict between ethical practices and acceptable profits. Indeed, the first is a necessary precondition for the second.[8]

To be sure, we can, at least in theory, behave like saints without a code to describe how we are behaving. But a written document reinforces an intention to be ethical—as a reminder, as a guide, and as a focus for the solidarity of the corporate officers in their attempts to run the company along the lines it lays down. And beyond this, there is the first concern mentioned: that the public is, probably justifiably, concerned over the proclivities of the business community and interested in seeing tangible proof of its intention to behave.

So a public commitment to ethics serves at least two functions: it addresses the concerns of the public and it reinforces (and clarifies) a bottom-line-justified interest in ethical behavior on the part of the officers. A third reason to take ethics seriously, address the subject explicitly, and articulate provisions to enforce it, is simple realism. As Freeman and Gilbert point out, as long as organizations are composed of human beings, no organizational task can proceed, nor can any cogent corporate strategy be formulated, without recognizing that these human beings have values. Their "First Axiom of Corporate Strategy," "Corporate strategy must reflect an understanding of the values of organizational members and stakeholders," is derived directly from the discovery that the human players in the corporate enterprise very often act in accordance with personal and cultural ethical imperatives, and that the corporation relegates itself to irrelevance if it fails to recognize this fact. Their second Axiom, "Corporate strategy must reflect an understanding of the ethical nature of strategic choice," acknowledges the interaction between corporate direction and private value. It is essential that the choices made by management in strategic planning meet the ethical standards implicit in the stakeholders' values.[9] The authors note the current fashion for describing strategy formulation as if persons did not exist, and point out at some length the errors of such attempts.[10]

2. WHY CODES FAIL

We sometimes take note of "widespread skepticism" as to the effectiveness of codes and the motivation behind their development. That skepticism bears some examination. Oddly, the doubts do not seem to have their roots in the business community, whose opinions are captured above. It seems to originate in the academic community of the business schools, possibly due to misunderstandings on the nature of valid corporate codes. LaRue Tone Hosmer states well the prevailing error:

> Ethical codes are statements of the norms and beliefs of an organization. These norms and beliefs are generally proposed, discussed, and defined by the senior executives in the firm and then published and distributed to all of the members. Norms, of course, are standards of behavior; they are the ways the senior people in the organization want the others to act when confronted with a given situation.[11]

Again,

> The beliefs in an ethical code are standards of thought; they are the ways that the senior people in the organization want others to think.[12]

With that understanding, no wonder that he must immediately insist that "[t]his is not censorship"! Although that insistence is hardly reinforced with his following, "the intent is to encourage ways of thinking and patterns of attitudes that will lead towards the wanted behavior."

And with both of those understandings in place, again it is not surprising that his evaluation of codes is negative: "Do ethical codes work? Are they helpful in conveying to all employees the moral standards selected by the board of directors and president? Not really."[13] The problem with the code he describes is not only that it is not effective—taking no essential account of the nature of the business, let alone the pre-existing commitments of the people to whom it is supposed to apply, how could it be?—but that it is not ethical. The basis for its norms is, it appears, completely subjective, founded on the whim of whoever happens to be in the executive offices the day that it occurs to a CEO to write a code of ethics; its application is coercive, being conceived by a more powerful group to apply to a less powerful group (but not to themselves); and there is no built-in check to see that it will actually help the company and its employees achieve the ends of the business. In short, it fails by any standards of reasonableness, and why on earth any firm would be interested in such a code is puzzling beyond the norm for such writings. (As Richard DeGeorge points out, we are occasionally willing to allow short lists of rules to be simply imposed on us, as long as the author is reliably known to be God. Senior officers, even CEO's, are not God.)[14]

While we have Hosmer's example before us, we may take the opportunity to extract some more general ethical principles from the critique. The code he describes was brought into existence by a few people in a few remote offices, enlisting the energies of none of the lower-ranking employees of the company. For this reason it fails on any measure of democracy, that understanding of governance that holds participation in policy formulation to be a part of justice; and it fails on any estimate of likely relevance to the situation of those excluded employees. The temptations that beset the stockman and secretary are best known to them, and it is inherently unwise to draw up rules without drawing on their experience. To avoid both sets of failures, it is essential to include as many employees as possible in the development process. This imperative we may call the *principle of participation.*

Second, the content of the code is completely unspecified save by reference to its authors—its provisions are those that strike the CEO and his golfing buddies as good, at the time they write it. Given their understandings of justice (see above and below), we are not inspired to confidence in their intuitions, but that is quite beside the point. Subjective presentations of this type can never qualify as imperatives with the authority of ethics. The provisions of a code must be reasoned, logically consistent, defended by reasoned argument, and coherent with the usual understandings of ethics: they must demonstrate respect for the individual, a commitment to justice, and sensitivity to the rights and interests of all parties affected by corporate action. We may call this requirement the *principle of validity.*

Third, it is assumed that the code is written by the senior officers, but that they themselves are not bound by it, and are therefore by implication perfectly free to ignore it or defy it if that is what they want to do. No liberty could be more destructive. People will do not as they are told, but as it is modeled to them; the company's values are trumpeted in the acts of the highest ranking employees, and need appear nowhere else. Again there is a violation of justice, in the development of a set of rules from which a privileged few shall be exempt, and again there is gross inattention to effectiveness. Whatever we may not know about codes, we know for sure that the real culture of a corporation will be embodied in the behavior of the senior officers, especially the CEO, and that it is imperative to secure the allegiance and the compliance of those persons for a code to be taken seriously; we may call this imperative the *principle of authenticity.* Hosmer's understanding of a corporate code violates all three principles, and condemns itself to ineffectiveness through its violations.

In the limiting case, then, a purported "code" can be no more than some authority's attempt to impose whimsical rules, which are bound to fail. A second type of code that is doomed to failure is the oracular code, confined to bare rules or ideals, no matter how derived or promulgated, with no commentary or explanation grounding the rule in experience.

> The difficulty with many codes is not that they prescribe what is immoral, but that they fail to be truly effective in helping members of the profession or company to act morally. To be moral means not only doing what someone says is right, but also knowing *why* what one does is right, and assuming moral responsibility for the action. How were the provisions of the code arrived at? On what moral bases do the injunctions stand?[15]

The standard instruction at the end of such codes, to discuss any dilemmas with the legal office, won't do it; they don't know morality. Implicit in this objection is a strong suggestion that the code must serve an educational function. This is correct; we will come back to this point.

A third and common way for codes to fail is through failure of the highest executives to take the provisions seriously, not only as they apply to themselves (the principle of authenticity, above), but as they apply to the company's management policies (especially "management by objectives") and other standard procedures. If the CEO honestly believes in the provisions, and takes the lead in modeling and enforcing them, if top management follows suit, and if the company's reward and punishment structure reinforces those provisions consistently, the code may well achieve its purpose even if it fails as a model of logical coherence. If they do not [do] so, there is very little chance that anyone else will either, at least when no one is watching. "Management needs to understand the real dynamics of its own organization. For example, how do people get ahead in the company? What conduct is actually rewarded, what values are really being instilled in employees?"[16] And the modeling and enforcement must be spread throughout the company. As Andy Sigler, CEO of Champion International and initiator of one of the best corporate codes in existence, put it, "Making speeches and sending letters just doesn't do it. You need a culture and peer pressure that spells out what is acceptable and isn't and why. It involves training, education, and follow-up."[17] For example, the institutionalization of any code must include protection from retaliation by supervisors against whistleblowers.[18] Kenneth Arrow would go further, arguing that any effective code must not only be fused into the corporate culture, but "accepted by the significant operating institutions and transmitted from one generation of executives to the next through standard operating procedures [and] through education in business schools."[19]

3. HOW CODES SUCCEED

The first condition for success is a commitment to the promotion of ethical behavior in a company—not to better public relations, nor to more certain deterrence of Federal inspectors, nor to the terror of an occasional bad apple, but to make the whole company a better and finer employer, producer, resident and citizen. For starters, the business community must take a leaf from the book of the professions, who have seen themselves as moral communities from the outset.[20] Like the professions, the corporation must take its status as a moral agent seriously. (There is almost a note of surprise in Leonard Brooks' observation that nowadays, there is a public expectation that if managers are caught *in flagrante delicto* [in the act of committing a misdeed], as they sometimes are, they will be punished. "This is a significant change because it is signalling that our society no longer regards the interests of the corporation or its shareholders to be paramount in importance. Neither corporate executives nor professionals can operate with impunity any longer, because society now expects them to be accountable.")[21] It certainly does.

From that basic commitment should follow a commitment to a process aimed at gathering that ethos from, and infusing it throughout, the entire company. Our first and third specifications, the principle of participation and the principle of authenticity, are two phases of that process commitment. The whole company (starting from the top) must commit itself to the development of the corporate code; the whole company (including the most junior members) must contribute to the process of deliberation; and the whole company (again, especially the top) must be, and feel, bound to obey and to exemplify it.

The imperative of validity is no more than a remote test of the coherence of the content. In accordance with the examples set by the professions, it is not essential for a cede to be a model of academic ethics. The requirement that the code be in conformity with theory does not mean that the code must explicitly signal the kind of reasoning that validates it. Earlier in this enterprise academicians were perhaps too insistent, and codecrafters too self-conscious, on this point; earlier discussions of the issue of corporate and professional codes were known to break down on the issue of "consequentialist vs. deontological moral reasoning." Both are necessarily included in the development of a corporate ethic. As Robin and Reidenbach point out, maintaining a certain kind of "ethical profile" (e.g. strong customer orientation for a sales-driven industry) is absolutely essential for the bottom line—there is no more utilitarian requirement. Yet the "core values" extracted from that profile (e.g. "Treat customers with respect and honesty,... the way you would want your family treated") can be derived from any system of primary duties, and are deontological in form and function. Any good formulation of a company's creed should be subject to verification by both kinds of moral reasoning.[22]

As Robin and Reidenbach emphasize, the code must be drawn to reflect the aims of the particular set of business practices with which the company is concerned. The ruling ideal of the code might equally be integrity of the practitioners, the excellence of craftsmanship, or the dedication to serve the client/customer, depending on the type of business it is. One of the first principles of "excellence" in the running of any company—the imperative to "stick to the knitting"—entails that a code for one industry, or one kind of company, need not apply with equal force to any others.

Along that line, be it noted that there are many reasons why a code cannot be all things to all people. Critics with certain key areas of interest, for instance, will often discover limits in codes that might not occur to the rest of us. Pat Werhane, for instance, complains that codes "usually tell the employee what he or she is not permitted to do, but they seldom spell out worker rights."[23] She goes on to argue that they tend to turn employees into legalists, obedient to the letter of the regulation but ignorant of its moral spirit.

The solution to both problems may lie in the shift of focus from dead rule to living dialogue. I am inclined to argue that the real value of the code does not lie in the finished product, rules with explanations that all must obey, but in the process by which it came to be. The first call for participation is an invitation to the employee to look into his conscience, discover his own moral commitments, and attempt to prioritize and formulate them. This may be the first time he has ever been asked to take on that job, and the educational value is enormous. The second phase of the participatory process includes the discovery of community consensus, a dialogue in which the employee must test his perceptions against those of others, re-examine and perhaps replace those that do not meet the test, and discover the defenses of those that do. However the code emerges, we will have much more articulate employees at the end of the process than we had at the beginning. And in this articulation is implicit genuine self-awareness: the employee now has his moral beliefs where he can see and get at them, and can be educated to apply them in new and creative ways should the situation around him change.

And it will change. Change was always a fact in the American business community, and very rapid, almost chaotic, change an occasional reality. Now, as Tom Peters points out, partly at his instigation, it has become a conscious policy. The continuation of that dialogue is needed especially as firms radically reorganize themselves, destroying the traditional departmental divisions and job descriptions. In the absence of traditional guides, all members of the corporation will need new and extraordinary norms to govern practice, and there is no substitute for a dialogical process in place as the change happens.[24]

ENDNOTES

1. Leonard J. Brooks, "Corporate Codes of Ethics," *Journal of Business Ethics* 8 (1989):117–129, p. 119.

2. W. Michael Hoffman and Jennifer Mills Moore, *Business Ethics*, second edition. New York: McGraw Hill, 1990, p. 2.

3. Gerald F. Cavanagh, *American Business Values*, second edition. Englewood Cliffs, New Jersey: Prentice-Hall, 1984, p. 159.

4. Raymond C. Baumhart, S. J., "How Ethical Are Businessmen?" *Harvard Business Review* 39 (July–August 1961):166–71.

5. George C. S. Benson, "Codes of Ethics," *Journal of Business* 8 (1989):305–319, p. 306.

6. W. Michael Blumenthal, "New Business Watchdog Needed," *The New York Times*, May 25, 1975, F1; and "R_x for Reducing the Occasion of Corporate Sin," *Advanced Management Journal* 42 (Winter 1977):4–13.

7. Touche Ross, *Ethics in American Business: An Opinion Survey of Key Business Leaders on Ethical Standards and Behavior*. New York: Touche Ross, 1988, p. 14. The sample included only chief executive officers of companies with $500 million or more in

annual sales, deans of business schools and members of Congress.

8. *Corporate Ethics: A Prime Business Asset*. New York: The Business Roundtable, 1988, p. 9.

9. R. Edward Freeman and Daniel R. Gilbert, Jr., *Corporate Strategy and the Search for Ethics*. Englewood Cliffs, New Jersey: Prentice-Hall, 1988, pp. 6–7.

10. *Loc. cit.* See also p. 138, and p. 197, n.25.

11. LaRue Tone Hosmer, *The Ethics of Management*. Homewood, Illinois: Irwin, 1987, p. 153.

12. *Ibid.* p. 154.

13. *Loc. cit.* p. 154.

14. Richard T. DeGeorge, *Business Ethics*, third edition. New York, Macmillan, 1990, p. 390.

15. DeGeorge, *op. cit.* p. 391.

16. William H. Shaw, *Business Ethics*. Belmont, California: Wadsworth Publishing Company, 1991, p. 175.

17. Andrew Sigler, CEO of Champion International, cited in "Businesses Are Signing Up for Ethics 101," *Business Week*, February 15, 1988, p. 56.

18. Leonard J. Brooks, "Corporate Codes of Ethics," *Journal of Business Ethics* 8 (1989):117–129, p. 124.

19. Kenneth J. Arrow, "Social Responsibility and Economic Efficiency," *Public Policy* 21 (Summer 1973):42.

20. Mark S. Frankel, "Professional Codes: Why, How, and With What Impact?" *Journal of Business Ethics* 8 (1989):109–115, p. 110.

21. Brooks, *op. cit.* p. 119.

22. Donald P. Robin and R. Eric Reidenbach, *Business Ethics: Where Profits Meet Value Systems*. Englewood Cliffs, New Jersey: Prentice-Hall, 1989, pp. 94–95.

23. Patricia H. Werhane, *Persons, Rights and Corporations*. Englewood Cliffs, New Jersey: Prentice-Hall, Inc. 1985, p. 159.

24. See Tom Peters, "Get Innovative or Get Dead (part one)," *California Management Review* 33 (Fall 1990):9–26.

POSTSCRIPT

Are Corporate Codes of Ethics Just for Show?

Why might a corporation's management decide to develop a corporate code of ethics, to sponsor or join lectures and workshops on ethics, or to hire consultants to run "ethics training programs" for their middle managers? There are numerous possible answers to this question: The company may be in the headlines again for falsifying time sheets for government projects and management wishes to project a righteous image before sentencing; employees may be stealing supplies and the employers want to make their people more moral in order to cut costs; or managers may simply believe that ethics as a principle is important to the company.

There may be no single answer to that question in any given case. Surely, given the fiduciary obligations of management to the shareholders, and given the expectations of the community, the managers will stress different motivations for community service at shareholders' meetings. This is probably as it should be; people are complex beings and operate from mixed motivations in most areas of life. There may be no need to insist on purity of motive before an ethics project begins. Motives, after all, come immediately under scrutiny in any consideration of ethics, and it is natural to search for ulterior ones. Whatever the motivation, are efforts to improve corporate behavior often successful? Should we promote the adoption of corporate codes of ethics in all, some, or no companies?

SUGGESTED READINGS

Peter Drucker, "What is Business Ethics?" *The Public Interest* (Spring 1981).

Catherine C. Langlois and Bodo B. Schlegelmilch, "Do Corporate Codes of Ethics Reflect National Character? Evidence from Europe and the United States," *Journal of International Business Studies* (November 1990).

Maurica Lefebvre and Jang B. Singh, "The Content and Focus of Canadian Corporate Codes of Ethics," *Journal of Business Ethics* (October 1992).

Robert Solomon and Kristine Hanson, *It's Good Business* (Atheneum, 1985).

PART 2

Human Resources: The Corporation and the Employee

The workforce is changing. Employees in the United States and Canada, and to a lesser extent elsewhere in the world, are becoming very diverse: many ethnic groups are represented in the workplace, women and men are approaching equality in numbers in most fields, and an array of protected conditions—such as age, ethnicity, disability, and religious persuasion—are making corporate life complicated for employers. Employees are more aware of their rights and more willing to demand that their employers honor them than they've ever been. What can business do to protect the rights of this diverse group while protecting its own economic interests?

- Should Women Have the Same Right to Work as Men?

- Are Programs of Preferential Treatment Unjustifiable?

- Does Blowing the Whistle Violate Company Loyalty?

- Should Concern for Drug Abuse Overrule Concerns for Employee Privacy?

ISSUE 6

Should Women Have the Same Right to Work as Men?

YES: George J. Annas, from "Fetal Protection and Employment Discrimination—The *Johnson Controls* Case," *The New England Journal of Medicine* (September 5, 1991)

NO: Hugh M. Finneran, from "Title VII and Restrictions on Employment of Fertile Women," *Labor Law Journal* (April 1980)

ISSUE SUMMARY

YES: George J. Annas, a professor of law and medicine, argues that women may not be legally excluded from traditionally male jobs without some real relation of gender to job performance. He maintains that health risks to children not yet conceived do not constitute such a relation and that, therefore, women's rights to equal employment cannot be abridged on that rationale.

NO: Hugh M. Finneran, former senior labor counsel for PPG Industries, Inc., holds that preventing women from coming into contact with substances that can deform or destroy a growing embryo is a legitimate excuse for excluding women from certain jobs.

Workplaces often abound with nasty and unpleasant substances, chemical and otherwise. Fortunately, very few of them are really hazardous to health, and of those that are, the worst (such as coal dust, which leads to black lung disease) are well known. Most worrisome are the "quiet hazards," substances that are associated with adverse physical reactions and suspected to be the cause of damage to various other organ and physiological systems but that are not surely proven to do any real and lasting damage.

Among the most troubling of these quiet hazards are those that attack us where we are most vulnerable—in the reproductive systems. Germ cells, the sperm for men and the ova for women, are both the most carefully segregated of the body's systems—they are almost immune from damage from germs coursing through our blood, for instance—and the most vulnerable to damage, for damage to those cells may pass on, in unpredictable ways, to the next generation.

Reproductive damage is divided into two categories: Some substances directly affect the sperm and ova and cause changes that can damage any child that is conceived by the union of those cells. Such substances are called *muta-*

gens because they cause mutations in the germ plasma. The second category, called *teratogens*, is even more frightening; they attack the developing embryo in the womb, interfering with the complex physiological reactions and anatomical development of the first several weeks of a human's life, causing deformities of limbs, organs, and the nervous system that are usually, but not always, incompatible with life.

With mutagens, men and women are on equal footing. Mutagens may affect the germ cells of both sexes, so it is equally possible for both sexes to pass adverse effects down to their children. Therefore, women may not be excluded from a work environment in which there is a risk of infection any more than men can. This was the first finding of the *Johnson Controls* case, which is discussed by George J. Annas in the following selection.

The second finding is more controversial. When it is believed that a substance in a workplace is a teratogen, the danger is not to the worker (male or female) but to the developing child in the womb of a female worker. There is no *prima facie* reason to object to a rule excluding children from a workplace that contains a substance that is demonstrably dangerous to children but not to adults. But teratogens do not affect young children, or babies, or (it is believed) even fetuses at the stage where the mother is visibly pregnant. They affect development most at its earliest stages, in the first few weeks after the embryo is implanted in the uterus. But at that stage, the woman herself usually does not know that she is pregnant, let alone her employer. All the damage has been done by the time she knows that there is an embryo at risk.

It seems that the only practicable way to protect these children is to exclude from that workplace any woman who *might* become pregnant; that is, any woman of childbearing age not provably sterile. It could be argued that the exclusion is not sexist: both male and female embryos (the at-risk groups) are being excluded from the workplace by simply excluding all potential embryo-carriers from the workplace. At the same time, it is sexist because although women must be excluded, there is no reason to exclude men. Is this illegal? The arbiters of the *Johnson Controls* case say it is.

Hugh M. Finneran wrote the selection that follows before *Johnson Controls*, but the issues he raises are still ethically significant. Whatever the law says, he suggests, in order to protect the new equality for women, we should make special efforts to protect the most vulnerable of workplace participants—especially since there is no way for an embryo to consent to the risk.

Ask yourself, as you read these selections, whether or not attempts to reach total equality between women and men have gone too far. Are there some aspects of life in which gender equality is impossible? Also ask yourself if society should attempt to maintain some wall of protection for the vulnerable (such as children) that does not exist for the not-so-vulnerable. Should compassion for and protection of weaker persons take precedence over individual rights?

YES

George J. Annas

FETAL PROTECTION AND EMPLOYMENT DISCRIMINATION—THE *JOHNSON CONTROLS* CASE

Employers have historically limited women's access to traditionally male, high-paying jobs.[1] In one famous case early in this century, the U.S. Supreme Court upheld an Oregon law that forbade hiring women for jobs that required more than 10 hours of work a day in factories. The Chief Justice explained that this restriction was reasonable because "healthy mothers are essential to vigorous offspring" and preserving the physical well-being of women helps "preserve the strength and vigor of the race."[2] This rationale was never particularly persuasive, and women's hours have not been limited in traditionally female, low-paid fields of employment, such as nursing. Although such blatant sex discrimination in employment is a thing of the past, the average man continues to earn "almost 50 percent more per hour than does the average woman of the same race, age, and education."[3]

The contemporary legal question has become whether employers can substitute concern for fetal health for concern for women's health as an argument for limiting job opportunities for women. The U.S. Supreme Court decided in March 1991 that the answer is no and that federal law prohibits employers from excluding women from job categories on the basis that they are or might become pregnant.[4] All nine justices agreed that the "fetal-protection policy" adopted by Johnson Controls, Inc., to restrict jobs in the manufacture of batteries to men and sterile women was a violation of law, and six of the nine agreed that federal law prohibits any discrimination solely on the basis of possible or actual pregnancy. The ruling in *International Union* v. *Johnson Controls* applies to all employers engaged in interstate commerce, including hospitals and clinics.

Title VII of the Civil Rights Act of 1964 forbids employers to discriminate on the basis of race, color, religion, sex, or national origin. Explicit discrimination on the basis of religion, sex, or national origin can be justified only

From George J. Annas, "Fetal Protection and Employment Discrimination—The *Johnson Controls* Case," *The New England Journal of Medicine*, vol. 325, no. 10 (September 5, 1991), pp. 740–743. Copyright © 1991 by The Massachusetts Medical Society. Reprinted by permission.

if the characteristic is a "bona fide occupational qualification." The federal Pregnancy Discrimination Act of 1978 made it clear that sex discrimination includes discrimination "on the basis of pregnancy, childbirth, or related conditions."[5]

THE FETAL-PROTECTION POLICY OF JOHNSON CONTROLS

Beginning in 1977, Johnson Controls advised women who expected to have children not to take jobs involving exposure to lead, warned women who took such jobs of the risks entailed in having a child while being exposed to lead, and recommended that workers consult their family doctors for advice. The risks were said to include a higher rate of spontaneous abortion as well as unspecified potential risks to the fetus. Between 1979 and 1983, eight employees became pregnant while their blood lead levels were above 30 µg per deciliter (1.45 µmol per liter) (a level the Centers for Disease Control had designated as excessive for children). Although there was no evidence of harm due to lead exposure in any of the children born to the employees, a medical consultant for the company said that he thought hyperactivity in one of the children "could very well be and probably was due to the lead he had."[6]

In 1982, apparently after consulting medical experts about the dangers to the fetus of exposure to lead, the company changed its policy from warning to exclusion:

… women who are pregnant or who are capable of bearing children will not be placed into jobs involving lead exposure or which could expose them to lead through the exercise of job bidding, bumping, transfer, or promotion rights.

The policy defined women capable of bearing children as all women except those who "have medical confirmation that they cannot bear children."

In 1984, a class-action suit was brought challenging the policy as a violation of Title VII of the Civil Rights Act of 1964. In 1988, a federal district court ruled in favor of Johnson Controls, primarily on the basis of depositions and affidavits from physicians and environmental toxicologists regarding the damage that exposure to lead could cause in developing fetuses, children, adults, and animals.[7] The U.S. Court of Appeals for the Seventh Circuit affirmed this decision in 1989 in a seven-to-four opinion.[6] The majority based its opinion primarily on the medical evidence of potential harm to the fetus and on their view that federal law permitted employers to take this potential harm into account in developing employment policies.

THE SUPREME COURT'S DECISION

The U.S. Supreme Court unanimously reversed the decision in an opinion written by Justice Harry Blackmun. The Court had no trouble finding that the bias in the policy was "obvious," since "fertile men, but not fertile women, are given a choice as to whether they wish to risk their reproductive health for a particular job."[4] The Court noted that the company did not seek to protect all unconceived children, only those of its female employees. The policy was based on the potential for pregnancy and, accordingly, directly in conflict with the Pregnancy Discrimination Act of 1978. The key to the case was determining whether the absence of pregnancy or the absence of the potential to become pregnant was a bona fide occupational qualification for a job in battery manufacturing.

Employment discrimination is permitted "in those certain instances where religion, sex, or national origin is a bona fide occupational qualification reasonably necessary to the normal operation of that particular business or enterprise."[4] The Court's approach was to determine whether Johnson Controls' fetal-protection policy came within the scope of those "certain instances." The statutory language requires that the occupational qualification affect "an employee's ability to do the job."[4] The Court determined that the defense was available only when it went to the "essence of the business" or was "the core of the employee's job performance."[4]

The Court had previously allowed a maximum-security prison for men to refuse to hire women guards because "the employment of a female guard would create real risks of safety to others if violence broke out because the guard was a woman." Thus, sex was seen as reasonably related to the essence of the guard's job: maintaining prison security. Similarly, other courts had permitted airlines to lay off pregnant flight attendants if it was considered necessary to protect the safety of passengers. The Court agreed that protecting the safety or security of customers was related to the essence of the business and was legitimate.

The welfare of unconceived fetuses, however, did not fit into either category of exception. In the Court's words, "No one can disregard the possibility of injury to future children; the BFOQ [bona fide occupational qualification], however, is not so broad that it transforms this deep social concern into an essential aspect of battery making." Limitations involving pregnancy or sex "must relate to ability to perform the duties of the job.... Women as capable of doing their jobs as their male counterparts may not be forced to choose between having a child and having a job." The Court concluded that Congress had left the welfare of the next generation to parents, not employers: "Decisions about the welfare of future children must be left to the parents who conceive, bear, support, and raise them rather than to the employers who hire those parents."[4]

The Court finally addressed potential tort liability should a fetus be injured by its mother's occupational exposure and later sue the company. The Court wrote that since the Occupational Safety and Health Administration (OSHA) had concluded that there was no basis for excluding women of childbearing age from exposure to lead at the minimal levels permitted under its guidelines, the likelihood of fetal injury was slight. And even if injury should occur, the injured child would have to prove that the employer had been negligent. If the employer followed OSHA guidelines and fully informed its workers of the risks involved, the Court concluded that liability seemed "remote at best." Thus, just as speculation about risks to children not yet conceived has nothing to do with job performance, speculation about future tort liability—at least one step further removed from harm to the fetus—is not job-related.

THE CONCURRING OPINIONS

Justice Byron White wrote the main concurring opinion for himself, Chief Justice William Rehnquist, and Justice Anthony Kennedy. Although they agreed with the outcome in this case, they dissented from the bona fide occupational-qualification analysis as it applied to tort liability, and warned that the case could be used to undercut certain privacy rights. These three justices believed that under some circumstances it should be permissible for employers to exclude women from employment on the grounds that their fetuses could be injured and sue the employers (the women themselves could not sue because they would be covered by workers' compensation as their exclusive remedy). Their rationale was that parents cannot waive the right of their children to sue, that the parents' negligence will not be imputed to the children, and that even in the absence of negligence, "it is possible that employers will be held strictly liable, if, for example, their manufacturing process is considered."[4] Avoiding such liability was, in the view of these justices, a safety issue relevant to the bona fide occupational-qualification standard.

The other point made by the three justices was relegated to a footnote, but it is of substantial interest. They argued that the Court's opinion could be read to outlaw considerations of privacy as a justification for employment discrimination on the basis of sex because considerations of privacy would not directly relate to the employees' ability to do the job or to customers' safety. They cited cases in which the privacy-related wishes of some patients to be cared for by nurses and nurses' aides of the same sex had been upheld as a bona fide occupational qualification, including an instance regarding the sex of nurses' aides in a retirement home[8] and a policy excluding male nurses from obstetrical practice in one hospital.[9] The justices in the majority responded to this issue by saying simply, "We have never addressed privacy-based sex discrimination and shall not do so here because the sex-based discrimination at issue today does not involve the privacy interests of Johnson Controls' customers."[4] This issue has been left for another day, but it should be noted that the obstetrical-nurse case rests on outmoded judicial stereotyping of obstetricians as men and nurses as women.[10]

IMPLICATIONS OF THE DECISION

The Court took the language of the Pregnancy Discrimination Act seriously, correctly observing that "concern for a woman's existing or potential offspring historically has been the excuse for denying women equal employment opportunities."[4] The purpose of the act was to end such employment discrimination, and the Court's opinion in *Johnson Controls* holds that recasting sex discrimination in the name of fetal protection is illegal. Johnson Controls had argued that its policy was ethical and socially responsible and that it was meant only to prevent exposing the fetus to avoidable risk. Judge Frank Easterbrook probably had the most articulate response to this concern in his dissent from the appeals-court decision:

There is a strong correlation between the health of the infant and prenatal medical care; there is also a powerful link between the parents' income and infants' health, for higher income means better nutrition, among other things.... Removing women from well-paying jobs (and the attendant health insurance), or denying women access to these jobs, may reduce the risk from lead while also reducing levels of medical care and quality of nutrition.[6]

Judge Easterbrook argued that ultimately fetal-protection policies cannot require "zero risk" but must be based on reasonable risk. He correctly noted that it is good and reasonable to worry about the health of workers and their future children. But,

to insist on *zero* risk... is to exclude women from industrial jobs that have been a male preserve. By all means let society lend its energies to improving the prospects of those who come after us. Demanding zero risk produces not progress but paralysis.[6]

The same zero-risk analysis can, of course, be applied to the possibility of tort liability as seen from the industry's perspective. The industry would like its risk to be zero. Six of the nine judges agreed that it is close to zero, or at least remote. As a factual matter, there has been only one recorded case of a child's bringing a lawsuit for injuries suffered while the mother was pregnant and continued to work. In this case, the jury found in favor of the employer, even though there was evidence that the employer had violated OSHA safety standards.[11] Two thirds of the justices on the U.S. Supreme Court think that state tort liability is preempted so long as the employer follows federal law, informs workers of the risks, and is not negligent. Added to this is the extraordinarily difficult issue of causation, even if the employer is negligent. Putting the two together may not eliminate all risk of liability, but the risk is as small as can reasonably be expected.

It has been persuasively suggested that fetal-protection policies that affect only women are based on the view that women are "primarily biologic actors" and not economic ones and that men are only economic actors who have no "biologic connections and responsibilities to their families."[12] The decision in *Johnson Controls* continues the legal and social movement to provide equality of opportunity in the workplace. It does not eliminate the duty to minimize workplace exposure to toxic substances. Indeed, it would be a hollow victory for women to gain the right to be exposed to the same high levels of mutagens and other toxic substances that men are exposed to. The real challenge for public policy remains to turn industry's focus away from new methods of sex discrimination and toward new ways to reduce workplace hazards. In this area, physicians continue to have a prominent role.

Physicians specializing in occupational health should continue to work to reduce exposure to toxic substances in the workplace for all workers (by replacing such agents with other, less toxic substances, reducing their volume, and encouraging the use of protective gear). In addition, all workers should be warned about the health risks of all clinically important exposures that cannot be avoided, and encouraged to be monitored for the early signs of damage. Personal physicians should take a careful occupational history and be sufficiently informed to be able to tell their patients about the risks of exposure to various substances, including what is known about their mutagenicity and teratogenicity.* Armed with this information, workers—both men and women—will be able to make informed decisions about their jobs and the risks they are willing to run to keep

---

* [Mutagenicity is the capacity to cause mutations; teratogenicity is the capacity to cause developmental malformations.—Ed.]

them, as well as to pressure management intelligently to make the workplace safer.

Congress and the Court have made a strong statement about the use of fetal protection as a rationale to control or restrict the activities and decisions of women: the ultimate decision maker must be the worker herself. This policy is consistent with good medical practice as well—as is evident, for instance, in the policy of the American College of Obstetricians and Gynecologists on "maternal–fetal conflicts."[13] To paraphrase Justice Blackmun, it is no more appropriate for physicians to attempt to control women's opportunities and choices on the basis of their reproductive role than it is for the courts or individual employers to do so.

REFERENCES

1. Becker ME. From *Muller v. Oregon* to fetal vulnerability policies, 53 U. Chicago Law Rev. 1219 (1986).

2. Muller v. Oregon, 208 U.S. 412 (1908).

3. Fuchs VR. Sex differences in economic well-being. Science 1986; 232:459–64.

4. International Union v. Johnson Controls, 111 S.CT. 1196 (1991).

5. Pregnancy Discrimination Act of 1978, 92 Stat. 2076, 42 U.S.C. sec 2000e (k).

6. International Union v. Johnson Controls, 886 F.2d 871 (7th Cir. 1989) (en banc).

7. International Union v. Johnson controls, 680 F. Supp. 309 (E.D. Wis. 1988).

8. Fesel v. Masonic Home of Delaware, 447 F. Supp. 1346 (D.Del. 1978).

9. Buckus v. Baptist Medical Center, 510 F. Supp. 1191 (E.D.Ark. 1981).

10. Sex in the delivery room: is the nurse a boy or a girl? In: Annas GJ. Judging medicine. Clifton, N.J.: Humana Press, 1988:53–6.

11. Security National Bank v. Chloride Industrial Battery, 602 F. Supp. 294 (D.Kan. 1985).

12. Becker ME. Can employers exclude women to protect children? JAMA 1990; 264:2113–7.

13. American College of Obstetricians and Gynecologists Committee opinion no. 55, Committee on Ethics. Patient choice: maternal-fetal conflict. Washington, D.C.: American College of Obstetricians and Gynecologists, 1987.

NO

Hugh M. Finneran

TITLE VII AND RESTRICTIONS ON EMPLOYMENT OF FERTILE WOMEN

During the decade of the 1970s, there was a rapid expansion of the female work force accompanied by a simultaneous expansion of scientific knowledge concerning hazards of exposure to toxic substances in the workplace. Health hazards in industry present serious legal, medical, and sociological issues.

Recently, a dramatic awareness of the hazards to the employee's reproductive capacity, i.e., miscarriage, stillbirth, and birth defects, has materialized. The hazard to the reproductive capacity and fetal damage is not a unique problem for female workers. Rather, it is a problem which may impact upon all workers. This article, however, will restrict its analysis to factual situations where the employer considers the problems of exposure to chemicals as uniquely, or primarily, arising out of the female physiology and either restricts or refuses to hire females with childbearing ability. Physical conditions other than chemical substances may also be harmful to the fetus, i.e., radiation, heat stress, vibration, and noise, but will not be treated in this article....

Title VII of the Civil Rights Act of 1964 incorporates two theories of discrimination which must be considered in a legal analysis of restrictions (the term "restriction" includes a refusal to hire) placed on females because of health hazards. These are: disparate treatment and policies, practices, or procedures with disparate impact not justified by business necessity.

Two types of substances will be considered in this article: teratogens and mutagens. Teratogens are substances that can harm the fetus after conception by entering the placenta. Mutagens are substances that can cause a change in the genetic material in living cells.

DISPARATE TREATMENT

The Supreme Court in *International Brotherhood of Teamsters v. United States* stated: "Disparate treatment... is the most easily understood type of discrimination. The employer simply treats some people less favorably than others because of their race, color, religion, sex, or national origin. Proof of discriminatory motive is critical, although it can in some situations be inferred from the mere fact of differences in treatment...."

From Hugh M. Finneran, "Title VII and Restrictions on Employment of Fertile Women," *Labor Law Journal*, vol. 31, no. 4 (April 1980). Published and copyrighted © 1980 by Commerce Clearing House, Inc., 4025 W. Peterson Avenue, Chicago, IL 60646. Reprinted by permission.

The Equal Employment Opportunity Commission and the United States Department of Labor on February 1, 1980, issued, for comment, Interpretive Guidelines on Employment Discrimination and Reproductive Hazards. "An employer/contractor whose work environment involves employee exposure to reproductive hazards shall not discriminate on the basis of sex (including pregnancy or childbearing capacity) in hiring, work assignment, or other conditions of employment."

An employer's policy of protecting female employees from reproductive hazards by depriving them of employment opportunities without any scientific data is a per se violation of Title VII. The Guidelines' position, however, is that the exclusion of women with childbearing ability from the workplace is a per se violation. To arrive at such a conclusion without an analysis of the precise scientific and medical evidence is an erroneous and indefensible legal standard. Thus, an employer's exclusion of females on the basis of their susceptibility to the mutagenic effects of a toxic substance should not be a per se violation but should be analyzed under the rubric of disparate treatment or adverse impact.

One line of inquiry under the disparate treatment analysis would be whether the mutagenic substance has reproductive hazards for male and female employees. If the particular chemical substance has a mutagenic effect on male and female employees, the obvious question is why female workers are treated differently. The answer may be scientifically explained, but it raises the issue of disparate treatment. Indeed, the employer should consider whether there are any other substances in the workplace, other than the substance relied on to exclude the female, which have mutagenic effects on males.

In essence, if the basis for the exclusion is the mutagenic characteristics of a substance, the employer would have to treat all employees, male and female, who are exposed to mutagenic effects in the same manner. The employer may face a serious possibility of a Title VII violation for disparate treatment unless the scientific justification for the differential treatment is very persuasive.

In establishing a prima facie case of sex discrimination, under the principles of *McDonnell Douglas Corp. v. Green* a female must show that: she belongs to a protected class; she applied or was qualified for a job for which the employer was seeking applicants; and despite her qualifications, she was rejected. She also must prove that, after her rejection, the employer continued to seek applicants with her qualifications.

Applying the *McDonnell Douglas* principles to a restriction on female employment, the female could establish a prima facie case of sex discrimination if a chemical substance has a mutagenic effect on the males but only females are excluded from exposure to the hazard by the employer's restrictive policy. In this assumed factual situation, the very basis for the restriction would be applicable to either of sex discrimination, the employer has the burden of proving the existence of a business necessity or a bona fide occupational qualification. Of course, proof of compelling scientific data that the degree or severity of risk was substantially greater might alter the existence of a prima facie case, but the court more likely would consider such evidence as an affirmative defense.

GENDER-BASED CLASSIFICATION

Varying the factual assumptions, let us consider the existence of a work environment in which the chemical substance is a teratogen and an employer restricts the employment of females with childbearing ability. In these circumstances, the employer could argue that the exclusion is based on a neutral health factor rather than sex-based criteria. Since teratogens by definition harm a fetus after conception, the safety hazard is present only for females with childbearing ability and cannot affect males or females without childbearing ability. Thus, a strong argument could be presented that the exclusion of females based upon the teratogenic effect of a chemical substance is a health classification and is not gender based.

In *Geduldig v. Aiello*, the Supreme Court ruled that the exclusion of pregnancy-related disabilities from a state disability system was not sex discrimination but was a distinction based on physical condition "by dividing potential recipients into two groups—pregnant women and non-pregnant persons." Likewise, *General Electric Co. v. Gilbert* viewed pregnancy classifications as not being gender based.

At least one commentator has criticized the relevance of *Gilbert* and *Aiello* to the restriction of female employment in toxic workplaces, because the classification suffers from overinclusiveness since "many women in the excluded class delay or plan to avoid childbearing and thus face no additional risk at all." This contention is small comfort to an employer, however, since women have been known to change their plans and birth-control techniques are not universally effective.

Furthermore, some teratogens are cumulative and remain in the body long after the exposure has ceased. The legal issue is more complex where there is a restriction on the employment of a woman with childbearing ability where teratogens are present but mutagens with adverse reproductive effects present in the workplace affect males on whom no restrictions are placed.

The Pregnancy Disability Amendment to Title VII may have a bearing on the issue of whether the classification is gender based. "The terms 'because of sex' or 'on the basis of sex' include, but are not limited to, because of or on the basis of pregnancy, childbirth, or related medical conditions...."

The Pregnancy Amendment to Title VII does not state expressly that the terms "because of sex" or "on the basis of sex" includes a woman's childbearing ability or potential. The Guidelines, however, interpret "childbearing capacity" as prohibited by the Amendment. Such an interpretation is not without some doubt as to its validity. Nevertheless, if the Guidelines' construction is correct, a distinction based on childbearing ability would be considered gender-based disparate treatment. The practical consequences may be minimal since exclusions or restrictions on the employment of females with childbearing ability has a disparate impact and is best analyzed in this context.

DISPARATE IMPACT

The Supreme Court in *Griggs v. Duke Power Co.* held: "Under the Act, practices, procedures, or tests neutral on their face, and even neutral in terms of intent, cannot be maintained if they operate to 'freeze' the status quo of prior discriminatory employment practices." Thus,

Griggs ruled that the employer's requirement of a high school diploma or passage of a test as a condition of employment was a prima facie race violation of Title VII, unless these requirements are a "business necessity." "The Act proscribes not only overt discrimination but also practices that are fair in form but discriminatory in operation. The touchstone is business necessity."

In *Dothard v. Rawlinson*, the Supreme Court held that the employer violated Title VII by requiring a minimum height of five feet two inches and a weight of 120 pounds for prison guards since the policy had a disparate impact on women. Likewise, *Nashville Gas Co. v. Satty* is relevant to the issue. In *Satty*, the employer denied accumulated seniority to female employees returning from pregnancy leaves of absence. The Court held that an employer may not "burden female employees in such a way as to deprive them of employment opportunities because of their different role." The conclusion appears inescapable that an employer's restriction on the employment of women with childbearing ability, and this includes restrictions limited to specific jobs, is a prima facie violation of Title VII's proscriptions against sex discrimination under *Griggs*, *Dothard*, and *Satty*.

BONA FIDE OCCUPATIONAL QUALIFICATION

Two affirmative defenses must be considered: bona fide occupational qualification [BFOQ] and business necessity. Title VII provides an affirmative defense to a charge of sex discrimination where sex "is a bona fide occupational qualification reasonably necessary to the normal operation of that particular business or enterprise...."

The Guidelines state: "narrow exception [for BFOQ] pertains only to situations where all or substantially all of the protected class is unable to perform the duties of the job in question. Such cannot be the case in the reproductive hazards setting, where exclusions are based on the premise of danger to the employee or fetus and not on the ability to perform." Under *Weeks v. Southern Bell Telephone & Telegraph Co.*, an employer relying on the bona fide occupational qualification exception "has the burden of proving that he had reasonable cause to believe, that is, a factual basis for believing, that all or substantially all women would be unable to perform safely and efficiently the duties of the job involved."

In the absence of medical evidence to the contrary, an employer's assumption is that all, or substantially all, females have the capacity of bearing children. Thus, the area of controversy will probably center on the issue of whether the safety of the fetus or future generations is reasonably necessary to the normal operation of the employer's business. However, plaintiffs may argue that all or substantially all females are not at risk since not all females plan to have a family.

Courts have sustained decisions by bus companies not to hire drivers over specified ages as being a BFOQ justified by increased safety hazards for third persons. In *Hodgson v. Greyhound Lines, Inc.*, the company refused to consider applications for intercity bus drivers from individuals thirty-five years of age or older. The Seventh Circuit held that the company was not guilty of age discrimination, since its hiring policy was a BFOQ justified by the increased hazards to third persons caused by hiring older drivers. "Greyhound must demonstrate that it has a rational basis in fact to believe that elimination of its maximum hiring age will increase the likelihood of risk of harm to its passengers. Greyhound need only demonstrate however a minimal increase in risk of harm for it is enough to show that elimination of the hiring policy might jeopardize the life of one more person than might otherwise occur under the present hiring practice."

The Fifth Circuit in *Usery v. Tamiami Trail Tours, Inc.*, in upholding the company's refusal to hire bus drivers over forty years of age, found that the policy was a BFOQ. The company had demonstrated "that the passenger-endangering characteristics of over-forty job applicants cannot practically be ascertained by some hiring test other than automatic exclusion on the basis of age."

The language of the BFOQ exception under the Age Discrimination Act is essentially the same as the language of the BFOQ exception under Title VII of the Civil Rights Act. Cases in the airline industry also have considered third-party safety as a sufficient BFOQ in situations involving involuntary pregnancy leaves of absence for flight attendants.

The concept of concern for third parties is sufficiently elastic to include the unborn. It is submitted that society, including employers, has an obligation to avoid action which will have an adverse effect on the health and well-being of future generations. With all the present concerns about the protection of our environment and endangered species, an enlightened judiciary should not callously turn its back on generations unborn. Indeed, on the more mundane and pragmatic basis, it is of the essence of a business venture to operate safely in a manner which avoids costly tort liability.

BUSINESS NECESSITY

The business necessity defense may also justify the exclusionary or restrictive practice. In order to prove this defense, the employer has the burden of establishing that: the practice is necessary to the safe and efficient operation of the business; the purpose must be sufficiently compelling to override the adverse impact; and the practice must carry out the business purpose. The employer also must establish that there are not acceptable alternative policies or practices which would better accomplish the business purpose or accomplish it with lesser adverse impact on the protected class.

PRENATAL INJURY

Since the safe and efficient operation is premised on the need to protect the fetus, tort law relating to prenatal injuries is pertinent. The potential tort liability bears on the necessity for the exclusion. The law of Texas will be reviewed in regard to prenatal injuries. Texas was selected because of its large petrochemical industry.

The parents of a child suffering prenatal injuries resulting in its death have cause of action under the Texas wrongful death statute, provided the child was born alive and was viable at the time the injury was inflicted. In so ruling, the court stated that the statutory requirement of the Texas wrongful death statute, that the deceased has suffered an injury for which he could have recovered damages had he survived, was met. This holding of necessity implied that the Texas Supreme Court recognized a cause of action for a surviving child who is born alive with a birth defect caused by prenatal injuries.

For a child born with birth defects, the cause of action exists for prenatal injuries at any time during pregnancy.

The Texas courts apparently have not yet decided whether parents have a cause of action under the wrongful death statute in cases where a child is stillborn due to prenatal injuries. The inquiry in such a case would revolve around the issue of whether a fetus is a person within the meaning of the wrongful death statute. Other state courts interpreting their wrongful death statutes have split on the issue.

Assuming that liability is established, Texas courts allow surviving parents to recover damages under the wrongful death act to compensate them for the pecuniary value of the child's service that would have been rendered during minority, less the cost and expense of the child's support, education, and maintenance, as well as economic benefits reasonably expected to have been contributed after reaching majority.

While it is generally held that some evidence of pecuniary loss is necessary to support a wrongful death judgment, the Texas courts have recognized that such proof cannot be supplied with any certainty or accuracy in cases involving young infants. Therefore, they leave the damages question largely to the discretion of the jury. Of course, a prenatally injured infant who manages to survive would be able to sue for his own personal injuries, including pain and suffering, loss of earning capacity, and any other damages, if applicable. Recognizing the "deep pocket syndrome," employers have a reasonable basis for being concerned about large tort recoveries.

The female employee's willing and informed consent to the assumption of the risk is not binding to the unborn child. Hence, obtaining a waiver from the female employee is an act with no legal significance other than documenting the employer's awareness of the unavoidably unsafe condition of the workplace for the fetus for use against the employer in tort litigation.

The employer should not be required to assume the risk of significant tort liability which could threaten the very existence of the enterprise, depending on the financial assets of the employer and the severity of injuries. Courts have required employers in discrimination cases to assume additional expense to achieve compliance with Title VII (costs of validation studies, loss of customer patronage, and training costs), but it is submitted that the magnitude of the risks of exposure to prenatal injuries and reproduction hazards should result in a different decision. The financial impact on the employer is important but certainly not the most important factor. A lifetime of suffering by future generations is worthy of societal concern. The Civil Rights Act does not exist in a vacuum.

Whether the purpose of the restriction is sufficiently compelling to override the adverse impact on women and is necessary to accomplish the employer's business purpose of ensuring a safe workplace without reproductive hazards will be decided by the scientific and medical data relating to the severity of the health hazard of the particular substance.

LESS RESTRICTIVE ALTERNATIVES

Under the business necessity principles of *Robinson v. Lorillard*, the employer must demonstrate the absence of "less restrictive alternatives" before relying on the affirmative defense. The Guidelines indicate that four factors should be considered. These are: whether the employer is complying with applicable occupational federal, state, and local safety and health laws; respirators or other protective devices are used to minimize or eliminate the hazard; product substitution is used; and affected employees are transferred without loss of pay or other benefits to areas of the plant where the reproductive hazard is minimal or nonexistent.

The employer's obligation to comply with its safety obligations under the Occupational Safety and Health Act is eminently reasonable, provided that it is recognized that the employer's obligation under OSHA only requires the use of technologically and economically feasible engineering and administrative controls. If engineering and administrative controls are not feasible, the employer must protect his employees by the use of personal protective devices. It is fair and reasonable to require an employer to satisfy his legal obligations under safety and health laws before excluding females from the workplace.

To suggest, however, that the employers change their products or provide rate retention for employees restricted from hazardous exposure is extreme and without legislative support. If Congress had intended to require substitution of products and rate retention for employees under Title VII, it would have done so explicitly. When, as here, these matters are at best tangentially related to nondiscrimination, Title VII is silent on the subject, and wages and rates of pay and seniority of workers transferred to jobs other than their usual jobs are mandatory subjects of collective bargaining, then a reasonable interpretation of the legislation is that Title VII does not impose this obligation of management.

If an employer intends to sustain his business necessity defense, there must be evidence that the employer has explored the feasible alternatives to imposing restrictions on the employment of fertile females. One alternative which must be considered is a system for individual screening and evaluation with restrictions imposed on the female only if she becomes pregnant. Serious medical questions are posed by this alternative. Indeed, for some teratogenic substances the first weeks of pregnancy are the most critical. During this period, a woman may not know that she is pregnant, and sophisticated tests may not reveal the pregnancy. The administration of such a program might raise serious personnel problems since female employees might object to continuous monitoring to determine whether they are pregnant.

CONCLUSION

The decade of the 1970s was the era of the testing cases under Title VII. The decade of the 1980s will be the era of large class actions involving the exclusion of fertile females from exposure to reproductive hazards.

On the extreme of one side will be those arguing that Title VII rejects these protections as Victorian, romantic paternalism which deprives the individual woman of the power to decide whether the economic benefits justify the risks. On the other extreme, some employers will argue that any possible risk of harm to the female's offspring require her exclusion.

An informed judiciary should consider not only the economic interests of the female employee and the employer but the societal concern for the quality and happiness of future generations as well.

The Supreme Court in *Roe v. Wade* recognized that a state may properly assert important interests in protecting potential life. After evaluating the level, duration, and manner of exposure in the specific employer's workplace, if there is reputable scientific evidence of a recognized reproductive hazard, either from a mutagen with significantly greater risk for female workers or a teratogen, the employer should be allowed to exclude females from that workplace if the business necessity criteria are satisfied. The employer should have the right and, indeed, the duty and obligation to operate his facility with due concern for the safety and health of future generations.

POSTSCRIPT

Should Women Have the Same Right to Work as Men?

The *Johnson Controls* decision holds that excluding women from workplaces, except on the genuine inability of a woman to do the job, is illegal. The fetal protection policy, designed to protect the fetus and not the woman, is therefore illegal. But is it wrong? The answer to this question turns on a commitment of values: values concerning equality, especially equality between the sexes; values concerning the family and reproduction; and, significantly, values concerning the bottom line and the conditions of labor. The problem at Johnson Controls, Inc., was that there was lead in the atmosphere, which is why the company had adopted the contested policy. Some argue that there was a simpler way out, that all gender issues, fetal protection issues, Occupational Safety and Health Administration (OSHA) issues, and others would be solved if the employers, Johnson Controls, had just eliminated the lead problem.

The issue of tort liability dominated the *Johnson Controls* case. Management argued, unsuccessfully, that leaving the women in the workplace was a sure invitation to horrendous lawsuits. The Court found instead that the mother's right to compensation, should her fetus be damaged by the lead, was waived, since she was covered by workman's compensation. But, considering that the fetus was not covered by workman's compensation and had waived no rights whatsoever, do you agree with this argument?

SUGGESTED READINGS

"Comparable Worth in Industrialized Countries," *Monthly Labor Review* (November 1992).

Julia Flynn, "Julia Stasch Raises the Roof for Feminism," *Business Week* (January 25, 1993).

Val Hammond, "Opportunity 2000: A Culture Change Approach to Equal Opportunity," *Women in Management Review* (1992).

Harry A. Jessell, "Court Overturns FCC Gender Preference," *Broadcasting* (February 24, 1992).

Joanne D. Leck and David M. Saunders, "Hiring Women: The Effects of Canada's Employment Equity Act," *Canadian Public Policy* (June 1992).

Peter Lurie, "The Law as They Found It: Disentangling Gender-Based Affirmative Action Programs from Croson," *University of Chicago Law Review* (Fall 1992).

Charlene Marmer Solomon, "Are White Males Being Left Out?" *Personnel Journal* (November 1991).

John Southerst, "Public Policy: What Price Fairness?" *Canadian Business* (December 1991).

ISSUE 7

Are Programs of Preferential Treatment Unjustifiable?

YES: Lisa H. Newton, from "Reverse Discrimination as Unjustified," *Ethics* (July 1973)

NO: Richard Wasserstrom, from "A Defense of Programs of Preferential Treatment," *National Forum: The Phi Kappa Phi Journal* (Winter 1978)

ISSUE SUMMARY

YES: Professor of philosophy Lisa H. Newton argues that programs of preferential treatment represent reverse discrimination and are therefore antimerit and unjust. These programs replace fair procedures with political positioning and open preferential avenues to minorities.

NO: Professor of philosophy Richard Wasserstrom maintains that society is not fair and merit based to begin with, and he argues that there is no inconsistency in objecting to racist and sexist discrimination while favoring preferential treatment.

When the civil rights movement in the United States began with the 1961 sit-ins at the lunch counters in Atlanta, Georgia, and the boycott of the buses in Montgomery, Alabama, racial discrimination meant that just because you were black, you would not get the good job, you would not get into the good school, you would not be served at the counter, and you would sit at the back of the bus. Leaders of the civil rights movement argued that such discrimination was devoid of sense, truth, or justice, and that all people should be treated equally, without attention to skin color. Ultimately, the Supreme Court ruled in favor of blacks, and racial discrimination in public places was forbidden.

A decade later, supporters of the women's liberation movement stressed many of the same points on behalf of women. Since the laws against discrimination were already in place, the goal of this second campaign was to change social policy. Society yielded for both movements and opened doors for African Americans and for women that had not been previously open to them in the history of the world.

So society had taken some steps toward racial and gender equality, but there was an enormous gap between a society with a little less discrimination in it and the dream of a fully equal society. A fully equal society was unlikely to come about if the normal procedures, even scrupulously fair normal procedures, were allowed to work unaided. Only the lowest positions of society were open to the newly recognized power minorities, and given the background conditions, they would make very few gains in the foreseeable future.

Consider the possibilities of hiring a black vice president at a major corporation shortly after the antidiscrimination laws were passed. Vice presidential positions are open only to those with managerial experience, and because of a history of discrimination, no African Americans held positions in middle management. Entry-level managerial positions were open to African Americans, but they were also open to all MBAs on a basis of equal opportunity. And because of the same history of discrimination, there were almost no African American MBAs or graduates of good colleges to enter those MBA programs, or even ambitious graduates of good high schools, because most of them were from areas that had a legal history of racial segregation in their schools. Even in grammar school, histories of neighborhood discrimination resulted in lower scores and aspirations for African American children. Patterns of poverty, cultural deprivation, systematic extinction of hope and effort, and poor education rendered African Americans (and, for some fields, women) less prepared than their white male contemporaries to advance in the educational, professional, and business worlds. Laws were passed in the 1960s proclaiming equal opportunity across the land, but all racist and sexist attitudes did not magically disappear. With the change in laws, it still took generations for real equality to get a foothold; that was enough time for racist and sexist attitudes to be reinforced by the inferior performance of African Americans and women in tasks for which they had (deliberately) not been prepared.

Programs of preferential treatment were created to advance the pace of integration. No one has ever advocated putting anyone in a job he or she simply could not do, but some writers believe that efforts to advance women and minority candidates up the corporate ladder as rapidly as possible could be justified in light of past injustices. Once there, the minorities could serve as excellent role models for others and would do a great deal to wipe out the negative stereotypes about the capabilities of certain races and genders. To other writers, such practices seem to invite the very abuses that brought about the civil rights movement to begin with.

Ask yourself, as you read these selections, how you would choose to establish justice in our society. Lisa H. Newton argues that we are bound to follow strict merit-based procedures, come what may. Richard Wasserstrom counters with appeals to the actual social realities addressed by affirmative action programs. Note that both utilitarian and deontological arguments are employed by both sides. Both authors point to the social evils that will follow should the other's policy be implemented, and both cite justice as requiring their own policy.

YES

Lisa H. Newton

REVERSE DISCRIMINATION AS UNJUSTIFIED

I have heard it argued that "simple justice" requires that we favor women and blacks in employment and educational opportunities, since women and blacks were "unjustly" excluded from such opportunities for so many years in the not so distant past. It is a strange argument, an example of a possible implication of a true proposition advanced to dispute the proposition itself, like an octopus absent-mindedly slicing off his head with a stray tentacle. A fatal confusion underlies this argument, a confusion fundamentally relevant to our understanding of the notion of the rule of law.

Two senses of justice and equality are involved in this confusion. The root notion of justice, progenitor of the other, is the one that Aristotle (*Nichomachean Ethics* 5.6; *Politics* 1.2; 3.1) assumes to be the foundation and proper virtue of the political association. It is the condition which free men establish among themselves when they "share a common life in order that their association bring them self-sufficiency"—the regulation of their relationship by law, and the establishment, by law, of equality before the law. Rule of law is the name and pattern of this justice; its equality stands against the inequalities—of wealth, talent, etc.—otherwise obtaining among its participants, who by virtue of that equality are called "citizens." It is an achievement—complete, or, more frequently, partial—of certain people in certain concrete situations. It is fragile and easily disrupted by powerful individuals who discover that the blind equality of rule of law is inconvenient for their interests. Despite its obvious instability, Aristotle assumed that the establishment of justice in this sense, the creation of citizenship, was a permanent possibility for men and that the resultant association of citizens was the natural home of the species. At levels below the political association, this rule-governed equality is easily found; it is exemplified by any group of children agreeing together to play a game. At the level of political association, the attainment of this justice is more difficult, simply because the stakes are so much higher for each participant. The equality of citizenship is not something that happens of its own accord, and without the expenditure of a fair amount of effort it will collapse into the rule of a powerful few over an apathetic many. But at least it has been achieved, at some times in some

From Lisa H. Newton, "Reverse Discrimination as Unjustified," *Ethics*, vol. 83, no. 4 (July 1973). Copyright © 1973 by The University of Chicago. Reprinted by permission of University of Chicago Press.

places; it is always worth trying to achieve, and eminently worth trying to maintain, wherever and to whatever degree it has been brought into being.

Aristotle's parochialism is notorious; he really did not imagine that persons other than Greeks could associate freely in justice, and the only form of association he had in mind was the Greek *polis*. With the decline of the *polis* and the shift in the center of political thought, his notion of justice underwent a sea change. To be exact, it ceased to represent a political type and became a moral ideal: the ideal of equality as we know it. This ideal demands that all men be included in citizenship—that one Law govern all equally, that all men regard all other men as fellow citizens, with the same guarantees, rights, and protections. Briefly, it demands that the circle of citizenship achieved by any group be extended to include the entire human race. Properly understood, its effect on our associations can be excellent: it congratulates us on our achievement of rule of law as a process of government but refuses to let us remain complacent until we have expanded the associations to include others within the ambit of the rules, as often and as far as possible. While one man is a slave, none of us may feel truly free. We are constantly prodded by this ideal to look for possible unjustifiable discrimination, for inequalities not absolutely required for the functioning of the society and advantageous to all. And after twenty centuries of pressure, not at all constant, from this ideal, it might be said that some progress has been made. To take the cases in point for this problem, we are now prepared to assert, as Aristotle would never have been, the equality of sexes and of persons of different colors. The ambit of American citizenship, once restricted to white males of property, has been extended to include all adult free men, then all adult males including ex-slaves, then all women. The process of acquisition of full citizenship was for these groups a sporadic trail of half-measures, even now not complete; the steps on the road to full equality are marked by legislation and judicial decisions which are only recently concluded and still often not enforced. But the fact that we can now discuss the possibility of favoring such groups in hiring shows that over the area that concerns us, at least, full equality is presupposed as a basis for discussion. To that extent, they are full citizens, fully protected by the law of the land.

It is important for my argument that the moral ideal of equality be recognized as logically distinct from the condition (or virtue) of justice in the political sense. Justice in this sense exists *among* a citizenry, irrespective of the number of the populace included in that citizenry. Further, the moral ideal is parasitic upon the political virtue, for "equality" is unspecified—it means nothing until we are told in what respect that equality is to be realized. In a political context, "equality" is specified as "equal rights"—equal access to the public realm, public goods and offices, equal treatment under the law—in brief, the equality of citizenship. If citizenship is not a possibility, political equality is unintelligible. The ideal emerges as a generalization of the real condition and refers back to that condition for its content.

Now, if justice (Aristotle's justice in the political sense) is equal treatment under law for all citizens, what is injustice? Clearly, injustice is the violation of that equality, discriminating for or against a group of citizens, favoring them with special immunities and privileges or depriving them of those guaranteed to the others. When the southern employer refuses to hire blacks in white-collar jobs, when Wall Street will only hire women as secretaries with new titles, when Mississippi high schools routinely flunk all black boys above ninth grade, we have examples of injustice, and we work to restore the equality of the public realm by ensuring that equal opportunity will be provided in such cases in the future. But of course, when the employers and the schools *favor* women and blacks, the same injustice is done. Just as the previous discrimination did, this reverse discrimination violates the public equality which defines citizenship and destroys the rule of law for the areas in which these favors are granted. To the extent that we adopt a program of discrimination, reverse or otherwise, justice in the political sense is destroyed, and none of us, specifically affected or not, is a citizen, a bearer of rights—we are all petitioners for favors. And to the same extent, the ideal of equality is undermined, for it has content only where justice obtains, and by destroying justice we render the ideal meaningless. It is, then, an ironic paradox, if not a contradiction in terms, to assert that the ideal of equality justifies the violation of justice; it is as if one should argue, with William Buckley, that an ideal of humanity can justify the destruction of the human race.

Logically, the conclusion is simple enough: all discrimination is wrong prima facie because it violates justice, and that goes for reverse discrimination too. No violation of justice among the citizens may be justified (may overcome the prima facie objection) by appeal to the ideal of equality, for that ideal is logically dependent upon the notion of justice. Reverse discrimination, then, which attempts no other justification than an appeal to equality, is wrong. But let us try to make the conclusion more plausible by suggesting some of the implications of the suggested practice of reverse discrimination in employment and education. My argument will be that the problems raised there are insoluble, not only in practice but in principle.

We may argue, if we like, about what "discrimination" consists of. Do I discriminate against blacks if I admit none to my school when none of the black applicants are qualified by the tests I always give? How far must I go to root out cultural bias from my application forms and tests before I can say that I have not discriminated against those of different cultures? Can I assume that women are not strong enough to be roughnecks on my oil rigs, or must I test them individually? But this controversy, the most popular and well-argued aspect of the issue, is not as fatal as two others which cannot be avoided: if we are regarding the blacks as a "minority" victimized by discrimination, what is a "minority"? And for any group— blacks, women, whatever—that has been discriminated against, what amount of reverse discrimination wipes out the initial discrimination? Let us grant as true that women and blacks were discriminated against, even where laws forbade such discrimination, and grant for the sake of argument that a history of discrimination must be wiped out by reverse discrimination. What follows?

First, are there other groups which have been discriminated against? For they should have the same right of restitution. What about American Indians, Chicanos, Appalachian Mountain whites, Puerto Ricans, Jews, Cajuns, and

Orientals? And if these are to be included, the principle according to which we specify a "minority" is simply the criterion of "ethnic (sub) group," and we're stuck with every hyphenated American in the lower-middle class clamoring for special privileges for *his* group—and with equal justification. For be it noted, when we run down the Harvard roster, we find not only a scarcity of blacks (in comparison with the proportion in the population) but an even more striking scarcity of those second-, third-, and fourth-generation ethnics who make up the loudest voice of Middle America. Shouldn't they demand *their* share? And eventually, the WASPs will have to form their own lobby, for they too are a minority. The point is simply this: there is no "majority" in America who will not mind giving up just a bit of their rights to make room for a favored minority. There are only other minorities, each of which is discriminated against by the favoring. The initial injustice is then repeated dozens of times, and if each minority is granted the same right of restitution as the others, an entire area of rule governance is dissolved into a pushing and shoving match between self-interested groups. Each works to catch the public eye and political popularity by whatever means of advertising and power politics lend themselves to the effort, to capitalize as much as possible on temporary popularity until the restless mob picks another group to feel sorry for. Hardly an edifying spectacle, and in the long run no one can benefit: the pie is no larger—it's just that instead of setting up and enforcing rules for getting a piece, we've turned the contest into a free-for-all, requiring much more effort for no larger a reward. It would be in the interests of all the participants to reestablish an objective rule to govern the process, carefully enforced and the same for all.

Second, supposing that we do manage to agree in general that women and blacks (and all the others) have some right of restitution, some right to a privileged place in the structure of opportunities for a while, how will we know when that while is up? How much privilege is enough? When will the guilt be gone, the price paid, the balance restored? What recompense is right for centuries of exclusion? What criterion tells us when we are done? Our experience with the Civil Rights movement shows us that agreement on these terms cannot be presupposed: a process that appears to some to be going at a mad gallop into a black takeover appears to the rest of us to be at a standstill. Should a practice of reverse discrimination be adopted, we may safely predict that just as some of us begin to see "a satisfactory start toward righting the balance," others of us will see that we "have already gone too far in the other direction" and will suggest that the discrimination ought to be reversed again. And such disagreement is inevitable, for the point is that we could not *possibly* have any criteria for evaluating the kind of recompense we have in mind. The context presumed by any discussion of restitution is the context of rule of law: law sets the rights of men and simultaneously sets the method for remedying the violation of those rights. You may exact suffering from others and/or damage payments for yourself if and only if the others have violated your rights; the suffering you have endured is not sufficient reason for them to suffer. And remedial rights exist only where there is law: primary human rights are useful guides to legislation but cannot stand as reasons for awarding remedies for injuries sustained. But then, the context presupposed by any discussion of restitution is the context of preexistent full citizenship. No remedial rights could exist for the excluded; neither in law nor in logic does there exist a right to *sue* for a standing to sue.

From these two considerations, then, the difficulties with reverse discrimination become evident. Restitution for a disadvantaged group whose rights under the law have been violated is possible by legal means, but restitution for a disadvantaged group whose grievance is that there was no law to protect them simply is not. First, outside of the area of justice defined by the law, no sense can be made of "the group's rights," for no law recognizes that group or the individuals in it, qua members, as bearers of rights (hence *any* group can constitute itself as a disadvantaged minority in some sense and demand similar restitution). Second, outside of the area of protection of law, no sense can be made of the violation of rights (hence the amount of the recompense cannot be decided by any objective criterion). For both reasons, the practice of reverse discrimination undermines the foundation of the very ideal in whose name it is advocated; it destroys justice, law, equality, and citizenship itself, and replaces them with power struggles and popularity contests.

NOTE

1. A version of this paper was read at a meeting of the Society for Women in Philosophy in Amherst, Massachusetts, November 5, 1972.

NO

Richard Wasserstrom

A DEFENSE OF PROGRAMS OF PREFERENTIAL TREATMENT

Many justifications of programs of preferential treatment depend upon the claim that in one respect or another such programs have good consequences or that they are effective means by which to bring about some desirable end, e.g., an integrated, equalitarian society. I mean by "programs of preferential treatment" to refer to programs such as those at issue in the *Bakke* case—programs which set aside a certain number of places (for example, in a law school) as to which members of minority groups (for example, persons who are non-white or female) who possess certain minimum qualifications (in terms of grades and test scores) may be preferred for admission to those places over some members of the majority group who possess higher qualifications (in terms of grades and test scores).

Many criticisms of programs of preferential treatment claim that such programs, even if effective, are unjustifiable because they are in some important sense unfair or unjust. In this paper I present a limited defense of such programs by showing that two of the chief arguments offered for the unfairness or injustice of these programs do not work in the way or to the degree supposed by critics of these programs.

The first argument is this. Opponents of preferential treatment programs sometimes assert that proponents of these programs are guilty of intellectual inconsistency, if not racism or sexism. For, as is now readily acknowledged, at times past employers, universities, and many other social institutions did not have racial or sexual quotas (when they did not practice overt racial or sexual exclusion), and many of those who were most concerned to bring about the eradication of those racial quotas are now untroubled by the new programs which reinstitute them. And this, it is claimed, is inconsistent. If it was wrong to take race or sex into account when blacks and women were the objects of racial and sexual policies and practices of exclusion, then it is wrong to take race or sex into account when the objects of the policies have their race or sex reversed. Simple considerations of intellectual consistency—of what it means to give racism or sexism as a reason for condemning these social policies and practices—require that what was a good reason then is still a good reason now.

From Richard Wasserstrom, "A Defense of Programs of Preferential Treatment," *National Forum: The Phi Kappa Phi Journal*, vol. 58, no 1 (Winter 1978), pp. 15–18. Copyright © 1978 by *National Forum: The Phi Kappa Phi Journal*. Reprinted by permission.

The problem with this argument is that despite appearances, there is no inconsistency involved in holding both views. Even if contemporary preferential treatment programs which contain quotas are wrong, they are not wrong for the reasons that made quotas against blacks and women pernicious. The reason why is that the social realities do make an enormous difference. The fundamental evil of programs that discriminated against blacks or women was that these programs were a part of a larger social universe which systematically maintained a network of institutions that unjustifiably concentrated power, authority, and goods in the hands of white male individuals, and which systematically consigned blacks and women to subordinate positions in the society.

Whatever may be wrong with today's affirmative action programs and quota systems, it should be clear that the evil, if any, is just not the same. Racial and sexual minorities do not constitute the dominant social group. Nor is the conception of who is a fully developed member of the moral and social community one of an individual who is either female or black. Quotas that prefer women or blacks do not add to an already relatively overabundant supply of resources and opportunities at the disposal of members of these groups in the way in which the quotas of the past did maintain and argument the overabundant supply of resources and opportunities already available to white males.

The same point can be made in a somewhat different way. Sometimes people say that what was wrong, for example, with the system of racial discrimination in the South was that it took an irrelevant characteristic, namely race, and used it systematically to allocate social benefits and burdens of various sorts. The defect was the irrelevance of the characteristic used—race—for that meant that individuals ended up being treated in a manner that was arbitrary and capricious.

I do not think that was the central flaw at all. Take, for instance, the most hideous of the practices, human slavery. The primary thing that was wrong with the institution was not that the particular individuals who were assigned the place of slaves were assigned there arbitrarily because the assignment was made in virtue of an irrelevant characteristic, their race. Rather, it seems to me that the primary thing that was and is wrong with slavery is the practice itself—the fact of some individuals being able to own other individuals and all that goes with that practice. It would not matter by what criterion individuals were assigned; human slavery would still be wrong. And the same can be said for most if not all of the other discrete practices and institutions which comprised the system of racial discrimination even after human slavery was abolished. The practices were unjustifiable—they were oppressive—and they would have been so no matter how the assignment of victims had been made. What made it worse still, was that the institutions and the supporting ideology all interlocked to create a system of human oppression whose effects on those living under it were as devastating as they were unjustifiable.

Again, if there is anything wrong with the programs of preferential treatment that have begun to flourish within the past ten years, it should be evident that the social realities in respect to the distribution of resources and opportunities make the difference. Apart from everything else, there is simply no way in which all of these programs taken together could plausibly be viewed as capable of relegating white males to the kind of genuinely oppressive status characteristically bestowed upon women and blacks by the dominant social institutions and ideology.

The second objection is that preferential treatment programs are wrong because they take race or sex into account rather than the only thing that does matter—that is, an individual's qualifications. What all such programs have in common and what makes them all objectionable, so this argument goes, is that they ignore the persons who are more qualified by bestowing a preference on those who are less qualified in virtue of their being either black or female.

There are, I think, a number of things wrong with this objection based on qualifications, and not the least of them is that we do not live in a society in which there is even the serious pretense of a qualification requirement for many jobs of substantial power and authority. Would anyone claim, for example, that the persons who comprise the judiciary are there because they are the most qualified lawyers or the most qualified persons to be judges? Would anyone claim that Henry Ford II is the head of the Ford Motor Company because he is the most qualified person for the job? Part of what is wrong with even talking about qualifications and merit is that the argument derives some of its force from the erroneous notion that we would have a meritocracy were it not for programs of preferential treatment. In fact, the higher one goes in terms of prestige, power and the like, the less qualifications seem ever to be decisive. It is only for certain jobs and certain places that qualifications are used to do more

than establish the possession of certain minimum competencies.

But difficulties such as these to one side, there are theoretical difficulties as well which cut much more deeply into the argument about qualifications. To begin with, it is important to see that there is a serious inconsistency present if the person who favors "pure qualifications" does so on the ground that the most qualified ought to be selected because this promotes maximum efficiency. Let us suppose that the argument is that if we have the most qualified performing the relevant tasks we will get those tasks done in the most economical and efficient manner. There is nothing wrong in principle with arguments based upon the good consequences that will flow from maintaining a social practice in a certain way. But it is inconsistent for the opponent of preferential treatment to attach much weight to qualifications on this ground; because it was an analogous appeal to the good consequences that the opponent of preferential treatment thought was wrong in the first place. That is to say, if the chief thing to be said in favor of strict qualifications and preferring the most qualified is that it is the most efficient way of getting things done, then we are right back to an assessment of the different consequences that will flow from different programs, and we are far removed from the considerations of justice or fairness that were thought to weigh so heavily against these programs.

It is important to note, too, that qualifications—at least in the educational context—are often not connected at all closely with any plausible conception of social effectiveness. To admit the most qualified students to law school, for example—given the way qualifications are now determined—is primarily to admit those who have the greatest chance of scoring the highest grades at law school. This says little about efficiency except perhaps that these students are the easiest for the faculty to teach. However, since we know so little about what constitutes being a good, or even successful lawyer, and even less about the correlation between being a very good law student and being a very good lawyer, we can hardly claim very confidently that the legal system will operate most effectively if we admit only the most qualified students to law school.

To be at all decisive, the argument for qualifications must be that those who are the most qualified deserve to receive the benefits (the job, the place in law school, etc.) because they are the most qualified. The introduction of the concept of desert now makes it an objection as to justice or fairness of the sort promised by the original criticism of the programs. But now the problem is that there is no reason to think that there is any strong sense of "desert" in which it is correct that the most qualified deserve anything.

Let us consider more closely one case, that of preferential treatment in respect to admission to college or graduate school. There is a logical gap in the inference from the claim that a person is most qualified to perform a task, e.g., to be a good student, to the conclusion that he or she deserves to be admitted as a student. Of course, those who deserve to be admitted should be admitted. But why do the most qualified deserve anything? There is simply no necessary connection between academic merit (in the sense of being most qualified) and deserving to be a member of a student body. Suppose, for instance, that there is only one tennis court in the community. Is it clear that the two best tennis players ought to be the ones permitted to use it? Why not those who were there first? Or those who will enjoy playing the most? Or those who are the worst and, therefore, need the greatest opportunity to practice? Or those who have the chance to play least frequently?

We might, of course, have a rule that says that the best tennis players get to use the court before the others. Under such a rule the best players would deserve the court more than the poorer ones. But that is just to push the inquiry back on stage. Is there any reason to think that we ought to have a rule giving good tennis players such a preference? Indeed, the arguments that might be given for or against such a rule are many and varied. And few if any of the arguments that might support the rule would depend upon a connection between ability and desert.

Someone might reply, however, that the most able students deserve to be admitted to the university because all of their earlier schooling was a kind of competition, with university admission being the prize awarded to the winners. They deserve to be admitted because that is what the rule of the competition provides. In addition, it might be argued, it would be unfair now to exclude them in favor of others, given the reasonable expectations they developed about the way in which their industry and performance would be rewarded. Minority-admission programs, which inevitably prefer some who are less qualified over some who are more qualified, all possess this flaw.

There are several problems with this argument. The most substantial of them is that it is an empirically implausible picture of our social world. Most of what are regarded as the decisive characteristics for higher education have a great deal to do with things over which the individual has neither control nor responsibility: such things as home environment, socioeconomic class of parents, and, of course, the quality of the primary and secondary schools attended. Since individuals do not deserve having had any of these things vis-á-vis other individuals, they do not, for the most part, deserve their qualifications. And since they do not deserve their abilities they do not in any strong sense deserve to be admitted because of their abilities.

To be sure, if there has been a rule which connects say, performance at high school with admission to college, then there is a weak sense in which those who do well at high school deserve, for that reason alone, to be admitted to college. In addition, if persons have built up or relied upon their reasonable expectations concerning performance and admission, they have a claim to be admitted on this ground as well. But it is certainly not obvious that these claims of desert are any stronger or more compelling than the competing claims based upon the needs of or advantages to women or blacks from programs of preferential treatment. And as I have indicated, all rule-based claims of desert are very weak unless and until the rule which creates the claim is itself shown to be a justified one. Unless one has a strong preference for the status quo, and unless one can defend that preference, the practice within a system of allocating places in a certain way does not go very far at all in showing that that is the right or the just way to allocate those places in the future.

A proponent of programs of preferential treatment is not at all committed to the view that qualifications ought to be wholly irrelevant. He or she can agree that, given the existing structure of any institution, there is probably some minimal set of qualifications without which one cannot participate meaningfully within the institution. In addition, it can be granted that the qualifications of those involved· will affect the way the institution works and the way it affects others in the society. And the consequences will vary depending upon the particular institution. But all of this only establishes that qualifications, in this sense, are relevant, not that they are decisive. This is wholly consistent with the claim that race or sex should today also be relevant when it comes to matters such as admission to college or law school. And that is all that any preferential treatment program—even one with the kind of quota used in the *Bakke* case—has ever tried to do.

I have not attempted to establish that programs of preferential treatment are right and desirable. There are empirical issues concerning the consequences of these programs that I have not discussed, and certainly not settled. Nor, for that matter, have I considered the argument that justice may permit, if not require, these programs as a way to provide compensation or reparation for injuries suffered in the recent as well as distant past, or as a way to remove benefits that are undeservedly enjoyed by those of the dominant group. What I have tried to do is show that it is wrong to think that programs of preferential treatment are objectionable in the centrally important sense in which many past and present discriminatory features of our society have been and are racist and sexist. The social realities as to power and opportunity do make a fundamental difference. It is also wrong to think that programs of preferential treatment are in any strong sense either unjust or unprincipled. The case for programs of preferential treatment could, therefore, plausibly rest both on the view that such programs are not unfair to white males (except in the weak, rule-dependent sense described above) and on the view that it is unfair to continue the present set of unjust—often racist and sexist—institutions that comprise the social reality. And the case for these programs could rest as well on the proposition that, given the distribution of power and influence in the United States today, such programs may reasonably be viewed as potentially valuable, effective means by which to achieve admirable and significant social ideals of equality and integration.

POSTSCRIPT

Are Programs of Preferential Treatment Unjustifiable?

What kind of society do we want to live in? It is not enough to say that justice in society is important. We must also ask whether equality in opportunity is an adequate stand-in for equality of result. Is procedural justice enough for us when it does not yield substantial justice?

What values weigh in the balance in the attempt to come to terms with the issue of preferential treatment? Clearly, individual interest is going to be affected, and social patterns are going to change. Industries that were completely dominated by white males in the 1950s now employ African Americans and women in managerial positions.

Throughout the effort to create an equal society, it will be important to preserve the freedom to compete in America and to select the best product, service, or vendor on the free market. The tension between the values of the free society and the equal society is troubling, as is evident in the recent Supreme Court decisions on affirmative action, which show an unmistakable trend against affirmative action provisions.

Are we backing off from a commitment to a thoroughly integrated society? The conservative (or strict constructionist) Supreme Court seems to avoid reasoning with the ends to be achieved in sight (a teleological method), preferring instead to reason from the strictest principles of established law to the narrowest possible extension of those principles, with little regard to the consequences (a deontological view). A liberal (or judicial activist) Court would attempt to use the power of constitutional interpretation to realize the ideals of the society.

SUGGESTED READINGS

Robert K. Bobinson, Billie Morgan, and T. Yohannan, "Affirmative Action Plans in the 1990s: A Double-Edged Sword?" *Public Personnel Management* (Summer 1992).

Paula Dwyer and Tim Smart, "The Price of Discrimination May Well Go Up," *Business Week* (August 13, 1990).

James P. McCarty, "Eliminate Reverse Discrimination in Group LTD," *Life Association News* (August 1992).

Robert J. Nobile, "Can There Be Too Much Diversity?" *Personnel* (August 1991).

Herman Schwartz, "In Defense of Affirmative Action," in Leslie Dunbar, ed., *Minority Report* (Pantheon Books, 1984).

ISSUE 8

Does Blowing the Whistle Violate Company Loyalty?

YES: Sissela Bok, from "Whistleblowing and Professional Responsibility," *New York University Education Quarterly* (Summer 1980)

NO: Robert A. Larmer, from "Whistleblowing and Employee Loyalty," *Journal of Business Ethics* (vol. 11, 1992)

ISSUE SUMMARY

YES: Philosopher Sissela Bok asserts that although blowing the whistle is often justified, it does involve dissent, accusation, and a breach of loyalty to the employer.

NO: Robert A. Larmer, an associate professor of philosophy, argues that attempting to stop illegal or unethical company activities may be the highest type of company loyalty an employee can display.

Whistle-blowing occurs when an employee discovers a wrong at his or her place of employment and exposes it, thereby saving lives or a great deal of money, but almost always at great expense to him- or herself. Since the readings that follow are theoretical, some specific cases might be useful. In "The Whistle Blowers' Morning After," *The New York Times* (November 9, 1986), N. R. Kleinfeld portrays five of the early whistle-blowers, some of whom have become famous as case studies in business schools across the country. Each one has an interesting story to tell; each claims that if he had it to do over again he would, for he likes living with a clear conscience. But each has also paid a price: great stress, sometimes ill health, career loss, financial ruin, and/or loss of friends and family.

Charles Atchinson blew the whistle on the Comanche Park nuclear plant in Glen Rose, Texas, a power station that was unsafe. It cost him his job, plunged him into debt from which he is still trying to recover, and left emotional scars on his family. Kermit Vandivier, who blew the whistle on the B. F. Goodrich Aircraft Brakes scandal, also lost his job. He has a new career as a journalist. James Pope claimed that the Federal Aviation Administration (FAA) found in 1975 an effective device, known as an airborne collision avoidance system, that would prevent mid-air crashes; but it chose instead to pursue an inferior device it had had a hand in developing. Mr. Pope was "retired" early by the FAA. The most famous whistle-blower of all may be A. Ernest Fitzgerald (*The*

High Priests of Waste; The Pentagonists), the Air Force cost analyst who found huge cost overruns on Lockheed cargo planes that were being developed for the Air Force. After his revelations, he was discharged from the Air Force. He fought for 13 years to be reinstated, which he was, at full rank, in 1982. The common thread of these stories is that when someone detected a wrong and properly reported it, he was demoted, labeled a troublemaker, and disciplined or fired, even when the evidence was very much in his favor. All of them, incidentally, initially believed in their organizations, and not only were all of them sure that they were acting in an ethical manner, all of them also believed that they would be thanked for their efforts and diligence.

Professors Myron Peretz Glazer and Penina Migdal Glazer, in *The Whistle Blowers: Exposing Corruption in Government and Industry* (Basic Books, 1989), tell the story of 55 whistle-blowers—why they did what they did, and what the consequences were for themselves and their families. The Glazers found that the dominant trait in these whistle-blowers was a strong belief in individual responsibility. As one of the spouses of a whistle-blower stated, "A corrupt system can happen only if the individuals who make up that system are corrupt. You are either going to be part of the corruption or part of the forces working against it. There isn't a third choice. Someone, someday, has to take a stand; if you don't, maybe no one will. And that is wrong."

The Glazers write that the strong belief in individual responsibility that drove these ethical resisters was often supported by professional ethics, religious values, or allegiance to a community. But the personal costs of public disclosure were high, and the results were less than satisfactory. In some cases the accused corporations made no changes. The whistle-blowers, however, had to recreate careers, relocate, and settle for less money in new jobs. For most resisters, the worst part was the devastating months or even years of dislocation, unemployment, and temporary jobs. In response to a question posed by the Glazers, 21 of the whistle-blowers advised other potential whistle-blowers to "forget it" or to "leak the information without your name attached." If blowing the whistle is unavoidable, however, then "be prepared to be ostracized, have your career come to a screeching halt, and perhaps even be driven into bankruptcy."

As you read the following selections, think about these cases and others you may have heard about. Consider the motivations involved in whistle-blowing and whether they reflect loyalty or disloyalty to the company. How would you view an instance of whistle-blowing if you or your company were the target? Who deserves the greatest consideration in potential whistle-blowing situations: the individual, the company, or the public?

YES

Sissela Bok

WHISTLEBLOWING AND PROFESSIONAL RESPONSIBILITY

"Whistleblowing" is a new label generated by our increased awareness of the ethical conflicts encountered at work. Whistleblowers sound an alarm from within the very organization in which they work, aiming to spotlight neglect or abuses that threaten the public interest.

The stakes in whistleblowing are high. Take the nurse who alleges that physicians enrich themselves in her hospital through unnecessary surgery; the engineer who discloses safety defects in the braking systems of a fleet of new rapid-transit vehicles; the Defense Department official who alerts Congress to military graft and overspending: all know that they pose a threat to those whom they denounce and that their own careers may be at risk.

MORAL CONFLICTS

Moral conflicts on several levels confront anyone who is wondering whether to speak out about abuses or risks or serious neglect. In the first place, he must try to decide whether, other things being equal, speaking out is in fact in the public interest. This choice is often made more complicated by factual uncertainties: Who is responsible for the abuse or neglect? How great is the threat? And how likely is it that speaking out will precipitate changes for the better?

In the second place, a would-be whistleblower must weigh his responsibility to serve the public interest against the responsibility he owes to his colleagues and the institution in which he works. While the professional ethic requires collegial loyalty, the codes of ethics often stress responsibility to the public over and above duties to colleagues and clients. Thus the United States Code of Ethics for Government Servants asks them to "expose corruption wherever uncovered" and to "put loyalty to the highest moral principles and to country above loyalty to persons, party, or government."[1] Similarly, the largest professional engineering association requires members to speak out against abuses threatening the safety, health, and welfare of the public.[2]

From Sissela Bok, "Whistleblowing and Professional Responsibility," *New York University Education Quarterly*, vol. 11 (Summer 1980), pp. 2–7. Copyright © 1980 by Sissela Bok. Reprinted by permission.

A third conflict for would-be whistle-blowers is personal in nature and cuts across the first two: even in cases where they have concluded that the facts warrant speaking out, and that their duty to do so overrides loyalties to colleagues and institutions, they often have reason to fear the results of carrying out such a duty. However strong this duty may seem in theory, they know that, in practice, retaliation is likely. As a result, their careers and their ability to support themselves and their families may be unjustly impaired.[3] A government handbook issued during the Nixon era recommends reassigning "undesirables" to places so remote that they would prefer to resign. Whistleblowers may also be downgraded or given work without responsibility or work for which they are not qualified; or else they may be given many more tasks than they can possibly perform. Another risk is that an outspoken civil servant may be ordered to undergo a psychiatric fitness-for-duty examination,[4] declared unfit for service, and "separated" as well as discredited from the point of view of any allegations he may be making. Outright firing, finally, is the most direct institutional response to whistleblowers.

Add to the conflicts confronting individual whistleblowers the claim to self-policing that many professions make, and professional responsibility is at issue in still another way. For an appeal to the public goes against everything that "self-policing" stands for. The question for the different professions, then, is how to resolve, insofar as it is possible, the conflict between professional loyalty and professional responsibility toward the outside world. The same conflicts arise to some extent in all groups, but professional groups often have special cohesion and claim special dignity and privileges.

The plight of whistleblowers has come to be documented by the press and described in a number of books. Evidence of the hardships imposed on those who chose to act in the public interest has combined with a heightened awareness of professional malfeasance and corruption to produce a shift toward greater public support of whistleblowers. Public service law firms and consumer groups have taken up their cause; institutional reforms and legislation have been proposed to combat illegitimate reprisals.[5]

Given the indispensable services performed by so many whistleblowers, strong public support is often merited. But the new climate of acceptance makes it easy to overlook the dangers of whistleblowing: of uses in error or in malice; of work and reputations unjustly lost for those falsely accused; of privacy invaded and trust undermined. There comes a level of internal prying and mutual suspicion at which no institution can function. And it is a fact that the disappointed, the incompetent, the malicious, and the paranoid all too often leap to accusations in public. Worst of all, ideological persecution throughout the world traditionally relies on insiders willing to inform on their colleagues or even on their family members, often through staged public denunciations or press campaigns.

No society can count itself immune from such dangers. But neither can it risk silencing those with a legitimate reason to blow the whistle. How then can we distinguish between different instances of whistleblowing? A society that fails to protect the right to speak out even on the part of those whose warnings turn out to be spurious obviously opens the door to political repression. But from the moral point of view there are important differences between the aims, messages, and methods of dissenters from within.

NATURE OF WHISTLEBLOWING

Three elements, each jarring, and triply jarring when conjoined, lend acts of whistleblowing special urgency and bitterness: dissent, breach of loyalty, and accusation.

Like all dissent, whistleblowing makes public a disagreement with an authority or a majority view. But whereas dissent can concern all forms of disagreement with, for instance, religious dogma or government policy or court decisions, whistleblowing has the narrower aim of shedding light on negligence or abuse, or alerting to a risk, and of assigning responsibility for this risk.

Would-be whistleblowers confront the conflict inherent in all dissent: between conforming and sticking their necks out. The more repressive the authority they challenge, the greater the personal risk they take in speaking out. At exceptional times, as in times of war, even ordinarily tolerant authorities may come to regard dissent as unacceptable and even disloyal.[6]

Furthermore, the whistleblower hopes to stop the game; but since he is neither referee nor coach, and since he blows the whistle on his own team, his act is seen as a violation of loyalty. In holding his position, he has assumed certain obligations to his colleagues and clients. He may even have subscribed to a loyalty oath or a promise of confidentiality. Loyalty to colleagues and to clients comes to be pitted against loyalty to the public interest, to those who may be injured unless the revelation is made.

Not only is loyalty violated in whistleblowing, hierarchy as well is often opposed, since the whistleblower is not only a colleague but a subordinate. Though aware of the risks inherent in such disobedience, he often hopes to keep his job.[7] At times, however, he plans his alarm to coincide with leaving the institution. If he is highly placed, or joined by others, resigning in protest may effectively direct public attention to the wrongdoing at issue.[8] Still another alternative, often chosen by those who wish to be safe from retaliation, is to leave the institution quietly, to secure another post, and then to blow the whistle. In this way, it is possible to speak with the authority and knowledge of an insider without having the vulnerability of that position.

It is the element of accusation, of calling a "foul," that arouses the strongest reactions on the part of the hierarchy. The accusation may be of neglect, of willfully concealed dangers, or of outright abuse on the part of colleagues or superiors. It singles out specific persons or groups as responsible for threats to the public interest. If no one could be held responsible—as in the case of an impending avalanche—the warning would not constitute whistleblowing.

The accusation of the whistleblower, moreover, concerns a present or an imminent threat. Past errors or misdeeds occasion such an alarm only if they still affect current practices. And risks far in the future lack the immediacy needed to make the alarm a compelling one, as well as the close connection to particular individuals that would justify actual accusations. Thus an alarm can be sounded about safety defects in a rapid-transit system that threaten or will shortly threaten passengers, but the revelation of safety defects in a system no longer in use, while

of historical interest, would not constitute whistleblowing. Nor would the revelation of potential problems in a system not yet fully designed and far from
implemented.[9]

Not only immediacy, but also speci-
ficity, is needed for there to be an alarm
capable of pinpointing responsibility. A
concrete risk must be at issue rather than
a vague foreboding or a somber predic-
tion. The act of whistleblowing differs in
this respect from the lamentation or the
dire prophecy. An immediate and specific
threat would normally be acted upon by
those at risk. The whistleblower assumes
that his message will alert listeners to
something they do not know, or whose
significance they have not grasped because it has been kept secret.

The desire for openness inheres in
the temptation to reveal any secret,
sometimes joined to an urge for self-
aggrandizement and publicity and the
hope for revenge for past slights or
injustices. There can be pleasure, too—
righteous or malicious—in laying bare
the secrets of co-workers and in setting
the record straight at last. Colleagues
of the whistleblower often suspect his
motives: they may regard him as a crank,
as publicity-hungry, wrong about the
facts, eager for scandal and discord, and
driven to indiscretion by his personal
biases and shortcomings.

For whistleblowing to be effective, it
must arouse its audience. Inarticulate
whistleblowers are likely to fail from the
outset. When they are greeted by apathy,
their message dissipates. When they
are greeted by disbelief, they elicit no
response at all. And when the audience
is not free to receive or to act on the
information—when censorship or fear
of retribution stifles response—then the
message rebounds to injure the whistleblower. Whistleblowing also requires the
possibility of concerted public response:
the idea of whistleblowing in an anarchy
is therefore merely quixotic.

Such characteristics of whistleblowing
and strategic considerations for achieving an impact are common to the noblest
warnings, the most vicious personal attacks, and the delusions of the paranoid.
How can one distinguish the many acts
of sounding an alarm that are genuinely
in the public interest from all the petty,
biased, or lurid revelations that pervade
our querulous and gossip-ridden society?
Can we draw distinctions between different whistleblowers, different messages,
different methods?

We clearly can, in a number of cases.
Whistleblowing may be starkly inappropriate when in malice or error, or when
it lays bare legitimately private matters
having to do, for instance, with political
belief or sexual life. It can, just as clearly,
be the only way to shed light on an ongoing unjust practice such as drugging
political prisoners or subjecting them
to electroshock treatment. It can be the
last resort for alerting the public to an
impending disaster. Taking such clear-
cut cases as benchmarks, and reflecting
on what it is about them that weighs so
heavily for or against speaking out, we
can work our way toward the admittedly
more complex cases in which whistleblowing is not so clearly the right or
wrong choice, or where different points
of view exist regarding its legitimacy—
cases where there are moral reasons both
for concealment and for disclosure and
where judgments conflict....

INDIVIDUAL MORAL CHOICE

What questions might those who consider sounding an alarm in public ask

themselves? How might they articulate the problem they see and weigh its injustice before deciding whether or not to reveal it? How can they best try to make sure their choice is the right one? In thinking about these questions it helps to keep in mind the three elements mentioned earlier: dissent, breach of loyalty, and accusation. They impose certain requirements—of accuracy and judgment in dissent; of exploring alternative ways to cope with improprieties that minimize the breach of loyalty; and of fairness in accusation. For each, careful articulation and testing of arguments are needed to limit error and bias.

Dissent by whistleblowers, first of all, is expressly claimed to be intended to benefit the public. It carries with it, as a result, an obligation to consider the nature of this benefit and to consider also the possible harm that may come from speaking out: harm to persons or institutions and, ultimately, to the public interest itself. Whistleblowers must, therefore, begin by making every effort to consider the effects of speaking out versus those of remaining silent. They must assure themselves of the accuracy of their reports, checking and rechecking the facts before speaking out; specify the degree to which there is genuine impropriety; consider how imminent is the threat they see, how serious, and how closely linked to those accused of neglect and abuse.

If the facts warrant whistleblowing, how can the second element—breach of loyalty—be minimized? The most important question here is whether the existing avenues for change within the organization have been explored. It is a waste of time for the public as well as harmful to the institution to sound the loudest alarm first. Whistleblowing has to remain a last alternative because of its destructive side effects: it must be chosen only when other alternatives have been considered and rejected. They may be rejected if they simply do not apply to the problem at hand, or when there is not time to go through routine channels or when the institution is so corrupt or coercive that steps will be taken to silence the whistleblower should he try the regular channels first.

What weight should an oath or a promise of silence have in the conflict of loyalties? One sworn to silence is doubtless under a stronger obligation because of the oath he has taken. He has bound himself, assumed specific obligations beyond those assumed in merely taking a new position. But even such promises can be overridden when the public interest at issue is strong enough. They can be overridden if they were obtained under duress or through deceit. They can be overridden, too, if they promise something that is in itself wrong or unlawful. The fact that one has promised silence is no excuse for complicity in covering up a crime or a violation of the public's trust.

The third element in whistleblowing—accusation—raises equally serious ethical concerns. They are concerns of fairness to the persons accused of impropriety. Is the message one to which the public is entitled in the first place? Or does it infringe on personal and private matters that one has no right to invade? Here, the very notion of what is in the public's best "interest" is at issue: "accusations" regarding an official's unusual sexual or religious experiences may well appeal to the public's interest without being information relevant to "the public interest."

Great conflicts arise here. We have witnessed excessive claims to executive privilege and to secrecy by government officials during the Watergate scandal in order to cover up for abuses the public had every right to discover. Conversely, those hoping to profit from prying into private matters have become adept at invoking "the public's right to know." Some even regard such private matters as threats to the public: they voice their own religious and political prejudices in the language of accusation. Such a danger is never stronger than when the accusation is delivered surreptitiously. The anonymous accusations made during the McCarthy period regarding political beliefs and associations often injured persons who did not even know their accusers or the exact nature of the accusations.

From the public's point of view, accusations that are openly made by identifiable individuals are more likely to be taken seriously. And in fairness to those criticized, openly accepted responsibility for blowing the whistle should be preferred to the denunciation or the leaked rumor. What is openly stated can more easily be checked, its source's motives challenged, and the underlying information examined. Those under attack may otherwise be hard put to defend themselves against nameless adversaries. Often they do not even know that they are threatened until it is too late to respond. The anonymous denunciation, moreover, common to so many regimes, places the burden of investigation on government agencies that may thereby gain the power of a secret police.

From the point of view of the whistleblower, on the other hand, the anonymous message is safer in situations where retaliation is likely. But it is also often less likely to be taken seriously. Unless the message is accompanied by indications of how the evidence can be checked, its anonymity, however safe for the source, speaks against it.

During the process of weighing the legitimacy of speaking out, the method used, and the degree of fairness needed, whistleblowers must try to compensate for the strong possibility of bias on their part. They should be scrupulously aware of any motive that might skew their message: a desire for self-defense in a difficult bureaucratic situation, perhaps, or the urge to seek revenge, or inflated expectations regarding the effect their message will have on the situation. (Needless to say, bias affects the silent as well as the outspoken. The motive for holding back important information about abuses and injustice ought to give similar cause for soul-searching.)

Likewise, the possibility of personal gain from sounding the alarm ought to give pause. Once again there is then greater risk of a biased message. Even if the whistleblower regards himself as incorruptible, his profiting from revelations of neglect or abuse will lead others to question his motives and to put less credence in his charges. If, for example, a government employee stands to make large profits from a book exposing the inequities in his agency, there is danger that he will, perhaps even unconsciously, slant his report in order to cause more of a sensation.

A special problem arises when there is a high risk that the civil servant who speaks out will have to go through costly litigation. Might he not justifiably try to make enough money on his public revelations—say, through books or public speaking—to offset his losses? In so doing he will not strictly speaking have *profited* from his revelations: he merely avoids being financially crushed by their sequels. He will nevertheless still be suspected at the time of revelation, and his message will therefore seem more questionable.

Reducing bias and error in moral choice often requires consultation, even open debate[10]: methods that force articulation of the moral arguments at stake and challenge privately held assumptions. But acts of whistleblowing present special problems when it comes to open consultation. On the one hand, once the whistleblower sounds his alarm publicly, his arguments will be subjected to open scrutiny; he will have to articulate his reasons for speaking out and substantiate his charges. On the other hand, it will then be too late to retract the alarm or to combat its harmful effects, should his choice to speak out have been ill-advised.

For this reason, the whistleblower owes it to all involved to make sure of two things: that he has sought as much and as objective advice regarding his choice as he can *before* going public; and that he is aware of the arguments for and against the practice of whistleblowing in general, so that he can see his own choice against as richly detailed and coherently structured a background as possible. Satisfying these two requirements once again has special problems because of the very nature of whistleblowing: the more corrupt the circumstances, the more dangerous it may be to seek consultation before speaking out. And yet, since the whistleblower himself may have a biased view of the state of affairs, he may choose not to consult others when in fact it would be not only safe but advantageous to do so; he may see corruption and conspiracy where none exists.

NOTES

1. Code of Ethics for Government Service passed by the U.S. House of Representatives in the 85th Congress (1958) and applying to all government employees and office holders.

2. Code of Ethics of the Institute of Electrical and Electronics Engineers, Article IV.

3. For case histories and descriptions of what befalls whistleblowers, see Rosemary Chalk and Frank von Hippel, "Due Process for Dissenting Whistle-Blowers," *Technology Review* 81 (June–July 1979); 48–55; Alan S. Westin and Stephen Salisbury, eds., *Individual Rights in the Corporation* (New York: Pantheon, 1980); Helen Dudar, "The Price of Blowing the Whistle," *New York Times Magazine,* 30 October 1979, pp. 41–54; John Edsall, *Scientific Freedom and Responsibility* (Washington, D.C.: American Association for the Advancement of Science, 1975), p. 5; David Ewing, *Freedom Inside the Organization* (New York: Dutton, 1977); Ralph Nader, Peter Petkas, and Kate Blackwell, *Whistle Blowing* (New York: Grossman, 1972); Charles Peter and Taylor Branch, *Blowing the Whistle* (New York: Praeger, 1972).

4. Congressional hearings uncovered a growing resort to mandatory psychiatric examinations.

5. For an account of strategies and proposals to support government whistleblowers, see Government Accountability Project, *A Whistleblower's Guide to the Federal Bureaucracy* (Washington, D.C.: Institute for Policy Studies, 1977).

6. See, e.g., Samuel Eliot Morison, Frederick Merk, and Frank Friedel, *Dissent in Three American Wars* (Cambridge: Harvard University Press, 1970).

7. In the scheme worked out by Albert Hirschman in *Exit, Voice and Loyalty* (Cambridge: Harvard University Press, 1970), whistleblowing represents "voice" accompanied by a preference not to "exit," though forced "exit" is clearly a possibility and "voice" after or during "exit" may be chosen for strategic reasons.

8. Edward Weisband and Thomas N. Franck, *Resignation in Protest* (New York: Grossman, 1975).

9. Future developments can, however, be the cause for whistleblowing if they are seen as resulting from steps being taken or about to be taken that render them inevitable.

10. I discuss these questions of consultation and publicity with respect to moral choice in chapter 7 of Sissela Bok, *Lying* (New York: Pantheon, 1978); and in *Secrets* (New York: Pantheon Books, 1982), Ch. IX and XV.

NO

Robert A. Larmer

WHISTLEBLOWING AND EMPLOYEE LOYALTY

Whistleblowing by an employee is the act of complaining, either within the corporation or publicly, about a corporation's unethical practices. Such an act raises important questions concerning the loyalties and duties of employees. Traditionally, the employee has been viewed as an agent who acts on behalf of a principal, i.e., the employer, and as possessing duties of loyalty and confidentiality. Whistleblowing, at least at first blush, seems a violation of these duties and it is scarcely surprising that in many instances employers and fellow employees argue that it is an act of disloyalty and hence morally wrong.[1]

It is this issue of the relation between whistleblowing and employee loyalty that I want to address. What I will call the standard view is that employees possess *prima facie* duties of loyalty and confidentiality to their employers and that whistleblowing cannot be justified except on the basis of a higher duty to the public good. Against this standard view, Ronald Duska has recently argued that employees do not have even a *prima facie* duty of loyalty to their employers and that whistleblowing needs, therefore, no moral justification.[2] I am going to criticize both views. My suggestion is that both misunderstand the relation between loyalty and whistleblowing. In their place I will propose a third more adequate view.

Duska's view is more radical in that it suggests that there can be no issue of whistleblowing and employee loyalty, since the employee has no duty to be loyal to his employer. His reason for suggesting that the employee owes the employer, at least the corporate employer, no loyalty is that companies are not the kinds of things which are proper objects of loyalty. His argument in support of this rests upon two key claims. The first is that loyalty, properly understood, implies a reciprocal relationship and is only appropriate in the context of a mutual surrendering of self-interest. He writes,

> It is important to recognize that in any relationship which demands loyalty the relationship works both ways and involves mutual enrichment. Loyalty is

From Robert A. Larmer, "Whistleblowing and Employee Loyalty," *Journal of Business Ethics*, vol. 11 (1992), pp. 125–128. Copyright © 1992 by D. Reidel Publishing Co., Dordrecht, Holland, and Boston, U.S.A. Reprinted by permission of Kluwer Academic Publishers.

incompatible with self-interest, because it is something that necessarily requires we go beyond self-interest. My loyalty to my friend, for example, requires I put aside my interests some of the time.... Loyalty depends on ties that demand self-sacrifice with no expectation of reward, e.g., the ties of loyalty that bind a family together.[3]

The second is that the relation between a company and an employee does not involve any surrender of self-interest on the part of the company, since its primary goal is to maximize profit. Indeed, although it is convenient, it is misleading to talk of a company having interests. As Duska comments,

A company is not a person. A company is an instrument, and an instrument with a specific purpose, the making of profit. To treat an instrument as an end in itself, like a person, may not be as bad as treating an end as an instrument, but it does give the instrument a moral status it does not deserve...[4]

Since, then, the relation between a company and an employee does not fulfill the minimal requirement of being a relation between two individuals, much less two reciprocally self-sacrificing individuals, Duska feels it is a mistake to suggest the employee has any duties of loyalty to the company.

This view does not seem adequate, however. First, it is not true that loyalty must be quite so reciprocal as Duska demands. Ideally, of course, one expects that if one is loyal to another person that person will reciprocate in kind. There are, however, many cases where loyalty is not entirely reciprocated, but where we do not feel that it is misplaced. A parent, for example, may remain loyal to an erring teenager, even though the teenager demonstrates no loyalty to the parent. Indeed, part of being a proper parent is to demonstrate loyalty to your children whether or not that loyalty is reciprocated. This is not to suggest any kind of analogy between parents and employees, but rather that it is not nonsense to suppose that loyalty may be appropriate even though it is not reciprocated. Inasmuch as he ignores this possibility, Duska's account of loyalty is flawed.

Second, even if Duska is correct in holding that loyalty is only appropriate between moral agents and that a company is not genuinely a moral agent, the question may still be raised whether an employee owes loyalty to fellow employees or the shareholders of the company. Granted that reference to a company as an individual involves reification and should not be taken too literally, it may nevertheless constitute a legitimate shorthand way of describing relations between genuine moral agents.

Third, it seems wrong to suggest that simply because the primary motive of the employer is economic, considerations of loyalty are irrelevant. An employee's primary motive in working for an employer is generally economic, but no one on that account would argue that it is impossible for her to demonstrate loyalty to the employer, even if it turns out to be misplaced. All that is required is that her primary economic motive be in some degree qualified by considerations of the employer's welfare. Similarly, the fact that an employer's primary motive is economic does not imply that it is not qualified by considerations of the employee's welfare. Given the possibility of mutual qualification of admittedly primary economic motives, it is fallacious to argue that employee loyalty is never appropriate.

In contrast to Duska, the standard view is that loyalty to one's employer is appropriate. According to it, one has an obligation to be loyal to one's employer and, consequently, a *prima facie* duty to protect the employer's interests. Whistleblowing constitutes, therefore, a violation of duty to one's employer and needs strong justification if it is to be appropriate. Sissela Bok summarizes this view very well when she writes

> the whistleblower hopes to stop the game; but since he is neither referee nor coach, and since he blows the whistle on his own team, his act is seen as a violation of loyalty. In holding his position, he has assumed certain obligations to his colleagues and clients. He may even have subscribed to a loyalty oath or a promise of confidentiality. Loyalty to colleagues and to clients comes to be pitted against loyalty to the public interest, to those who may be injured unless the revelation is made.[5]

The strength of this view is that it recognizes that loyalty is due one's employer. Its weakness is that it tends to conceive of whistleblowing as involving a tragic moral choice, since blowing the whistle is seen not so much as a positive action, but rather the lesser of two evils. Bok again puts the essence of this view very clearly when she writes that "a would-be whistleblower must weigh his responsibility to serve the public interest *against* the responsibility he owes to his colleagues and the institution in which he works" and "that [when] their duty [to whistleblow] ... *so overrides loyalties to colleagues and institutions*, they [whistleblowers] often have reason to fear the results of carrying out such a duty."[6]

The employee, according to this understanding of whistleblowing, must choose between two acts of betrayal, either her employer or the public interest, each in itself reprehensible.

Behind this view lies the assumption that to be loyal to someone is to act in a way that accords with what that person believes to be in her best interests. To be loyal to an employer, therefore, is to act in a way which the employer deems to be in his or her best interests. Since employers very rarely approve of whistleblowing and generally feel that it is not in their best interests, it follows that whistleblowing is an act of betrayal on the part of the employee, albeit a betrayal made in the interests of the public good.

Plausible though it initially seems, I think this view of whistleblowing is mistaken and that it embodies a mistaken conception of what constitutes employee loyalty. It ignores the fact that

> the great majority of corporate whistleblowers... [consider] themselves to be very loyal employees who... [try] to use 'direct voice' (internal whistleblowing),... [are] rebuffed and punished for this, and then... [use] 'indirect voice' (external whistleblowing). They... [believe] initially that they... [are] behaving in a loyal manner, helping their employers by calling top management's attention to practices that could eventually get the firm in trouble.[7]

By ignoring the possibility that blowing the whistle may demonstrate greater loyalty than not blowing the whistle, it fails to do justice to the many instances where loyalty to someone constrains us to act in defiance of what that person believes to be in her best interests. I am not, for example, being disloyal to a friend if I refuse to loan her money for an investment I am sure will bring her financial ruin; even if she bitterly reproaches me for denying her what is so obviously a golden opportunity to make a fortune.

A more adequate definition of being loyal to someone is that loyalty involves acting in accordance with what one has good reason to believe to be in that person's best interests. A key question, of course, is what constitutes a good reason to think that something is in a person's best interests. Very often, but by no means invariably, we accept that a person thinking that something is in her best interests is a sufficiently good reason to think that it actually is. Other times, especially when we feel that she is being rash, foolish, or misinformed we are prepared, precisely by virtue of being loyal, to act contrary to the person's wishes. It is beyond the scope of this paper to investigate such cases in detail, but three general points can be made.

First, to the degree that an action is genuinely immoral, it is impossible that it is in the agent's best interests. We would not, for example, say that someone who sells child pornography was acting in his own best interests, even if he vigorously protested that there was nothing wrong with such activity. Loyalty does not imply that we have a duty to refrain from reporting the immoral actions of those to whom we are loyal. An employer who is acting immorally is not acting in her own best interests and an employee is not acting disloyally in blowing the whistle.[8] Indeed, the argument can be made that the employee who blows the whistle may be demonstrating greater loyalty than the employee who simply ignores the immoral conduct, inasmuch as she is attempting to prevent her employer from engaging in self-destructive behaviour.

Second, loyalty requires that, whenever possible, in trying to resolve a problem we deal directly with the person to whom we are loyal. If, for example, I am loyal to a friend I do not immediately involve a third party when I try to dissuade my friend from involvement in immoral actions. Rather, I approach my friend directly, listen to his perspective on the events in question, and provide an opportunity for him to address the problem in a morally satisfactory way. This implies that, whenever possible, a loyal employee blows the whistle internally. This provides the employer with the opportunity to either demonstrate to the employee that, contrary to first appearances, no genuine wrongdoing had occurred, or, if there is a genuine moral problem, the opportunity to resolve it.

This principle of dealing directly with the person to whom loyalty is due needs to be qualified, however. Loyalty to a person requires that one acts in that person's best interests. Generally, this cannot be done without directly involving the person to whom one is loyal in the decision-making process, but there may arise cases where acting in a person's best interests requires that one act independently and perhaps even against the wishes of the person to whom one is loyal. Such cases will be especially apt to arise when the person to whom one is loyal is either immoral or ignoring the moral consequences of his actions. Thus, for example, loyalty to a friend who deals in hard narcotics would not imply that I speak first to my friend about my decision to inform the police of his activities, if the only effect of my doing so would be to make him more careful in his criminal dealings. Similarly, a loyal employee is under no obligation to speak first to an employer about the employer's immoral actions, if the only response of the employer will be to take care to cover up wrongdoing.

Neither is a loyal employee under obligation to speak first to an employer if it is clear that by doing so she placed herself in jeopardy from an employer who will retaliate if given the opportunity. Loyalty amounts to acting in another's best interests and that may mean qualifying what seems to be in one's own interests, but it cannot imply that one take no steps to protect oneself from the immorality of those to whom one is loyal. The reason it cannot is that, as has already been argued, acting immorally can never really be in a person's best interests. It follows, therefore, that one is not acting in a person's best interests if one allows oneself to be treated immorally by that person. Thus, for example, a father might be loyal to a child even though the child is guilty of stealing from him, but this would not mean that the father should let the child continue to steal. Similarly, an employee may be loyal to an employer even though she takes steps to protect herself against unfair retaliation by the employer, e.g., by blowing the whistle externally.

Third, loyalty requires that one is concerned with more than considerations of justice. I have been arguing that loyalty cannot require one to ignore immoral or unjust behaviour on the part of those to whom one is loyal, since loyalty amounts to acting in a person's best interests and it can never be in a person's best interests to be allowed to act immorally. Loyalty, however, goes beyond considerations of justice in that, while it is possible to be disinterested and just, it is not possible to be disinterested and loyal. Loyalty implies a desire that the person to whom one is loyal take no moral stumbles, but that if moral stumbles have occurred that the person be restored and not simply punished. A loyal friend is not only someone who sticks by you in times of trouble, but someone who tries to help you avoid trouble. This suggests that a loyal employee will have a desire to point out problems and potential problems long before the drastic measures associated with whistleblowing become necessary, but that if whistleblowing does become necessary there remains a desire to help the employer.

In conclusion, although much more could be said on the subject of loyalty, our brief discussion has enabled us to clarify considerably the relation between whistleblowing and employee loyalty. It permits us to steer a course between the Scylla of Duska's view that, since the primary link between employer and employee is economic, the ideal of employee loyalty is an oxymoron, and the Charybdis of the standard view that, since it forces an employee to weigh conflicting duties, whistleblowing inevitably involves some degree of moral tragedy. The solution lies in realizing that to whistleblow for reasons of morality is to act in one's employer's best interests and involves, therefore, no disloyalty.

NOTES

1. The definition I have proposed applies most directly to the relation between privately owned companies aiming to realize a profit and their employees. Obviously, issues of whistleblowing arise in other contexts, e.g., governmental organizations or charitable agencies, and deserve careful thought. I do not propose, in this paper, to discuss whistleblowing in these other contexts, but I think my development of the concept of whistleblowing as positive demonstration of loyalty can easily be applied and will prove useful.

2. Duska, R.: 1985, 'Whistleblowing and Employee Loyalty', in J. R. Desjardins and J. J. McCall, eds., *Contemporary Issues in Business Ethics* (Wadsworth, Belmont, California), pp. 295–300.

3. Duska, p. 297.

4. Duska, p. 298.

5. Bok, S.: 1983, 'Whistleblowing and Professional Responsibility', in T. L. Beauchamp and N. E. Bowie, eds., *Ethical Theory and Business*, 2nd ed. (Prentice-Hall Inc., Englewood Cliffs, New Jersey), pp. 261–269, p. 263.

6. Bok, pp. 261–2, emphasis added.

7. Near, J. P. and P. Miceli: 1985, 'Organizational Dissidence: The Case of Whistle-Blowing', *Journal of Business Ethics* 4, pp. 1–16, p. 10.

8. As Near and Miceli note 'The whistle-blower may provide valuable information helpful in improving organizational effectiveness… the prevalence of illegal activity in organizations is associated with declining organizational performance' (p. 1).

The general point is that the structure of the world is such that it is not in a company's long-term interests to act immorally. Sooner or later a company which flouts morality and legality will suffer.

POSTSCRIPT

Does Blowing the Whistle Violate Company Loyalty?

Whistle-blowing is a difficult choice. What would you do when faced with such a choice? The corporation is not the only setting for whistle-blowers. Would you report a friend for drug abuse, cheating on exams, or stealing? How do you weigh the possibility of damage done to the community against the security of your own career (some damage done to many people versus much damage done to a few people)? If you see only painful consequences if you blow the whistle, does that settle the problem—or does simple justice and fidelity to law have a claim of its own, as A. Ernest Fitzgerald has argued?

Should we, as a society, protect the whistle-blower with legislation designed to discourage corporate retaliation? Richard T. DeGeorge and Alan F. Westin, two of the earliest business ethics writers to take whistle-blowing seriously, agree that companies should adopt policies that preclude the need for employees to blow the whistle. "The need for moral heroes," DeGeorge concludes in *Business Ethics*, 2d ed. (Macmillan, 1986), "shows a defective society and defective corporations. It is more important to change the legal and corporate structures that make whistle blowing necessary than to convince people to be moral heroes." In *Whistle Blowing: Loyalty and Dissent in the Corporation* (McGraw-Hill, 1981), Westin writes, "The single most important element in creating a meaningful internal system to deal with whistle blowing is to have top leadership accept this as a management priority. This means that the chief operating officer and his senior colleagues have to believe that a policy which encourages discussion and dissent, and deals fairly with whistle-blowing claims, is a good and important thing for their company to adopt.... They have to see it, in their own terms, as a moral duty of good private enterprise."

SUGGESTED READINGS

Rosemary Chalk, "Doing Right and Wrongdoing," *Technology Review* (February/March 1993).

Natalie Kandekar, "Contrasting Consequences: Bringing Charges of Sexual Harassment Compared With Other Cases of Whistleblowing," *Journal of Business Ethics* (vol. 9, no. 2, 1990).

Marcia P. Miceli, Janet P. Near, and Charles R. Schwenk, "Who Blows the Whistle and Why?" *Industrial and Labor Relations Review* (October 1991).

Kenneth Silverstein, "Proposed Whistle-Blowing Law Puts Corporations on Notice," *Corporate Cashflow* (December 1992).

ISSUE 9

Should Concern for Drug Abuse Overrule Concerns for Employee Privacy?

YES: Michael A. Verespej, from "Drug Users—Not Testing—Anger Workers," *Industry Week* (February 17, 1992)

NO: Jennifer Moore, from "Drug Testing and Corporate Responsibility: The 'Ought Implies Can' Argument," *Journal of Business Ethics* (vol. 8, 1989)

ISSUE SUMMARY

YES: Michael A. Verespej, a writer for *Industry Week*, argues that workers are the hardest hit when their coworkers use drugs and suggests that, for this reason, a majority of employees are tolerant of drug testing.

NO: Jennifer Moore, a researcher of business ethics and business law, asserts that a right is a right and that any utilitarian concerns that employers can cite to justify drug testing should not override the right of the employee to dignity and privacy on the job.

In 1928, U.S. Supreme Court justice Louis Brandeis defined the right of privacy as "the right to be let alone, the most comprehensive of rights and the right most valued by civilized men." The constitutional origins of that right are hazy, found variously in the Fourth Amendment (prohibiting illegal searches and seizures), the Fifth Amendment (prohibiting compulsory testimony), and parts of the Ninth Amendment. But the U.S. Constitution only limits *government* action, and worried Americans increasingly find that their employers can be a more dangerous threat to their privacy.

What right does an employee have to be "let alone" by his or her employer? Historically, none at all. Dictatorial employers had no qualms about making and enforcing rules governing not only job performance but dress and personal behavior on the job as well. Many also had rules for off-the-job behavior. School boards, for example, routinely enforced rules that required teachers to abstain from smoking and drinking, to attend church regularly, and to limit courting to one day a week. But with the advent of organized labor, the freedom of the employer to dictate the employee's lifestyle off the job almost disappeared. On-the-job requirements also ceased to be absolute. Although certain obvious safety rules could be enforced (such as prohibiting alcohol on the job and requiring that safety equipment be worn), the presumption was that rules should not be extended beyond necessity. Until very recently, we had seemed to be approaching an understanding that the employee's choices of amusements and associations off the job were sacrosanct and that his or her personal style of dress and grooming on the job could be regulated only to the extent that such appearances were reasonably job-related.

Then came drugs. Unlike alcohol, drugs can be easily concealed in one's clothing and cannot be detected on a person's breath after they are consumed. Seasoned foremen who would have no trouble spotting the slurred speech and wobbly walk caused by alcohol may not be able to detect drug use in their employees. The effect of drug use on judgment and behavior, especially for such people as pilots, bus drivers, and military personnel, can and does cause deaths.

While many may agree that this fact alone justifies testing for on-the-job drug use, there are many factors that complicate the issue. First, the only tests currently available to determine drug use are seriously invasive (unlike the Breathalyzer test for alcohol, for instance). In practice, the tester must take a blood sample from the worker or require the worker to give up a urine sample. The blood test requires a needle stick that some find painful and terrifying, and the urination must be observed to ensure that the test is valid—at an imaginable cost in embarrassment to the worker and to the observer. Second, the tests cannot distinguish between drug-use behavior on the job and off the job. Marijuana smoked on a Friday night may show up in urine that is expelled on the following Tuesday. So the worker subjected to testing at random may find his off-the-job activities severely restricted by the tests. To be sure, no one is interested in condoning off-the-job drug use, but the move from on-the-job regulation to 24-hour regulation is an unintended consequence that raises further legal and ethical issues.

Third, the tests are not always accurate. Most employers have a policy that if an employee fails one drug test, he or she can take another in order to ensure accuracy. If the employee fails twice, he or she is out. But the tests are only, at best, 90 to 95 percent accurate. That means that 1 out of 10, or at best 1 out of 20, will yield a false positive (the employee will appear to have drugs in his or her system). One out of 100, or at best 1 out of 400, will yield a false positive upon retest of a false positive. But some firms have thousands of workers. Is it fair to impose a testing routine that commits gross injustice once in 100 cases—or even only once in 400 cases?

Ask yourself, as you read these selections, how society ought to balance the conflicting demands of privacy for the worker and safety for society. Given the doubts surrounding the practice, is routine randomized drug testing justified? On the other hand, given the terrible dangers that attend drug use on the job, can we afford to do without it?

YES

Michael A. Verespej

DRUG USERS—NOT TESTING—
ANGER WORKERS

Drug testing by companies still elicits an emotional response from employees. But it's a far different one from four years ago.

Back then, readers responding to an IW [*Industry Week*] survey angrily protested workplace drug testing as an invasion of privacy and argued that drug testing should be reserved for occasions in which there was suspicion of drug use or in an accident investigation.

Today's prevailing view, based on a recent IW survey covering essentially the same questions, stands as a stark contrast. Not only do fewer employees see drug testing as an invasion of privacy, but a significantly higher percentage think that companies should extend the scope of drug testing to improve safety and productivity in the workplace.

Why aren't employees as leery of workplace drug testing as they were four years ago?

First, both the numbers and the comments suggest that employees and managers are less worried that inaccurate drug tests will brand them as drug users. Just 19.3% of those surveyed say that they consider drug testing an invasion of privacy, compared with 30% in the earlier survey.

Second, the tight job market appears to have made non-drug-users resent the presence of drug users in the workplace. Third, in contrast to four years ago, employees and managers are more concerned about the potential safety problems that drug users cause them than whatever invasion of privacy might result from a drug test. The net result: Unlike four years ago, employee thinking is now in sync with the viewpoints held for some time by top corporate management. "Job safety and performance are more important than the slight invasion of privacy caused by drug testing," asserts Lee Taylor, plant manager at U.S. Gypsum Co.'s Siguard, Utah, facility. "Freedom and privacy end when others are likely to be injured," adds the president of a high-tech business in Fort Collins, Colo.

G. A. Holland, chief estimator for a Bloomfield, Conn., construction firm, agrees: "Drug testing may be an invasion of privacy, but, because drug use puts others in danger, [drug testing] is an acceptable practice. The safety of employees overrides the right to privacy of another." Adds D. S. McRoberts, manager of a Green Giant food-processing plant in Buhl, Idaho: "The risks employees put themselves and their peers under when they use drugs justify testing."

Perhaps the most blunt response comes from Louis Krivanek, a consulting engineer with Omega Induction Services, Warren, Mich.: "I certainly wouldn't ride with a drinking alcoholic. Why should I work with a drug addict not under control?"

And the anti-drug-user attitude is not just a safety issue, either. "Drug users are also a financial risk to the employer," declares John Larkin, president of Overland Computer, Omaha, Nebr. "It's time to begin thinking about the health and welfare of the company," says William Pence, vice president and general manager of Kantronics Inc., Lawrence, Kans. "Drug testing is simply a preventive measure to ensure the future stability of a company."

The competitive factor also appears to be influencing workers' viewpoints. "A drug-free environment must exist if the quality of product and process is to be continuously improved," writes one employee.

"Productivity and company survival are too important to trust to an employee with a drug problem," says Jack VerMeulen, director of quality assurance at C-Line Products, Des Plaines, Ill. "Employees are a company's most valuable assets, and those assets must perform at the peak of their ability. Test them." One could argue that workers—and managers—have simply become conditioned to drug testing in the workplace because it is no longer the exception, but the rule. After all, 56% of the managers responding to the survey—twice as many

as four years ago—say their companies have drug-testing programs in place.

But the real reason for the change in opinion appears to be that four years of day-in, day-out experience with workplace drug problems have made managers and employees less tolerant of users. The attitude appears to be: Drug users are criminals and shouldn't be protected by the absence of a drug-testing program.

"Users are, by definition, criminals," declares Nick Benson, senior automation engineer at Babcock & Wilcox, Lynchburg, Va. "Drug users are breaking the law," states Naomi Walter, a data-processing specialist at Gemini Marketing Associates, Carthage, Mo. "So why let them get an advantage?"

Layoffs and plant and store closings are also behind the new lack of tolerance for the drug user. "I believe that if a company is paying a person to work for them," says one IW reader, "that person should be drug-free. A job is a privilege, not a right."

* * *

That lack of tolerance is reflected in significantly changed ideas of who in the workplace should be tested for drug use. A significantly higher percentage of respondents think that more workers should be tested at random or that *all* employees should be tested.

More than 45% of IW readers—compared with 29.6% four years ago—say that drug tests should be conducted at random. And 70.5% think all employees should be required to take drug tests. Only 60% felt that way in the last IW drug-testing survey. Not surprisingly, then, the percentage of readers who would take a drug test and who think that employers should be able to test employees for drug use is now 93%; it was 88% four years ago.

But several attitudes haven't changed. Workers and managers still think that when companies use drug testing, they should be required to offer rehabilitation through employee-assistance programs, that management should be tested as well as employees, and that alcohol problems are equally troublesome. "Employers should be prepared to help—not just fire someone if the drug or alcohol abuse is exposed," says H. A. Dellicker, programming manager at Siemens Nixdorf, Burlington, Mass. "You need a properly monitored rehabilitation program."

Readers are just as adamant that if the majority of employees is to be tested, then everyone should be included—all the way up to the CEO. "Drug testing should be conducted on all employees, from top management down to the lowest position," asserts Sharon Hyitt, a drafting technician at Varco Pruden Buildings, Van Wert, Ohio. And IW readers contend that any drug-testing program should test for alcohol abuse as well. "Drug testing stops short," argues a reader in Muncie, Ind. "Alcoholism is more widespread in our workplace and just as destructive."

A plant superintendent in Ohio agrees and laments, "Alcohol is the most abused drug in our workplace, but it is not covered under our testing program. While the 'heavy' drugs get the spotlight because of the violence associated with their distribution, alcohol does the most damage in the workplace."

A product-testing engineer agrees, "Alcohol should be included in the tests and then perhaps lunch-time drinking would decrease. Why is it O.K. for those who have three-martini lunches to come back to work and try to function?"

NO

Jennifer Moore

DRUG TESTING AND CORPORATE RESPONSIBILITY: THE "OUGHT IMPLIES CAN" ARGUMENT

In the past few years, testing for drug use in the workplace has become an important and controversial trend. Approximately 30% of Fortune 500 companies now engage in some sort of drug testing or screening, as do many smaller firms. The Reagan administration has called for mandatory testing of all federal employees. Several states have already passed drug testing laws; others will probably consider them in the future. While the Supreme Court has announced its intention to rule on the testing of federal employees within the next few months, its decision will not settle the permissibility of testing private employees. Discussion of the issue is likely to remain lively and heated for some time.

Most of the debate about drug testing in the workplace has focused on the issue of privacy rights. Three key questions have been: Do employees have privacy rights? If so, how far do these extend? What kinds of considerations outweigh these rights? I believe there are good reasons for supposing that employees do have moral privacy rights,[1] and that drug testing usually (though not always) violates these, but privacy is not my main concern in this paper. I wish to examine a different kind of argument, the claim that because corporations are responsible for harms committed by employees while under the influence of drugs, they are entitled to test for drug use.

This argument is rarely stated formally in the literature, but it can be found informally quite often.[2] One of its chief advantages is that it seems, at least at first glance, to bypass the issue of privacy rights altogether. There seems to be no need to determine the extent or weight of employees' privacy rights to make the argument work. It turns on a different set of principles altogether, that is, on the meaning and conditions of responsibility. This is an important asset, since arguments about rights are notoriously difficult to settle. Rights claims frequently function in ethical discourse as conversation-stoppers or non-negotiable demands.[3] Although it is widely recognized that rights are not absolute, there is little consensus on how far they extend, what kinds of considerations should be allowed to override them, or even how to go

From Jennifer Moore, "Drug Testing and Corporate Responsibility: The 'Ought Implies Can' Argument," *Journal of Business Ethics*, vol. 8 (1989), pp. 279–287. Copyright © 1989 by D. Reidel Publishing Co., Dordrecht, Holland, and Boston, U.S.A. Reprinted by permission of Kluwer Academic Publishers.

about settling these questions. But it is precisely these thorny problems that proponents of drug testing must tackle if they wish to address the issue on privacy grounds. Faced with the claim that drug testing violates the moral right to privacy of employees, proponents of testing must either (1) argue that drug testing does not really violate the privacy rights of employees;[4] (2) acknowledge that drug testing violates privacy rights, but argue that there are considerations that override those rights, such as public safety; or (3) argue that employees have no moral right to privacy at all.[5] It is not surprising that an argument that seems to move the debate out of the arena of privacy rights entirely appears attractive.

In spite of its initial appeal, however, I will maintain that the argument does not succeed in circumventing the claims of privacy rights. Even responsibility for the actions of others, I will argue, does not entitle us to do absolutely anything to control their behavior. We must look to rights, among other things, to determine what sorts of controls are morally permissible. Once this is acknowledged, the argument loses much of its force. In addition, it requires unjustified assumptions about the connection between drug testing and the prevention of drug-related harm

AN "OUGHT IMPLIES CAN" ARGUMENT

Before we can assess the argument, it must be set out more fully. It seems to turn on the deep-rooted philosophical connection between responsibility and control. Generally, we believe that agents are not responsible[6] for acts or events that they could not have prevented. People are responsible for their actions

only if, it is often said, they "could have done otherwise". Responsibility implies some measure of control, freedom, or autonomy. It is for this reason that we do not hold the insane responsible for their actions. Showing that a person lacked the capacity to do otherwise blocks the normal moves of praise or blame and absolves the agent of responsibility for a given act.

For similar reasons, we believe that persons cannot be obligated to do things that they are incapable of doing, and that if they fail to do such things, no blame attaches to them. Obligation is empty, even senseless, without capability. If a person is obligated to perform an action, it must be within his or her power. This principle is sometimes summed up by the phrase "ought implies can". Kant used it as part of a metaphysical argument for free will, claiming that if persons are to have obligations at all, they must be autonomous, capable of acting freely.[7] The argument we examine here is narrower in scope, but similar in principle. If corporations are responsible for harms caused by employees under the influence of drugs, they must have the ability to prevent these harms. They must, therefore, have the freedom to test for drug use

But the argument is still quite vague. What exactly does it mean to say that corporations are "responsible" for harms caused by employees? There are several possible meanings of "responsible". Not all of these are attributable to corporations, and not all of them exemplify the principle that "ought implies can". The question of how or whether corporations are "responsible" is highly complex, and we cannot begin to answer it in this paper.[8] There are, however, four distinct senses of "responsible" that appear with some regularity in the argument. They can be characterized, roughly, as follows: (a) legally liable; (b) culpable or guilty; (c) answerable or accountable; (d) bound by an obligation. The first is purely legal; the last three have a moral dimension.

Legal Liability

We do hold corporations legally liable for the negligent acts of employees under the doctrine of *respondeat superior* ("let the master respond"). If an employee harms a third party in the course of performing his or her duties for the firm, it is the corporation which must compensate the third party. *Respondeat superior* is an example of what is frequently called "vicarious liability". Since the employee was acting on behalf of the firm, and the firm was acting through the employee when the harmful act was committed, liability is said to "transfer" from the employee to the firm. But it is not clear that such liability on the part of the employer implies a capacity to have prevented the harm. Corporations are held liable for accidents caused by an employee's negligent driving, for example, even if they could not have foreseen or prevented the injury. While some employee accidents can be traced to corporate negligence,[9] there need be no fault on the part of the corporation for the doctrine of *respondeat superior* to apply. The doctrine of *respondeat superior* is grounded not in fault, but in concerns of public policy and utility. It is one of several applications of the notion of liability without fault in legal use today.

Because it does not imply fault, and its attendant ability to have done otherwise, legal liability or responsibility **a** cannot be used successfully as part of an "ought implies can" argument. Holding corporations legally liable for harms committed

by intoxicated employees while at the same time forbidding drug-testing is not inconsistent. It could simply be viewed as yet another instance of liability without fault. Of course, one could argue that the notion of liability without fault is itself morally unacceptable, and that liability ought not to be detached from moral notions of punishment and blame. This is surely an extremely important claim, but it is beyond the scope of this paper. The main point to be made here is that we must be able to attribute more than legal liability to corporations if we are to invoke the principle of "ought implies can". Corporations must be responsible in sense **b, c,** or **d**—that is, *morally responsible*—if the argument is to work.

Moral Responsibility

Are corporations morally responsible for harms committed by intoxicated employees? Perhaps the most frequently used notion of moral responsibility is sense **b**, what I have called "guilt" or "culpability".[10] I have in mind here the strongest notion of moral responsibility, the sense that is prevalent in criminal law. An agent is responsible for an act in this sense if the act can be imputed to him or her. An essential condition of imputability is the presence in the agent of an intention to commit the act, or *mens rea*.[11] But does an employer whose workers use drugs satisfy the *mens rea* requirement? The requirement probably would be satisfied if it could be shown that the firm intended the resulting harms, ordered its employees to work under the influence of drugs, or even, perhaps (though this is less clear) turned a blind eye to blatant drug abuse in the workplace.[12] But these are all quite farfetched possibilities. It is reasonable to assume that most corporations do not intend the harms caused by their employees, and that they do not order employees to use drugs on the job. Drug use is quite likely to be prohibited by company policy. If corporations are morally responsible for drug-related harms committed [by] employees, then, it is not in sense **b.**

Corporations might, however, be morally responsible for harms committed by employees in another sense. An organization acts through its employees. It empowers its employees to act in ways in which they otherwise would not act by providing them with money, power, equipment, and authority. Through a series of agreements, the corporation delegates its employees to act on its behalf. For these reasons, one could argue that corporations are responsible, in the sense of "answerable" or "accountable" (responsibility **c**), for the harmful acts of their employees. Indeed, it could be argued that if corporations are not morally responsible for these acts, they are not morally responsible for any acts at all, since corporations can only act through their employees.[13] To say that corporations are responsible for the harms of their employees in sense **c** is to say more than just that a corporation must "pay up" if an employee causes harm. It is to assign fault to the corporation by virtue of the ways in which organizational policies and structures facilitate and direct employees' actions.[14]

Moreover, corporations presumably have the same obligations as other agents to avoid harm in the conduct of their business. Since they conduct their business through their employees, it could plausibly be argued that corporations have an obligation to anticipate and prevent harms that employees might cause in the course of their employment. If this reasoning is correct, corporations are morally responsible for the drug-related harms of employees in sense **d**—that is, they are under an obligation to prevent those harms. The "ought implies can" argument, then, may be formulated as follows:

1. If corporations have obligations, they must be capable of carrying them out, on the principle of "ought implies can".

2. Corporations have an obligation to prevent harm from occurring in the course of conducting their business

3. Drug use by employees is likely to lead to harm.

4. Corporations must be able to take steps to eliminate (or at least reduce) drug use by employees.

5. Drug testing is an effective way to eliminate/reduce employee drug use.

6. Therefore corporations must be permitted to test for drugs.[15]

THE LIMITS OF CORPORATE AUTONOMY

This is surely an important argument, one that deserves to be taken seriously. The premise that corporations have an obligation to prevent harm from occurring in the conduct of their business seems unexceptionable and consistent with the actual moral beliefs of society. There is not much question that drug use by employees, especially regular drug use or drug use on the job, leads to harms of various kinds. Some of these are less serious than others, but some are very serious indeed: physical injury to consumers, the public, and fellow employees—and sometimes even death.[16]

Moreover, our convictions about the connections between responsibility or obligation and capability seem unassailable. Like other agents, if corporations are to have obligations, they must have the ability to carry them out. The argument seems to tell us that corporations are only able to carry out their obligations to prevent harm if they can free themselves of drugs. To prevent corporations from drug testing, it implies, is to prevent them from discharging their obligations. It is to cripple corporate autonomy just as we would cripple the autonomy of an individual worker if we refused to allow him to "kick the habit" that prevented him from giving satisfactory job performance.

But this analogy between corporate and individual autonomy reveals the initial defect in the argument. Unlike human beings, corporations are never fully autonomous selves. On the contrary, their actions are always dependent upon individual selves who are autonomous. Human autonomy means self-determination, self-governance, self-control. Corporate autonomy, at least as it is understood here, means control over others. Corporate autonomy is essentially derivative. But this means that corporate acts are not the simple sorts of acts generated by individual persons. They are complex. Most importantly, the members of a corporation are frequently not the agents, but the objects, of "corporate" action. A good deal of corporate action, that is, necessitates doing something not only *through* corporate employees, but *to* those employees.[17] The act of eliminating drugs from the workplace is an act of this sort. A corporation's ridding itself of drugs is not like an individual person's "kicking the habit". Rather, it is one group of persons making another group of persons give up drug use.

This fact has important implications for the "ought implies can" argument. The argument is persuasive in situations in which carrying out one's obligations requires only *self*-control, and does not involve controlling the behavior of others. Presumably there are no restrictions on what one may do to oneself in order to carry out an obligation.[18] But a corporation is not a genuine "self", and there *are* moral limits on what one person may do to another. Because this is so, we cannot automatically assume that the obligation to prevent harm justifies employee drug testing. Of course this does not necessarily mean that drug testing is *unjustified*. But it does mean that before we can determine whether it is justified, we must ask what is permissible for one person or group of persons to do to another to prevent a harm for which they are responsible.

Are there any analogies available that might help to resolve this question? It is becoming increasingly common to hold a hostess responsible (both legally and morally) for harm caused by a drunken guest on the way home from her party. In part, this is because she contributes to the harm by serving her guest alcohol. It is also because she knows that drunk driving is risky, and has a general obligation to prevent harm. What must she be allowed to do to prevent harms of this kind? Persuade the guest to spend the night on the couch? Surely. Take her car keys away from her? Perhaps. Knock her out and lock her in the bathroom until morning? Surely not.

Universities are occasionally held legally and morally responsible for harms committed by members of fraternities—destruction of property, gang rapes, and injuries or death caused by hazing. What may they do to prevent such harms? They may certainly withdraw institutional recognition and support from the fraternity, refusing to let it operate on the campus. But may they expel students who live together off-campus in fraternity-like arrangements? Have university security guards police these houses, covertly or by force? These questions are more difficult to answer.

We sometimes hold landlords morally (though not legally) responsible for tenants who are slovenly, play loud music, or otherwise make nuisances of themselves. Landlords are surely permitted to cancel the leases of such tenants, and they are justified in asking for references from previous landlords to prevent future problems of this kind. But it is not clear that a landlord may delve into a tenant's private life, search his room, or tap his telephone in order to anticipate trouble before it begins.

Each of these situations is one in which one person or group of persons is responsible, to a greater or a lesser degree, for the prevention of harm by others, and needs some measure of control in order to carry out this responsibility.[19] In each case, there is a fairly wide range of actions which we would be willing to allow the first party, but there are some actions which we would rule out. Having an obligation to prevent the harms of others seems to permit us some forms of control, but not all. At least one important consideration in deciding what kinds of actions are permissible is the *rights* of the controlled parties.[20] If these claims are correct, we must examine the rights of employees in order to determine whether drug testing is justified. The relevant right in the case of drug testing is the right to privacy. The "ought implies can" argument, then, does not circumvent the claims of privacy rights as it originally seemed to do.

THE AGENCY ARGUMENT

A proponent of drug testing might argue, however, that the relation between employers and employees is significantly different from the relation between hosts and guests, universities and members of fraternities, or landlords and tenants. Employees have a special relation with the firm that employs them. They are *agents*, hired and empowered to act on behalf of the employer. While they act on the business of the firm, it might be argued, they "are" the corporation. The restrictions that apply to what one independent agent may do to another thus do not apply here.

But surely this argument is incorrect, for a number of reasons. First, if it were correct, it would justify anything a corporation might do to control the behavior of an employee—not merely drug testing, but polygraph testing, tapping of telephones, deception, psychological manipulation, whips and chains, etc.[21] There are undoubtedly some people who would argue that some of these procedures are permissible, but few would argue that all of them are. The fact that even some of them appear not to be suggests that we believe there are limits to what corporations may do to control employees, and that one consideration in determining these limits is the employees' rights.

Secondly, the argument implies that employees give up their own autonomy completely when they sign on as agents, and become an organ or piece of the corporation. But this cannot be true. Agency is a moral and contractual relationship of the kind that can only obtain between two independent, autonomous parties. This relationship could not be sustained if the employee ceased to be autonomous upon signing the contract. Employees are not slaves, but autonomous agents capable of upholding a contract. Moreover, we expect a certain amount of discretion in employees in the course of their agency. Employees are not expected to follow illegal or immoral commands of their employers, and we find them morally and legally blameworthy when they do so. That we expect such independent judgment of them suggests that they do not lose their autonomy entirely.[22]

Finally, if the employment contract were one in which employees gave up all right to be treated as autonomous human beings, then it would not be a legitimate or morally valid contract. Some rights are considered "inalienable"—people are forbidden from negotiating them away even if it seems advantageous to them to do so. The law grants recognition to this fact through anti-discrimination statutes, minimum wage legislation, workplace health and safety standards, etc. Even if I would like to, I may not trade away, for example, my right not to be sexually harassed or my right to know about workplace hazards.

Again, these arguments do not show that drug testing is unjustified. They do show, however, that *if* drug testing is justified, it is not because the "ought implies can" argument bypasses the issue of employee rights, but because drug testing does not impermissibly violate those rights.[23] To think that obligation, or responsibility for the acts of others, can circumvent rights claims is to misunderstand the import of the "ought implies can" principle. The principle tells us that there is a close connection between obligation or responsibility and capability. But it does not license us to disregard the rights of others any more than it guarantees us the physical conditions

that make carrying out our obligations possible. It may well prove that employees' right to privacy, assuming they have such a right, is secondary to some more weighty consideration. I take up this question briefly below. What has been shown here is that the issue of the permissibility of drug testing will not and cannot be settled *without* a close scrutiny of privacy rights. If we are to decide the issue, we must eventually determine whether employees have privacy rights, how far they extend, and what considerations outweigh them—precisely the difficult questions the "ought implies can" argument sought to avoid.

IS DRUG TESTING NECESSARY?

The "ought implies can" argument also has another serious flaw. The argument turns on the claim that forbidding drug testing prevents corporations from carrying out their obligation to prevent harm. But this is only true if drug testing is *necessary* for preventing drug-related harm. If it is merely one option among many, the forbidding drug testing still leaves a corporation free to prevent harm in other ways. For the argument to be sound, in other words, premise 5 would have to be altered to read, "drug testing is a necessary element in any plan to rid the workplace of drugs."

But it is not at all clear that drug testing *is* necessary to reduce drug use in the workplace. Its necessity has been challenged repeatedly. In a recent article in the *Harvard Business Review,* for example, James Wrich draws on his experience in dealing with alcoholism in the workplace and suggests the use of broadbrush educational and rehabilitative programs as alternatives to testing. Corporations using such programs to combat alcohol problems, Wrich reports, have achieved tremendous reductions in absenteeism, sick leave, and on-the-job accidents.[24] Others have argued that impaired performance likely to result in harm could be easily detected by various sorts of performance-oriented tests—mental and physical dexterity tests, alertness tests, flight simulation tests, and so on. These sorts of procedures have the advantage of not being controversial from a rights perspective.[25]

Indeed, many thinkers have argued that drug testing is not only unnecessary, but is not even an effective way to attack drug use in the workplace. The commonly used and affordable urinalysis tests are notoriously unreliable. They have a very high rate both of false negatives and of false positives. At best the tests reveal, not impaired performance or even the presence of a particular drug, but the presence of metabolites of various drugs that can remain in the system long after any effects of the drug have worn off.[26] Because they do not measure impairment, such tests do not seem well-tailored to the purpose of preventing harm—which, after all, is the ultimate goal. As Lewis Maltby, vice president of a small instrumentation company and an opponent of drug testing, puts it,

... [T]he fundamental flaw with drug testing is that it tests for the wrong thing. A realistic program to detect workers whose condition put the company or other people at risk would test for the condition that actually creates the danger.[27]

If these claims are true, there is no real connection between the obligation to prevent harm and the practice of drug testing, and the "ought implies can" argument provides no justification for drug testing at all.[28]

CONCLUSION

I have made no attempt here to determine whether drug testing does indeed violate employees' privacy rights. The analysis ... above suggests that we have reason to believe that employees have some rights. Once we accept the notion of employee rights in general, it seems likely that a right to privacy would be among them, since it is an important civil right and central for the protection of individual autonomy. There are also reasons, I believe, to think that most drug testing violates the right to privacy. These claims need much more defense than they can be given here, and even if they are true, this does not necessarily mean that drug testing is unjustified. It does, however, create a *prima facie* case against drug testing. If drug testing violates the privacy rights of employees, it will be justified only under very strict conditions, if it is justified at all. It is worth taking a moment to see why this is so.

It is generally accepted in both the ethical and legal spheres that rights are not absolute. But we allow basic rights to be overridden only in special cases in which some urgent and fundamental good is at stake. In legal discourse, such goods are called "compelling interests".[29] While there is room for some debate about what counts as a "compelling interest", it is almost always understood to be more than a merely private interest, however weighty. Public safety might well fall into this category, but private monetary loss probably would not. While more needs to be done to determine what kinds of interests justify drug testing, it seems clear that if testing does violate the basic rights of employees, it is only justified in extreme cases—far less often than it is presently used. Moreover, we believe that overriding a right is to be avoided wherever possible, and is only justified when doing so is *necessary* to serve the "compelling interest" in question. If it violates rights, then drug testing is only permissible if it is necessary for the protection of an interest such as public safety and if there is no other, morally preferable, way of accomplishing the same goal. As we have seen above, however, it is by no means clear that drug testing meets these conditions. There may be better, less controversial ways to prevent the harm caused by drug use; if so, these must be used in preference to drug testing, and testing is unjustified. And if the attacks on the effectiveness of drug testing are correct, testing is not only unnecessary for the protection of public safety, but does not serve any "compelling interest" at all.

What do these conclusions tell us about the responsibility of employers for preventing harms caused by employees? If it is decided that drug testing is morally impermissible, then there can be no duty to use it to anticipate and prevent harms. Corporations who fail to use it cannot be blamed for doing so. They cannot have a moral obligation to do something morally impermissible. Moreover, if it turns out that there is no other effective way to prevent the harms caused by drug use, then it seems to me we may not hold employers morally responsible for those harms. This seems to me unlikely to be the case—there probably are other effective measures to control drug abuse in the workplace. But corporations can be held responsible only to the extent that they are permitted to act. It would

not be inconsistent, however, to hold corporations legally liable for the harms caused by intoxicated employees under the doctrine of *respondeat superior*, even if drug testing is forbidden, for this kind of liability does not imply an ability to have done otherwise.

NOTES

1. Employees do not, of course, have legal privacy rights, although the courts seem to be moving slowly in this direction. Opponents of testing usually claim that employees have *moral* rights to privacy, even if these have not been given legal recognition. See, for example, Joseph Des Jardins and Ronald Duska, "Drug Testing in Employment", in *Business Ethics: Readings and Cases in Corporate Morality*, 2nd edition, ed. W. M. Hoffman and J. M. Moore (McGraw-Hill, forthcoming).

2. See, for example, "Work-Place Privacy Issues and Employer Screening Policies," Richard Lehr and David Middlebrooks, *Employee Relations Law Journal* 11, 407. Lehr and Middlebrooks cite the argument as one of the chief justifications for drug testing used by employers. I have also encountered the argument frequently in discussion with students, colleagues, and managers.

3. Ronald Dworkin has referred to rights as moral "trumps". This kind of language tends to suggest that rights overwhelm all other considerations, so that when they are flourished, all that opponents can do is subside in silence. Rights are frequently asserted this way in everyday discourse, and in this sense rights claims tend to close, rather than open, the door to fruitful ethical dialogue.

4. In his article "Privacy, Polygraphs, and Work," *Business and Professional Ethics Journal* 1, Fall, 1981, 19, George Brenkert has developed the idea that my privacy is violated when some one acquires information about me that they are not entitled, by virtue of their relationship to me, to have. My mortgage company, for example, is entitled to know my credit history; a prospective sexual partner is entitled to know if I have any sexually transmitted diseases. Thus their knowledge of this information does not violate my privacy. One could argue that employers are similarly entitled to the information obtained by drug tests, and that drug testing does not violate privacy for this reason. A somewhat different move would be to argue that testing does not violate privacy because employees give their "consent" to ... drug testing as part of the employment contract. For a sustained attack on these and other Type 1 arguments, see Joseph Des Jardins and Ronald Duska, "Drug Testing in Employment".

5. One might defend this position on the ground that the employer "owns" the job and is therefore entitled to place any conditions he wishes on obtaining or keeping it. The problem with this argument is that it seems to rule out *all* employee rights, including such basic ones as the right to organize and bargain collectively, or the right not to be discriminated against, which have solid legal as well as ethical grounding. It also implies that ownership overrides all other considerations, and it is not at all clear that this is true. One might take the position that by accepting a job, an employee has agreed to give up all his rights save those actually specified in the employment contract. But this makes the employment contract look like an agreement in which employees sell themselves and accept the status of things without rights. And it overlooks the fact that we believe there are some things ("inalienable" rights) that persons ought not to be permitted to bargain away. Alex Michalos has discussed some of the limitations of the employment contract in "The Loyal Agent's Argument", in *Ethical Theory and Business*, 2nd edition, ed. Tom L. Beauchamp and Norman E. Bowie (Englewood Cliffs, NJ: Prentice-Hall, 1983), p. 247.

6. The term "responsibility" is deliberately left ambiguous here. Several different meanings of it are examined below.

7. See Immanuel Kant, *Critique of Practical Reason*, trans. Lewis White Beck (Indianapolis: Bobbs-Merril, 1956), p. 30.

8. In this paper I have tried to avoid getting embroiled in the question of whether or not corporations are themselves "moral agents", which has been the question to dominate the corporate responsibility debate. The argument I offer here does, I believe, have important implications for the problem of corporate agency, but does not require me to take a stand on it here. I am content to have those who reject the notion of corporations as moral agents read my references to corporate responsibility as shorthand for some complex form of individual or group responsibility.

9. One example would be negligent hiring, which is an increasingly frequent cause of action against an employer. Employers can also be held negligent if they give orders that lead to harms that they ought to have foreseen. Domino's Pizza is now under suit because it encouraged its drivers to deliver pizzas as fast as possible, a policy that accident victims claim should have been expected to cause accidents.

10. This understanding of moral responsibility often seems to overshadow other notions. In an article on corporate responsibility, for example, Manuel Velasquez concludes that because corporations are not responsible in this sense, they are "not responsible for anything they do". "Why Corporations Are Not Responsible For Anything They Do", *Business and Professional Ethics Journal* 2, Spring, 1983, 1.

11. There is also an *actus reus* requirement for this type of responsibility—that is, the act must be traceable to the voluntary bodily movements of the agent. Obviously, corporations do not have bodies, but the people who work for them do. The question, then, has become when may we call an act by one member of the corporation a "corporate act". If it is possible to do so at all, the decisive feature is probably the presence of some sort of corporate "intention." This is why I focus on intention here, and why intention has been central to the discussion of corporate responsibility.

12. There are some, like Velasquez, who hold that a corporation can never satisfy the *mens rea* requirement because this would require a collective mind. If this were true, the argument would collapse at the outset. Others believe that a *mens rea* can be attributed to corporations metaphorically, if it can be shown that company policy includes an "intention" to harm, and it is this model I follow here.

13. There are, of course, those who take precisely this position. See Velasquez, "Why Corporations Are Not Responsible For Anything They Do".

14. See, for example, Peter French, *Collective and Corporate Responsibility* (New York: Columbia University Press, 1984).

15. It is tempting to conclude from this argument that drug testing is not only permissible, but obligatory, but this is not the case. The reason why it is not provides a clue to one of the major weaknesses of the argument. Drug testing would be obligatory only if it were *necessary* for the prevention of harm due to drug use, but it is not clear that this is so. But [it] also means that it is not clear that corporations are deflected from their duty to prevent harm by a prohibition against drug testing. See below for a fuller discussion of this problem.

16. For example, it has been claimed that employees who use drugs cause four times as many work-related accidents as do other employees. The highly publicized Conrail crash in 1987 was determined to be drug-related. Of course there are harms to the company itself as well, in the form of higher absenteeism, lowered productivity, higher insurance costs, etc. But since these types of harm raise the question of what a company may do to preserve its self-interest, rather than what it may do to prevent harms to others for which they are responsible, I focus here on harm to employees, consumers, and the public.

17. In our eagerness to assign "corporate responsibility", this fact has frequently been overlooked. This in turn has led, I believe, to an oversimplified view of corporate action. I discuss this problem more fully in a paper in progress entitled "The Paradox of Corporate Autonomy".

18. It is an interesting question whether there are limitations on what individuals can do to themselves to control their own behavior. What about

individuals who undergo hypnosis, or who have their jaws wired shut in order to lose weight? Are they violating their own rights? Undermining their own autonomy? It could be argued plausibly that these kinds of things are not permissible, on the Kantian ground that we have a duty not to treat ourselves as merely as means to an end. Of course, if there are such restrictions, it makes the "ought implies can" argument as applied to corporations even weaker.

19. None of these analogies is perfect. In the case of the hostess and guest, for example, the guest is clearly intoxicated. This is rarely true of employees who are tested for drugs; if the employee were visibly intoxicated, there would be no need to test. Moreover, in the hostess/guest case the hostess contributes directly to the intoxication. There are important parallels, however. In each case one party is held morally (and in two of the cases, legally) responsible for harms caused by others. Moreover, the first parties are responsible in close to the same way that employers are responsible for the acts of their employees: they in some sense "facilitate" the harmful acts, they have some capacity to prevent those acts, and they are thus viewed as having an obligation to prevent them. One main difference, of course, is that employees are "agents" of their employers....

20. There are other, utility-related considerations, as well—for example, harm to employees who are unjustly dismissed, a demoralized workforce, the costs of testing, etc. I concentrate here on rights because they have been the primary focal point in the drug testing debate.

21. The assumption here is that persons are entitled to do whatever they wish to themselves. See Note 18.

22. See Michalos, "The Loyal Agent's Argument".

23. Some violations of right, of course, are permissible....

24. James T. Wrich, "Beyond Testing: Coping with Drugs at Work", *Harvard Business Review* Jan.–Feb. 1988, 120.

25. See Des Jardins and Duska, "Drug Testing in Employment", and Lewis Maltby, "Why Drug Testing is a Bad Idea", *Inc.* June 1987. While other sorts of tests also have the potential to be abused, they are at least a direct measurement of something that an employer is entitled to know—performance capability. Des Jardins and Duska offer an extended defense of this sort of test.

26. See Edward J. Imwinkelreid, "False Positive", *The Sciences*, Sept.–Oct. 1987, 22. Also David Bearman, "The Medical Case Against Drug Testing", *Harvard Business Review* Jan.–Feb. 1988, 123.

27. Maltby, "Why Drug Testing is a Bad Idea", pp. 152–153.

28. It could still be argued that drug testing *deters* drug use, and thus has a connection with preventing harm, even though it doesn't directly provide any information that enables companies to prevent harm. This is an important point, but it is still subject to the restrictions discussed in the previous section. Not everything that has a deterrent value is permissible. It is possible that a penalty of capital punishment would provide a deterrent for rapists, or having one's hand removed deter shoplifting, but there are very few advocates for these penalties. Effectiveness is not the only issue here; rights and justice are also relevant.

29. The principle that fundamental rights may not be overridden by the state unless doing so is necessary to serve a "compelling state interest" is a principle of constitutional law, but it also reflects our moral intuitions about when it is appropriate to override rights. The legal principle would not apply to all cases of drug testing in the workplace because many of these involve private, rather than state, employees. But the principle does provide us with useful guidelines in the ethical sphere. Interestingly, Federal District Judge George Revercomb recently issued an injunction blocking the random drug testing of Justice Department employees on the ground that it did not serve a compelling state interest. Since there was no evidence of a drug problem among the Department's employees, the Judge concluded, there is no threat that would give rise to a compelling interest. See "Judge Blocks Drug Testing of Justice Department Employees", *New York Times* July 30, 1988, 7.

POSTSCRIPT

Should Concern for Drug Abuse Overrule Concerns for Employee Privacy?

In the controversy over drug testing, the two sides seem to be reasoning from different moral principles and to different consequences. The proponents of randomized drug testing cite the principle of Least Harm: left to themselves to take drugs, the workforce is likely to turn out terribly harmful results—damaged products, derailed trains, and the pervasive negligence that makes products unsafe and the workplace dangerous.

At least some professions—such as firefighter, peace officer, and airplane pilot—are not only incompatible with drug use but are also so important to the public's safety and vulnerable to public distrust that the public thus deserves assurances that such employees are demonstrably drug free. For the sake of those assurances alone there should be a policy of random drug testing for those occupations. Meanwhile, the threat of being tested should deter those workers from using drugs; this deterrence provides a separate consequentialist argument for the testing.

The opponents of drug testing, however, find more harm than good resulting from drug testing. Given the potential for error, good employees will be not only fired but stigmatized; the morale of the workforce will suffer as the invasions of privacy threaten the dignity and self-esteem of the worker; and the atmosphere of suspicion built up by the testing policy will result in worker resentment.

Both sides also cite nonconsequentialist arguments to their conclusions. Those in favor of drug testing cite the importance of subordinating individual freedom to community interest in times of emergency, and they find worker resentment of drug testing not only suspicious (what are they trying to hide?) but also antisocial and obstructionist. Those against drug testing cite the importance of individual privacy and dignity—especially against the kind of invasion that drug testing entails—and further cite the importance of maintaining trust between employer and employee, which is violated by drug testing policies.

Troubling for both sides is the scope of the principle. After all, why stop with drugs? Once the employer has a license to regulate personal habits for the greater good of the customer, the company, and society, why not put that license to work in other areas? Can the employer tell the employees not to smoke tobacco, on or off the job? It would be to an employer's advantage since health insurance costs are reduced for companies with smoke-free environments. What about alcohol? Alcohol is at least as dangerous as other recreational drugs, with far-reaching effects on areas as diverse as family happiness, general health, and safety on the roads. Can employers regulate dating habits among their employees similar to the old school boards' practices? And what about AIDS? What if any role should testing for HIV infection play in the workplace?

Finally, once testing for these dangers has begun, who will keep the records of those who fail, and who will have access to those records? Publicly revealing negative results of any test could constitute defamation of character. How could the confidentiality of employee records be ensured?

It is difficult to predict the future of drug testing in the workplace. If it is to be allowed—and, according to the surveys reported by Verespej, it should—more reliable tests are needed on the front line. There is now a very expensive test for which 99.9 percent accuracy is claimed, which is often used as a backup if an employee fails a drug test once. But generally, it is not used to screen candidates for employment, so there is still the risk of excluding good employees because of false positives or ruining credibility with too many false negatives. Primarily, drugs are not a company problem or an affliction of American business or capitalism. They are proliferating in the society at large, and until drugs are removed from the street, there is little hope of getting them out of the workplace. Under these circumstances, it seems that the certainty of invasion outweighs the possibility of preventing drug use. On the other hand, the corporations may be the perfect place to begin to confront drug abuse.

SUGGESTED READINGS

Richard L. Berke, "The Post-Arrest Drug Test Gets a Foothold," *The New York Times* (April 2, 1989).

Rob Brookler, "Industry Standards in Workplace Drug Testing," *Personnel Journal* (April 1992).

Bruce A. Campbell, "Alcohol and Drug Abuse in the Workplace: Major Problem or Myth?" *R. F. Goodell Business Quarterly* (Autumn 1990).

Jonathan S. Franklin, "Undercover in Corporate America," *The New York Times* (January 29, 1989).

Michael Janofsky, "Drug Use and Workers' Rights," *The New York Times* (December 28, 1993).

Charles L. Redel and Augustus Abbey, "The Arbitration of Drug Use and Testing in the Workplace," *Arbitration Journal* (March 1993).

J. K. Ross III and B. J. Middlebrook, "AIDS Policy in the Work Place, Will You Be Ready?" *Advanced Management Journal* (Winter 1990).

Barbara Steinburg, "Foolproofing Drug Tests Results," *Business and Health* (December 1990).

Kimberly A. Weber and Robin E. Shea, "Drug Testing: The Necessary Evil," *Bobbin* (August 1991).

PART 3

Moving the Product: Marketing and Consumer Dilemmas

What right does a consumer have that the product he or she buys will cause no harm? At the start of the twentieth century, the buyer tended to be stuck with a purchase, however reached, and responsible for her or his own safety in using the product. This is no longer the rule governing product liability. In this section, we look at four cases: advertising, in and of itself; the marketing of a product that is essentially harmful (tobacco); the production and marketing of a car that may or may not contain a dangerous design flaw (the Pinto); and the marketing and pricing of pharmaceuticals. Questions of intent and effect are inextricably linked in all four cases.

■ Are Pharmaceutical Price
  Controls Justifiable?

■ Is Advertising Fundamentally Deceptive?

■ Product Liability: Was Ford to Blame in the
  Pinto Case?

■ Should Tobacco Advertising
  Be Banned?

ISSUE 10

Are Pharmaceutical Price Controls Justifiable?

YES: Richard A. Spinello, from "Ethics, Pricing and the Pharmaceutical Industry," *Journal of Business Ethics* (August 1992)

NO: Pharmaceutical Manufacturers Association, from "Price Controls in the Economy and the Health Sector," *Backgrounder* (April 1993)

ISSUE SUMMARY

YES: Philosopher Richard A. Spinello argues that the pharmaceutical industry should regulate its prices in accordance with the principles of distributive justice, with special attention to the needs of the least advantaged.

NO: The Pharmaceutical Manufacturers Association, an association of 93 manufacturers of pharmaceutical and biological products who support high manufacturing standards and ethical business practices, argues that price controls are historically counterproductive in providing scarce goods for the consumer, especially in the health care sector.

How shall we distribute the scarce valuable products of our society? Current economic philosophies offer two alternatives: the free market and public provision. In a free market, tradable goods or money or services are exchanged between buyers and sellers, at a rate acceptable to both. This system assumes that everyone can bring enough money or goods or services to the exchange process to have their needs met. A public commodity, on the other hand, is available to all, as needed; police protection is a good example of a public commodity. Where does health care and the products that are essential to health care fall in this division?

Before the 1900s, in the United States, physicians charged fees for visits, which the patient was expected to pay; all pharmaceuticals were sold at essentially what the market would bear; and the industry was profitable. The suffering of those who could not afford health care was occasionally relieved by private charity and by religious orders that set up hospitals for the poor. But on the whole, medical care and all that went with it was a marketable good.

In this century, several nations began to make health care available to all through public taxation, on the same basis as police and fire protection. The medical treatments available under socialized medicine, as it is called, included most of the treatments that were previously available only to those who could pay for them through the private sector.

The rationale for this extension of benefits was simple enough: we are all dependent for our prosperity on the productivity of the nation—that is, the productivity of its citizens—and that depends upon the national level of health. It makes sense to oppose disease and promote health with the same energy spent on opposing enemy armies and promoting sound fiscal policy. Early public health movements financed clean water and universal inoculations at public expense; medical treatments and drugs were a direct extension of this idea.

In nations that have socialized their health care provision, there have always been disputes over the acceptable boundaries of medical coverage: Should cosmetic surgery be covered? What about elaborate reconstructive surgery for the very old? Weight loss treatments? Psychiatric care, not including emergencies? However, treatment of disease—AIDS, for example—is always covered, and here is where the dispute begins.

The United States has never fully subscribed to socialized health care provision (or of socialized anything, for that matter), and there is no tax money allocated to underwrite the cost of manufacturing drugs. As part of its federal police power, the United States does have the legal apparatus to control prices of essential commodities if the lawmakers feel that these prices are unconscionably high. But are price controls justified to equalize access to essential medications?

The dispute centers on two points: First, do pharmaceutical companies have an obligation to take into account the needs of the poorest customers in setting their prices (in accordance with the principles of justice), or may they restrict sales to only those who can pay full price? Second, if price controls were established, would they work in practice to achieve the ends of justice, or would they bring about negative consequences, such as the shutting down of drug research?

In the following selections, Richard A. Spinello argues that the principles of distributive justice justify the implementation of price controls. On the opposing side, the Pharmaceutical Manufacturers Association, in a paper prepared by Van Dyk Associates, Inc., a public policy consulting firm in Washington, D.C., reports that past attempts to administer price controls have all failed. Ask yourself, as you read these selections, what kind of arguments are being deployed by the disputants. Do the moral arguments advanced by Spinello carry enough weight to require a practical response? Do the empirical arguments advanced by the Pharmaceutical Manufacturers Association that price controls are ineffective in practice render the theoretical arguments irrelevant?

YES

Richard A. Spinello

ETHICS, PRICING AND THE PHARMACEUTICAL INDUSTRY

INTRODUCTION

A perennial ethical question for the pharmaceutical industry has been the aggressive pricing policies pursued by most large drug companies. Criticism has intensified in recent years over the high cost of new conventional ethical drugs and the steep rise in prices for many drugs already on the market. One result of this public clamor is that the pricing structure of this industry has once again come under intense scrutiny by government agencies, Congress, and the media.

The claim is often advanced that these high prices and the resultant profits are unethical and unreasonable. It is alleged that pharmaceutical companies could easily deliver less expensive products without sacrificing research and development. It is quite difficult to assess, however, what constitutes an unethical price or an unreasonable profit. Where does one draw the line in these nebulous areas? We will consider these questions as they relate to the pharmaceutical industry with the understanding that the normative conclusions reached in this analysis might be applicable to other industries which market *essential* consumer products. Our primary axis of discussion, however, will be the pharmaceutical industry where the issue of pricing is especially complex and controversial.

THE PROBLEM

Beyond any doubt, instances of questionable and excessive drug prices abound. Azidothymide or AZT is one of the most prominent and widely cited examples. This effective medicine is used for treating complications from AIDS. The Burroughs-Wellcome Company has been at the center of a spirited controversy over this drug for establishing such a high price— AZT treatment often costs as much as $6500 a year, which is prohibitively expensive for many AIDS patients, particularly those with inadequate

From Richard A. Spinello, "Ethics, Pricing and the Pharmaceutical Industry," *Journal of Business Ethics*, vol. 11 (August 1992), pp. 617–626. Copyright © 1992 by D. Reidel Publishing Co., Dordrecht, Holland, and Boston, U.S.A. Reprinted by permission of Kluwer Academic Publishers.

insurance coverage. The company has steadfastly refused to explicate how it arrived at this premium pricing level, but industry observers suggest that this important drug was priced to be about the same as expensive cancer therapy.[1] ...

ETHICAL QUESTIONS

The behavior of Burroughs and the tendency of most drug companies to charge premium prices for breakthrough medicines raises serious moral issues which defy easy answers and simple solutions. As Clarence Walton observed, "no other area of managerial activity is more difficult to depict accurately, assess fairly, and prescribe realistically in terms of morality than the domain of price" (1969, p. 209). This difficulty is compounded in the pharmaceutical industry due to the complications involved in ascertaining the true cost of production.

To be sure, every business is certainly entitled to a *reasonable profit* as a reward to its investors and a guarantee of long-term stability. But the difficulty is judging a reasonable profit level. When, if ever, do profits become "unreasonable?" It is even more problematic to determine if that profit is "unethical," especially if it is the result of premium prices.

Obviously, the issue of ethical or fair pricing assumes much greater significance when the product or service in question is not a luxury item but an essential one such as medicine. Few are concerned about the ethics of pricing a BMW or a waterfront condo in Florida. But the matter is quite different when dealing with vital commodities like food, medicine, clothing, housing, and education. Each of these goods has a major impact on our basic well-being

and our ability to achieve any genuine self-fulfillment. Given the importance of these products in the lives of all human beings, one must consider how equitably they are priced since pricing will determine their general availability. Along these lines several key questions must be raised. Should free market, competitive forces determine the price of "essential" goods such as pharmaceuticals? Is it morally wrong to charge exceptionally high prices even if the market is willing to pay that price? Is it ethical to profit excessively at the expense of human suffering? Finally, how can we even begin to define what constitutes reasonable profits?

Also, the issue of pricing must be considered in the context of the pharmaceutical industry's lofty performance guidelines for return on assets, return on common equity, and so forth. On what authority are such targets chosen over other goals such as the widest possible distribution of some breakthrough pharmaceutical that can save lives or improve the quality of life? Pharmaceutical companies would undoubtedly contend that this authority emanates from the expectations of shareholders and other key stakeholders such as members of the financial community. In addition, these targets are a result of careful strategic planning that focuses on long-term goals.

But a key question persistently intrudes here. Should *other* viewpoints be considered? Should the concerns and needs of the sick be taken into account, especially in light of the fact that they have such an enormous stake in these issues? In other words, as with many business decisions, there appear to be stark tradeoffs between superior financial performance versus humane empathy and fairness. Should corporations consider the "human cost" of their objectives for excellent performance? And what role, if any, should fairness or justice play in pricing decisions? It is only by probing these difficult and complex questions that we can make progress in establishing reasonable norms for the pricing of pharmaceuticals.

... The strategic decisions of large organizations "inevitably involve social as well as economic consequences, inextricably intertwined" (Mintzberg, 1989, p. 173). Thus such firms are social agents whether they like it or not. It is virtually impossible to maintain neutrality on these issues and aspire to some sort of apolitical status. The point for the pharmaceutical industry and the matter of pricing seems clear enough. The refusal to take "non-economic" criteria into account when setting prices is itself a moral and social decision which inevitably affects society. Companies have a choice—either they can explicitly consider the social consequences of their decisions or they can be blind to those consequences, deliberately ignoring them until the damage is perceived and an angry public raises its voice in protest.

If companies do choose, however, to be attentive and *responsible* social agents they must begin to cultivate a broader view of their environment and their obligations. To begin with, they must treat those affected by their decisions as people with an important stake in those decisions. This stakeholder model, which has become quite popular with many executives, allows corporations to link strategic decisions such as pricing with social and ethical concerns. By recognizing the legitimacy of its stakeholders such as consumers and employees, managers will better appreciate all the negative as well as positive consequences of their decisions. Moreover, an honest stakeholder analysis will compel them to explore the financial and human implications of those decisions. This will enable corporations to become more responsible social agents, since explicit attention will be given to the social dimension of their various strategic decisions.

... According to Goodpaster and Matthews, the most effective solution to this and most other moral dilemmas is one "that permits or encourages corporations to exercise independent, non-economic judgment over matters that face them in their short- and long-term plans and operations" (1989, p. 161). In other words, the burden of morality and social responsibility does not lie in the marketplace or in the hand of government regulation but falls directly on the corporation and its managers.

Companies that do aspire to such moral and social responsibility will adopt *the moral point of view*, which commits one to view positively the interest of others, including various stakeholder groups. Moreover, the moral point of view assigns primacy to virtues such as justice, integrity, and respect. Thus, the virtuous corporation is analogous to the virtuous person: each exhibits these moral qualities and acts according to the principle that the single-minded pursuit of one's own selfish interests is a violation of moral standards and an offense to the community. The moral point of view also assumes that both the corporation and the individual thrive in an environment of cooperative interaction which can only be realized when one turns from a narrow self-interest to a wider interest in others.

PRICING POLICIES AND JUSTICE

This brings us back to the specific moral question of fair pricing policies for the pharmaceutical industry. The moral issue at stake here concerns justice and more precisely distributive justice. As we have remarked, justice has always been considered a primary virtue and thus it is an indispensable component of the moral point of view. According to Aristotle, justice "is not a part of virtue but the whole of excellence or virtue" (1962, p. 114). Thus, there can be no virtue without justice. This implies that if corporations are serious about assimilating the moral point of view and exercising their capacity for responsible behavior, they must strive to be just in their dealings with both their internal and external constituencies. Moreover, traditional discussions on justice in the works of philosophers such as Aristotle, Hume, Mill, and Rawls have emphasized distributive justice, which is concerned with the fair distribution of society's benefits and burdens. This seems especially relevant to the matter of ethical pricing policies.

Corporations which control the distribution of essential products such as ethical drugs like AZT can be just or unjust in the way they distribute these products. When premium prices are charged for such goods an artificial scarcity is created, and this gives rise to the question of how equitably this scarce resource is being allocated. The consequence of a premium pricing strategy whose objective is to garner high profits would appear to be an inequitable distribution pattern. As we have seen, due to the expensiveness of AZT and similar drugs they are often not available to the poor and lower middle class unless their insurance plans cover this expense or they can somehow secure government assistance which has not been readily forthcoming. However, if this distribution pattern can be considered unjust, what determines a just distribution policy?

There are, of course, many conceptions of distributive justice which would enable us to answer this question. Some stress individual merit (each according to his ability) while others are more egalitarian and stress an equal distribution of society's goods and services. Given a wide array of different theories on justice, where does the manager turn for some guidance and straightforward insights?

One of the most popular and plausible conceptions of justice is advanced by John Rawls in his well known work, *A Theory of Justice*. A thorough treatment of this complex and prolix work is beyond the scope of this essay. However, a concise summary of Rawls' work should reveal its applicability to the problem of fair pricing. Rawls' conception of justice, which is predicated on the Kantian idea of personhood, properly emphasizes the equal worth and universal dignity of all persons. All rational persons have a dual capacity: they possess the ability to develop a rational plan to pursue their own conception of the good life along with the ability to respect this same capacity of self-determination in others. This Kantian ideal underlies the choice of the two principles of justice in the original position. Furthermore, this choice is based on the assumption that the "protection of Kantian self-determination for all persons depends on certain formal guarantees—the equal rights and liberties of democratic citizenship—plus guaranteed access to certain material resources" (Doppelt, p. 278). In short, the essence of justice as fairness means that persons are entitled to an extensive system of liberties *and* basic material goods.

Unlike pure egalitarian theories, however, Rawls stipulates that inequities are consistent with his conception of justice so long as they are compatible with universal respect for Kantian personhood. This implies that such inequities should not be tolerated if they interfere with the basic rights, liberties, and material benefits all deserve as Kantian persons capable of rational self-determination. In other words, Rawls espouses the detachment of the distribution of primary social goods from one's merit and ability because these goods are absolutely essential for our self-determination and self-fulfillment as rational persons. These primary goods include "rights and liberties, opportunities and power, income and wealth" (Rawls, 1971, p. 92). Whatever one's plan or conception of the good life, these goods are the necessary means to realize that plan, and hence everyone would prefer more rather than less primary goods. Their unequal distribution in a just society should only be allowed if such a distribution would benefit directly the least advantaged of that society (the difference principle).

The key element in Rawls' theory for our purposes is the notion that there are material benefits everyone deserves as Kantian persons. The exercise of one's capacity for free self-determination requires a certain level of material well-being and not just the guarantee of abstract and formal rights such as freedom of expression and equal opportunity. Thus the primary social goods involve some material goods, like income and wealth. To a certain extent health care (including medicine) should be considered as one of the primary social goods since it is obviously necessary for the pursuit of one's rational life plan. Therefore, the distribution of health care should not be contingent upon ability and merit. Also it would be untenable to justify an inequitable distribution of this good by means of Rawls' difference principle. It is difficult to imagine a scenario in which the unequal distribution of health care in our society would be more beneficial to the least advantaged than a more equal distribution which would assure all consumers access to hospital care, medical treatment, medicines, and so forth. If we assume that the least advantaged (a group which Rawls never clearly defines) are the indigent who are also suffering from certain ailments, there is no advantage to any inequity in the distribution of health care. Unlike other primary goods such as income and wealth it cannot be distributed in such a way that a greater share for certain groups will benefit the least advantaged. In short, this is a zero sum game—if a person is deprived of medical treatment or pharmaceutical products due to premium pricing policies that person has lost a critical opportunity to save his life, cure a disease, reduce suffering, and so on.

Thus, at least according to this Rawlsian view of justice with its Kantian underpinnings, there seems to be little room for the unequal distribution of a vital commodity such as health care in a just society. It follows, then, that the just pharmaceutical corporation must be far more diligent and consider very carefully the implications of pricing policies for an equitable distribution of its products. The alternative is government intervention in this process, and as we have seen, this has the potential to yield gross inefficiencies and ultimately be self-defeating. If these corporations charge premium prices and garner excessive profits from their pharmaceutical products, the end result will be the deprivation of these goods for certain classes of people. Such a pricing pattern systematically worsens the situation of the least advantaged in society, violates the respect due them as Kantian persons, and seriously impairs their capacity for free self-determination.

It should be emphasized, however, that this concern for justice does not imply that pharmaceutical companies should become charities by distributing these drugs free of charge or at prices so low they must sustain meager profits or even losses. To be sure, their survival, long-term stability, and ongoing research are also vital to society and can only be guaranteed through substantial profits. Thus, the demand for justice which we have articulated must be balanced with the need to realize key economic objectives which guarantee the long-term stability of this industry. As Kenneth Goodpaster notes, "the responsible organization aims at congruence between its moral and nonmoral aspirations" (1984, p. 309). In other words, it does not see goals of justice and economic viability as mutually exclusive, but will attempt to manage the joint achievement of both objectives.

We are arguing, then, that pharmaceutical companies should seek to balance their legitimate concern for profit and return on investment with an equal consideration of the crucial importance of distributive justice. There must be an explicit recognition that for the afflicted certain pharmaceutical products are critical for one's well-being; hence they are as important as any primary social good and are deserved by every member of society. As a result these products should be distributed on the widest possible basis, but in a way that permits companies to realize a realistic and reasonable level of profitability.

It is, of course, quite difficult to define a "reasonable level of profitability." In many respects the definition of "reasonable" is the crux of the matter here. Unfortunately, as outsiders to the operations of drug companies we are ill prepared to judge whether development costs for certain drugs are inflated or truly necessary. As a result, these corporations must be trusted to arrive at their own definition of a reasonable profit, given the level of legitimate costs involved in researching and developing the drug in question. But we can look to some case histories for meaningful examples that would serve as a guide to a more general definition. One of the most famous controversies over drug prices concerned the Hoffman-LaRoche corporation and the United Kingdom in which the government's Monopoly Commission alleged that Hoffman-LaRoche was charging excessive prices for valium and librium in order to subsidize its research and preserve its monopoly position. In the course of the prolonged deliberations between the British government and the company reasonable profits were defined as "profits no higher than is necessary to obtain the 'desired' performance of industry from the point of view of the economy as a whole."[2] In general, then, under normal circumstances reasonable profits for a particular product should be consistent with the average return for the industry. Exceptions might be made to this rule of average returns if the risks and costs of development are inordinately and unavoidably high.

Thus, based on this Rawlsian ideal of justice I propose the following thesis regarding ethical pricing for pharmaceutical companies: for those drugs which are truly essential the just corporation will aim to charge prices that will assure the widest possible distribution of these products consistent with a reasonable level of profitability. In other words, these companies will seek to minimize the deprivation of material benefits which are needed by all persons for their self-realization by imposing restraints on their egocentric interests in premium prices and excessive profits.... Moreover, we must present some sort of methodology for reaching this determination.

... The more critical the product and the less likely it will be affordable to certain segments of society, the more prominent should be the consideration given to distributive justice in pricing policy deliberations. Justice cannot be the exclusive concern in these deliberations, but must be given its proportionate weight depending upon the way in which the questions in this framework are addressed. Thus, as pricing decisions duly consider factors such as production and promotion costs, etc., they should also take into account the element of distributive justice. Clearly, however, drugs that are less important for society because they deal with less serious ailments should not be subject to the same demands of justice as those for diseases which are truly life threatening or debilitating. Hence drug companies should have much more flexibility in pricing medicines for these less critical ailments....

This analysis does not by any means eliminate the frustrations regarding ethical pricing which were cited earlier by Walton. We can offer no definitive, quantitative formulae or comprehensive criteria to assure that pricing in this industry will always be fair and just. As with most moral decisions, much will depend on the individual judgment and moral sensitivity of the managers making those decisions.... It seems beyond doubt that responsible and fair pricing in the pharmaceutical industry is a serious moral imperative, since for so many consumers it is a matter of well-being or infirmity and perhaps even life or death.

We might consider once again the wisdom of Aristotle on this topic of justice. In the *Nicomachean Ethics* he writes that "we call those things 'just' which produce and preserve happiness for the social and political community" (1962, p. 113). If corporations respond to the demands of justice for the sake of the common good, it will help promote the elusive goal of a just community and a greater harmony between the corporation and its many concerned stakeholders.

NOTES

1. Holzman, D.: 1988, 'New Wonder Drugs at What Price?', *Insight* (March 21), pp. 54–55. For more recent data on drug prices see 'Maker of Schizophrenia Drug Bows to Pressure to Cut Costs', *The New York Times* (Dec. 6, 1990), pp. A1 and D3.

2. 'F. Hoffman-LaRoche and Company A.G.', Harvard Business School Case Study in Matthews, Goodpaster, Nash (eds.), *Policies and Persons* (McGraw Hill Book Company: N.Y., 1985).

REFERENCES

Aristotle: 1962, *Nicomachean Ethics*, trans. by M. Oswald (Library of Liberal Arts, Bobbs Merrill Company, Inc., Indianapolis).

Doppelt, G.: 1989, 'Beyond Liberalism and Communitarianism: Towards a Critical Theory of Social Justice', *Philosophy and Social Criticism* 14 (No. 3/4).

Goodpaster, K.: 1984, 'The Concept of Corporate Responsibility', in T. Regan (ed.), *Just Business: New Introductory Essays in Business Ethics* (Random House, New York).

Goodpaster, K. and Matthews, J.: 1989, 'Can a Corporation Have a Conscience', in K. Andrews (ed.), *Ethics in Practice* (Harvard Business School Press, Boston).

Mintzberg, H.: 1989, 'The Case for Corporate Social Responsibility', in A. Iannone (ed.), *Contemporary Moral Controversies in Business* (Oxford University Press, New York).

Rawls, J.: 1971, *A Theory of Justice* (Harvard University Press, Cambridge).

Walton, C.: 1969, *Ethos and the Executive* (Prentice Hall, Inc., Englewood Cliffs, N.J.).

NO

Pharmaceutical Manufacturers
Association

PRICE CONTROLS IN THE ECONOMY
AND THE HEALTH SECTOR

EXECUTIVE SUMMARY

The current national focus on health care reform has revived discussion of price controls as a possible policy instrument.

Such discussion is predictable because health-sector costs consistently have risen faster than the general rate of price inflation and—in part because of unintended inflationary consequences created by health-reform programs of the 1960s—have tended to be resistant to government efforts to date to contain them. If, as anticipated, current contemplated reform includes dramatic expansion of health system access, additional pressures for cost containment will be created.

This brief paper examines experience with price controls historically and, then, since World War II in the U.S. health sector. Major points:

1. Price controls have been attempted in many times and places dating back 40 centuries. Except in those times and places where national unity and consensus made controls easily enforceable—for instance, in World War II Great Britain where the country quite literally was fighting for its survival—they generally have failed. Moreover, when controls have been ended, inflation typically has equalled or exceeded the rate which would have been reached without controls. In the meantime, economic growth has been inhibited.

2. Controls, when applied, quickly create artificial scarcities, resource misallocations, and black markets. Large bureaucratic structures are required for administration. Problems of enforcement and equity arise. Since controls interfere with normal market mechanisms, issues of fairness (both to consumers and producers) quickly present themselves. Public support for controls quickly erodes.

3. In the United States, those government officials who have administered price controls universally counsel against their further use. These judgments

From Pharmaceutical Manufacturers Association, "Price Controls in the Economy and the Health Sector," *Backgrounder* (April 1993). Copyright © 1993 by The Pharmaceutical Manufacturers Association. Reprinted by permission. Prepared independently for the Pharmaceutical Manufacturers Association by Van Dyk Associates, Inc., Washington, D.C.

are made, typically, on practical as well as theoretical bases.

4. In the health sector, the federal government has made numerous attempts since World War II to freeze or selectively control costs. None of these efforts has slowed a steady rise in health sector inflation.

5. The experience with overall drug-price controls has been limited in this country to Nixon-era controls. Their effect, however, was the same as with controls generally. Prices rose sharply after their relaxation.

6. Internationally, drug price controls also have proved ineffective. Additionally, they have reduced research into breakthrough drugs in countries where they have been adopted.

7. New health-sector price controls could be expected to create the same effects that prior controls have done. Alternative means of health-sector cost containment are available and already have been applied on a limited basis. All would be felt only over a longer period.

Summary: When faced with near-term general or sectoral inflation, national leaders often have turned to price controls. Such controls create enormous distortions and in the end do not quell inflation. Imperfect but applicable means of cost containment suggest themselves in the current effort toward health care reform....

CLEAR LESSONS FROM THE EXPERIENCE OF THE UNITED STATES AND OTHER NATIONS WITH PRICE CONTROLS

From Hammurabi, Babylonia, and the Roman Empire to the 1970s experiences of the United States, Japan, Canada, and Australia, price controls have been tried.

And in every single instance, with the possible exception of wartime Britain, they have been found wanting. They basically did not work. Their only certain result in any country has been to reduce production. And such losses in production usually mean a profit squeeze, less investment in plant and equipment and in R&D [research and development], and less growth in the future.

Another lesson learned: All the great monetary stabilizers of this century have been classical economists who insisted upon balanced budgets and government living within its means at home and abroad, without borrowing from the central bank or printing more paper money of its own.

Not one resorted to price controls because all knew from previous history that price controls, freezes and "rollbacks" simply produced scarcities and artificial distortions.

Treasury Secretary Lloyd Bentsen, while Vice Chairman of the Congressional Joint Economic Committee in 1978, chaired a hearing in which he noted that one of the problems he had seen with wage and price controls was that there were so many ways that they could be evaded. His assessment:

"Mandatory wage and price controls don't stop inflation any more than the Maginot line stopped the defeat of the French Army. And they are not going to protect the American consumer from all of the hurt and the damage of inflation.... The Joint Economic Committee... found that the mere prospect of controls... resulted in a substantial increase to the consumers of this country and additional inflation because of manufacturers increasing prices in anticipation of the wage demands that resulted...."

PRICE CONTROLS IN THE U.S. HEALTH SECTOR

Since World War II the federal government has made several attempts to control health care costs, either by freezing prices across the board or by imposing selective controls on individual sectors such as hospitals or physicians. None of these initiatives has slowed the steady rise in what Americans are paying for health care through taxes, through private insurance, or out of their own pockets.

Throughout this period, any savings achieved by controls in one sector have been offset by increased spending in others. Economies achieved by shorter patient stays in hospitals have been erased by higher payments for nursing home and home health care. Hospitals barred from adding new beds have poured the money into new outpatient facilities and expensive diagnostic equipment. Placing a ceiling on prices that doctors could charge for treatments or office visits simply has produced a larger number of treatments or office visits. Indeed, Medicare administrators drawing up a new "resource-based" schedule of allowable physician fees have factored into their calculations the assumption that doctors automatically would offset half the reduction in their rates of payment by an increase in billings.

No scheme yet tried has produced actual dollars-and-cents savings. No scheme could—short of central government control of all health care costs and spending. And were that attempted, it would produce... shortages, dislocations, and other problems....

This section will examine... health care price controls initiated at the federal level in the last 50 years, and show how and why they failed. (The wage-price stabilization program during the Korean War is not discussed because professional fees, such as doctor bills and hospital charges, were excluded from controls.) It will then sketch alternative cost control initiatives mounted in the private sector, often with government support, that offer more hope for moderating health care inflation than does price regulation....

The Steady Expansion of Federally-Funded Health Services

... [I]n the U.S. experience, price controls have not stemmed the growth of health care spending. As a government program, price controls necessarily exist in a political environment where other pressures are operating in the direction of greater spending. Each year, Congressional budgetmakers make significant cuts in Administration Medicare and Medicaid requests—almost always through cuts to providers. Yet each year, actual payments increase.

Why is it that, despite the "success" of PPS [Prospective Payment System] in halving the growth of inpatient hospital costs (the single largest segment of the Medicare program), total spending for hospital care by Medicare and Medicaid has doubled in the seven years after PPS over the seven years before—from $230 billion to $460 billion?

Why has total federal spending for Medicaid increased by 73 percent in just the last two years while Medicare spending was rising far less rapidly?

The answer: At the same time the government was administering its price controls, it was taking other actions that raised its health care costs. Example:

• In the same legislation in which Congress froze physician fees, it required

Medicaid to cover more children and more low income pregnant women and extended Medicare to mammographies.

• At the same time it reduced provider fees for Medicare, it was mandating states to cover expensive and medically-questionable treatments under Medicaid, for which it provides half the funds.

• At the same time it was implementing the RVS fee schedule [a revised payment system for Medicare physicians, begun in 1992], Congress significantly extended Medicare benefits for nursing homes, home health and hospice care.

The same political thinking that makes price controls attractive to them makes it hard for policymakers to restrain themselves from sweetening government health benefits packages to enlist Congressional and interest-group support. This bit of history is instructive in view of the declared objective of the Clinton Administration to extend health insurance to the 37 million uninsured while at the same time reducing health care costs.

PRICE CONTROLS ON PHARMACEUTICALS

Conclusions about the wisdom of price controls in the pharmaceutical sector must be drawn primarily from the experience of other countries. The United States has had only one experience with such controls—during the wage-price freeze of the Nixon Administration. Most other industrialized countries have long tried to regulate drug prices and outlays as part of their broader programs of national health insurance. Only the United States and Denmark leave pricing to the competitive marketplace.

The U.S. Experience

The Nixon Administration Wage and Price Stabilization programs tried to control drug prices, with these results:

• In the three years prior to the program, the drug component of the Consumer Price Index had risen only 3 percent, considerably less than health care cost inflation generally.

• During the period of controls (April, 1971 through October, 1974) the Index increased by only 1.5 percent.

• As soon as controls were lifted, however, the typical "catch-up" effect was seen. Between 1975 and 1977, drug prices rose almost 12 percent. When the last impacts of price controls had faded from the economy, prices were probably higher than they would have been without controls.

Controls also were ineffective in curbing spending on drugs.

In the three years before they were instituted, patient drug costs rose by an average of $378 million a year. During the three control years, they rose $515 million a year. In the three years after, they rose $600 million a year....

Effects of Drug Price Controls Beyond Prices

... [I]t is clear that price controls on drugs in other countries have uniformly failed to accomplish their goal. It also is clear why controls, which are supposed to hold down spending, have had the opposite effect. If government decides for a pharmaceutical company how much it can charge for its products, the company has little incentive to conduct the extremely expensive search for truly innovative and breakthrough therapies. The odds against a drug in development making it to market are 5,000 to 1. Even when a drug advances to where it is actually tested in clinical trials on patients, the odds against its being marketed are 10 to 1. Unless there is pricing freedom, the financial reward is just not worth the risk.

Many firms in nations with strict price controls largely have abandoned the search for breakthrough drugs. Funds that might have been used for research have been shifted to increased promotion and marketing of existing drugs, seeking increased demand as a way of maintaining revenues in the face of controlled prices. Foreign firms also engage in low-risk research and development to come up [with] "new" drugs that are not innovative, and only marginally better than existing therapies, but are nonetheless eligible for higher controlled prices than the older drugs in their inventory.

A study of the French pharmaceutical industry, which was responsible for only 3 world class drugs between 1975 and 1989, concluded that "the calibre of research [has] deteriorated because severe price control has encouraged French companies to give priority to small therapeutic improvements which are useful in price negotiations." Of Japan, Dr. Heinz Redwood, a British researcher and policy analyst, says "There is a pronounced tendency to develop 'Japanese drugs for Japan' rather than for world health care. This is largely the result of the Japanese system of price regulation... which grants very high prices for new drugs, whilst putting heavy pricing pressure on older drugs."

In Italy, the Ruoppolo Commission, created to revamp the price control system to give greater encouragement to innovative activity, reported that:

"The virtual freezing of the price of old products... has acted as a decisive incentive in the search by companies for new registrations in order to obtain more up-to-date prices; and then, by means of appropriate promotion, induce a prescription shift from the old to the new [drug]."

Were price controls to touch off the same syndrome here, it could have a profound effect not only on the nature of this country's pharmaceutical industry but on world health. The international community depends on innovative U.S. industry to provide it with new medicines. Almost 50 percent of the new drugs effective enough to be marketed globally in the past 20 years have been developed in the U.S. In biotechnology and immunology, it is 70 percent.

What Will Happen If New Price Controls Are Placed On Health Care?

Given previous experience with price controls generally, and on what has happened when they have been imposed in different forms upon the U.S. health care system, it is not difficult to speculate what will happen if federal policymakers impose what have been called "interim cost containment measures" to hold the line on prices for the period—probably several years—that will pass before a new national health insurance system can be passed into law, implemented by regulations, survive the inevitable court challenges, and actually begin to operate throughout the country.

1. Investment funds that would have flowed into the development of new medical technology, new cures for disease and other advances will be diverted to other, more economically attractive channels.

2. The economic incentive to enter the health care field will decline, eventually

leading to a shortage of physicians and other trained personnel.

3. Providers will continue to find ways to "game" the system, reducing hoped-for savings. To counter this, government will impose increasing supervision, restrictions, and paperwork on the activities of health care professionals.

4. The quality of health care will suffer. Physicians will spend less time with patients and there will be fewer drugs in hospital formularies. Shortages and waiting lists will develop as they have in other countries. Those who can afford it will try to preserve their current quality of care by creating a separate, privately-funded privileged system of health care as exists in Britain. This alternative system in turn will draw the best professionals and force the quality of care given the rest of us lower.

5. The inherent contradiction between universal system access and simultaneous cost containment inevitably will lead to de facto rationing of care. The Medicaid experience is instructive here. As Medicaid has become the largest item in their budgets, many states have severely restricted reimbursement under the program. Many doctors have responded by refusing to take Medicaid patients. To expand eligibility for Medicaid, the state of Oregon has had to adopt a rationing system, barring payment for whole categories of treatments. Similarly, Great Britain denies expensive surgery to patients over a certain age.

Alternative to Controls Which Could Contain Costs

Health care costs can be contained without the distortions created by controls.

Most of the measures listed below now are being practiced in the health care system—many with the support and encouragement of government. Others are readily available. Strong incentives to use these measures would occur under "managed competition" schemes for health care reform.

• Expansion of Health Maintenance Organizations, group practice associations, and other organizations under which health care practitioners have no incentives to perform unneeded services.

• Expansion of Preferred Provider Organizations and other arrangements in which physicians give up higher fees for an assured caseload.

• Greater emphasis on prevention, early intervention, wellness, and lifestyle changes to lower the incidence of disease and the necessity for surgery.

• Requiring second opinions before surgery and other expensive services.

• Living wills, which give terminal patients the right to appoint someone to decide when to stop the use of high-cost technology whose only purpose is to prolong life according to its clinical definition.

• Drug utilization review systems, that are consistent with the principles developed by the American Medical Association, the American Pharmaceutical Association, and the Pharmaceutical Manufacturers Association. Such systems detect and correct inappropriate prescribing practices as well as fraud and abuse.

• Encouraging medical innovation, including the development of cost-effective therapies such as drugs as a cure for major diseases and a substitute for surgery.

• Greater research on the "outcomes" of alternative treatments, to spread knowledge among physicians about the most effective treatments and therapies.

- Education of patients so they can work more knowledgeably with their doctors. Patient information should be more widely available on computer networks.
- Tort reform to reduce the practice of "defensive" medicine to avoid malpractice suits which, according to the American Medical Association, costs the health care system $15 billion a year.
- Measures to reduce redundancy of expensive technologies and equipment in the same markets—i.e., where several hospitals and clinics in the same area invest in the same costly technologies whereas demand might justify only one such facility.
- The imposition of substantial deductibles and/or co-payments on the insured so as to require patients to make prudent choices about health expenditures. (A Rand Corporation study has shown that patients, when required to write a check on each physician visit, make visits with less frequency.)
- Voluntary industry measures to limit drug-price increases, with or without antitrust waivers, with provision for monitoring by credible third-party agency.

None of the above measures, of course, can be expected to produce immediate and dramatic reductions in health-sector inflation—particularly if implemented while health-sector access simultaneously is being dramatically expanded. Nor can they counteract and overcome those factors which plague the U.S. health system more greatly than those of other Western countries: High rates of poverty, violent crime, homelessness, aging, AIDS and drug abuse.

The aforementioned measures are appropriate ways of maintaining quality while reducing costs. Any government involvement should be designed to increase incentives to adopt such measures.

But the government cannot have it both ways by adopting incentives for the marketplace to manage care *and* government price controls on the components of care. To manage care, providers and insurers must invest significant fiscal and human resources into restructuring, expanding and monitoring health care delivery. Why invest when price controls will likely reward those providers who were most inefficient in the old fragmented system? Attempts to solve the data needs equity issues and enforcement rules would further slow enactment of proper incentives.

At the same time, however, it can be predicted with relative certainty that, given past international and U.S. experience, health-sector as well as other price controls—even when applied short-term—lead to distortions and, over time, do not result in net cost reductions.

POSTSCRIPT

Are Pharmaceutical Price Controls Justifiable?

The United States is more committed to the free market than any other developed nation. Consequently, the arguments advanced by the Pharmaceutical Manufacturers Association against pharmaceutical price controls tend to be accepted for all cases: attempts to regulate the market must fail. According to the laws of the market, if we try to support prices (as with the products of American farms), we will drive buyers from the market and tempt inefficient suppliers to stay in, both moves tending to drive prices *down*. Without price supports, prices would likely recover on their own as enthusiastic buyers outbid each other for the reduced amount of product. On the other hand, as in the case of pharmaceuticals, if we try to control prices, we will drive suppliers from the market and truncate the healthy process of competition that would have brought prices down naturally. Meanwhile, the company's reward for, and means for, pursuing research into better drugs would be destroyed.

But the principles of justice, which govern us as surely as the laws of supply and demand, require that we make our economic arrangements keeping in mind the fate of the least advantaged among us. Does the market do that? Which do we hold more dear, the liberty of the market or justice in distribution? As Spinello notes, people who have AIDS are dying. Is it likely that this fact will eventually persuade pharmaceutical manufacturers to accept price controls?

SUGGESTED READINGS

Judy Chaconas, "Providers Offer Prescription for Medicaid Drug-Pricing Law," *Trustee* (December 1991).

Joseph A. DiMasi et al., "The Cost of Innovation in the Pharmaceutical Industry," *Journal of Health Economics* (vol. 10, 1991).

David Hanson, "Report on Drug R & D Fuels Attack on Prices," *Chemical and Engineering News* (March 8, 1993).

Office of Technology Assessment, *Pharmaceutical R & D: Costs, Risks and Rewards* (Government Printing Office, 1993).

David Pryor, "Drugs *Must* Be Made Affordable," *The New York Times* (March 7, 1993).

Pamela Zurer, "NIH Weighs Role in Drug Pricing," *Chemical and Engineering News* (December 21, 1992).

ISSUE 11

Is Advertising Fundamentally Deceptive?

YES: Roger Crisp, from "Persuasive Advertising, Autonomy, and the Creation of Desire," *Journal of Business Ethics* (vol. 6, 1987)

NO: John O'Toole, from *The Trouble With Advertising* (Chelsea House, 1981)

ISSUE SUMMARY

YES: Philosopher Roger Crisp argues that persuasive advertising removes the possibility of real decision-making by manipulating consumers without their knowledge, and for no good reason, and thus destroys personal autonomy.

NO: John O'Toole, president of the American Association of Advertising Agencies, argues that advertising is only salesmanship functioning in the paid space and time of mass media and that it is no more coercive than an ordinary salesperson.

Advertisers do one thing—they persuade us to buy products that otherwise we would not buy. If we would buy the products anyway, there would be no point in producers spending the money to purchase magazine space or television time to display ads. That advertising seems necessary in today's market and is used to sell everything from cars to movies raises the question of whether the art of promotion aids the consumer or cons consumers into throwing money away on products they neither need nor desire.

Where, in pure capitalism, is there room for salesmanship? According to Scottish economist Adam Smith (1723–1790), the decision to buy is based solely on need, price, and (perceived) quality. The customer desires the exchange and wants to maximize the value obtained by it. But human psychology does not necessarily work as Smith's theory postulates. When some people shop, they are often tired and in a hurry, and they will buy the first thing they see that satisfies a need and that falls within an acceptable range of price and quality. As a matter of fact, they may buy the first thing that grabs their attention and looks attractive—and therein is the sales pitch. Attention and attractiveness are the keys to sales, and the customer's hypothesized needs, plans, and comparisons may have very little to do with the actual decision to buy.

Salesmanship, then, works in defiance of and at variance with the rational satisfaction of need in the free market. The salesman will not succeed in inducing people to buy things they never thought of or conceived a use for because he does not have the time to plant the idea of some new need and help it to grow. But when a willing buyer wanders into the market, the aggressive salesman can certainly accelerate the decision to buy and influence the buyer to choose one vendor rather than another.

If the salesman has more time, however, can he produce new needs? Suppose the national widgetmaker makes twice too many widgets one year, and there is no real need for the excess. Could he hire a salesman to persuade people that widgets make fine lawn ornaments (a use no one had thought of), that lawn ornaments are essential to the good life (also unthought), and that, therefore, they truly need his widgets? According to Smith's theory, consumers should see through such a ploy, and no sale would ever take place. But here is where advertising enters the consumer's life as a picture or a fantasy of a life more valuable than his or her own. By associating this beautiful life with a product, not really an object of need but beginning to seem so, the advertiser can build up an inclination to buy, well away from the point of sale, and predispose a consumer first to pay attention to, and then to *need*, the manufacturer's product. Sales, in that case, are not need driven, proceeding from the customer's life and needs, but are product driven, proceeding from the producer's desire to sell and the advertiser's skill.

In the following selections, Roger Crisp is primarily interested in the effect of advertising on the individual and the problems of preserving any notion of autonomy in a world overrun with persuasive messages. John O'Toole does not try to present advertising as an objective exercise in consumer education. But if salesmanship in the marketplace is acceptable, and it surely seems to be, then what possible objection can there be to extending salesmanship to the print and broadcast media?

Ask yourself, as you read these selections, how *you* react to advertising. Do you think about it? Talk back to it? Absorb it? Can you think of an advertisement that really changed your idea of what was good and valuable and worth buying? Should there be limits on pitches beyond the federal prohibition of outright deception? Why? Is advertising just clean fun that fools no one, entertains us, and in a thoroughly harmless way persuades us to try something we might like?

179

YES

Roger Crisp

PERSUASIVE ADVERTISING, AUTONOMY, AND THE CREATION OF DESIRE

In this paper, I shall argue that all forms of a certain common type of advertising are morally wrong, on the ground that they override the autonomy of consumers.

One effect of an advertisement might be the creation of a desire for the advertised product. How such desires are caused is highly relevant as to whether we would describe the case as one in which the autonomy of the subject has been overridden. If I read an advertisement for a sale of clothes, I may rush down to my local clothes store and purchase a jacket I like. Here, my desire for the jacket has arisen partly out of my reading the advertisement. Yet, in an ordinary sense, it is based on or answers to certain properties of the jacket—its colour, style, material. Although I could not explain to you why my tastes are as they are, we still describe such cases as examples of autonomous action, in that all the decisions are being made by me: What kind of jacket do I like? Can I afford one? And so on. In certain other cases, however, the causal history of a desire may be different. Desires can be caused, for instance, by subliminal suggestion. In New Jersey, a cinema flashed sub-threshold advertisements for ice cream onto the screen during movies, and reported a dramatic increase in sales during intermissions. In such cases, choice is being deliberately ruled out by the method of advertising in question. These customers for ice cream were acting 'automatonously', rather than autonomously. They did not buy the ice cream because they happened to like it and decided they would buy some, but rather because they had been subjected to subliminal suggestion. Subliminal suggestion is the most extreme form of what I shall call, adhering to a popular dichotomy, persuasive, as opposed to informative, advertising. Other techniques include puffery, which involves the linking of the product, through suggestive language and images, with the unconscious desires of consumers for power, wealth, status, sex, and so on; and repetition, which is self-explanatory, the name of the product being 'drummed into' the mind of the consumer.

The obvious objection to persuasive advertising is that it somehow violates the autonomy of consumers. I believe that this objection is correct, and that, if one adopts certain common-sensical standards for autonomy, non-persuasive forms of advertising are not open to such an objection. Very high standards for autonomy are set by Kant, who requires that an agent be entirely external to the causal nexus found in the ordinary empirical world, if his or her actions are to be autonomous. These standards are too high, in that it is doubtful whether they allow *any* autonomous action. Standards for autonomy more congenial to common sense will allow that my buying the jacket is autonomous, although continuing to deny that the people in New Jersey were acting autonomously. In the former case, we have what has come to be known in recent discussions of freedom of the will as *both* free will *and* free action. I both decide what to do, and am not obstructed in carrying through my decision into action. In the latter case, there is free action, but not free will. No one prevents the customers buying their ice cream, but they have not themselves made any genuine decision whether or not to do so. In a very real sense, decisions are made for consumers by persuasive advertisers, who occupy the motivational territory properly belonging to the agent. If what we mean by autonomy, in the ordinary sense, is to be present, the possibility of decision must exist alongside.

Arrington (1981) discusses, in a challenging paper, the techniques of persuasive advertising I have mentioned, and argues that such advertising does not override the autonomy of consumers. He examines four notions central to autonomous action, and claims that, on each count, persuasive advertising is exonerated on the charge we have made against it. I shall now follow in the footsteps of Arrington, but argue that he sets the standards for autonomy too low for them to be acceptable to common sense, and that the charge therefore still sticks.

(a) *Autonomous desire:* Arrington argues that an autonomous desire is a first-order desire (a desire for some object, say, Pongo Peach cosmetics) accepted by the agent because it fulfils a second-order desire (a desire about a desire, say, a desire that my first-order desire for Pongo Peach be fulfilled), and that most of the first-order desires engendered in us by advertising are desires that we do accept. His example is an advertisement for Grecian Formula 16, which engenders in him a desire to be younger. He desires that both his desire to be younger and his desire for Grecian Formula 16 be fulfilled.

Unfortunately, this example is not obviously one of persuasive advertising. It may be the case that he just has this desire to look young again rather as I had certain sartorial tastes before I saw the ad about the clothes sale, and then decides to buy Grecian Formula 16 on the basis of these tastes. Imagine this form of advertisement: a person is depicted using Grecian Formula 16, and is then shown in a position of authority, surrounded by admiring members of the opposite sex. This would be a case of puffery. The advertisement implies that having hair coloured by the product will lead to positions of power, and to one's becoming more attractive to the opposite sex. It links, by suggestion, the product with my unconscious desires for power and sex. I may still claim that I am buying the product because I want to look young again. But the real reasons for my purchase are my unconscious desires for power and sex, and the link made between the product and the fulfillment of those desires by the advertisement. These reasons are not reasons I could avow to myself as good reasons for buying the product, and, again, the possibility of decision is absent.

Arrington's claim is that an autonomous desire is a first-order desire which we accept. Even if we allow that it is possible for the agent to consider whether to accept or to repudiate first-order desires induced by persuasive advertising, it seems that all first-order desires induced purely by persuasive advertising will be non-autonomous in Arrington's sense. Many of us have a strong second-order desire not to be manipulated by others without our knowledge, and for no good reason. Often, we are manipulated by others without our knowledge, but for a good reason, and one that we can accept. Take an accomplished actor: much of the skill of an actor is to be found in unconscious body-language. This manipulation we see as essential to our being entertained, and thus acquiesce in it. What is important about this case is that there seems to be no diminution of autonomy. We can still judge the quality of the acting, in that the manipulation is part of its quality. In other cases, however, manipulation ought not to be present, and these are cases where the ability to decide is importantly diminished by the manipulation. Decision is central to the theory of the market-process: I should be able to decide whether to buy product A or product B, by judging them on their merits. Any manipulation here I shall repudiate as being for no good reason. This is not to say, incidentally, that once the fact that my desires are being manipulated by others has been made transparent to me, my desire will lapse. The people in New Jersey would have been unlikely to cease their craving for ice cream, if we had told them that their desire had been subliminally induced. But they would no longer have voiced acceptance of this desire, and, one assumes, would have resented the manipulation of their desires by the management of the cinema.

Pace Arrington, it is no evidence for the claim that most of our desires are autonomous in this sense that we often return to purchase the same product over and over again. For this might well show that persuasive advertising has been supremely efficient in inducing non-autonomous desires in us, which we are unable even to attempt not to act on, being unaware of their origin. Nor is it an argument in Arrington's favour that certain members of our society will claim not to have the second-order desire we have postulated. For it may be that this is a desire which we can see is one that human beings *ought* to have, a desire which it would be in their interests to have, and the lack of which is itself evidence of profound manipulation.

(b) *Rational desire and choice:* One might argue that the desires induced by advertising are often irrational, in the sense that they are not present in an agent in full possession of the facts about the product. This argument fails, says Arrington, because if we require *all* the facts about a thing before we can desire that thing, then all our desires will be irrational; and if we require only the *relevant* information, then prior desires determine the relevance of information. Advertising may be said to enable us to fulfil these prior desires, through the transfer of information, and the supplying of means to ends is surely a paradigm example of rationality.

But, what about persuasive, as opposed to informative, advertising? Take puffery. Is it not true that a person may buy Pongo Peach cosmetics, hoping for an adventure in paradise, and that the product will not fulfil these hopes? Are they really in possession of even the relevant facts? Yes, says Arrington. We wish to purchase *subjective* effects, and these are genuine enough. When I use Pongo Peach, I will experience a genuine feeling of adventure.

Once again, however, our analysis can help us to see the strength of the objection. For a desire to be rational, in any plausible sense, that desire must at least not be induced by the interference of other persons with my system of tastes, against my will and without my knowledge. Can we imagine a person, asked for a reason justifying their purchase of Pongo Peach, replying: "I have an unconscious desire to experience adventure, and the product has been linked with this desire through advertising'? If a desire is to be rational, it is not necessary that all the facts about the object be known to the agent, but one of the facts about that desire must be that it has not been induced in the agent through techniques which the agent cannot accept. Thus, applying the schema of Arrington's earlier argument, such a desire will be repudiated by the agent as non-autonomous and irrational.

Arrington's claim concerning the subjective effects of the products we purchase fails to deflect the charge of overriding autonomy we have made against persuasive advertising. Of course, very often the subjective effects will be lacking. If I use Grecian Formula 16, I am unlikely to find myself being promoted at work, or surrounded by admiring members of the opposite sex. This is just straight deception. But even when the effects do manifest themselves, such advertisements have still overridden my autonomy. They have activated desires which lie beyond my awareness, and over behaviour flowing from which I therefore have no control. If these claims appear doubtful, consider whether this advertisement is likely to be successful: 'Do you have a feeling of adventure? Then use this brand of cosmetics'. Such an advertisement will fail, in that it appeals to a *conscious* desire, either which we do not have, or which we realise will not be fulfilled by purchasing a certain brand of cosmetics. If the advertisement were for a course in mountain-climbing, it might meet with more success. Our conscious self is not so easily duped by advertising, and this is why advertisers make such frequent use of the techniques of persuasive advertising.

(c) *Free choice:* One might object to persuasive advertising that it creates desires so covert that an agent cannot resist them, and that acting on them is therefore neither free nor voluntary. Arrington claims that a person acts or chooses *freely* if they can adduce considerations which justify their act in their mind; and *voluntarily* if, had they been aware of a reason for acting otherwise, they could have done so. Only occasionally, he says, does advertising prevent us making free and voluntary choices.

Regarding free action, it is sufficient to note that, according to Arrington, if I were to be converted into a human robot, activated by an Evil Genius who has implanted electrodes in my brain, my actions would be free as long as I could cook up some justification for my behaviour. I want to dance this jig because I enjoy dancing. (Compare: I want to buy this ice cream because I like ice cream.) If my argument is right, we are placed in an analogous position by persuasive advertising. If we no longer mean by freedom of action the mere non-obstruction of behaviour, are we still ready to accept that we are engaged in free action? As for whether the actions of consumers subjected to persuasive advertising are voluntary in Arrington's sense, I am less optimistic than he is. It is likely, as we have suggested, that the purchasers of ice cream or Pongo Peach would have gone ahead with their purchase even if they had been made aware that their desires had been induced in them by persuasive advertising. But they would now claim that they themselves had not made the decision, that they were acting on a desire engendered in them which they did not accept, and that there was, therefore, a good reason for them not to make the purchase. The unconscious is not obedient to the commands of the conscious, although it may be forced to listen.

In fact, it is odd to suggest that persuasive advertising does give consumers a choice. A choice is usually taken to require the weighing-up of reasons. What persuasive advertising does is to remove the very conditions of choice.

(d) *Control or manipulation:* Arrington offers the following criteria for control:

A person C controls the behaviour of another person P if (1) C intends P to act in a certain way A, (2) C's intention is causally effective in bringing about A, and (3) C intends to ensure that all of the necessary conditions of A are satisfied. He argues that advertisements tend to induce a desire for X, given a more basic desire for Y. Given my desire for adventure, I desire Pongo Peach cosmetics. Thus, advertisers do not control consumers, since they do not intend to produce all of the necessary conditions for our purchases.

Arrington's analysis appears to lead to some highly counter-intuitive consequences. Consider, again, my position as human robot. Imagine that the Evil

Genius relies on the fact that I have certain basic unconscious desires in order to effect his plan. Thus, when he wants me to dance a jig, it is necessary that I have a more basic desire, say, ironically, for power. What the electrodes do is to jumble up my practical reasoning processes, so that I believe that I am dancing the jig because I like dancing, while, in reality, the desire to dance stems from a link between the dance and the fulfilment of my desire for power, forged by the electrodes. Are we still happy to say that I am not controlled? And does not persuasive advertising bring about a similar jumbling-up of the practical reasoning processes of consumers? When I buy Pongo Peach, I may be unable to offer a reason for my purchase, or I may claim that I want to look good. In reality, I buy it owing to the link made by persuasive advertising between my unconscious desire for adventure and the cosmetic in question.

A more convincing account of behaviour control would be to claim that it occurs when a person causes another person to act for reasons which the other person could not accept as good or justifiable reasons for the action. This is how brainwashing is to be distinguished from liberal education, rather than on Arrington's ground that the brainwasher arranges all the necessary conditions for belief. The student can both accept that she has the beliefs she has because of her education and continue to hold those beliefs as true, whereas the victim of brainwashing could not accept the explanation of the origin of her beliefs, while continuing to hold those beliefs. It is worth recalling the two cases we mentioned at the beginning of this paper. I can accept my tastes in dress, and do not think that the fact that their origin is unknown to me detracts from my autonomy, when I choose to buy the jacket. The desire for ice cream, however, will be repudiated, in that it is the result of manipulation by others, without good reason.

It seems, then, that persuasive advertising does override the autonomy of consumers, and that, if the overriding of autonomy, other things being equal, is immoral, then persuasive advertising is immoral.

An argument has recently surfaced which suggests that, in fact, other things are not equal, and that persuasive advertising, although it overrides autonomy, is morally acceptable. This argument was first developed by Nelson (1978), and claims that persuasive advertising is a form of informative advertising, albeit an indirect form. The argument runs at two levels: first, the consumer can judge from the mere fact that a product is heavily advertised, regardless of the form or content of the advertisements, that that product is likely to be a market-winner. The reason for this is that it would not pay to advertise market-losers. Second, even if the consumer is taken in by the content of the advertisement, and buys the product for that reason, he is not being irrational. For he would have bought the product *anyway*, since the very fact that it is advertised means that it is a good product. As Nelson says:

It does not pay consumers to make very thoughtful decisions about advertising. They can respond to advertising for the most ridiculous, explicit reasons and still do what they would have done if they had made the most careful judgements about their behaviour. 'Irrationality' is rational if it is cost-free.

Our conclusions concerning the mode of operation of persuasive advertising, however, suggest that Nelson's argument cannot succeed. For the first level to work, it would have to be true that a purchaser of a product can evaluate that product on its own merits, and then decide whether to purchase it again. But, as we have seen, consumers induced to purchase products by persuasive advertising are not buying those products on the basis of a decision founded upon any merit the products happen to have. Thus, if the product turns out to be less good than less heavily advertised alternatives, they will not be disappointed, and will continue to purchase, if subjected to the heavy advertising which induced them to buy in the first place. For this reason, heavy persuasive advertising is not a sign of quality, and the fact that a product is advertised does not suggest that it is good. In fact, if the advertising has little or no informative content, it might suggest just the opposite. If the product has genuine merits, it should be possible to mention them. Persuasive advertising, as the executives on Madison Avenue know, can be used to sell anything, regardless of its nature or quality.

For the second level of Nelson's argument to succeed, and for it to be in the consumer's interest to react even unthinkingly to persuasive advertising, it must be true that the first level is valid. As the first level fails, there is not even a *prima facie* reason for the belief that it is in the interest of the consumer to be subjected to persuasive advertising. In fact, there are two weighty reasons for doubting this belief. The first has already been hinted at: products promoted through persuasive advertising may well not be being sold on their merits, and may, therefore, be bad products, or products that the consumer would not desire on being confronted with unembellished facts about the product. The second is that this form of 'rational irrationality' is anything but cost-free. We consider it a great cost to lose our autonomy. If I were to demonstrate to you conclusively that if I were to take over your life, and make your decisions for you, you would have a life containing far more of whatever you think makes life worth living, apart from autonomy, than if you were to retain control, you would not surrender your autonomy to me even for these great gains in other values. As we mentioned above in our discussion of autonomous desire, we have a strong second-order desire not to act on first-order desires induced in us unawares by others, for no good reason, and now we can see that that desire applies even to cases in which we would *appear* to be better off in acting on such first-order desires.

Thus, we may conclude that Nelson's argument in favour of persuasive advertising is not convincing. I should note, perhaps, that my conclusion concerning persuasive advertising echoes that of Santilli (1983). My argument differs from his, however, in centering upon the notions of autonomy and causes of desires acceptable to the agent, rather than upon the distinction between needs and desires. Santilli claims that the arousal of a desire is not a rational process, unless it is preceded by a knowledge of actual needs. This, I believe, is too strong. I may well have no need of a new tennis-racket, but my desire for one, aroused by informative advertisements in the newspaper, seems rational enough. I would prefer to claim that a desire is autonomous and at least *prima facie* rational if it is not induced in the agent without his knowledge and for no good reason, and allows ordinary processes of decisionmaking to occur.

Finally, I should point out that, in arguing against all persuasive advertising, unlike Santilli, I am not to be interpreted as bestowing moral respectability upon all informative advertising. Advertisers of any variety ought to consider whether the ideological objections often made to their conduct have any weight. Are they, for instance, imposing a distorted system of values upon consumers, in which the goal of our lives is to consume, and in which success is measured by one's level of consumption? Or are they entrenching attitudes which prolong the position of certain groups subject to discrimination, such as women or homosexuals? Advertisers should also carefully consider whether their product will be of genuine value to any consumers, and, if so, attempt to restrict their campaigns to the groups in society which will benefit (see Durham, 1984). I would claim, for instance, that all advertising of tobacco-based products, even of the informative variety, is wrong, and that some advertisements for alcohol are wrong, in that they are directed at the wrong audience. Imagine, for instance, a liquor-store manager erecting an informative bill-board opposite an alcoholics' rehabilitation centre. But these are secondary questions for prospective advertisers. The primary questions must be whether they are intending to employ the techniques of persuasive advertising, and, if so, how those techniques can be avoided.

ACKNOWLEDGEMENT

I should like to thank Dr. James Griffin for helpful discussion of an earlier draft of this paper.

REFERENCES

Arrington, R.: 1982, 'Advertising and Behaviour Control,' *Journal of Business Ethics* I, 1

Durham, T.: 1984, 'Information, Persuasion, and Control in Moral Appraisal of Advertising Strategy,' *Journal of Business Ethics* III, 3

Nelson, P.: 1978, 'Advertising and Ethics,' in *Ethics, Free Enterprise, and Public Policy,* (eds.) R. De George and J. Pichler, New York: Oxford University Press

Santilli, P.: 1983, 'The Informative and Persuasive Functions of Advertising: A Moral Appraisal,' *Journal of Business Ethics* II, 1.

NO
John O'Toole

THE TROUBLE WITH ADVERTISING

Advertising is an inescapable part of almost everyone's life in America. Thus, almost everyone has an attitude about the subject. And the attitudes, as expressed, seem extremely negative, in terms of both the product and those who produce it.

Back in 1975, Dr. Margaret Mead was quoted in one of our too-numerous trade journals as saying. "The only reason many people are in advertising is because no other business would pay them so much money." She added, "Most advertising people don't believe in the products they advertise or the words they are writing about their clients' products." In *The Lonely Crowd*, sociologist David Riesman writes, "Why, I ask, isn't it possible that advertising as a whole is a fantastic fraud, presenting an image of America taken seriously by no one, least of all by the advertising men who create it?"

According to a survey done in 1978 by Market Facts, Inc. for *Advertising Age* magazine, 43 percent of respondents not involved in advertising chose my craft as the one with "the lowest ethical standards." In 1977, a Gallup poll revealed the relative ranking of 20 occupational groups in terms of honesty and ethical standards. The public rated advertising practitioners 19th, just after labor union leaders and state officeholders. We did, however, beat car salesmen. The same year, a Harris survey asked respondents how much confidence they had in the people who ran various institutions. Ad agencies ranked last. Humorist Kin Hubbard once characterized us this way: "It used to be that a fellow went on the police force when all else failed, but today he goes into the advertising game."

Now, I am no more insensitive to boors, scam artists, dolts and loudmouths than the next person. And over something more than a quarter of a century in advertising, though I've encountered a few of each, I've not noticed a disproportionate representation in my craft—certainly no more than among the lawyers, doctors, journalists, accountants, academicians, clergymen, clerks, civil servants and businessmen I've met.

* * *

Why do people feel that way about us? Was it something we said? Where do these staunchly held and mainly negative impressions come from? Well, a book entitled *The Hucksters* made a mighty contribution. It was published in 1946 by Frederick Wakeman, who, I'm grieved to admit, worked for the same agency I work for now (but so did Alan Jay Lerner, whose lyrics for *Camelot* provided a cheerier type of fantasy).

The Hucksters depicted ad people as fast-talking, double-dealing, hard-drinking scoundrels who yielded every ethical point to unscrupulous clients. It would probably have faded away on the remainder shelves had it not been made into a movie starring Clark Gable. The film was a hit and reappears to this day, like a spirit that cannot find eternal rest, on late-night television. Subsequent movies developed the stereotype into a character as morally impoverished as those in *The Hucksters* but far less acute. The adman became an exploitable hustler who was usually played by Jack Lemmon. With a few refinements, this persona surfaced as second banana in the television series *Bewitched*, in which Dick York added the further dimension of ineptitude.

Then, of course, self-destructive and self-serving advertising people contributed their share to what they perceived as an increasingly popular myth. Autobiographical books detailing the zany goings-on inside advertising agencies "where anything can happen and usually does" began to proliferate. Most bore the same relationship to advertising as *Dr. Doolittle* does to zoology, but the public loved them because they amused and didn't challenge the mind by questioning the stereotype. Foremost among these was *From Those Wonderful Folks Who Brought You Pearl Harbor* by Jerry della Femina. Jerry works hard at being an enfant terrible and masking the fact that he's a serious advertising practitioner. He succeeded at both in his book.

All of this has shaped the impressions people have of those of us in advertising. But it's not the whole story. There have been novels and TV programs and films aplenty about corrupt congressmen, venal businessmen and crooked lawyers, yet members of those occupations can attend cocktail parties relatively unassailed. The reason is that their activities affect most people indirectly or through third parties. At least the products of their efforts are less proximate, less numerous and less ubiquitous than is advertising.

Attitudes about advertising, which color attitudes about those who practice it, are obviously a concern to me. Because of the importance of advertising to a system that produces a lot of good living and good jobs for a lot of good people, it's worth looking into what those attitudes are, what has caused them, who is at fault, and what can be done about it.

In the first instance, it's important to separate public attitudes—those measured by polling a sample of citizens representing all of us—from the attitudes of specialized publics: educators, journalists, consumer advocates and government. Each of the latter influence public opinion to some extent and should be looked at in terms of how and how much.

Whatever the influences, public attitudes toward advertising do not bring cheer to the heart of one who makes his living at it. A 1980 study by Yankelovich, Skelly & White reported that 70 percent of the American population was concerned with truth, distortion and exaggeration in advertising. A 1979 Louis Harris poll showed 81 percent feeling that "the claims for most products advertised on TV are exaggerated," and 52 percent saying that most or all TV advertising is "seriously misleading."

A survey conducted by my own company in 1977 found 36 percent of the national sample objecting to most TV advertising; the adjectives chosen most frequently were "dumb" and "juvenile." A 1974 study done by our industry association indicated that 59 percent of the respondents believed "most advertising insults the intelligence of the average consumer." It's interesting to note, however, that in the same study 88 percent said that advertising is essential and 57 percent that advertising results in better products.

The professional critics come at us from a somewhat different direction. Since there are few more professional or critical than John Kenneth Galbraith, let us begin with him. In *The New Industrial State*, Galbraith says, "In everyday parlance, this great machine, and the demanding and varied talents that it employs are said to be engaged in selling goods. In less ambiguous language, it means that it is engaged in the management of those who buy goods." Similarly, in his book *The Sponsor: Notes on a Modern Potentate*, Columbia University professor Erik Barnouw defines television advertising as "selling the unnecessary."

Philip Slater writes, in *The Pursuit of Loneliness*, "If we define pornography as any message from any communication medium that is intended to arouse sexual excitement, then it is clear that most advertisements are covertly pornographic." Novelist Mary McCarthy attacks us thusly in *On the Contrary*: "The thing, however, that repels us in these advertisements is their naive falsity to life. Who are these advertising men kidding? ... Between the tired, sad, gentle faces of the subway riders and the grinning Holy Families of the Ad-Mass, there exists no possibility of even a wishful identifica-

tion." I could go on and on were it not for a narrow threshold for self-inflicted pain. I'll conclude with a definition of advertising by Fred Allen: "85 percent confusion and 15 percent commission."

The criticisms leveled against advertising by the general public are clearly of a different nature from those of the specialized groups. The people are faulting advertising on what it's doing wrong or what it's not doing well enough or what it's doing too much of. The specialists are criticizing advertising on the basis of a totally different set of standards. The distinction is important because it explains why the advertising industry often responds so ineptly to its professional critics. It's hard to come up with answers when you not only don't understand the question but can't conceive why anyone would ask it.

The fact is that academicians, journalists, consumer advocates and government regulators criticize—and dislike—advertising because it isn't something else.

It accomplishes little to carry on about automobiles because they weren't made to fly or to reproach dogs because they don't climb trees. It is not in the nature of dogs to do what cats do, nor were the evolutionary forces that produced them guided by any imperative to develop that capacity. By the same token, it accomplishes little to condemn advertising because it isn't journalism or education or entertainment. It is fruitless to hold that advertising should be hidden, since it is not advertising if it's not seen. And it is witless to excoriate advertising for having arcane powers to brainwash or to make people act against their will when it clearly wouldn't and couldn't function as advertising if it did.

Yet such charges form the case made against advertising by many professional critics. Before I answer them, it's important for all of us to understand what advertising actually *is*. Only then can we put aside criticism based on what it isn't and get down to the positive challenge of making it better.

Archeologists have discovered evidence of some kind of advertising among the artifacts of every civilization that communicated by writing. The moment one man began growing or raising more than he needed and saw the opportunity to have what someone else was producing, the concept of bartering was born. Now, the only way to extend bartering beyond the chance encounter of two individuals with corresponding needs and surpluses was for each to post what he had and what he wanted in a public place where many could learn about it. The introduction of currency simplified the process by allowing people to post only what they were offering.

This "poster" concept dominated advertising for millennia. Its elements were the item or service offered, the name and location of the offerer, and sometimes the price. Often the most gifted artists of the era were employed to visualize for the prospect what he would receive for his money. Toulouse-Lautrec was one, and the graphics he created to lure customers into the Moulin Rouge now hang in the great art museums of the world.

Such embellishments brought a new dimension of creativity to the simple exposition of product, seller and price but did not change the basic approach; the poster remained the principal form of advertising until relatively recent years. As newspapers and magazines appeared, the poster concept was transferred to paid space in their pages. Early advertising agencies did little to advance the craft and develop its potential, for they had been formed essentially as brokers of space. They bought advertising space in quantity from newspapers and magazines at a 15 percent discount, then sold it to advertisers at full price. To justify this "commission," they counseled their clients on what to put in that space. But such advice was a relatively simple sideline to the space-brokering function since the poster concept more or less limited the information to product, seller and price.

In fact, in the early 1900s, the generally accepted definition of advertising was the one coined by the leading agency of the time (still in business today), N. W. Ayer. Ayer said advertising was "keeping your name before the public." But all that was to change with the new century. As a result of two men meeting in Chicago, the real energy of advertising was unlocked, its enormous potential tapped, and its true nature revealed.

One spring afternoon in 1904, in an office building at Wabash and Randolph Streets that was eventually replaced by Marshall Field's department store, two men were chatting. One was Ambrose Thomas, one of the founders of the Lord & Thomas advertising agency. The other was a bright young man named Albert Lasker, who, it was already apparent, would soon be running the agency.

Following a polite knock, an office boy came in with a note and handed it to Thomas. Upon reading it, Thomas snorted and gave it to Lasker. The note said: "I am downstairs in the saloon, and I can tell you what advertising is. I know that you don't know. It will mean much to me to have you know what it is and it will mean much to you. If you wish to know what advertising is, send the word 'yes' down by messenger." It was signed by a John E. Kennedy.

Thomas asked Lasker if he had ever heard of the man, and when Lasker said he hadn't, Thomas decided Kennedy was probably mad and wasn't worth wasting time on. But Lasker, who was dissatisfied with the concept of "keeping your name before the public," was willing to take a chance. He sent down for Kennedy, and the two spent an hour in Lasker's office. Then they headed for the saloon downstairs, not to emerge until midnight.

Kennedy was a former Royal Canadian Mounted Policeman, a dashing, mustachioed chap who in 1904 was employed as a copywriter for an elixir known as Dr. Shoop's Restorative. What he said to Lasker that day resulted in his being hired on the spot for the unheard-of salary of $28,000 a year. Within 24 months, he was making $75,000.

What did he say to Lasker? Simply this: "Advertising is salesmanship in print."

It seems so simple and obvious today. But what this definition did in 1904 was to change the course of advertising completely and make possible the enormous role it now plays in our economy. For, by equating the function of an advertisement with the function of a salesman who calls on a prospect personally, it revealed the true nature of advertising.

For the first time, the concept of persuasion, which is the prime role of a salesman, was applied to the creation of advertising. Information was considered in a new light, since information is what a salesman must be equipped with and what he uses to persuade. An ad was seen as a means of conveying the personality of the advertiser, just as a good salesman reflects the standards of his company. Reason and logic became part of advertising planning. And so, for the first time, did the consumer.

With its possibilities revealed, advertising exploded. Now it could be refined, made more effective and applied to new tasks. Agencies proliferated, and those that understood the new definition flourished. None flourished more than Lord & Thomas, the birthplace of the revolution. Under Albert Lasker's leadership it became the biggest, most successful agency of its time.

* * *

Advertising, then, is salesmanship functioning in the paid space and time of mass media. To criticize it for being that, for being true to its nature, is to question whether it should be permitted—a position taken by only the most rabid, none of whom have come up with a reasonable substitute for its role in the economy. And to criticize it for not being something else—something it might resemble but by definition can never be—is equally fruitless. Yet much of the professional criticism I spoke of has its feet planted solidly on those two pieces of shaky ground.

As a format of conveying information, advertising shares certain characteristics with journalism, education, entertainment and other modes of communication. But it cannot be judged by the same standards because it is essentially something else. This point is missed by many in government, both the regulators and the elected representatives who oversee the regulators.

The Federal Trade Commission was pushing not too long ago for one of those quasi-laws they call a Trade Regulation Ruling (when they were empowered to write the law of the land, I don't know; but that's another argument). This particular TRR would have required an ad or commercial for any product claiming to be nutritious to list all its nutritive elements. For two reasons advertising cannot comply with such a requirement and still end up as advertising.

One, advertising is salesmanship, and good salesmanship does not countenance boring the prospect into glassy-eyed semiconsciousness. Yet I am sure—and consumers on whom sample ads and commercials were tested agreed—that a lengthy litany of niacin, riboflavin, ascorbic acid and so on is as interesting as watching paint dry.

Less subjective is the fact that such a listing can't be given for many good, wholesome products within the confines of a 30-second commercial. Since that's the standard length today, the end result of the proposed TRR would have been to ban those products from television advertising. The FTC staff did not consider that advertising necessarily functions in the paid space and time of mass media. Adding 20 or more seconds of Latin makes that impossible.

This example illustrates the problems that can arise when regulators try to dictate what must go into advertising. An FTC attorney named Donald F. Turner was quoted by Professor Raymond Bauer in a piece for the *Harvard Business Review* as saying, "There are three steps to informed choice. (1) The consumer must know the product exists. (2) The consumer must know how the product performs. (3) He must know how it performs compared to other products. If advertising only performs step one and appeals on other than a performance basis, informed choice cannot be made."

This is probably true in an ad for a new floor wax from S. C. Johnson or an antiperspirant from Bristol-Myers. But what about a new fragrance from Max Factor? How do you describe how Halston performs compared with other products? Is it important for anyone to know? Is it salesmanship to make the attempt? Or suppose you're advertising Coca-Cola. There can't be many people left in the world who don't know Coke exists or how it performs. Granted, there may be a few monks or aborigines who don't know how it performs in relation to other products, but you can't reach them through advertising. So why waste the time or space?

The reason Coca-Cola advertises is to maintain or increase a level of awareness about itself among people who know full well it exists and what it tastes like, people whom other beverage makers are contacting with similar messages about their products. Simple information about its existence and its popularity—information that triggers residual knowledge in the recipient about its taste and other characteristics—is legitimate and sufficient. It does what a salesman would do.

On the other hand, advertising for a big-ticket item—an automobile, for instance—would seemingly have to include a lot of information in order to achieve its end. But the advertising is not attempting to sell the car. It is an advance salesman trying to persuade the prospect to visit a showroom. Only there can the principal salesman do the complete job. Turner's definition is neither pertinent nor possible in the case of automobiles. In such cases mass communications media cannot convey the kind of information one needs in order to "know how the product performs" or to "know how it performs compared to other products." You have to see it, kick the tires, ask the salesman questions about it, let the kids try out the windshield wipers. And surely you have to drive it.

In the paid space and time of mass media, the purpose of automobile advertising is to select the prospect for a particular car and, on the basis of its appeal to his income, life-style or basic attitudes, to persuade him he's the person the designers and engineers had in mind when they created this model. If the information is properly chosen and skillfully presented, it will point out the relevance of the car to his needs and self-image sufficiently to get him into the showroom. Then it's up to the salesman to sell him the car—but with a different package of information, including the tactile and experiential, than could be provided in the ad.

From time to time some government regulator will suggest that advertising information should be limited to price and function. But consider how paleolithic that kind of thinking is. Restricting advertising to a discussion of price and function would eliminate, among other things, an equally essential piece of information: what kind of people make and market this product or provide this service.

The reputation, quality standards, taste and responsibility of the people who put out a product is information that's not only important to the consumer but is increasingly demanded by the consumer. It's information that can often outweigh price and function as these differences narrow among products within the same category. It's information that is critical to the advertising my agency prepares for clients like Johnson's Wax, Sunkist Growers, Hallmark, Sears and many others. Advertising would not be salesmanship without it. Put it this way: if surgeons advertised and you had a hot appendix, would you want the ads to be limited to price and function information?

The government regulators, and the consumer advocates dedicated to influencing them, do not understand what advertising is and how it is perceived by the consumer. And their overwhelming fear that one is always trying to deceive the other leads them to demand from advertising the kind of product information that characterizes *Consumer Reports*. They expect advertising to be journalism, and they evaluate it by journalistic standards. Since it is not, advertising, like the ugly duckling, is found wanting.

* * *

It is not in the nature of advertising to be journalistic, to present both sides, to include information that shows the product negatively in comparison with other entries in the category (unless, of course, the exclusion of such information would make the ad misleading or product usage hazardous). For example, advertising for Sunkist lemons, which might point out the flavor advantages of fresh lemons over bottled juice, should not be expected to remind people that fresh lemons can't be kept as long as a bottle of concentrate. Information is selected for journalism—or should be—to provide the recipient with as complete and objective an account as possible. Information is selected for advertising to persuade the recipient to go to a showroom or make a mental pledge to find the product on a store shelf.

Advertising, like the personal salesman, unabashedly presents products in their most favorable light. I doubt that there's a consumer around who doesn't understand that. For instance, would you, in a classified ad offering your house for sale, mention the toilet on the second floor that doesn't flush? I doubt that even a conscience as rigorous as Ralph Nader's would insist, in an ad to sell his own used car, on information about that worn fan belt or leaky gasket. No reader would expect it. Nor does anyone expect it from our clients.

Information, as far as advertising is concerned, is anything that helps a genuine prospect to perceive the applicability of a product to his or her individual life, to understand how the product will solve a problem, make life easier or better, or in some way provide a benefit. When the knowledge can't safely be assumed, it also explains how to get the product. In other words, it's salesmanship.

It is not witchcraft, another craft government regulators and otherwise responsible writers are forever confusing with mine. For the same reasons people like to believe that someone is poisoning our water supply or, as in the Joseph McCarthy era, that pinkos proliferate in our government and are trying to bring it down, someone is always rejuvenating the idea of subliminal advertising.

Subliminal advertising is defined as advertising that employs stimuli operating below the threshold of consciousness. It is supposed to influence the recipient's behavior without his being aware of any communication taking place. The most frequently cited example, never fully verified, involved a movie theater where the words "Drink Coke" were flashed on the screen so briefly that while the mind recorded the message, it was not conscious of receiving it. The result was said to be greatly increased sales of Coca-Cola at the vending counter.

I don't like to destroy cherished illusions, but I must state unequivocally that there is no such thing as subliminal advertising. I have never seen an example of it, nor have I ever heard it seriously discussed as a technique by advertising people. Salesmanship is persuasion involving rational and emotional tools that must be employed on a conscious level in order to effect a conscious decision in favor of one product over its competitive counterparts, and in order to have that decision remembered and acted upon at a later time. Furthermore, it's demeaning to assume that the human mind is so easily controlled that anyone can be made to act against his will or better judgment by peremptory commands he doesn't realize are present.

Even more absurd is the theory proposed by Wilson Bryan Key in a sleazy book entitled *Subliminal Seduction.* From whatever dark motivations, Key finds sexual symbolism in every ad and commercial. He points it out to his readers with no little relish, explaining how, after reducing the prospect to a pliant mass of sexual arousal, advertising can get him to buy anything. There are some who might envy Mr. Key his ability to get turned on by a photograph of a Sunkist orange.

Most professional critics are much less bizarre in their condemnations. Uninformed about the real nature of advertising, perhaps, but not mad. For instance, they often ascribe recondite powers to advertising—powers that it does not have and that they cannot adequately define—because it is not solely verbal. Being for the most part lawyers and academics, they are uncomfortable with information conveyed by means other than words. They want things spelled out, even in television commercials, despite the fact that television is primarily a visual medium. They do not trust graphic and musical information because they aren't sure that the meaning they receive is the same one the consumer is receiving. And since they consider the consumer much more gullible and much less astute than they, they sound the alarm and then charge to the rescue. Sorcery is afoot.

Well, from time immemorial, graphics and music have been with us. I suspect each has been part of the salesman's tool kit for as long as they have been salesmen. The songs of medieval street vendors and Toulouse-Lautrec's Jane Avril attest.

A mouth-watering cake presented photographically as the end benefit of Betty Crocker Cake Mix is just as legitimate as and more effective than a verbal description. The mysteriously exuberant musical communication "I Love New York" honestly conveys the variety of experiences offered by New York State; it is not witchcraft. It is not to be feared unless you fear yourself. But perhaps that is the cradle that spawns consumer advocates and government regulators. There is something murky in that psyche, some kink in the mentality of those who feel others are incapable of making mundane decisions for themselves, something Kafka-like in the need to take over the personal lives of Americans in order to protect them from themselves.

I read with growing disquiet a document put out by the Federal Trade Commission in 1979 entitled *Consumer Information Remedies*. In discussing how to evaluate consumer information, they wrote, "The Task Force members struggled long and hard to come up with a universally satisfactory definition of the *value* of consumer information. Should the Commission consider a mandatory disclosure to be a valuable piece of information, for instance, if it were later shown that although consumers understood the information, they did not use it when making purchase decisions? Is there a value in improving the *quality* of

market decisions through the provision of relevant information, or is it necessary for the information to change behavior to have value?" The ensuing "remedies" make it clear that the staff really judges the value of a mandatory disclaimer by the degree to which it changes consumer behavior in the direction they are seeking.

But wait a minute. I'm a consumer, too. Who are they to be wondering what to do with me next if I understand but choose to ignore some dumb disclaimer they've forced an advertiser to put in his ad? It's my God-given right to ignore any information any salesman presents me with—and an ad, remember, is a salesman. And what's this about changing behavior? Well, mine is going to change if the employees of a government I'm paying for start talking like that out loud. It's going to get violent.

Later in the same document, the staff addresses "Sub-Optional Purchases." While I have no quarrel with their intent, I find my hackles rising as they define the problem in terms of people "misallocating resources," consumers wasting their dollars on "products that do not best satisfy their needs." Listen, fellows, those are *my* resources you're talking about. Those are *my* dollars, what there is of them after you guys in Washington have had your way with my paycheck. I'm going to allocate them as I damn well please. And if I want to waste a few on products that do not best satisfy my needs—an unnutritious but thoroughly delicious hot dog at the ball park, for example—try to stop me.

Perhaps I, in return, am seeking evidence of conspiracy. Perhaps I'm looking under beds. But I think I understand the true nature of government bureaucrats. They, on the other hand, do not understand that of advertising. They and other professional critics—the journalists, consumerists, academicians—don't understand that it's not journalism or education and cannot be judged on the basis of objectivity and exhaustive, in-depth treatment. Thorough knowledge of a subject cannot be derived from an advertisement but only from a synthesis of all relevant sources: the advertising of competitors, the opinions of others, the more impartial reports in newspapers, magazines and, increasingly, television.

The critics also don't understand that advertising isn't witchcraft, that it cannot wash the brain or coerce someone to buy what he doesn't want. It shouldn't be castigated for what it cannot and does not purport to do. And it isn't entertainment, either. A commercial should offer some reward to the viewer in return for his time, but that reward need not always take the form of entertainment. Sometimes the tone should be serious, even about seemingly frivolous subjects. Hemorrhoids are not funny to those who have them.

Advertising sometimes resembles other fields, just as an elephant resembles a snake to the blind man who feels its trunk, and a tree to another who feels its leg. But advertising is really salesmanship functioning in the paid space and time of mass media.

POSTSCRIPT

Is Advertising Fundamentally Deceptive?

The issue in advertising comes down to social expectation. If advertising is a gentle put-on expected and appreciated by all, a way of displaying a product for sale that might persuade a customer to try it once, and no more than that, then surely it is a harmless addition to the pages and airwaves of our experience. Advertising can be uplifting, appealing, funny, and even beautiful. If advertising remains only in the inessential margins of our lives, it can do no real harm. The manufacturer of the advertised product obtains value from having people try his product just once, and from that value comes the justification to hire the advertising firm and to place the messages in print or on the air. This placement in turn funds the magazines and the entertainment of radio and television, and it therefore brings otherwise unobtainable value to our lives. There seems to be no moral percentage in insisting on the strict theoretical line, that if advertising in any way influences you to spend a penny on anything that you would not have bought if not for the advertising, then it is manipulative and wrong.

But what if it is *not* at the margins of our lives? Those who take advertising more seriously hold that the practice is wrong because it distorts our perception of what is socially valuable and of what is personally redeeming.

The first line of attack on the advertising industry was developed originally by economist John Kenneth Galbraith in *The Affluent Society*. Galbraith was interested not so much in the decision to buy one good rather than another in the market but the decision to allot funds to the private rather than to the public sector. The decision to vote for or against taxes to buy public goods, after all, is an economic decision. Galbraith argued that since only private firms purchase advertising space and time, advertising distorts the normal decision-making process of a society in favor of the purchase of private goods (cars, swimming pools, and video games, for example) and against the selection of public goods (such as clean air, better roads, and pleasant parks), thus systematically starving the public sector in favor of the private. For Galbraith, then, advertising is not only a nuisance but a seriously unethical strategy to funnel the national wealth into the hands of the industrialists and away from public needs.

The second line of reasoning notes the psychological targets of typical advertising. People are weak, vulnerable, and plagued, on occasion, by feelings of inadequacy and social inferiority. These feelings are not at all marginal but go to the core of the social creatures that we are. They are painful, and we are grateful for relief. Advertising learns to ask questions that expose our vulnerabilities and then answers the questions with products that explicitly promise to strengthen us at those weak points. The deception of advertising is not in the lies that the advertisers tell but in the implication that there are products that can remedy the fear and imperfections of the human condition itself. As such, advertising is doubly harmful: it leads us to believe falsehoods about what will and will not make us smarter, more popular, thinner, more attractive to the opposite sex, and in all other ways the better social person many of us would like to be. More importantly, it portrays the weakness of human nature only as a deplorable and shameful condition, not to be acknowledged or faced in company with others who share it, but to be quickly remedied before others notice. Fortunately, the advertising says, the remedy for human inadequacies, in the form of the advertised product, is at hand. If you cannot or do not purchase it, you have only yourself to blame for your continuing social failures.

In this manner humans are stripped of the real means to help them cope with their weaknesses—the support of other humans with similar weaknesses. Instead, they are isolated in their feelings of inadequacy and left with a false remedy that can never do what it so glowingly promises to do. When the false remedy is only a perfume that promises to make you fantastically attractive, one may still argue that no *real* harm is done, and that you really do enjoy the fantasy. But when the false remedy is a cigarette that purports to turn you into a strong and self-sufficient cowboy, then the purveyance of images and the law and practices that condone it begin to appear harmful.

Is advertising a fraud and a deception, the more fraudulent advertising being the more successful, or is advertising a harmless practice of American business, helping the economy by keeping goods, especially new goods, flowing?

SUGGESTED READINGS

Robert L. Arrington, "Advertising and Behavior Control," *Journal of Business Ethics* (1981).

Sissela Bok, *Lying: Moral Choice in Public and Private Life* (Pantheon Books, 1978).

William A. Cook, "Truth, in the Eye of the Beholder?" *Journal of Advertising Research* (December 1991).

John Fraedrich, O. C. Ferrell, and William Pride, "An Empirical Examination of Three Machiavellian Concepts: Advertisers vs. The General Public," *Journal of Business Ethics* (September 1989).

John Kenneth Galbraith, *The Affluent Society*, 3rd ed. (Houghton Mifflin, 1976).

Jonathan Karl, "Lotto Baloney," *The New Republic* (March 4, 1991).

Peter Nelson, "Advertising and Ethics," in Richard T. DeGeorge and Joseph A. Pichler, eds., *Ethics, Free Enterprise, and Public Policy: Original Essays on Moral Issues in Business* (Oxford University Press, 1978).

ISSUE 12

Product Liability: Was Ford to Blame in the Pinto Case?

YES: Mark Dowie, from "Pinto Madness," *Mother Jones* (September/October 1977)

NO: Ford Motor Company, from "Closing Argument by Mr. James Neal," Brief for the Defense, *State of Indiana v. Ford Motor Company*, U.S. District Court, South Bend, Indiana (January 15, 1980)

ISSUE SUMMARY

YES: Award-winning investigative journalist Mark Dowie alleges that Ford Motor Company deliberately put an unsafe car—the Pinto—on the road, causing hundreds of people to suffer burn deaths and horrible disfigurement. He argues that the related activities of Ford's executives, both within the company and in dealing with the public and the government, were criminal.

NO: James Neal, chief attorney for Ford Motor Company during the Pinto litigation, argues to the jury that Ford cannot be held responsible for deaths that were caused by others—such as the driver of the van that struck the victims—and that there is no proof of criminal intent or negligence on the part of Ford.

On August 10, 1978, three girls had stopped their car, a 1973 Ford Pinto, on U.S. Highway 22 near Goshen, Indiana, and were about to get under way again when they were struck from the rear at high speed by a van. The car immediately burst into flames, and the girls had no chance to escape before the flames reached them.

The blame for these girls' deaths fell not on the driver of the van but on the manufacturer of the Pinto. Questions that were asked were: What was wrong with the car? Why did it burst into flames so quickly? Mark Dowie, then–general manager of business operations of the magazine *Mother Jones*, had argued a year earlier that there was a great deal wrong with the Pinto. Dowie's argument, which is reprinted here, is based on data obtained for him by some disaffected Ford engineers. In it, he suggests that the Pinto had been rushed into production without adequate testing; that it had a vulnerable fuel system that would rupture with any rear-end collision; that even though the vulnerability was discovered before production, Ford had hurried the Pinto to the market anyway; and that successful lobbying thereafter had prevented government regulators from instituting a requirement for a safer gas tank. Most suggestive to the public was a document supplied by one of the engineers, an estimate of the probable costs of refitting valves to prevent fire in a rollover accident. It was a cost-benefit analysis that placed a dollar value on human life—among the estimates were the probability of a fatal accident, the amount of money needed to settle a lawsuit for the loss of a life, and the amount of money needed to do the refitting so that there would be less chance for that loss of life—and concluded that it was more economical to accept the higher probability of death occurring and then settle the suits as they come. The document caused serious damage to Ford Motor Company's reputation, and it is not likely to ever be entirely forgiven.

Ford endured two sets of court appearances as a result of this article. More common, and successful, were the civil suits, alleging culpable negligence that damaged the rights of other individuals. But the state of Indiana also brought a public prosecution for *criminal* negligence, and James Neal's brief, which also follows, was prepared for that trial.

The 1916 case *McPherson v. Buick* helps set the stage for this debate. In this case, McPherson successfully sued the Buick Motor Company for injury sustained as a direct result of a poorly manufactured product. This was the first instance of a consumer's suing a manufacturer (as opposed to the seller), and it marked the transfer of product liability cases from the form of action known as "contract" to the form of action known as "tort" (in this case, negligence). The logic is that not only is an individual agreement breached when a shoddy product injures a consumer but a general obligation on the part of a manufacturer (an implied "warrant of merchantability") to avoid putting an unsafe product on the market is not met. Given the myriad ways that people can injure themselves, that obligation seems to be very broad indeed.

With regard to the Pinto case, was Ford guilty of deliberate malfeasance? Was it a series of unlucky decisions made in good faith? Or was this just a very unfortunate accident? Ask yourself, while reading these selections, what conditions need to be satisifed in order to attribute "responsibility" to any person or company. Also, what kinds of risks do people assume when buying a car, a motorcycle, or a can of tuna fish? For what is the manufacturer responsible? Should we be willing to assume more risks in the enormously competitive market that prevails among small automobiles? Does the product liability suit unjustly cripple American efforts to compete in highly competitive industries? Is this something we should worry about?

YES   Mark Dowie

PINTO MADNESS

One evening in the mid-1960s, Arjay Miller was driving home from his office in Dearborn, Michigan, in the four-door Lincoln Continental that went with his job as president of the Ford Motor Company. On a crowded highway, another car struck his from the rear. The Continental spun around and burst into flames. Because he was wearing a shoulder-strap seat belt, Miller was unharmed by the crash, and because his doors didn't jam he escaped the gasoline-drenched, flaming wreck. But the accident made a vivid impression on him. Several months later, on July 15, 1965, he recounted it to a U.S. Senate subcommittee that was hearing testimony on auto safety legislation. "I still have burning in my mind the image of that gas tank on fire," Miller said. He went on to express an almost passionate interest in controlling fuel-fed fires in cars that crash or roll over. He spoke with excitement about the fabric gas tank Ford was testing at that very moment. "If it proves out," he promised the senators, "it will be a feature you will see in our standard cars."

Almost seven years after Miller's testimony, a woman, whom for legal reasons we will call Sandra Gillespie, pulled onto a Minneapolis highway in her new Ford Pinto. Riding with her was a young boy, whom we'll call Robbie Carlton. As she entered a merge lane, Sandra Gillespie's car stalled. Another car rear-ended hers at an impact speed of 28 miles per hour. The Pinto's gas tank ruptured. Vapors from it mixed quickly with the air in the passenger compartment. A spark ignited the mixture and the car exploded in a ball of fire. Sandra died in agony a few hours later in an emergency hospital. Her passenger, 13-year-old Robbie Carlton, is still alive; he has just come home from another futile operation aimed at grafting a new ear and nose from skin on the few unscarred portions of his badly burned body. (This accident is real; the details are from police reports.)

Why did Sandra Gillespie's Ford Pinto catch fire so easily, seven years after Ford's Arjay Miller made his apparently sincere pronouncements—the same seven years that brought more safety improvements to cars than any other period in automotive history? An extensive investigation by *Mother Jones* over

From Mark Dowie, "Pinto Madness," *Mother Jones*, vol. 2, no. 8 (September/October 1977). Copyright © 1977 by Mark Dowie. Reprinted by permission.

the past six months has found these answers:

• Fighting strong competition from Volkswagen for the lucrative small-car market, the Ford Motor Company rushed the Pinto into production in much less than the usual time.

• Ford engineers discovered in pre-production crash tests that rear-end collisions would rupture the Pinto's fuel system extremely easily.

• Because assembly-line machinery was already tooled when engineers found this defect, top Ford officials decided to manufacture the car anyway—exploding gas tank and all—*even though Ford owned the patent on a much safer gas tank.*

• For more than eight years afterwards, Ford successfully lobbied, with extraordinary vigor and some blatant lies, against a key government safety standard that would have forced the company to change the Pinto's fire-prone gas tank.

By conservative estimates Pinto crashes have caused 500 burn deaths to people who would not have been seriously injured if the car had not burst into flames. The figure could be as high as 900. Burning Pintos have become such an embarrassment to Ford that its advertising agency, J. Walter Thompson, dropped a line from the end of a radio spot that read "Pinto leaves you with that warm feeling."

Ford knows the Pinto is a firetrap, yet it has paid out millions to settle damage suits out of court, and it is prepared to spend millions more lobbying against safety standards. With a half million cars rolling off the assembly lines each year, Pinto is the biggest-selling subcompact in America, and the company's operating profit on the car is fantastic. Finally,

in 1977, new Pinto models have incorporated a few minor alterations necessary to meet that federal standard Ford managed to hold off for eight years. Why did the company delay so long in making these minimal, inexpensive improvements?

• Ford waited eight years because its internal "cost-benefit analysis," *which places a dollar value on human life,* said it wasn't profitable to make the changes sooner.

Before we get to the question of how much Ford thinks your life is worth, let's trace the history of the death trap itself. Although this particular story is about the Pinto, the way in which Ford made its decision is typical of the U.S. auto industry generally. There are plenty of similar stories about other cars made by other companies. But this case is the worst of them all.

* * *

The next time you drive behind a Pinto (with over two million of them on the road, you shouldn't have much trouble finding one), take a look at the rear end. That long silvery object hanging down under the bumper is the gas tank. The tank begins about six inches forward of the bumper. In late models the bumper is designed to withstand a collision of only about five miles per hour. Earlier bumpers may as well not have been on the car for all the protection they offered the gas tank.

Mother Jones has studied hundreds of reports and documents on rear-end collisions involving Pintos. These reports conclusively reveal that if you ran into that Pinto you were following at over 30 miles per hour, the rear end of the car would buckle like an accordion, right up to the back seat. The tube leading to the gas-tank cap would be ripped away from the tank itself, and gas would immediately begin sloshing onto the road around the car. The buckled gas tank would be jammed up against the differential housing (that big bulge in the middle of your rear axle), which contains four sharp, protruding bolts likely to gash holes in the tank and spill still more gas. Now all you need is a spark from a cigarette, ignition, or scraping metal, and both cars would be engulfed in flames. If you gave that Pinto a really good whack—say, at 40 mph—chances are excellent that its doors would jam and you would have to stand by and watch its trapped passengers burn to death.

This scenario is no news to Ford. Internal company documents in our possession show that Ford has crash-tested the Pinto at a top-secret site more than 40 times and that *every* test made at over 25 mph without special structural alteration of the car has resulted in a ruptured fuel tank. Despite this, Ford officials denied under oath having crash-tested the Pinto.

Eleven of these tests, averaging a 31-mph impact speed, came before Pintos started rolling out of the factories. Only three cars passed the test with unbroken fuel tanks. In one of them an inexpensive light-weight plastic baffle was placed between the front of the gas tank and the differential housing, so those four bolts would not perforate the tank. (Don't forget about that little piece of plastic, which costs one dollar and weighs one pound. It plays an important role in our story later on.) In another successful test, a piece of steel was placed between the tank and the bumper. In the third test car the gas tank was lined with a rubber bladder. But none of these protective alterations was used in the mass-produced Pinto.

In pre-production planning, engineers seriously considered using in the Pinto the same kind of gas tank Ford uses in the Capri. The Capri tank rides over the rear axle and differential housing. It has been so successful in over 50 crash tests that Ford used it in its Experimental Safety Vehicle, which withstood rear-end impacts of 60 mph. So why wasn't the Capri tank used in the Pinto? Or, why wasn't that plastic baffle placed between the tank and the axle—something that would have saved the life of Sandra Gillespie and hundreds like her? Why was a car known to be a serious fire hazard deliberately released to production in August of 1970?

* * *

Whether Ford should manufacture subcompacts at all was the subject of a bitter two-year debate at the company's Dearborn headquarters. The principals in this corporate struggle were the then-president Semon "Bunky" Knudsen, whom Henry Ford II had hired away from General Motors, and Lee Iacocca, a spunky Young Turk who had risen fast within the company on the enormous success of the Mustang. Iacocca argued forcefully that Volkswagen and the Japanese were going to capture the entire American subcompact market unless Ford put out its own alternative to the VW Beetle. Bunky Knudsen said, in effect: let them have the small-car market; Ford makes good money on medium and large models. But he lost the battle and later resigned. Iacocca became president and almost immediately began a rush program to produce the Pinto.

Like the Mustang, the Pinto became known in the company as "Lee's car." Lee Iacocca wanted that little car in the showrooms of America with the 1971 models.

So he ordered his engineering vice president, Bob Alexander, to oversee what was probably the shortest production planning period in modern automotive history. The normal time span from conception to production of a new car model is about 43 months. The Pinto schedule was set at just under 25.

... Design, styling, product planning, advance engineering and quality assurance all have flexible time frames, and engineers can pretty much carry these on simultaneously. Tooling, on the other hand, has a fixed time frame of about 18 months. Normally, an auto company doesn't begin tooling until the other processes are almost over: you don't want to make the machines that stamp and press and grind metal into the shape of car parts until you know all those parts will work well together. *But Iacocca's speed-up meant Pinto tooling went on at the same time as product development.* So when crash tests revealed a serious defect in the gas tank, it was too late. The tooling was well under way.

When it was discovered the gas tank was unsafe, did anyone go to Iacocca and tell him? "Hell no," replied an engineer who worked on the Pinto, a high company official for many years, who, unlike several others at Ford, maintains a necessarily clandestine concern for safety. "That person would have been fired. Safety wasn't a popular subject around Ford in those days. With Lee it was taboo. Whenever a problem was raised that meant a delay on the Pinto, Lee would chomp on his cigar, look out the window and say 'Read the product objectives and get back to work.' "

The product objectives are clearly stated in the Pinto "green book." This is a thick, top-secret manual in green covers containing a step-by-step production plan for the model, detailing the metallurgy, weight, strength and quality of every part in the car. The product objectives for the Pinto are repeated in an article by Ford executive F. G. Olsen published by the Society of Automotive Engineers. He lists these product objectives as follows:

1. TRUE SUBCOMPACT
   • Size
   • Weight
2. LOW COST OF OWNERSHIP
   • Initial price
   • Fuel consumption
   • Reliability
   • Serviceability
3. CLEAR PRODUCT SUPERIORITY
   • Appearance
   • Comfort
   • Features
   • Ride and Handling
   • Performance

Safety, you will notice, is not there. It is not mentioned in the entire article. As Lee Iacocca was fond of saying, "Safety doesn't sell."

Heightening the anti-safety pressure on Pinto engineers was an important goal set by Iacocca known as "the limits of 2,000." The Pinto was not to weigh an ounce over 2,000 pounds and not to cost a cent over $2,000. "Iacocca enforced these limits with an iron hand," recalls the engineer quoted earlier. So, even when a crash test showed that that one-pound, one-dollar piece of plastic stopped the puncture of the gas tank, it was thrown out as extra cost and extra weight.

People shopping for subcompacts are watching every dollar. "You have to keep in mind," the engineer explained, "that the price elasticity on these subcompacts is extremely tight. You can price yourself right out of the market by adding $25 to the production cost of the model. And nobody understands that better than Iacocca."

Dr. Leslie Ball, the retired safety chief for the NASA manned space program and a founder of the International Society of Reliability Engineers, recently made a careful study of the Pinto. "The release to production of the Pinto was the most reprehensible decision in the history of American engineering," he said. Ball can name more than 40 European and Japanese models in the Pinto price and weight range with safer gas-tank positioning. Ironically, many of them, like the Ford Capri, contain a "saddle-type" gas tank riding over the back axle. *The patent on the saddle-type tank is owned by the Ford Motor Co.*

Los Angeles auto safety expert Byron Bloch has made an in-depth study of the Pinto fuel system. "It's a catastrophic blunder," he says. "Ford made an extremely irresponsible decision when they placed such a weak tank in such a ridiculous location in such a soft rear end. It's almost designed to blow up—premeditated."

A Ford engineer, who doesn't want his name used, comments: "This company is run by salesmen, not engineers; so the priority is styling, not safety." He goes on to tell a story about gas-tank safety at Ford.

Lou Tubben is one of the most popular engineers at Ford. He's a friendly, outgoing guy with a genuine concern for safety. By 1971 he had grown so concerned about gas-tank integrity that he asked his boss if he could prepare a presentation on safer tank design. Tubben and his boss had both worked on the Pinto and shared a concern for its safety. His boss gave him the go-ahead, scheduled a date for the presentation and invited all company engineers and key production planning personnel. When time came for the meeting, a grand total of two people showed up— Lou Tubben and his boss.

"So you see," continued the anonymous Ford engineer ironically, "there *are* a few of us here at Ford who are concerned about fire safety." He adds: "They are mostly engineers who have to study a lot of accident reports and look at pictures of burned people. But we don't talk about it much. It isn't a popular subject. I've never seen safety on the agenda of a product meeting and, except for a brief period in 1956, I can't remember seeing the word safety in an advertisement. I really don't think the company wants American consumers to start thinking too much about safety—for fear they might demand it, I suppose."

Asked about the Pinto gas tank, another Ford engineer admitted: "That's all true. But you miss the point entirely. You see, safety isn't the issue, trunk space is. You have no idea how stiff the competition is over trunk space. Do you realize that if we put a Capri-type tank in the Pinto you could only get one set of golf clubs in the trunk?"

* * *

Blame for Sandra Gillespie's death, Robbie Carlton's unrecognizable face and all the other injuries and deaths in Pintos since 1970 does not rest on the shoulders of Lee Iacocca alone. For, while he and his associates fought their battle against a safer Pinto in Dearborn, a larger war against safer cars raged in Washington. One skirmish in that war involved Ford's successful eight-year lobbying effort against Federal Motor Vehicle Safety Standard 301, the rear-end provisions of which would have forced Ford to redesign the Pinto.

But first some background:

During the early '60s, auto safety legislation became the *bête-noire* of American big business. The auto industry was the last great unregulated business, and if *it* couldn't reverse the tide of government regulation, the reasoning went, no one could.

People who know him cannot remember Henry Ford II taking a stronger stand than the one he took against the regulation of safety design. He spent weeks in Washington calling on members of Congress, holding press conferences and recruiting business cronies like W. B. Murphy of Campbell's Soup to join the anti-regulation battle. Displaying the sophistication for which today's American corporate leaders will be remembered, Murphy publicly called auto safety "a hula hoop, a fad that will pass." He was speaking to a special luncheon of the Business Council, an organization of 100 chief executives who gather periodically in Washington to provide "advice" and "counsel" to government. The target of their wrath in this instance was the Motor Vehicle Safety Bills introduced in both houses of Congress, largely in response to Ralph Nader's *Unsafe at Any Speed.*

By 1965, most pundits and lobbyists saw the handwriting on the wall and prepared to accept government "meddling" in the last bastion of free enterprise. Not Henry. With bulldog tenacity, he held out for defeat of the legislation to the very end, loyal to his grandfather's invention and to the company that makes it. But the Safety Act passed the House and Senate unanimously, and was signed into law by Lyndon Johnson in 1966.

While lobbying for and against legislation is pretty much a process of high-level back-slapping, press-conferencing and speech-making, fighting a regulatory agency is a much subtler matter. Henry headed home to lick his wounds in Grosse Pointe, Michigan, and a planeload of the Ford Motor Company's best brains flew to Washington to start the "education" of the new federal auto safety bureaucrats.

Their job was to implant the official industry ideology in the minds of the new officials regulating auto safety. Briefly summarized, that ideology states that auto accidents are caused not by *cars*, but by 1) people and 2) highway conditions.

This philosophy is rather like blaming a robbery on the victim. Well, what did you expect? You were carrying money, weren't you? It is an extraordinary experience to hear automotive "safety engineers" talk for hours without ever mentioning cars. They will advocate spending billions educating youngsters, punishing drunks and redesigning street signs. Listening to them, you can momentarily begin to think that it is easier to control 100 million drivers than a handful of manufacturers. They show movies about guardrail design and advocate the clear-cutting of trees 100 feet back from every highway in the nation. If a car is unsafe, they argue, it is because its owner doesn't properly drive it. Or, perhaps, maintain it.

In light of an annual death rate approaching 50,000, they are forced to admit that driving is hazardous. But the car is, in the words of Arjay Miller, "the safest link in the safety chain."

Before the Ford experts left Washington to return to drafting tables in Dearborn they did one other thing. They managed to informally reach an agreement with the major public servants who would be making auto safety decisions. This agreement was that "cost-benefit" would be an acceptable mode of analysis by Detroit and its new regulators. And as we shall see, cost-benefit analysis quickly became the basis of Ford's argument against safer car design.

* * *

Cost-benefit analysis was used only occasionally in government until President Kennedy appointed Ford Motor Company President Robert McNamara to be Secretary of Defense. McNamara, originally an accountant, preached cost benefit with all the force of a Biblical zealot. Stated in its simplest terms, cost-benefit analysis says that if the cost is greater than the benefit, the project is not worth it—no matter what the benefit. Examine the cost of every action, decision, contract, part, or change, the doctrine says, then carefully evaluate the benefits (in dollars) to be certain that they exceed the cost before you begin a program or—and this is the crucial part for our story—pass a regulation.

As a management tool in a business in which profits matter over everything else, cost-benefit analysis makes a certain amount of sense. Serious problems come, however, when public officials who ought to have more than corporate profits at heart apply cost-benefit analysis to every conceivable decision. The inevitable result is that they must place a dollar value on human life.

Ever wonder what your life is worth in dollars? Perhaps $10 million? Ford has a better idea: $200,000.

Remember, Ford had gotten the federal regulators to agree to talk auto safety in terms of cost-benefit analysis. But in order to be able to argue that various safety costs were greater than their benefits, Ford needed to have a dollar value

figure for the "benefit." Rather than be so uncouth as to come up with such a price tag itself, the auto industry pressured the National Highway Traffic Safety Administration to do so. And in a 1972 report the agency decided a human life was worth $200,725. (For its reasoning, see [Table 1].) Inflationary forces have recently pushed the figure up to $278,000.

Furnished with this useful tool, Ford immediately went to work using it to prove why various safety improvements were too expensive to make.

Nowhere did the company argue harder that it should make no changes than in the area of rupture-prone fuel tanks. Not long after the government arrived at the $200,725-per-life figure, it surfaced, rounded off to a cleaner $200,000, in an internal Ford memorandum. This cost-benefit analysis argued that Ford should not make an $11-per-car improvement that would prevent 180 fiery deaths a year. (This minor change would have prevented gas tanks from breaking so easily both in rear-end collisions, like Sandra Gillespie's, and in rollover accidents, where the same thing tends to happen.)

Ford's cost-benefit table [Table 2] is buried in a seven-page company memorandum entitled "Fatalities Associated with Crash-Induced Fuel Leakage and Fires." The memo argues that there is no financial benefit in complying with proposed safety standards that would admittedly result in fewer auto fires, fewer burn deaths and fewer burn injuries. Naturally, memoranda that speak so casually of "burn deaths" and "burn injuries" are not released to the public. They are very effective, however, with Department of Transportation officials indoctrinated in McNamarian cost-benefit analysis.

Table 1

What's Your Life Worth? Societal Cost Components for Fatalities, 1972 NHTSA Study

Component	1971 Costs
Future productivity losses	
Direct	$132,000
Indirect	41,300
Medical costs	
Hospital	700
Other	425
Property damage	1,500
Insurance administration	4,700
Legal and court	3,000
Employer losses	1,000
Victim's pain and suffering	10,000
Funeral	900
Assets (lost consumption)	5,000
Miscellaneous accident cost	200
Total per fatality: $200,725	

Here is a chart from a federal study showing how the National Highway Traffic Safety Administration has calculated the value of a human life. The estimate was arrived at under pressure from the auto industry. The Ford Motor Company has used it in cost-benefit analyses arguing why certain safety measures are not "worth" the savings in human lives. The calculation above is a breakdown of the estimated cost to society every time someone is killed in a car accident. We were not able to find anyone, either in the government or at Ford, who could explain how the $10,000 figure for "pain and suffering" had been arrived at.

All Ford had to do was convince men like John Volpe, Claude Brinegar and William Coleman (successive Secretaries of Transportation during the Nixon-Ford years) that certain safety standards would add so much to the price of cars that fewer people would buy them. This could damage the auto industry, which was still believed to be the bulwark of the American economy. "Compliance to these standards," Henry Ford II prophesied at more than one press conference, "will shut down the industry."

The Nixon Transportation Secretaries were the kind of regulatory officials big business dreams of. They understood and loved capitalism and thought like businessmen. Yet, best of all, they came into office uninformed on technical automo-

tive matters. And you could talk "burn injuries" and "burn deaths" with these guys, and they didn't seem to envision children crying at funerals and people hiding in their homes with melted faces. Their minds appeared to have leapt right to the bottom line—more safety meant higher prices, higher prices meant lower sales and lower sales meant lower profits.

So when J. C. Echold, Director of Automotive Safety (which means chief anti-safety lobbyist) for Ford wrote to the Department of Transportation—which he still does frequently, at great length—he felt secure attaching a memorandum that in effect says it is acceptable to kill 180 people and burn another 180 every year, *even though we have the technology that could save their lives for $11 a car.*

Table 2

$11 vs. a Burn Death: Benefits and Costs Relating to Fuel Leakage Associated With the Static Rollover Test Portion of FMVSS 208

Benefits
Savings: 180 burn deaths, 180 serious burn injuries, 2,100 burned vehicles. *Unit cost:* $200,000 per death, $67,000 per injury, $700 per vehicle. *Total benefit:* 180 × ($200,000) + 180 × ($67,000) + 2,100 × ($700) = $49.5 million.

Costs
Sales: 11 million cars, 1.5 million light trucks. *Unit cost:* $11 per car, $11 per truck. *Total cost:* 11,000,000 × ($11) + 1,500,000 × ($11) = $137 million.

From Ford Motor Company internal memorandum: "Fatalities Associated with Crash-Induced Fuel Leakage and Fires."

Furthermore, Echold attached this memo, confident, evidently, that the Secretary would question neither his low death/injury statistics nor his high cost estimates. But it turns out, on closer examination, that both these findings were misleading.

First, note that Ford's table shows an equal number of burn deaths and burn injuries. This is false. All independent experts estimate that for each person who dies by an auto fire, many more are left with charred hands, faces and limbs. Andrew McGuire of the Northern California Burn Center estimates the ratio of burn injuries to deaths at ten to one instead of the one to one Ford shows here. Even though Ford values a burn at only a piddling $67,000 instead of the $200,000 price of life, the true ratio obviously throws the company's calculations way off.

The other side of the equation, the alleged $11 cost of a fire-prevention device, is also a misleading estimation. One document that was *not* sent to Washington by Ford was a "Confidential" cost analysis *Mother Jones* has managed to obtain, showing that crash fires could be largely prevented for considerably *less* than $11

a car. The cheapest method involves placing a heavy rubber bladder inside the gas tank to keep the fuel from spilling if the tank ruptures. Goodyear had developed the bladder and had demonstrated it to the automotive industry. We have in our possession crash-test reports showing that the Goodyear bladder worked well. On December 2, 1970 (*two years before* Echold sent his cost-benefit memo to Washington), Ford Motor Company ran a rear-end crash test on a car with the rubber bladder in the gas tank. The tank ruptured, but no fuel leaked. On January 15, 1971, Ford again tested the bladder and again it worked. The total purchase and installation cost of the bladder would have been $5.08 per car. That $5.08 could have saved the lives of Sandra Gillespie and several hundred others.

* * *

When a federal regulatory agency like the National Highway Traffic Safety Administration (NHTSA) decides to issue a new standard, the law usually requires it to invite all interested parties to respond before the standard is enforced—a reasonable enough custom on the surface.

However, the auto industry has taken advantage of this process and has used it to delay lifesaving emission and safety standards for years. In the case of the standard that would have corrected that fragile Pinto fuel tank, the delay was for an incredible eight years.

The particular regulation involved here was Federal Motor Vehicle Safety Standard 301. Ford picked portions of Standard 301 for strong opposition back in 1968 when the Pinto was still in the blueprint stage. The intent of 301, and the 300 series that followed it, was to protect drivers and passengers *after* a crash occurs. Without question the worst postcrash hazard is fire. So Standard 301 originally proposed that all cars should be able to withstand a fixed barrier impact of 20 mph (that is, running into a wall at that speed) without losing fuel.

When the standard was proposed, Ford engineers pulled their crash-test results out of their files. The front ends of most cars were no problem—with minor alterations they could stand the impact without losing fuel. "We were already working on the front end," Ford engineer Dick Kimble admitted. "We knew we could meet the test on the front end." But with the Pinto particularly, a 20-mph rear-end standard meant redesigning the entire rear end of the car. With the Pinto scheduled for production in August of 1970, and with $200 million worth of tools in place, adoption of this standard would have created a minor financial disaster. So Standard 301 was targeted for delay, and, with some assistance from its industry associates, Ford succeeded beyond its wildest expectations: the standard was not adopted until the 1977 model year. Here is how it happened:

There are several main techniques in the art of combating a government safety standard: a) make your arguments in succession, so the feds can be working on disproving only one at a time; b) claim that the real problem is not X but Y (we already saw one instance of this in "the problem is not cars but people"); c) no matter how ridiculous each argument is, accompany it with thousands of pages of highly technical assertions it will take the government months or, preferably, years to test. Ford's large and active Washington office brought these techniques to new heights and became the envy of the lobbyists' trade.

The Ford people started arguing against Standard 301 way back in 1968 with a strong attack of technique b). Fire, they said, was not the real problem. Sure, cars catch fire and people burn occasionally. But statistically auto fires are such a minor problem that NHTSA should really concern itself with other matters.

Strange as it may seem, the Department of Transportation (NHTSA's parent agency) didn't know whether or not this was true. So it contracted with several independent research groups to study auto fires. The studies took months which was just what Ford wanted.

The completed studies, however, showed auto fires to be more of a problem than Transportation officials ever dreamed of. Robert Nathan and Associates, a Washington research firm, found that 400,000 cars were burning up every year, burning more than 3,000 people to death. Furthermore, auto fires were increasing five times as fast as building fires. Another study showed that 35 per cent of all fire deaths in the U.S. occurred in automobiles. Forty per cent of all fire department calls in the 1960s were to vehicle fires—a public cost of $350 million a year, a figure that, incidentally, never shows up in cost-benefit analyses.

Another study was done by the Highway Traffic Research Institute in Ann Arbor, Michigan, a safety think-tank funded primarily by the auto industry (the giveaway there is the words "highway traffic" rather than "automobile" in the group's name). It concluded that 40 per cent of the lives lost in fuel-fed fires could be saved if the manufacturers complied with proposed Standard 301. Finally, a third report was prepared for NHTSA by consultant Eugene Trisko entitled "A National Survey of Motor Vehicle Fires." His report indicates that the Ford Motor Company makes 24 per cent of the cars on the American road, yet these cars account for 42 per cent of the collision-ruptured fuel tanks.

Ford lobbyists then used technique a)—bringing up a new argument. Their line then became: yes, perhaps burn accidents do happen, but rear-end collisions are relatively rare (note the echo of technique b) here as well). Thus Standard 301 was not needed. This set the NHTSA off on a new round of analyzing accident reports. The government's findings finally were that rear-end collisions were seven and a half times more likely to result in fuel spills than were front-end collisions. So much for that argument.

By now it was 1972; NHTSA had been researching and analyzing for four years to answer Ford's objections. During that time, nearly 9,000 people burned to death in flaming wrecks. Tens of thousands more were badly burned and scarred for life. And the four-year delay meant that well over 10 million new unsafe vehicles went on the road, vehicles that will be crashing, leaking fuel and incinerating people well into the 1980s.

Ford now had to enter its third round of battling the new regulations. On the "the problem is not X but Y" principle, the company had to look around for something new to get itself off the hook. One might have thought that, faced with all the latest statistics on the horrifying number of deaths in flaming accidents, Ford would find the task difficult. But the company's rhetoric was brilliant. The problem was not burns, but . . . impact! Most of the people killed in these fiery accidents, claimed Ford, would have died whether the car burned or not. They were killed by the kinetic force of the impact, not the fire.

And so once again, as in some giant underwater tennis game, the ball bounced into the government's court and the absurdly pro-industry NHTSA began another slow-motion response. Once again it began a time-consuming round of test crashes and embarked on a study of accidents. The latter, however, revealed that a large and growing number of corpses taken from burned cars involved in rear-end crashes contained no cuts, bruises or broken bones. They clearly would have survived the accident unharmed if the cars had not caught fire. This pattern was confirmed in careful rear-end crash tests performed by the Insurance Institute for Highway Safety. A University of Miami study found an inordinate number of Pintos burning on rear-end impact and concluded that this demonstrated "a clear and present hazard to all Pinto owners."

Pressure on NHTSA from Ralph Nader and consumer groups began mounting. The industry-agency collusion was so obvious that Senator Joseph Montoya (D-N.M.) introduced legislation about Standard 301. NHTSA waffled some more and again announced its intentions to promulgate a rear-end collision standard.

Waiting, as it normally does, until the last day allowed for response, Ford filed with NHTSA a gargantuan batch of letters, studies and charts now arguing that the federal testing criteria were unfair. Ford also argued that design changes required to meet the standard would take 43 months, which seemed like a rather long time in light of the fact that the entire Pinto was designed in about two years. Specifically, new complaints about the standard involved the weight of the test vehicle, whether or not the brakes should be engaged at the moment of impact and the claim that the standard should only apply to cars, not trucks or buses. Perhaps the most amusing argument was that the engine should not be idling during crash tests, the rationale being that an idling engine meant that the gas tank had to contain gasoline and that the hot lights needed to film the crash might ignite the gasoline and cause a fire.

Some of these complaints were accepted, others rejected. But they all required examination and testing by a weak-kneed NHTSA, meaning more of those 18-month studies the industry loves so much. So the complaints served their real purpose—delay; all told, an eight-year delay, while Ford manufactured more than three million profitable, dangerously incendiary Pintos. To justify this delay, Henry Ford II called more press conferences to predict the demise of American civilization. "If we can't meet the standards when they are published," he warned, "we will have to close down. And if we have to close down some production because we don't meet standards we're in for real trouble in this country."

* * *

While government bureaucrats dragged their feet on lifesaving Standard 301, a different kind of expert was taking a close look at the Pinto—the "recon man." "Recon" stands for reconstruction; recon men reconstruct accidents for police departments, insurance companies and lawyers who want to know exactly who or what caused an accident. It didn't take many rear-end Pinto accidents to demonstrate the weakness of the car. Recon men began encouraging lawyers to look beyond one driver or another to the manufacturer in their search for fault, particularly in the growing number of accidents where passengers were uninjured by collision but were badly burned by fire.

Pinto lawuits began mounting fast against Ford. Says John Versace, executive safety engineer at Ford's Safety Research Center, "Ulcers are running pretty high among the engineers who worked on the Pinto. Every lawyer in the country seems to want to take their depositions." (The Safety Research Center is an impressive glass and concrete building standing by itself about a mile from Ford World Headquarters in Dearborn. Looking at it, one imagines its large staff protects consumers from burned and broken limbs. Not so. The Center is the technical support arm of Jack Echold's 14-person anti-regulatory lobbying team in World Headquarters.)

When the Pinto liability suits began, Ford strategy was to go to a jury. Confident it could hide the Pinto crash tests, Ford thought that juries of solid American registered voters would buy the industry doctrine that drivers, not cars, cause accidents. It didn't work. It seems that juries are much quicker to see the truth than bureaucracies, a fact that gives one confidence in democracy. Juries began ruling against the company, granting million-dollar awards to plaintiffs.

"We'll never go to a jury again," says Al Slechter in Ford's Washington office. "Not in a fire case. Juries are just too sentimental. They see those charred remains and forget the evidence. No sir, we'll settle."

Settlement involves less cash, smaller legal fees and less publicity, but it is an indication of the weakness of their case. Nevertheless, Ford has been settling when it is clear that the company can't pin the blame on the driver of the other car. But, since the company carries $2 million deductible product-liability insurance, these settlements have a direct impact on the bottom line. They must therefore be considered a factor in determining the net operating profit on the Pinto. It's impossible to get a straight answer from Ford on the profitability of the Pinto and the impact of lawsuit settlements on it—even when you have a curious and mildly irate shareholder call to inquire, as we did. However, financial officer Charles Matthews did admit that the company establishes a reserve for large dollar settlements. He would not divulge the amount of the reserve and had no explanation for its absence from the annual report.

Until recently, it was clear that, whatever the cost of these settlements, it was not enough to seriously cut into the Pinto's enormous profits. The cost of retooling Pinto assembly lines and of equipping each car with a safety gadget like that $5.08 Goodyear bladder was, company accountants calculated, greater than that of paying out millions to survivors like Robbie Carlton or to widows and widowers of victims like Sandra Gillespie. The bottom line ruled, and inflammable Pintos kept rolling out of the factories.

In 1977, however, an incredibly sluggish government has at last instituted Standard 301. Now Pintos will have to have rupture-proof gas tanks. Or will they?

* * *

To everyone's surprise, the 1977 Pinto recently passed a rear-end crash test in Phoenix, Arizona, for NHTSA. The agency was so convinced the Pinto would fail that it was the first car tested. Amazingly, it did not burst into flame.

"We have had so many Ford failures in the past," explained agency engineer Tom Grubbs, "I felt sure the Pinto would fail."

How did it pass?

Remember that one-dollar, one-pound plastic baffle that was on one of the three modified Pintos that passed the pre-production crash tests nearly ten years ago? Well, it is a standard feature on the 1977 Pinto. In the Phoenix test it protected the gas tank from being perforated by those four bolts on the differential housing.

We asked Grubbs if he noticed any other substantial alterations in the rear-end structure of the car. "No," he replied, "the [plastic baffle] seems to be the only noticeable change over the 1976 model."

But was it? What Tom Grubbs and the Department of Transportation didn't know when they tested the car was that it was manufactured in St. Thomas, Ontario. Ontario? The significance of that becomes clear when you learn that Canada has for years had extremely strict rear-end collision standards.

Tom Irwin is the business manager of Charlie Rossi Ford, the Scottsdale, Arizona, dealership that sold the Pinto to

Tom Grubbs. He refused to explain why he was selling Fords made in Canada when there is a huge Pinto assembly plant much closer by in California. "I know why you're asking that question, and I'm not going to answer it," he blurted out. "You'll have to ask the company."

But Ford's regional office in Phoenix has "no explanation" for the presence of Canadian cars in their local dealerships. Farther up the line in Dearborn, Ford people claim there is absolutely no difference between American and Canadian Pintos. They say cars are shipped back and forth across the border as a matter of course. But they were hard pressed to explain why some Canadian Pintos were shipped all the way to Scottsdale, Arizona. Significantly, one engineer at the St. Thomas plant did admit that the existence of strict rear-end collision standards in Canada "might encourage us to pay a little more attention to quality control on that part of the car."

The Department of Transportation is considering buying an American Pinto and running the test again. For now, it will only say that the situation is under investigation.

* * *

Whether the new American Pinto fails or passes the test, Standard 301 will never force the company to test or recall the more than two million pre-1977 Pintos still on the highway. Seventy or more people will burn to death in those cars every year for many years to come. If the past is any indication, Ford will continue to accept the deaths.

According to safety expert Byron Bloch, the older cars could quite easily be retrofitted with gas tanks containing fuel cells. "These improved tanks would add at least 10 mph improved safety per-

formance to the rear end," he estimated, "but it would cost Ford $20 to $30 a car, so they won't do it unless they are forced to." Dr. Kenneth Saczalski, safety engineer with the Office of Naval Research in Washington, agrees. "The Defense Department has developed virtually fail-safe fuel systems and retrofitted them into existing vehicles. We have shown them to the auto industry and they have ignored them."

Unfortunately, the Pinto is not an isolated case of corporate malpractice in the auto industry. Neither is Ford a lone sinner. There probably isn't a car on the road without a safety hazard known to its manufacturer. And though Ford may have the best auto lobbyists in Washington, it is not alone. The anti-emission control lobby and the anti-safety lobby usually work in chorus form, presenting a well-harmonized message from the country's richest industry, spoken through the voices of individual companies—the Motor Vehicle Manufacturers Association, the Business Council and the U.S. Chamber of Commerce.

Furthermore, cost-valuing human life is not used by Ford alone. Ford was just the only company careless enough to let such an embarrassing calculation slip into the public records. The process of willfully trading lives for profits is built into corporate capitalism. Commodore Vanderbilt publicly scorned George Westinghouse and his "foolish" air brakes while people died by the hundreds in accidents on Vanderbilt's railroads.

The original draft of the Motor Vehicle Safety Act provided for criminal sanction against a manufacturer who willfully placed an unsafe car on the market. Early in the proceedings the auto industry lobbied the provision out of the bill. Since then, there have been those damage settlements, of course, but the only government punishment meted out to auto companies for non-compliance to standards has been a minuscule fine, usually $5,000 to $10,000. One wonders how long the Ford Motor Company would continue to market lethal cars were Henry Ford II and Lee Iacocca serving 20-year terms in Leavenworth for consumer homicide.

NO

CLOSING ARGUMENT BY MR. NEAL

If it please the Court, Counsel, ladies and gentlemen:

Not too many years ago our broad American Industry straddled the world like a giant.

It provided us with the highest standards of living ever known to man.

It was ended, eliminated, no more. Now it is an Industry weakened by deteriorating plants and equipment, weakened by lack of products, weakened by lack of manpower, weakened by inadequate capital, weakened by massive Government controls, weakened by demands on foreign oil and reeling from competition from foreign manufacturers.

I stand here today to defend a segment of that tattered Industry.

One company that saw the influx of foreign, small-made cars in 1967 and '68 and tried to do something about it, tried to build a small car with American labor that would compete with foreign imports, that would keep Americans employed, that would keep American money in America.

As State's witness, Mr. Copp, admitted, Ford Motor Company would have made more profit sticking to the bigger cars where the profit is.

That would have been the easiest way.

It was not the way Ford Motor Company took.

It made the Ford to compete. And this is no easy effort, members of the jury.

As even Mr. Copp admitted, the Automobile Industry is extremely regulated.

It has to comply with the Clean Air Act, the Safety Act, the Emissions Control Act, the Corporate Average Fuel Economy Act, the Safety Act, and OSHA as well as a myriad of Statutes and Regulations applicable to large and small businesses generally, and, again, as Mr. Copp admitted, it now takes twice as many Engineers to make a car as it did before all the massive Government controls.

Nevertheless, Ford Motor Company undertook the effort to build a subcompact, to take on the imports, to save jobs for Americans and to make a profit for its stockholders.

This rather admirable effort has a sad ending.

From U.S. District Court, South Bend, Indiana, *State of Indiana v. Ford Motor Company* (January 15, 1980).

On August 10, 1978, a young man gets into a van weighing over 4,000 pounds and heads towards Elkhart, Indiana, on a bad highway called "U.S. 33."

He has a couple of open beer bottles in his van, together with his marijuana which he may or may not have been smoking....

As he was cruising along on an open stretch of highway in broad daylight at at least 50 to 55 miles per hour, he drops his "smoke," ignores his driving and the road, and fails to see a little Pinto with its emergency flashers on stopped on the highway ahead.

He plows into the rear of the Pinto with enormous force and three young girls are killed.

Not the young man, but Ford Motor Company is charged with reckless homicide and arraigned before you.

I stand here to defend Ford Motor Company, and to tell you that we are not killers....

Mr. Cosentino gave you the definition of "reckless homicide" as "plain, conscious and unjustifiable disregard of harm, which conduct involves substantial deviation from acceptable standards of conduct."

This case and the elements of this case, strictly speaking, involve 40 days, July 1, 1978 to August 10, 1978, and the issue is whether, during that period of time, Ford Motor Company recklessly, as that term is defined, omitted to warn of a danger and repair, and that reckless omission caused the deaths involved....

[I]n my opening statement, I asked you to remember nine points, and I asked you to judge me, my client, by how well or how poorly we supported those nine points.

Let me run through briefly and just tick them off, the nine points, with you, and

then let me get down to discussing the evidence and record with respect to those nine points.

One, I said this was a badly-designed highway, with curbs so high the girls couldn't get off when they had to stop their car in an emergency.

Two, I said that the girls stopped there with their emergency flashers on, and this boy in a van weighing more than 4,000 pounds, with his eyes off the road, looking down trying to find the "smoke," rammed into the rear of that Pinto at at least 50 miles an hour, closing speed.

And by "closing speed," I mean the differential speed.

That is Points 1 and 2.

Point 3, I said the 1973 Pinto met every fuel-system integrity standard of any Federal, State or Local Government.

Point No. 4, I said, Ford Motor Company adopted a mandatory standard dealing with fuel-system integrity on rear-impact of 20 miles per hour moving-barrier, 4,000 pound moving-barrier, and I said that no other manufacturer in the world had adopted any standard, only Ford Motor Company.

Five, I said that the Pinto, it is not comparable to a Lincoln Continental, a Cadillac, a Mercedes Benz or that Ascona, or whatever that exotic car was that Mr. Bloch called—but I did say No. 5, it is comparable to other 1973 subcompacts.

No. 6, I said that... we would bring in the Engineers who designed and manufactured the Pinto, and I brought them from the stand, and they would tell you that they thought the Pinto was a good, safe car, and they bought it for themselves, their wives and their children to drive.

No. 7, I told you that we would bring in the statistics that indicated to us as to our state of mind that the Pinto performed as well or better than other subcompacts.

And, No. 8, I said we would nevertheless tell you that we decided to recall the Pinto in June of 1978, and having made that decision for the reasons that I—that I told you I would explain, we did everything in our power to recall that Pinto as quickly as possible, that there was nothing we could have done between July 1, 1978 and 8-10-1978, to recall the Pinto any faster.

And finally, No. 9, I said we would demonstrate that any car, any subcompact, any small car, and even some larger cars, sitting out there on Highway 33 in the late afternoon of August 10, 1978 and watching that van roar down that highway with the boy looking for his "smoke"—any car would have suffered the same consequences.

Those are the nine points I ask you to judge me by, and let me touch on the evidence, now, with respect to those nine points....

The van driver, Duggar, took his eyes off the road and off driving to look around the floor of the van for a "smoke."

Duggar had two open beer bottles in the car and a quantity of marijuana.

Duggar was not prosecuted for reckless homicide or for possession of marijuana, even though his prior record of conviction was:

November, '73, failure to yield right-of-way;

April, '76, speeding 65 miles an hour in a 45 mile an hour zone;

July, '76, running stop sign;

June, '77, speeding 45 in a 25 zone;

August, '77, driver's license suspended;

September, '77, driving with suspended license;

December, '77, license suspended again.

Mr. Cosentino, you got up in front of this jury and you cried.

Well, I cry, too, because Mr. Duggar is driving, and you didn't do anything about him with a record like that except say, "Come in and help me convict Ford Motor Company, and I will help you get probation."

We all cry.

But crying doesn't do any good, and it doesn't help this jury.

The big disputed fact in this case regarding the accident, ladies and gentlemen, is the closing speed. The differential speed, the difference between the speed the Pinto was going, if any, and the speed the van was going.

That is the big disputed fact in regard to this accident.

And whether the Pinto was stopped or not is relevant only as it affects closing speed....

Mr. Duggar testified—I guess he is great about speed, because while he's looking down there for his "smoke," he knows he is going 50 miles per hour in the van.

But he said he was going 50 miles per hour at the time of impact, and he said the Pinto was going 15.

But here is the same man who admits he was going at least 50 miles per hour and looking around down "on a clear day," trying to find the "smoke" and looked up only to see the Pinto ten feet ahead of him.

Here is a witness willing to say under oath that the Pinto was going 15 miles per hour, even though he had one-sixth of a second—one-sixth of a second to make the judgment on the speed.

Here is a witness who says he had the time to calculate the speed of the

Pinto but had no time even to try to apply brakes because there were no skid marks.

And here is a witness who told Dr. Galen Miller, who testified here, that— told him right after the accident that in fact the Pinto was stopped.

And here was a witness who made a deal with the State.

And here was a witness who's not prosecuted for recklessness.

And here is a witness who is not prosecuted for possession of marijuana.

So the State's proof from Mr. Alfred Clark through Mr. Duggar is kind of a smorgasbord or a buffet—you can go in and take your choice.

You can pick 15—5 miles per hour, if you want to as to differential speed, or you can take 35 miles per hour.

And the State, with the burden of proof says, "Here," "Here," "Here. I will give you a lot of choice."

"You want choices? I will give you choices. Here. Take 5. Take 15. 10, 15, 20, 25, 30, 35."

Because, ladies and gentlemen of the jury,—and I'm sure you are—the alternatives the State offers you are closing speeds of anywhere from 5 miles—on the low side—to 35 miles on the high side as a differential speed in this accident....

Mr. Toms, the former National Highway Traffic Safety Administrator, told you that in his opinion the 20 mile per hour rear-impact moving-barrier was a reasonable and acceptable standard of conduct for 1973 vehicles.

Why didn't Ford adopt a higher standard?

Mr. MacDonald, a man even Mr. Copp—do you remember this? Mr. Mac-Donald sitting on the stand, the father of the Pinto, as Mr. Cosentino called him—and he didn't deny it.

He says, "Yes, it is my car."

Mr. MacDonald, a man even Mr. Copp—on cross examination I asked him, I said:

"Q Mr. Copp, isn't it a fact that you consider Harold MacDonald an extremely safety-conscious Engineer?"

And he said:

"A Yes, sir."

Mr. MacDonald, that extremely safety-conscious Engineer, told you he did not believe a higher standard could be met for 1973 cars without greater problems, such as handling, where more accidents and death occur.

Mr. Copp, let's take the State's witness, Copp.

Mr. Copp admitted that even today, seven years later, the Federal Government Standard is only 30 miles per hour, 10 miles higher than what Ford adopted—voluntarily adopted for itself for 1973.

And Mr. Copp further testified that a 30 mile an hour would be equivalent only to a 31.5 or 32 mile car-to-car.

So, ladies and gentlemen of the jury, Mr. Cosentino tells you about, "Oh, isn't it terrible to put these cars out there, wasn't it awful—did you know?"

Well, do you know that today, the—today, 1980 model cars are required to meet only a 30 mile an hour rear-impact moving-barrier standard? 1980 cars.

And that that is equivalent to a 32 mile an hour car-to-car, and yet Ford Motor Company, the only company in the world, imposed upon itself a standard and made a car in 1973, seven years ago, that would meet 26 to 28 miles an hour, within 5, 6 or 7 miles of what the cars are required by law to meet today.

Mr. Cosentino will tell you, frankly, the cars today, in his judgment, are defective and he will prosecute.

What a chaos would evolve if the Government set the standard for automobiles and says, "That is reasonable," and then Local Prosecutors in the fifty states around the country start saying, "I am not satisfied, and I am going to prosecute the manufacturer."

Well, Mr. Cosentino may say that the standard should be 40.

The Prosecutor in Alabama may say, "No, it should be 50."

The Prosecutor in Alaska may say, "No, it should be 60."

And the Prosecutor in Tennessee—they say—you know, "I am satisifed—I am satisfied with 30," or, "I think it should be 70."

How can our companies survive?

Point 5, the 1973 Pinto was comparable in design and manufacture to other 1973 subcompacts.

I say again, ladies and gentlemen, we don't compare the Pinto with Lincolns, Cadillacs, Mercedes Benz—we ask you to compare the Pinto with the other three subcompacts.

Let's take the State's witnesses on this point first.

Mr. Bloch—Mr. Cosentino didn't mention Mr. Bloch, but I don't want him to be forgotten.

Mr. Bloch and Mr. Copp complain about the Pinto, and that is easy.

Let's descend to the particulars. Let's see what they really said.

Well, they complain about the metal, the gage of the metal in the fuel tank; you remember that?

And then on cross examination it was brought out that the general range of metal in fuel tanks ranged between twenty-three-thousandths of an inch and forty-thousandths of an inch.

That is the general range. Twenty-three-thousandths on the low to forty-thousandths on the high, and lo and behold, what is the gage of metal in the Pinto tank?

Thirty-five-thousandths.

And Mr. Bloch admits that it is in the upper third of the general range.

And they complain about the bumper on the Pinto.

And, remember, I said we would show that the Pinto was comparable to other '73 subcompacts.

They complain about the bumper, but then they admit on cross examination the Vega, the Gremlin, the Colt, the Pinto and the Toyota had about the same bumper.

And they complain of a lack of a protective shield between the tank and the axle, but they admitted on cross examination that no other 1973 car had such a shield, and Mr. Copp admits that there was no significant puncture in the 1973—in the Ulrich accident caused by the axle, and you remember I had him get up here and say, "Point out where this protective shield would have done something, where this puncture source we are talking about—" and you remember, it is so small—I can't find it now.

So much for the protective shield.

And then they complained about the insufficient rear structure in the Pinto, but they both admit that the Pinto had a left side rail hat section and that the Vega had none, nothing on either side, that the Pinto had shear plates, these plates in the trunk, and that neither the Vega, the Gremlin or the Colt or Toyota had any of these.

And the Vega used the coil-spring suspension, when the Pinto had a leaf-spring, and that was additional structure.

I am not going through all those—well, I will mention one more thing.

They talked about puncture sources, there is a puncture source there, puncture source here, but on cross examination, they end up by admitting that the puncture sources on all subcompacts have about the same—and in about the same space....

Mr. MacDonald testified, "Yes, I thought the Pinto was a reasonably safe car. I think the '73 Pinto is still a reasonably safe car, and I bought one, I drove it for years for myself."

Mr. Olsen—you remember little Mr. Frank Olsen?

He came in here, has his little eighteen-year-old daughter—he said, "I am an Engineer responsible for the Pinto. I think it is a safe car. I bought one for my little eighteen-year-old daughter, and she drove it for several years."

And Mr. Freers, the man who Mr. Cosentino objected to going over the fact that he was from Rose-Hullman, and on the Board of Trustees there—Mr. Freers said, "I like the Pinto. I am an Engineer responsible for the Pinto, and I bought a '73 Pinto for my young son and he drove it several years."

And then Mr. Feaheny says, "I am one of the Engineers responsible for the Pinto, and I bought one for my wife, the mother of my six children, and she drove it for several years."

Now, when Mr. Cosentino tried to say there was something phoney about that—he brought out their salaries.

And I—I don't know how to deal with the salary question.

It just seems to me to be so irrelevant, like some other things I am going to talk about in a minute that I am just going to simply say, "It is irrelevant," and go on.

But he said to these people—he suggested to you, suggested to these people, "Well, you make a lot of money, you can afford better than a Pinto."

Like, "You don't really mean you had a Pinto?"

And Mr. Feaheny says, "Yes, I could afford a more expensive car, but, you know, I—all of us, we have been fighting, we come out with something we thought would fight the imports, and we were proud of it, and our families were proud of it."

Do you think, ladies and gentlemen of the jury, that Mr. MacDonald was indifferent, reckless, when he bought and drove the Pinto?

He drives on the same roads, he has the—subject to the same reckless people that Mr. Cosentino didn't prosecute.

Do you think that Mr. Olsen was reckless and indifferent when he gave a Pinto to his eighteen-year-old daughter, a '73 Pinto?

Do you think that Mr. Freers was reckless when he gave one to his young son?...

Finally, ladies and gentlemen—not "finally," but Point No. 8: Notwithstanding all I have said, Ford Motor Company decided on June 8th, 1978, to recall the Pintos to improve fuel systems and did everything in its power to recall it as quickly as possible.

This is really what this case, I guess, is all about, because that period of time involved is July 1, 1978 until August 10, 1978.

And the Court will charge you, as I said, the elements are whether we recklessly failed to warn and repair during that period of time.

And whether that reckless omission, if any, caused the deaths.

And you may ask—and I think it is fair to ask—why recall the Pinto, the '73 Pinto, if it is comparable to other subcompacts, if statistics say it is performing as well as other '73 subcompacts?

And if Ford had a standard for '73 that no other manufacturer had?

And Feaheny and Mr. Misch told you why.

The Federal Government started an investigation. The publicity was hurting the Company.

They thought the Government was wrong, but they said, "You can't fight City Hall."

"We could fight and fight and we could go to Court and we could fight, but it's not going to get us anywhere. If we can improve it, let's do it and let's don't fight the Federal Government."

Maybe the Company should not have recalled the '73 Pinto.

Douglas Toms did not think, as he told you on the stand under oath, that the '73 Pinto should have been recalled.

He had information that the Pinto did as well as other cars;

That Pinto fire accidents equaled the total Pinto population or equaled the percentage of Pinto population to all car population.

And Mr. Bloch, on the other hand, says, "All of them should be recalled."

He said, "The Pinto should have been recalled."

He said, "The Vega should have been recalled."

He said, "The Gremlin should be recalled."

And he didn't know about the Dodge Colt.

Nevertheless, the Company did decide to recall the Pinto. And they issued widely-disseminated Press Releases on June 9, 1978.

It was in the newspapers, TV, radio, according to the proof in this case.

And thereafter the Government regulated what they did in the recall.

That is what Mr. Misch told you.

He said, "From the time we started—June 9, 1978—to August 10, Mr.—the Federal Government regulated what we did."

Now, Mr. Cosentino is prosecuting us.

And the Federal Government has regulated us.

Mr. Misch said, "The Federal Government reviewed what kind of Press Releases we should issue, what kind of Recall Letter we should issue, what kind of a Modification Kit that they would approve."

Even so—it is undisputed, absolutely undisputed that we did everything in our power to recall as fast as possible—nights, days, weekends.

And notwithstanding all of that, the first kit—the first complete kit was assembled August 1, 1978.

And on August 9, 1978, there were only 20,000 kits available for 1,600,000 cars.

And this was not Ford's fault. Ford was pushing the suppliers, the people who were outside the Company doing work for them.

And Mr. Vasher testified that he got the names of the current owners from R. L. Polk on July 17;

That the Ulrich name was not among them;

That he sent the Recall Letter in August to the original owner because he had no Ulrich name.

Now,—and he said he couldn't have gotten the Ulrich name by August 10.

Now, Mr. Cosentino said, "Well, the Ulrich Registration was on file with the State of Indiana and it is open to the public."

Well, Ford Motor Company doesn't know where these 1,600,000 cars are. It has to use R. L. Polk because they collect the information by the VIN Numbers.

If Ford Motor Company went to each state, they would go to fifty states and they would have each of the fifty states run through its files 1,600,000 VIN Numbers.

And Mr. Vasher, who is the expert in there, said it would take months and months to do that.

And, finally, ladies and gentlemen, the Government didn't approve the Modification Kit until August 15, 1978.

But the State says that we should have warned—we should have warned 1973 Pinto owners not to drive the car.

But the Government never suggested that.

Based on our information, and confirmed by the Toms testimony, our cars were performing as well—or better than—other '73 subcompacts.

As Mr. Misch so succinctly stated, "We would have been telling the Pinto owners to park their Pintos and get into another car no safer—and perhaps even less safe—than the Pinto."...

Well, we submit that the physical facts, the placement of the—the placement of the gasoline cap, where it is found, the testimony of Levi Woodard, and Nancy Fogo—demonstrate the closing speed in this case was at least 50 to 60 miles per hour.

Mr. Copp, the State's witness, testified that no small car made in America in 1973 would withstand 40 to 50 miles per hour—40 to 50 rear-impact. No small car made in America in 1973 would withstand a 40-plus mile per hour rear-impact.

The Dodge Colt would not have; the Vega could not have; the Gremlin would not have; and certainly even the Toyota would not have.

Mr. Habberstad told you that no small car—and some big cars—would have withstood this crash.

And he established by the crash-tests you have seen that the Vega could not withstand 50;

That the Gremlin could not withstand 50;

That the Toyota Corolla with the tank over the axle could not withstand 50;

And that even a full-sized Chevrolet Impala cannot withstand 50 miles per hour.

If it made no difference what kind of car was out there, members of the jury, how can Ford Motor Company have caused the deaths? ...

I am not here to tell you that the 1973 Pinto was the strongest car ever built.

I'm not here to tell you it is equal to a Lincoln, a Cadillac, a Mercedes—that funny car that Mr. Bloch mentioned.

I'm not here to tell you a stronger car couldn't be built.

Most of us, however, learn early in life that there is "no Santa Claus," and, "There's no such thing as a free lunch."

If the public wanted it, and could pay for it, and we had the gasoline to drive it, Detroit could build a tank of a car—a car that would withstand practically anything, a car that would float if a careless driver drove it into the water.

A car that would be invulnerable even to the "Duggars" of the world.

But, members of the jury, only the rich could afford it and they would have to stop at every other gasoline station for a refill.

I am here to tell you that the 1973 Pinto is comparable to other '73 subcompacts, including that Toyota, that Corolla with the tank over the axle.

I am here to tell you it was not designed by some mysterious figure you have never seen.

It was designed and manufactured by Harold MacDonald, Frank Olsen and Howard Freers.

I am here to tell you these are the decent men doing an honorable job and trying to do a decent job.

I am here to tell you that Harold Mac-Donald, Frank Olsen, and Howard Freers are not reckless killers.

Harold MacDonald is the same man, State's witness, Copp, called an "extremely safety-conscious individual."

Frank Olsen is the same "Frank Olsen" Mr. Copp said was a "good Engineer."

And Howard Freers is the same "Howard Freers" Mr. Copp said was a "man of honesty and integrity."

I am here to tell you that these men honestly believe and honestly believed that the 1973 Pinto was—and is—a reasonably safe car—so safe they bought it for their daughters, sons and family.

Do you think that Frank Olsen believed he was acting in plain, conscious, unjustifiable disregard of harm?

When he bought a '73 Pinto for his eighteen-year-old daughter?

Or Howard Freers, when he bought one for his young son?

I am here to tell you that the design and manufacture of an automobile is not an easy task;

That it takes time to know whether a change in one part of the 14,000 parts of a car will or will not cause greater problems elsewhere in the car or its performance.

I am here to tell you that safety is a matter of degree;

That no one can say that a car that will meet a 26 to 28 mile per hour rear-impact is unsafe and one that will meet a 30 to 32 impact is safe.

I am here to tell you that if this country is to survive economically, it is really time to stop blaming Industry or Business, large or small, for our own sins.

I am here to tell you that no car is now or ever can be safe when reckless drivers are on the road.

I am here to tell you that Ford Motor Company may not be perfect, but it is not guilty of reckless homicide.

Thank you, members of the jury.

And God bless you in your deliberations.

POSTSCRIPT

Product Liability: Was Ford to Blame in the Pinto Case?

Was Ford guilty? The jury said no, but the larger issue remains: Who takes responsibility when many factors combine to bring about an injury?

Consider the following: Ford Motor Company obeyed the law, but the law may not have been all that it *should* have been. The reason for this is that the Ford Motor Company spent a great deal of money lobbying Congress to prevent the release of new and higher legal safety standards in order to be able to sell the Pinto for a lower price and thus increase its market share and its profits. Is the government, through its agencies, guilty for not fulfilling its role as protector of the consumer? What was the government's duty at this point? To protect those consumers of the automobile? To protect the workers in the Ford Motor Company factories? To protect the American manufacturers against encroachments from foreign competition? Does government have some absolute duty in these cases, or are our legislators asked only to bring about the greatest good for the greatest number? How could they have done that in this case? Three girls are not very many. Could it be shown that all people who safely enjoyed their Pintos at the lower cost outweigh, in their happiness, the enormous unhappiness of the three dead girls and their families and friends?

Ford Motor Company found new structural allies when the criminal negligence case was brought against it. Under the U.S. Constitution, the legal system tends to protect the defendant in these cases. The tradition in the United States is to protect the rights of the individual against the interests of the community. In general, this is as it should be. In this case, the "individual" was one of the largest corporations in the world. However, legal traditions held true, and the rights of Ford were supported when the company was acquitted.

Manufacturers know how to make a safe car. They *could* build one like a tank and rig it to go no faster than 30 miles per hour, but very few people would buy it. So they make relatively unsafe cars that people will buy— lighter and faster, but more likely to crumple and burn in an accident. Is this trade-off acceptable to a nation that is used to making choices? Or should we be more diligent about eliminating threats to safety?

SUGGESTED READINGS

Lawrence A. Benningson and Arnold I. Benningson, "Product Liability: Manufacturers Beware!" *Harvard Business Review* (May–June 1974).

Richard T. DeGeorge, "Ethical Responsibilities of Engineers in Large Organizations: The Pinto Case," *Business and Professional Ethics Journal* (Fall 1981).

Richard A. Epstein, "Is Pinto a Criminal?" *Regulation* (March–April 1980).

Niles Howard and Susan Antilla, "What Price Safety? The 'Zero-Risk' Debate," *Dun's Review* (September 1979).

Alvin S. Weinstein et al., *Products Liability and the Reasonably Safe Product: A Guide for Management, Design and Marketing* (John Wiley, 1978).

ISSUE 13

Should Tobacco Advertising Be Banned?

YES: Mark Green, from "Luring Kids to Light Up," *Business and Society Review* (Spring 1990)

NO: John Luik, from "Government Paternalism and Citizen Rationality: The Justifiability of Banning Tobacco Advertising," *International Journal of Advertising* (vol. 9, 1990)

ISSUE SUMMARY

YES: Mark Green, the commissioner of Consumer Affairs in New York City, attacks a popular cigarette advertising campaign that seems to be aimed directly at children and claims that such unconscionable methods of advertising should be prevented.

NO: Professor of philosophy John Luik argues that restricting the freedom of commercial speech cannot be justified unless it is shown to be absolutely necessary to avoid certain harm, which has not been done in the case of tobacco advertising.

The quarrel here is specifically about tobacco advertising. Some background on the product is necessary to understand the problem with marketing it.

First, there is a good amount of evidence that smoking tobacco is hazardous to one's health. Wherever tobacco is consumed, mortality and morbidity rates go up in direct proportion to the amount of tobacco consumed, especially when the tobacco is smoked. Smoking cigarettes is the most common form of tobacco use.

Second, curbing the tobacco industry is, economically, very serious business. It is a multibillion-dollar industry that employs tens of thousands. It builds and finances schools, churches, state governments, and regional economies. It was America's first export product, and it remains one of the best. The market for tobacco is still growing all over the world, and the export of tobacco might be one of the most hopeful ways to reduce the U.S. trade deficit.

Third, there is no compulsion to smoke cigarettes and lots of encouragement not to smoke them. Yet, people do choose to smoke all the same. Setting aside the claim that just being in the same room with a smoker can harm nonsmokers, people should have a right to make decisions about their own health. The issue, as John Luik sees it, is that banning tobacco advertising would represent an erosion of citizen autonomy, or the basic freedom of American people to make their own choices with respect to their own lives.

The dilemma here begins before the first ad hits the page: There is reason to believe that certain sorts of behavior are harmful to those who engage in them. In the normal exercise of the police power of the state, we could try to make sure that people do not indulge in that behavior, either by educating the people to avoid it, by quietly abolishing the purveyors of the means to engage in it, or both. But some people will not abstain, and the tobacco industry is too big and economically important to be shut down without a very clear consensus that it should be done.

In this situation, the proposal to ban the advertising of tobacco from all media (it has already been banned from radio and television) has certain attractions. First, to underscore Mark Green's point, it would end the exposure of young people to the traditional images of sophistication and worldliness that go with smoking. This would strengthen the claims of the tobacco industry that they are not trying to lure new smokers into the habit but are only trying to communicate product information to those who are already smokers. Since the major function of advertising is to persuade a nonuser to try the product once, there is no reason to advertise tobacco. If smokers wish to receive product information, they can sign up to receive it. It is not clear, however, that there is any sense in which smokers need such information.

On the positive side, banning advertising would leave the industry alone to make money abroad. There are signs that it will continue to do this well. At present, American cigarettes are being sold and promoted abroad; America is encouraging farmers in the Third World to grow tobacco and sending agronomists to teach them how to do it. There seems to be no problem with Third World receptivity: Farmers enjoy growing a high-income crop; governments enjoy the taxes collected both on cigarette sales and on the income from the tobacco crops; and the tobacco customers of the developing countries, a large and growing population, enjoy having available to them products of a higher quality than their indigenous industry could provide. Whether or not Americans have a right to take advantage of that receptivity for their own profit is another question—closely related to the question of taking advantage of that receptivity at home.

Ask yourself, as you read the following selections, what weight should be given to human freedom, and what weight should be given to human welfare. In general, what is the responsibility of business in this dilemma? To serve customers what they want until the law tells it not to? Or to take a proactive stance and arrange business dealings so as to do the least harm and promote the most good for those affected by such dealings?

YES

Mark Green

LURING KIDS TO LIGHT UP

Earlier this year, Mark Green, the New York City Commissioner of Consumer Affairs, wrote the following letter to Louis V. Gerstner, Jr., the chairman and chief executive officer of RJR Nabisco. The letter appeals to the tobacco manufacturer to end its current Camel cigarette advertising campaign, which Green views as a thinly veiled attempt to lure children to start smoking.

As the father of two young children and the new Commissioner of Consumer Affairs, I am appalled at your "Smooth Character" Camel advertising campaign which risks addicting children to cigarettes.

I first noticed the prevalence and pitch of your ads in mid-January. On one day, I saw a Smooth Character poster when I bought a paper in the morning at the 86th Street and York Avenue newsstand, then another on the crosstown bus ("Un Tipo Suave," it read in Spanish), and yet another on the Lexington Avenue subway en route to work. Finally, later that day, I came across your huge, pull-out poster "suitable for framing" in *Rolling Stone*, along with language urging readers to send away for any of eight colorful posters. The posters involve cartoon characters such as your "Old Joe" camel and comely women, along with symbols one needn't be Freud to understand.

WHERE THERE'S SMOKE

However, it wasn't until I spotted the perforated fold at the bottom of the *Rolling Stone* poster, which allows readers to delete the congressionally mandated warning label, that I decided to write you to ask this question: Isn't this ad campaign an obvious attempt to lure children into smoking in violation of the tobacco industry's own 1964 code against advertising directed at children?

True, the *Rolling Stone* ad does say in extremely small print that a person sending in a coupon for posters is supposed to "certify that I am a smoker 21 years of age or older." On the other hand:

- Who puts posters up on their walls—kids or adults?
- Who watches and talks about cartoon characters—kids or adults?

From Mark Green, "Luring Kids to Light Up," *Business and Society Review,* vol. 73 (Spring 1990). Copyright © 1990 by Mark Green. Reprinted by permission.

- Who is impressionable enough to associate smoking with success and sex—kids or adults?
- Why do these advertisements run in magazines such as *Rolling Stone, National Lampoon,* and *Movies, U.S.A.,* which have so many teenage readers? (*Movies, U.S.A.* says its target is "a captive audience of one million moviegoers" who are, in its words, "youthful and image-conscious.")
- Was *Advertising Age* correct when it said on July 11, 1988, that "R. J. Reynolds is updating its Camel and Salem advertising to lure younger voters away from Marlboro country?"
- Why don't any of the posters one can order by mail have warning labels on them?

You know the adage that if something walks like a duck and quacks like a duck... it's a duck. Based on the most obvious circumstantial evidence, RJR's campaign is not a duck but a camel aimed directly at the health of our children. It was just such concerns that prompted the authors of *Barbarians at the Gate* to write of Theodore Forstmann, one of RJR's suitors, "Debating future demand in the teen market made him feel like a drug pusher."

Already, children in 1990 America live under multiple threats: One in five lives in poverty, the worst rate in the industrial West; more than a third in our city schools drop out before senior year; the United States has the highest rate of teenage pregnancy and one of the lowest investments in primary education among industrial nations; one-parent and no-parent families are on the rise, especially in minority areas. For those and other reasons, New York City Mayor David Dinkins made the welfare of children his top priority in his Inaugural Address last month. And today, at my swearing-in, I followed suit and pledged to focus on children as consumers.

UNCONSCIONABLE CAMEL?

At the same time, tobacco is not just another product. It is the number-one preventable cause of death and disease in America and the only product that causes disease and death in its normal use. The Surgeon General estimates that smoking causes nearly 400,000 premature deaths annually—or fifty times more than those who die from drug abuse; the Federal Office on Smoking and Health concluded in 1987 that smoking contributed to 16 percent of all deaths (heart disease, lung cancer, emphysema, etc.), including more than 2,500 deaths of infants attributed to smoking by the mother. And, of course, smoking is a very powerful addiction, as much so as alcohol and drugs. Indeed, even after undergoing heart and lung surgery, half of all smokers still continue their habit.

Consequently, the goal of public officials concerned with already imperiled children must be to discourage them from smoking in the first place. Some 80 percent of all adults who smoke began before or during their teen years; 50 percent of all smokers first lit up by age 13, and 25 percent by 11. Smoking can also be a "gateway" to illegal drugs: "Virtually all children involved in hard drug use," concluded Sen. Edward Kennedy (D-Mass.), "began with cigarettes." So if we can keep our teenagers tobacco-free, they will live longer, healthier lives.

Which brings me back to your Smooth Character advertising campaign. I am writing you as my first official act because there are few if any marketplace abuses worse than inducing children to smoke, and RJR's ads appear to be inherently misleading, if not unconscionable.

They're potentially misleading because their images convey that smoking a Camel leads to social success and happiness, not to disease and death. And in our MTV era, many kids get more information from images than words. It is very hard to square your ads with the *Tobacco Industry's Principles Covering Cigarette Advertising and Sampling*'s provision that "Cigarette advertising shall not suggest that smoking is essential to social prominence, distinction, success, or sexual attraction."

The ads are potentially unconscionable because they appear to be targeted to unsophisticated minors who feel immortal and are uniquely subject to peer pressure—and who may, as a result, get addicted for life, a shortened life at that. For example, 35 percent of high school seniors don't think that smoking a pack a day causes serious harm. And while 95 percent of high school smokers believe they will later stop smoking, eight years later only 25 percent of them have.

INDUSTRY ARGUMENTS

In reviewing the literature in your industry, I find that tobacco spokespeople make at least four arguments to frustrate government actions designed to reduce these health hazards—namely, paternalism, censorship, preemption, and advertising.

Legislation to restrict or even ban cigarette advertising, for example, is attacked as "paternalism" and "censorship." Of course, the Latin origin of paternalism is "pater," meaning like a father. But what's wrong with acting like a parent when government tries to protect children from harm?

As for censorship, there is no First Amendment right to sell or advertise a dangerous product, as four Supreme Court decisions over a half century make clear. Unlike political speech, commercial speech can be regulated, which is precisely what our consumer protection law does when it forbids false or misleading advertising. In any event, the worst censorship of all is a product that censors life itself.

Periodically, when local officials such as myself attempt to reduce this health hazard, industry holds up federal law as a bar. But the preemption clause that is cited applies to local attempts to add to the Federal Trade Commission's warning label, not to actions against, for example, misleading ads or unconscionable trade practices. Also, it's getting harder to maintain the fiction that warning labels on cigarette packs are sufficient disclosure when the FTC has twice described (in 1969 and 1981) the warning's "futility," when it doesn't even use provable words like "addiction," or "death," and when it is all but invisible on billboards, including your famous one in Times Square. Or, as satirist Calvin Trillin has written, "Anyone who wants to see that warning would have to have the sort of long-range vision usually associated with the pilot of an F-14."

Last, industry leaders argue that the $2.6–billion-plus spent on cigarette ads and other promotions—or $9 for every man, woman and child—doesn't persuade anyone to smoke. At best, it is said, these ads only influence a small percentage of existing smokers to switch among brands. Whether you personally believe this thesis or not, surely Madison Avenue doesn't.

Advertising experts agree that market expansion, especially for an industry that loses over 2 million consumers a year who die or quit, is an important objective of nearly all advertising. Emerson Foote, former chairman of McCann-Erickson, one of the world's largest advertising agencies, once remarked that "I am always amused by the suggestion that advertising, a function that has been shown to increase consumption of virtually every other product, somehow miraculously fails to work for tobacco products." Foote's view is seconded by advertising executive Charles Sharp, a former vice president of Ogilvy & Mather: "By depicting a product as an integral part of a highly desirable life-style and personal image, in addition to current users, an advertiser can attract individuals who do not currently use that product but who want to emulate that life-style [and] want to be like the people in the ads."

SIX QUESTIONS

Your industry finds itself in the ironic position of killing off your own consumers. A thousand times a day, or forty times an hour, there's a funeral and grieving because someone was addicted to smoking. If the public were told that a new product society could live without had killed forty people a year, there would be outrage and probably a legislative prohibition. Companies talking about their First Amendment right to sell such a product would be laughed out of court or Congress. Yet cigarettes kill not forty people a year but an hour.

A group of tobacco executives who have previously told us that smoking is not dangerous now tells us that $2.6 billion in advertising and promotion doesn't increase smoking and that cartoon posters that appeal to children

---

AD INDUSTRY FIDDLES WHILE AMERICA BURNS

There are nearly a dozen bills before Congress to restrict print advertising for tobacco products. As the pols in the smoke-free backrooms of Washington contemplate such legislation, not only the cigarette industry is worried.

The Leadership Council on Advertising, an advertising industry lobbying group, estimates that more than 4,000 jobs would be lost and 165 periodicals would fold if tobacco advertising were banned. This study, as reported in *Publishing News*, is "designed to diffuse some of the anti-tobacco din around the halls of Congress."

Of course, 4,000 jobs are about 1 percent of the number of people who die prematurely each year from diseases caused by smoking. And the study apparently does not account for the potential success of the legislation's goal: to reduce the number of smokers. If an ad ban were to work, people might live longer and, thus, buy and read more magazines. Up to 400,000 people is one heck of an untapped market.

---

weren't intended for children. Frankly, that insults our intelligence and injures the most vulnerable among us. And it makes my job as a parent that much harder.

Consequently, I'd like to solicit your responses to six questions, while preserving my options for possible future action. For if RJR now acts with the responsibility of, say, Johnson & Johnson during the Tylenol tragedy, it could yet find some common ground with concerned parents and avoid an outright ban on all advertising:

1. Since data proves that "the vast majority of new [smoking] recruits are children and teenagers," according to a health coalition including the American Cancer Society, do you still maintain that these Camel ads aren't intended for this very audience?

2. Isn't it inherently misleading to associate a disease-causing product such as smoking with attractive, healthy women?

3. Would you agree to immediately stop marketing all Smooth Character posters, especially since they lack federal warnings?

4. Would you agree to stop all Smooth Character ads on billboards within three months since viewers include children and since the warning label is essentially unreadable?

5. Would you agree to cease and desist your entire Smooth Character ad campaign by 1991, or before the 500th anniversary of Columbus' discovery of America *and* tobacco?

6. Would you consider supporting: (a) Rep. Henry Waxman's legislation allowing only informational cigarette ads without pictures (like securities ads); and (b) Sen. Edward Kennedy's bill, which encourages federally funded counter-advertising for undereducated cigarette consumers?

Mr. Gerstner, beyond any legal requirements, I am appealing to your demonstrated sense of civic obligation to avoid unnecessary disease and death. For prior to becoming chairman and CEO, you did serve on the National Cancer Advisory Board on Cancer Prevention and Early Detection, a body which urged America to evolve into a "tobacco-free" society by the year 2000. Given your personal sensitivity to this urgent topic, I hope RJR might now aspire to be a good corporate citizen and consider cooperative efforts to reduce the incidence of teenage smoking.

For kids' sake, I look forward to your prompt and favorable response.

NO   John Luik

GOVERNMENT PATERNALISM AND CITIZEN RATIONALITY: THE JUSTIFIABILITY OF BANNING TOBACCO ADVERTISING

The first assumption [that philosophers bring to any discussion of tobacco advertising] is the primacy of autonomy or individual liberty in a democratic society, a primacy that can normally be overridden only on the basis of two types of demonstration. One is that there is a conjunction of other significant values at issue and that this conjunction serves to diminish the foundational status of freedom in any given context. The other is that we can in fact produce a rational demonstration of the highest order that a course restricting individual autonomy is justified. It is thus not only that there must be a conjunction of other values which in a particular case outweigh freedom, but there must also be a demonstration of the most rigorous kind that the competing values can be secured only through the restriction of autonomy.

A second assumption that follows on from this is that when we speak about the goals for social policy and the justifications for government intervention—the two are not the same but we have, for convenience, conflated them—the only appropriate context in which we can speak of these goals is within the context of the primacy of autonomy. Thus the status of freedom as a basic value is always a legitimate consideration when any sort of social policy issue is at stake.

Having said this, an interesting paradox now emerges: what we are arguing for are two quite different and, one might say, peculiar senses of rationality. On the one hand we want to argue for individual autonomy which may include a large dose of irrational 'choice', and yet at the collective or social level we want to argue that social policies ought only to be undertaken on the most traditionally rational basis of analysis, so that when social policy decisions are being discussed or implemented we have the most stringent guarantees against irrational action. One might think that if one were going to hold society in general to stringent conditions of rationality, one would *not* allow individuals a high degree of eccentric irrationality. I hope that the reasons for this asymmetry will emerge in the course of these discussions.

From John Luik, "Government Paternalism and Citizen Rationality: The Justifiability of Banning Tobacco Advertising," *International Journal of Advertising*, vol. 9 (1990). Copyright © 1990 by *International Journal of Advertising*. Reprinted by permission of Cassell PLC, London.

The third assumption is what might be called the liberal presumption as advocated, for instance, by J. S. Mill in *On Liberty*. Essentially the liberal presumption is characterized by three different claims. The first is that one can make a reasonably clear distinction between actions that affect only oneself and actions that affect others. The second is that the individual is the best judge both of his own ends and the means necessary for the realization of those ends. The third is that government intervention in the life of a genuinely autonomous agent is justified only to prevent harm to others, never to prevent harm to self.

PATERNALISM AND INDIVIDUAL AUTONOMY

All of those assumptions are open to the objections of what can be described as classical paternalism. Classical paternalism wishes to assert that:

1. A cluster of values, not autonomy alone, assume primacy in a democratic society;

2. A clear distinction between self-regarding and other-regarding action is impossible to sustain;

3. Autonomy is frequently outweighed by other justifiable state interests in furthering happiness and welfare, broadly construed;

4. Individuals often do not understand their interests in the clearest way and often do not appreciate the means best suited to the actualization of those interests;

5. Individuals need to be assisted in furthering their 'real interests' and prevented from embarking on irrational courses of action such as the permanent alienation of the capacity for voluntary action.

Classical paternalism itself can be divided into two categories: strong and weak. The strong paternalist claims that if, for instance, an individual wants to walk across a bridge that he knows to be unsafe, then he is in some sense mentally deficient, if not long term at least temporarily, and we are justified in using the strongest measures—on compassionate grounds, even though they restrict autonomy—in preventing this individual from embarking on this course.

The strong paternalist can thus actually justify infringements on non-insane instances of autonomy (for example, starting to smoke) on what appear to be liberty-enhancing principles: namely, by keeping one alive we enhance one's autonomy. If in fact we allow you to fall off the bridge we allow you ultimately to destroy your autonomy. No one who is dead is autonomous. Therefore, although it appears that we are being paternalistic, what is being done is an action to enhance your long-term autonomy, which you have irrationally chosen to cast aside.

But the paternalist has a weaker sort of case which does not hinge on demonstrably insane action. The weaker paternalist case wants to claim that the State can justifiably intervene to prevent the action of a citizen or subject on two grounds: first, when the individual is about to make an unreasonable choice, not a *prima facie* insane choice but an unreasonable choice; second, when the individual is about to make a non-voluntary choice: that is, when the individual appears to be in the grip of a compulsion over which he has no control.

Here, of course, one encounters a related issue: the extent to which tobacco use is addictive and therefore a non-voluntary action. If in fact the tobacco user could be demonstrated to be non-voluntary, the plausibility of the paternalist argument is enormously strengthened, inasmuch as what one does by beginning to smoke is, it might be said, to surrender a significant degree of autonomy over the rest of one's life in the sense that one takes up a form of behavior which it is very difficult, if not impossible, to break.

Of course, the argument can still be made, despite the best efforts of the surgeon general, that there is no convincing evidence that this is in fact the case, and that there are millions of ex-smokers who can testify that autonomy is not surrendered. Even if that were not the case the autonomist would argue that the real commitment to freedom comes precisely at this point: that one is in fact willing to allow people to use their freedom to extinguish their freedom, in the same way in which democracy allows people to use free speech to campaign against democracy itself. The real test of a commitment to autonomy is precisely the extent to which one allows liberty to argue against itself. For the paternalist, however, tobacco advocacy could be an invitation to involuntary, perhaps unreasonable, action, and the question is, what justification could ever be given to allow someone to make that sort of advocacy? It is to this question—which lies at the heart of the debate over tobacco advertising bans—that we must now turn.

THE ANTI-PATERNALIST RESPONSE TO TOBACCO ADVERTISING BANS

A large measure of conceptual confusion, not to say controversy, that presently surrounds measures designed to prohibit the advertisement of tobacco products is due to the peculiar melange of empirical and theoretical issues that 'hazardous' product advertising in general and this type of 'hazardous' product advertising in particular generates. On the one hand there are the obviously empirical issues, such as the role of advertising in initiating and sustaining the use of tobacco products and the effectiveness of various measures designed to restrict advertising for such products in terms of reducing aggregate consumption. On the other hand, there are highly contentious theoretical issues about the ethics of hazardous product advertising, the status of commercial speech, and the legitimacy of governmental attempts to restrict certain types of speech and action. The paternalist justification for advertising prohibitions is based in a large measure on what might be called a mixed case argument; that is, an argument that relies on a mixture of empirical and theoretical elements.

Thus, the paradigm paternalist argument justifying tobacco advertising bans involves empirical arguments about the role of advertising in:

1. Establishing a general climate of legitimacy with respect to tobacco use;

2. Initiating new consumers, particularly minors, to tobacco use;

3. Increasing total tobacco consumption, whether aggregate or per capita;

4. Dissuading consumers from considering the health risks of tobacco use and from considering abandoning the products.

These arguments should be considered in harness with theoretical arguments about the merits of government paternalism in situations of non-rational and involuntary individual action. The paradigm paternalist argument is then constructed upon, first, the plausible association between tobacco use and certain forms of ill health; and second, the plausible connection between tobacco use and advertising, inasmuch as the decision to embark on a course of action injurious to health is so far outside the web of rational decision-making that it can only be the product of a factor like advertising that is designed to subvert rational choice. Given that the state has an interest in the health of its citizens, and given further that a particular product is threatening to citizens' health, then the state has a legitimate reason to curtail the use of that product through restricting advocacy on behalf of the product.

Now the anti-paternalist can counter this argument by initially noting that the required connections are not evident because:

1. Tobacco advertisements contain clear warnings about the dangers of tobacco products, warnings which provide a *prima facie* assurance that the users of these products are not ignorant as to the products' health risks;

2. It is not at all clear, given the evidence available, that advertising plays as substantial a role in individual decisions to begin smoking as do other cultural, socio-economic, and psychological factors (Childrens Research Unit, 1987); nor indeed that advertising is directed primarily to non-smokers rather than to existing smokers with a view to retaining or increasing a particular manufacturer's market share.

Without such connections the paternalist's argument is significantly weakened.

Weak Anti-Paternalism

Anti-paternalism is, however, a general term. As with classical paternalism, we can distinguish two types: weak and strong. The weak anti-paternalist attempts to assess the claim about tobacco and advertising on a strictly empirical basis. The weak anti-paternalist argues that the restriction of advertising and the imposition of bans, whether partial or total, in terms of tobacco products are justified if, and only if, the following conditions obtain.

First, bans are justified only if there is some extraordinarily significant objective at stake, or some important interest which the ban is designed to promote. Usually the implicit assumption is that the significant objective at stake is a reduction in smoking which would improve the overall health of the country, reduce health spending and result in people living longer.

The second condition is that bans are justified only if there is a rationally demonstrable connection between the significant objective, which is specified in the legislation, and the actual method that one is going to employ to achieve that objective. Here we return to the claim specified at the beginning of the essay: namely, that if any social policy issue is to be described as rational and acceptable in a democratic society, it has to meet a strictly defined test of rationality. If the policy could be shown in any sense to be irrational, causally or evidentially, then that would be a good reason to reject the policy. Thus the paternalist must satisfy us that there is a rational connection between the objectives specified, i.e., saving lives by reducing tobacco consumption, and the means chosen, in this case the advertising ban. This point will be discussed later in the article, but it seems clear that there is no decisive published evidence that can establish any rational connection between advertising bans and the objective of reducing tobacco consumption. Bans therefore fail this test and the legislation is by definition *prima facie* unreasonable.

The third condition is that individual autonomy, which we argued was a basic value in a democratic society, must be impaired as little as possible by the ban. In other words one must design a means to meet this objective and choose an instrument that reduces the scope of autonomy as little as possible. Otherwise, given that the autonomy of individual actors is significantly affected (in the case of advertisers it is obliterated by a total advertising ban), one fails to meet the condition that autonomy is impaired as little as possible.

Fourth, advertising bans are justified only if they do not infringe fundamental justice or equity. In other words, they preserve the equity of risk ventures across society. By 'risk ventures' we mean that the paternalistic intervention—in this case the advertising ban—cannot single out one risk venture unless other equally risky ventures are also considered fit candidates for government action. So if the use of tobacco products is relatively far down the list of risky ventures and other more, or equally risky, ventures are left untouched by the legislation, then that legislation is fundamentally unjust, since it has without justification impaired the equity status of risky ventures by prohibiting only one sort of risky venture.

Finally, bans are justified only if there is no other way, short of restricting autonomy, to secure these two objectives. In other words, if it could be rationally demonstrated that there is as much likelihood of achieving a reduction in tobacco use through some other method rather than a ban on commercial free speech, then it is imperative, if the paternalist case is to succeed, that the necessity of an advertising ban be shown. If you are going to totally eliminate a particular instance of commercial free speech, you have to be able to say, 'this total elimination is necessary because there is no other measure short of the measure that will achieve our necessary objective.'

Now, it is clear, based on the best empirical evidence about the role of advertising in (1) establishing a general climate of legitimacy with respect to tobacco use; (2) initiating new consumers, particularly minors, to tobacco use; (3) increasing total consumption; and (4) dissuading consumers from considering the health risks inherent in tobacco use and considering abandoning the product, that the paternalist argument justifying tobacco advertising bans can never meet conditions two, three, four and five. Whatever the sources, whether studies about adolescent smoking sponsored by the World Health Organisation (certainly no friend of the tobacco industry); studies which suggest that children begin smoking because of peer and parental influence; or comparative studies of smoking rates in countries that have bans (Norway and Finland) and those without bans (Britain and Austria) which suggest that a ban on all forms of tobacco advertising results—depending on which evidence one accepts as definitive—in either a higher consumption of tobacco products than before the ban, or a not significantly lower rate of consumption, there is no compelling evidence that advertising bans reduce smoking and thus save lives. It should also be noted that there is no compelling evidence of a causal link between advertising and smoking initiation and behaviour. Thus, we should not be surprised if there is no connection between advertising bans and reduced smoking. Without such causal links there can be no demonstrable connection between the objective of advertising bans and the means employed to realize that objective.

Moreover, such bans also violate conditions three, four and five in that a total ban, for example in Canada, does not impair autonomy as little as possible and, inasmuch as other equally risky forms of autonomous behaviour are not subjected to similar legislative intervention, the equity of risk venture is not preserved. Finally, even if there were evidence that advertising bans might reduce tobacco consumption, it is still incumbent on the paternalist to demonstrate that banning advertising is the only method whereby this objective can be achieved. Again, much of the evidence suggests that vigorous public education campaigns about the dangers of smoking and certain restrictions on smoking and sales to minors are more effective in reducing tobacco consumption than advertising bans, and they do not infringe autonomy in the unjustifiable ways that advertising bans do (Aaro et al., 1986, Allegrante et al., 1978, Bewley and Bland, 1977, Boddewyn, 1986, Leventhal and Cleary, 1980, Ross, 1973).

Strong Anti-Paternalism

So far we have spoken exclusively of weak anti-paternalism, but there is a second, perhaps more confident version of anti-paternalism: strong anti-paternalism that justifies tobacco advertising bans solely on the grounds of theoretical considerations. For the sake of the argument let us assume first that there is a demonstrable and universally accepted connection between the initiation and maintenance of juvenile and adult smoking and advertising, so that the empirical support for a ban must be conceded.

Secondly, let us concede for the purpose of argument that there is a significant and growing body of literature which shows that advertising bans do in fact work; that they do discourage the recruitment of new smokers; and that they do result in lessened consumption.

Strong anti-paternalists would argue, however, that even if this were the case, advertising bans would be unjustified because free and democratic societies place such a high value on freedom and autonomy that they are willing to risk, and indeed allow, a significant loss of life in order to preserve a value. History is replete with instances where a society places greater value on the continuance of society in a free and democratic way on the saving of individual lives. For instance, this is precisely what happens when society goes to war. We place a higher value on the maintenance of a particular kind of society than on saving individual lives. We may lose no lives if we capitulate but the democratic character of our society would be changed. Thus the first step in the argument is to establish the primacy of autonomy, even with the consequence of some individuals living shorter or less happy lives.

The next step is to demonstrate that any erosion of autonomy—as through an advertising ban—is an unacceptable erosion. This demonstration can be merely provisional. One could construct two different arguments, the first perhaps a little better than the second. The first is that arguments put forward by people who are in favour of restrictions on commercial free speech assume that it is legitimate to curtail commercial expression or commercial advocacy because commercial advocacy is, if not corrupt, then certainly of a much less distinguished character than other sorts of advocacy. In other words, commercial advocacy is about commerce; it is about economics and money-making, and economics and money-making play a peripheral role in society. Freedom of speech, on the other hand, was established to protect not the peripheral, but the important, primarily political, debates over societal issues.

There are several problems with this argument. The first is that, aside from anything, it reflects an extraordinary elitist view about the value of political speech. It is surely an arbitrary assumption that one form of speech can be characterized as peripheral and that commercial speech, precisely because it deals with economic choices, is therefore less important than political speech. This claim represents not merely an elitist, but also an antiquated view about the relative importance of political speech versus economic speech in society. A good argument could be made that the locus of autonomy and individual decision-making hinges for ordinary people far more on individual economic choices, such as the decision to buy certain products and to engage in certain practices, which in turn affect decisions to produce certain things, than on 'exalted political discourse'. A consequence of this argument is that it is necessary to maintain commercial free speech.

In other words the peculiar character of commercial free speech is that it affects the lives of ordinary people in a democracy far more than political free speech. Given the importance of individual economic decisions and their role in a democratic social order, it might be argued that we ought to reverse the traditional distinction and argue that commercial speech is more valuable in many contexts than political speech.

...[I]f one values democracy, then one values a particular form of citizen autonomy, and citizen autonomy is integrally connected with free speech in all of its varieties. When a society decides that certain forms of communications should be banned, it says, in effect, that there are some forms of communication that are too dangerous for a citizen to contemplate because the citizen may embark upon a course of action which society deems to be irrational. What this establishes is a socially defined notion of citizen rationality and a socially approved manner of living one's life. Certain social choices are closed by virtue of the fact that you cannot receive communications about those choices.

What strikes us as so offensive about restrictions of this sort is that they establish a paradigm of social rationality that in fact may be completely at odds with the majority of society. They open the door to a government-imposed definition of what constitutes acceptable risk-taking and unacceptable risk-taking, something that is a fundamentally subversive activity on the part of government in a democratic society. When the government assumes that there is an allowable conception of how one lives one's life in a rational way and a non-allowable conception, and then acts to censure information so that people do not even see other alternatives, then one arguably erodes autonomy in a fundamental sense. As Richard Arneson notes:

This failing is manifest when proposed paternalistic coercion would enhance someone's capacity for rationality by means of uprooting an irrational trait that is prominent in his self-conception or even in his ideal of himself. Consider the project of forcing adult education on a hillbilly who is suspicious of urban ways and identifies himself as a rural character. Somewhat similarly, the wild Heathcliff in *Wuthering Heights* would doubtless find his 'ability to rationally consider and carry out his own decisions' considerably enhanced if psychotherapy coercively administered should extirpate his self-destructive passion for Catherine Earnshaw. Note that no taint of sympathy for rural parochialism or for grotesque romanticism need color the judgment that paternalism is unacceptable in such instances. Rather these examples recall to us the conviction that rationality in the sense of economic prudence, the efficient adaptation of means to ends, is a value which we have no more reason to impose on an adult against his will for his own good than we have reason to impose any other value on paternalistic grounds. A vivid reminder that rationality may sometimes be alien to some humans is the circumstance that persons sometimes self-consciously choose to nurture an irrational quirk at the center of their personalities. Perhaps it is appropriate to deplore such a choice but not to coerce it (Arneson, 1980).

It could of course be argued that some erosion of autonomy is a necessary feature of social living, though the notion of a little erosion of autonomy might be as coherent as the idea of a little pregnancy. More important, however, is the fact that such arguments about autonomy and rationality miss a central feature of democratic life that has emerged over the last three hundred years: namely, the fact that by allowing individuals to shape the course of their lives, for better or worse, the State concedes to them the right to misorder and misshape their lives to a substantial degree. Consider, for instance, the rationale that might be given, and indeed was traditionally given, for state-enforced religious belief: namely, that the matter of individual salvation, eternal destiny, was far too significant to be left in the hands of the individual citizen. The State had a compelling 'state interest' in securing an individual's assent to religious truth, and in suppressing dissenting presentations of 'truth'.

Today, however, such an intrusion by the State into the rational ordering of an individual's life is universally considered inappropriate. The individual, whatever the cost in rationality and happiness, is left to pursue his own way with respect to his eternal outcome. But what the paternalist wishes to do is to revive state-imposed rationality, not with respect to religious belief, but with respect to health. Health moralism, as we might call it, proclaims that there is but one rational-healthy-moral way to live one's life, and inducements to divergent behaviour, e.g., tobacco advertisements, are not to be permitted. The question can thus legitimately be asked why, having abandoned one form of state-enforced rationality, the rationality of certain forms of religious belief and practice, we should accept, as consistent with autonomy, the imposition of another form of state-enforced rationality, health moralism?

Having once decided that there is an official standard of rationality, an acceptable life plan to which we must all conform, where do we stop? If we cannot trust the rationality of the smoker who concludes that his enjoyment of smoking is worth the risk of a shorter lifetime, can we trust the rationality of the overweight who regularly ignore our pleas to start an exercise programme, or the rationality of the red-meat eater who prefers his steak to the latest embodiments of lean cuisine, or the rationality of the credit-card addict who spends his way into insolvency, or the rationality of the lottery ticket buyer who, ignoring all the odds, still gambles his money? Surely these individuals are just as susceptible to the dangers of free speech that advertising presents as is the smoker.

If individuals wish to make assessments of risk, based on differing life plans and differing judgements of pleasure, then they should be allowed to do so. To put the case more specifically with respect to tobacco: there are no doubt smokers who would prefer to live shorter lives, if that is really the trade-off, in return for the pleasure they receive from smoking.

Free speech is about choices: about idiosyncratic choices and life plans, about the necessity of choices based on a fair hearing of all sides—popular and unpopular, socially condoned and socially condemned—of an issue. Free speech is also about confidence: confidence in autonomy as in the long run the foundational value of society, confidence that we have in ourselves and in others the right to make choices for ourselves, even if those choices are not the culturally approved ones. It is about the confidence that we have that dangers of suppressing certain forms of information and advocacy are always greater than the dangers of missing information and advocacy. And free speech is also about the tolerance that we have that permits all of us the chance to make what might well appear to others to be the wrong, the terribly wrong, choice.

In conclusion, the strong anti-paternalist cares too deeply about people to attempt to protect them against themselves, however attractive such a course of action might appear in the short term. Instead, the strong anti-paternalist turns to what might be called the paradox of democratic societies: namely, that democracy succeeds only because it allows the vigorous exercise of the very free speech that could destroy it, as the paradox of autonomy. The great compliment of democracy to human dignity is that through it we entrust to ourselves, not to a government, however well-intentioned, the task of ordering—and indeed perhaps misordering—our lives. And that compliment makes all the difference.

REFERENCES

Aaro, L. E., Wold, B., Kannas, L. & Rimpela, M. (1986) Health behaviour in schoolchildren, a WHO cross-national study. *Health Promotion*, **1**, pp. 17–33.

Allegrante, J. P., O'Rourke, R. W. & Tuncalp, S. A. (1978) Multivariate analysis of selected psychosocial behaviour. *Journal of Drug Education*, **7**, pp. 239–242.

Arneson, R. (1980) Mill versus Paternalism. *Ethics*, **90**, p. 474.

Bewley, B. R. & Bland, J. M. (1977) Academic performance and social factors related to cigarette smoking by schoolchildren. *British Journal of Preventive and Social Medicine*, **32**, pp. 18–24.

Boddewyn, J. (1986) *Tobacco Advertising Bans and Consumption in 16 Countries*. New York: International Advertising Association.

Children's Research Unit (1987) *An Examination of the Factors Influencing Juvenile Smoking Initiation in Canada*. Toronto: Children's Research Unit, Association of Canadian Advertising.

Leventhal, U. & Clary, P. D. (1980) The smoking problem: a review of the research and theory in behavioural risk modification. *Psychological Bulletin*, **88**, pp. 370–405.

Ross, R. (1973) Personality, social influence and cigarette smoking. *Journal of Health and Social Behaviour*. **14**, pp. 279–286.

POSTSCRIPT

Should Tobacco Advertising Be Banned?

The authors of these selections seem to argue past each other. In the name of autonomy, Luik wants to ensure a no-censorship policy for rational adults; in the name of harm prevention, Green wants to ensure protection of vulnerable adolescents from harmful messages. But since there is no practicable way of sending one set of messages to rational adults and another set to vulnerable adolescents, the question of advertising must remain as one question, and we may have to choose which of the two values is more important in this case.

When we cannot achieve agreement on the moral status of the endpoint or product of an inquiry—when we cannot decide which value is more important—we may simply have to agree that there is no just outcome and that each side has an equal right to prevail. But we may be able to agree on a just procedure, a way of reaching a decision that all can trust, and agree to accept whatever result the procedure yields, despite what our preference may have been to begin with. One just procedure would be to submit the proposal to ban advertising to the appropriate legislature and accept the results of the debate, the vote, and the acquiescence of the executive branch and the courts.

The following factors need to be held in mind as we consider this debate. On the side of the tobacco industry and of those who carry its message to the public:

1. Tobacco is legal. It is perfectly legal for adults to smoke cigarettes, and many people choose to do so. Concern for the health of children is entirely hypocritical if we continue to support the behavior from which we hope to protect them.

2. No one is forced to smoke. Tobacco consumption is free and voluntary.

3. Tobacco is a profitable crop for the United States, especially for certain regions of it. It would be a gross injustice to throw that many people out of work, particularly in today's economy.

On the opposing side, the following principles are governing:

1. We are under a general obligation to do no harm to our fellow human beings. Tobacco is harmful. Advertising tobacco will induce people to use it who otherwise would not. Therefore, advertising ought to be abolished.

2. We must show compassion in those cases where people may cause themselves pain, sickness, and general damage through ignorance or weakness when it is in our power to prevent those harms. We are often under an obligation to protect people from their own damaging habits, at least to the extent that we are aiding and abetting them in pursuing those habits.

3. Economically, the farmers and governors of the tobacco-producing states are convinced that tobacco is good for their economies. However, there is ultimately no future in a commodity that shortens the lives of its consumers.

The tobacco companies themselves have started diversifying as if all tobacco consumption would be outlawed tomorrow. Perhaps the same concern should be extended to the workers as has been extended to the investors. Which set of considerations should prevail in this debate?

SUGGESTED READINGS

Michele Barry, "The Influence of the U.S. Tobacco Industry on the Health, Economy, and Environment of Developing Countries," *The New England Journal of Medicine* (March 28, 1991).

Rae Corelli, "Smokers Go to War," *Macleans* (January 17, 1991).

David Scott Davis, "Selfish, Sanctimonious Anti-Smokers," *The New York Times* (January 27, 1989).

Kathleen Deveny, "With Help of Teens, Snuff Sales Revive," *The Wall Street Journal* (May 3, 1990).

Joseph R. DiFranza and John W. Richards, Jr., "RJR Nabisco's Cartoon Camel Promotes Camel Cigarettes to Children," *Journal of the American Medical Association* (December 11, 1991).

Michael Gartner, "Advertising Ban Could Be Hazardous to Smokers' Health," *The Wall Street Journal* (July 21, 1988).

Nancy R. Gibbs, Nancy Seufert, and Martha Smilgis, "All Fired Up Over Smoking," *Time* (April 18, 1988).

Patricia Bellew Gray, "Tobacco Firms Defend Smoker Liability Suits with Heavy Artillery," *The Wall Street Journal* (April 29, 1987).

Michael McCarthy, "Tobacco Critics See a Subtle Sell to Kids," *The Wall Street Journal* (May 3, 1990).

Morton Mintz, "The Nicotine Pushers: Marketing Tobacco to Children," *The Nation* (May 6, 1991).

Anastasia Toufexis and Dick Thompson, "A Not-So-Happy Anniversary," *Time* (January 23, 1989).

PART 4

Environmental Policy and Corporate Responsibility

Mankind's attempts to protect the environment have involved many conflicts over fundamental values. We know that the environment must be protected, but the natural environment cannot participate in our political processes as an interest group nor can it buy itself protection on the open market. So we have to put aside the fundamental model of human action as rule-governed competition; nature cannot compete. In this section, we consider debates on property rights and the environment and on the business aspects of one of the many ways we have attempted to mitigate the waste problem.

■ Should Property Rights Prevail Over Environmental Protection?

■ Is Incineration a Cost-Efficient Way to Dispose of Solid Waste?

ISSUE 14

Should Property Rights Prevail Over Environmental Protection?

YES: Richard Epstein, from "Property Rights and Environmental Protection," *Cato Policy Report* (May/June 1992)

NO: John Echeverria, from "Property Rights and Environmental Protection," *Cato Policy Report* (May/June 1992)

ISSUE SUMMARY

YES: Professor of law Richard Epstein notes that if the government takes a person's private property, it must pay that person the market value, or at least "fair compensation," for it. Epstein argues that if a law is passed that robs an individual's property of all value, that amounts to the same thing, and he or she should therefore be compensated.

NO: John Echeverria, a legal counsel to the National Audubon Society, argues that property rights have never included a right to do public harm and that environmental regulations, like other laws, do not violate a right to one's property.

The United States has always held the belief of liberty under law. However, the truth is that every law limits liberty in some way. Even though all American citizens have a right to liberty, every law infringes some possible rights, and every new law infringes some existing right. This is how it must be, for conditions change, needs evolve, and, above all, our knowledge base expands. It could be argued that all the major changes that have evolved in society during the twentieth century have come about because of the growth of knowledge. One of the largest areas of change-producing knowledge is the workings of the natural environment and environmental health.

As recently as two centuries ago, after 10,000 years of settled agricultural living, the connection between waterborne microorganisms and disease was not understood, the connection between airborne particulates and lung dysfunction was not understood, and the connection between sanitation in living habits—from latrine use to cleanliness of food and utensils—and general public health was a complete mystery. Infant and child mortality was unacceptably high in the most civilized societies as well as in the least, and epidemics raged through the cities periodically. People's lives were changed dramatically by knowledge (empirically grounded, if not scientifically grounded at the time) of connections between disease and unsanitary conditions and by government action following swiftly upon that knowledge. The government action inevitably limited liberty: the liberty to dispose of wastes indiscriminately as in the past, to use wells without controls as in the past, and to raise animals for food under the same unsanitary conditions as generations of farmers had in the past. The result of all that legislation is that we are currently alive in greater numbers and are far healthier than humans have been at any other time in history.

Knowledge continues to advance, including knowledge of the workings of the natural environment. On the downside, the success of the first wave of public health legislation has allowed a greater number of people than anticipated to occupy the fragile ecosystems of our salt- and fresh-water borders. The area under contention in *Lucas v. South Carolina Coastal Council*, the case that launches the debate that follows, would never have been inhabited by human beings a century or two ago; the mosquitoes from the swamps would have ensured that periodic epidemics of yellow fever and malaria swept the beaches clean of human inhabitants. Now we have the knowledge to protect ourselves from disease and other natural foes, and, consequently, nature cannot stop us from building on the barrier beaches and wetlands of our coasts.

As we have gained the technology to build on these fragile ecosystems, we have also learned why we should not: the marshes and the dunes should be left alone—unfilled, undug, undumped in—if we wish to preserve the larger life of the sea and the inland coastal areas. So where nature used to exercise its own rough zoning prerogatives by periodic disease and hurricane, legislation now steps in to ensure public health and safety in the long run.

The debate that follows turns on two points: First, is there any wisdom in creating the environmental protection legislation under question? Or are the agencies of government, the legislature and the regulatory agency, carrying the desire for ecosystem preservation too far, into what Richard Epstein calls "institutional overclaiming"? Second, whatever the wisdom of the legislation, does it constitute a "taking" under the Constitution, requiring compensation for the property owner whose property falls under the regulations? After all, there may be excellent, even compelling, reasons for a superhighway, but if you knock down my house in order to build it, you have to pay me for my house.

Ask yourself, as you read the following selections, what is really meant by the right of private property. Is property an exclusive "right" held *against* the commonwealth? Or is it primarily a "stewardship" held *within* the commonwealth, utilized by private parties for public good as well as private?

YES

Richard Epstein

PROPERTY RIGHTS AND ENVIRONMENTAL PROTECTION

In December 1986 David H. Lucas purchased two undeveloped waterfront lots, which were zoned for single-family homes, on the Isle of Palms, South Carolina. Lucas's intention was to build one home to sell and a second as his own residence. In 1988, after Hurricane Hugo, South Carolina passed the Beachfront Management Act [BMA], which prohibited all new construction beyond certain setback lines and thereby rendered Lucas's property essentially useless for the purposes he had intended. The trial court found that the BMA constituted a "taking" and awarded Lucas compensation. The South Carolina Supreme Court reversed that decision, and Lucas appealed to the U.S. Supreme Court, which will soon decide whether government must compensate property owners under the Fifth Amendment's takings clause when it forbids them to develop their land....

If you understand exactly what a comprehensive system of property rights entails, not only do you say that there is no opposition between property rights and environmentalism but you also say that property rights and environmental claims are mutually supportive when correctly understood.

Even though we recognize zones of autonomy, there have to be some limitations on what property owners can do with their own. It is in those limitations, I think, that one finds the effective reconciliation of property rights and environmental concerns.

The common law of nuisance, which developed over time to police disputes between property owners, is best understood as a mechanism designed to arbitrate and to reconcile disputes so as to maximize the value of each person's respective property holdings. The moment one starts to deviate from that understanding, there will be excesses in one direction or the other. If landowners, for example, are entitled to pollute more or less at will, then activities that are relatively small in value will be allowed to continue even though they cause enormous harms to other individuals. And if a system of land-use restrictions is imposed as a matter of positive law when there are no such externalities, relatively trivial gains will be exacted at the cost of enormous private losses. The system must maximize the value of inconsistent claims under general rules.

The eminent domain clause of the Fifth Amendment says, "Nor shall private property be taken for public use without just compensation." It says nothing of the justifications for governments' assuming control of property without compensating the owners—an activity that goes under the heading of police power. Therefore, to understand *Lucas* [*v. South Carolina Coastal Council*], we must first ask what kinds of activities engaged in by government *do* constitute a taking, that is, do move into the sphere of protected liberties. Then we must ask whether we can find some kind of public justification for the restrictions thus imposed.

On the first issue, it is quite clear that the common law did not draw a distinction that the constitutional lawyers insist on drawing: the modern claim that there is a vast distance between physical occupation by government and a mere regulation or restriction of use. That contemporary distinction is designed to say that we don't have to look closely at anything government does if it leaves a person in bare possession of his property.

In effect, the position of the environmentalists on this issue is, "We will allow you to keep the rind of the orange as long as we can suck out all of its juice for our own particular benefit." But exclusive possession of property is not an end in itself. The reason you want exclusive possession is to make some use of your property and if you can't make good use of it, you'd like to be able to sell or trade it to somebody else. The modern law essentially says that all those use and disposition decisions are subject to public veto.

What's wrong with that? Chiefly, it encourages a massive amount of irresponsible behavior on the part of government in its treatment of private endeavors. Essentially, a government now knows that it can attain 90 percent of its objectives and pay nothing. Why, then, would it ever bother to assume the enormous burden of occupying land for which it would then have to pay full market value? Thus, we see government regulations pushing further and further, regardless of private losses, which will never be reflected on the public ledgers—precisely the situation we find in *Lucas*.

We have in *Lucas* a change in value brought about, not because people don't want to live on the beach anymore, but because they are prohibited from using their land in the ordinary fashion. And the simplest question to ask is, what kinds of public benefits could justify that private loss?

Nobody on the Isle of Palms or anywhere else along the Carolina coast regards the restrictions in question as having been enacted for his benefit. We know that because before the regulation was imposed, land values were very high and appreciating rapidly; after the regulation was imposed, everybody who was subject to it was wiped out. When we see such a huge wipeout, we have to look for the explanation of the statute that caused it, not in the protection of the local community, but in external third-party interests who will gain something, although far less than the landowners have lost.

In the usual case, when we take property for public use, we want to make sure that there's no disproportionate burden on the affected parties, but that consideration is rightly discarded when we can say to a particular fellow that we're concentrating losses on him because he has done something of great danger to the public at large. So we now have to think about Mr. Lucas's one-family house sitting on the beach front and find in it the kind of terror that might be associated with heavy explosives or ongoing, menacing pollution.

Can we do it? I think the question almost answers itself. There is no way that we can get within a thousand miles of a common law nuisance on the facts of this particular case. There is no immediate threat of erosion. We're told we're really worried about the infliction of serious external harms. Can we get an injunction on the grounds that the roof might blow off a particular building and land in the hapless fields of a neighbor? The question again more or less answers itself.

The original statute made very little if any reference whatsoever to the problem of safety. It referred instead to promoting leisure among South Carolina citizens, promoting tourism, and promoting a general form of retreat. The moment we see safety introduced during litigation, we have to wonder whether it's a pretext for some other cause.

Another difficulty involves the breadth of the restriction. If the concern is hurricane damage, the appropriate solution is, not to limit the statute in question to just beach-front owners, but to pass a general order that says: after Hurricane Hugo, nobody is entitled to rebuild in South Carolina—in Charleston or anywhere else.

There's also the question of the relationship between means and ends. If there was $10 billion worth of damage attributable to the hurricane, at least $100 of that damage must have been attributable to flying debris and falling houses. That is a trivial problem, and even if it were serious, there are surely better ways of dealing with it. We might say, for example, that anybody whose house could be found littering the beach had to remove all debris.

We hear over and over again that the government's environmental programs will shrink in size if compensation is required in *Lucas*. Those programs *should* shrink, because when government is allowed to take without compensation, it claims too much for environmental causes relative to other kinds of causes that command equal attention. Unless we introduce a system that requires the government to take and pay when it restricts private use not associated with the prevention of harms, we'll face an institutional overclaiming problem. The expansion of government will become the major issue. The just compensation clause is designed to work a perfectly sensible and moderate accommodation, to force the government to make responsible choices.

... According to Mr. Echeverria, it would be within the state's power to order everybody who has a home on those islands to dismantle it immediately so that there would be no flying roofs to hurt anybody else. The state could order the demolition of old construction as well as enjoin new construction.

Moreover, the beach front is not the only area peculiarly exposed to the environmental and hurricane risks that we're talking about. What about Charleston? It's also exposed to those risks. Do we say, in effect, that in the name of environmental protection we must raze the entire city without compensation because somebody's house might fall on somebody else's?

This is not a question of environmental interaction. We now have a set of restrictions that promises to cause billions in private losses, and we've heard it said that we can stop houses from being knocked down by ordering them to be razed.

There is no sense of proportion or balance in Echeverria's position. An ounce of environmental angst is sufficient to allow draconian measures that forbid the very activities that enable people to use the environment constructively. This is a classic case of overclaiming, which occurs because the environmental lobby can go to the state legislature and say, "Let us have our way. You're not going to have to pay for this." And environmentalists can prove that the benefit is greater than the political cost. But that's the wrong test. From a social point of view, the *right* test is whether the benefit is greater than the cost inflicted on the property holders.

NO

John Echeverria

PROPERTY RIGHTS AND ENVIRONMENTAL PROTECTION

As everybody in this room knows, our national politics is driven by sound bites. The same is true in a judicial context. The hard facts of a particular case can make bad law, and the sound bite in this case is that David Lucas purchased a piece of property for about $1 million and two years later the South Carolina legislature passed a law that left him with nothing. But that's the sound bite, and the sound bite obscures the entirely genuine and legitimate goals that the South Carolina legislature had in mind—to prevent harms to the public, which are not trivial concerns.

My goal in this debate is to convince you that once you get past the sound bite of the impact on Lucas, you'll understand that the Supreme Court should and will conclude that there was no taking in this case. Before I get into it though, ... I want to try to correct the sound bite by reciting to you the facts of a case the Supreme Court dealt with in 1987. That case involved a similar kind of regulation and raised the same fundamental issues of principle but leads to quite a different sound bite. I am referring to *First English Evangelical Lutheran Church v. County of Los Angeles*. The church had set up a camp for handicapped children in a flood plain, and a fire occurred in the watershed upstream from the camp. The county recognized immediately that there was enormous danger, since the vegetation had been removed, that flood waters could come down the river and wipe out the camp. In fact, a storm did occur, a flood did occur and the camp was completely wiped out. In response, the county put in place an interim ordinance that said there could be no inhabitable structures, which could be wiped out once again, within the flood plain. When the Supreme Court got the case it did not resolve it on the merits. Instead, it used that case to reach the conclusion that a temporary taking is compensable under the Fifth Amendment. But in the dissenting opinion, several of the justices said there was no question that the ordinance was a valid public health and safety regulation and there was no taking. And Chief Justice Rehnquist said that the Court didn't have to touch that issue and would leave it to the lower courts to find out whether there had been a taking. The case was sent back to the lower courts. No taking was found, and

From John Echeverria, "Property Rights and Environmental Protection," *Cato Policy Report* (May/June 1992). Copyright © 1992 by The Cato Institute, Washington, DC. Reprinted by permission.

when the case went up for review, the Supreme Court, which probably has some understanding of sound bites itself, declined to review it.

Lucas, as it was actually presented to the trial court, is actually a fairly easy case, in my view. The Supreme Court should conclude that Lucas did not establish a taking because he presented his claim based on the completely preposterous theory that if he suffered economic harm, that alone, regardless of any other consideration, entitled him to compensation under the Fifth Amendment. The fact of the matter is that the Supreme Court has never held, and I predict will never hold, that economic injury, standing alone, is sufficient grounds for a Fifth Amendment claim. The Court has consistently rejected that way of thinking for several reasons. First, the Court has recognized that every piece of property held in the United States is subject to the condition that it can't be used to harm others. That goes back to common law. Property rights are not absolute. They're conditional upon a responsibility to the community in which one resides.

The Department of Justice recommended initially that the United States in its brief take the position that economic harm, standing alone, constitutes a taking. Happily, wiser heads prevailed, and the solicitor general filed a brief that specifically repudiated that theory.

Richard Epstein, in his amicus brief, admits that a complete wipeout does not, by itself, make out a taking. We disagree about the range of activities in which the government can engage to prevent public harm without providing compensation. But we agree that within that range of activities, the government can act to prevent harm and no compensation is due regard-less of the impact. I think it's on that issue that this case will basically turn.

Epstein's point, at least as I understand it from his brief, is that the burden of proof is on the government to show the legitimacy of the regulation, to show that it is in fact a public harm–prevention measure. But again, one doesn't have a property interest in harming others, and if the government is trying to prevent a landowner from harming others, then there's simply no taking.

I think that Epstein and I agree that there is a line between private property and the ability of people to impose external harms on others and to harm the general public by the use of property. The question is, where is that line drawn and on what side of the line does this particular regulation fall?

I submit that the harm the South Carolina legislature was trying to deal with here was both very real and very substantial. Barrier islands are not like other real estate. They literally migrate; they move. They're unconsolidated sandy sediments that migrate laterally up and down the shore and landward in response to the action of waves and winds. They are unstable areas that are very hazardous for construction. Barrier islands in the natural state provide the most important defense for coastal areas against the effects of storms, high winds, and storm surges associated with hurricanes. Building on the beach dune system, which destroys the dune, or trying to stabilize the dune fundamentally undermines the integrity of the system. Sand naturally moves from a dune down to the beach area, replenishing the beach and allowing it to serve as a barrier to storms. If the beach dune system is stabilized, its natural function is destroyed.

It is not simply a question of harm to somebody who builds on such an unstable area, although I think there are some reasons to support paternalism in some circumstances. It is also a question of harm to others. Landward properties depend on the defense provided by the beach dune system. If that system is destroyed, those properties are exposed to storm damage. Epstein belittled what the coastal geologists refer to as projectile damage, but it's a very real phenomenon. Buildings that are on the ocean shore in front of or on top of the dunes are particularly exposed to the effects of wind and storms. After Hurricane Hugo in South Carolina, the primary adverse effects on landward structures were found to be due precisely to exposed properties that were hurled landward. All of those risks also have to be considered in light of global warming and a consequent sea level rise—again, exacerbating the hazardous nature of construction on the ocean shore and the dangers to other property owners posed by such construction.

The South Carolina Beachfront Management Act is an entirely rational, thoughtful, well-tailored response to a public hazard. The first purpose of the act, and clearly the primary purpose as recited in the act itself, is to protect the public. The act recites the fact that beaches are important recreational areas and identifies other public purposes that are served by the beaches. But what is most clear is that the regulation at issue here is specifically tailored to address a public-hazard problem.

My final point, and perhaps the most important, is that the statute specifically provided that Mr. Lucas, if he believed the line drawn pursuant to the legislative scheme was unfair, could present evidence to the coastal council and explain that the line on his property should be drawn at a different point. He never took advantage of that opportunity. He simply said, "I've been hurt and I am entitled to compensation." I believe the Supreme Court will disagree.

POSTSCRIPT

Should Property Rights Prevail Over Environmental Protection?

Political conservatives and liberals tend to divide along different lines at different points in history. In the early nineteenth century, the conservatives believed that the right of the community came before the right of the individual, while the liberals championed individual liberty over community control and democratic equality over the traditional hierarchy. With regard to the current debate, this earlier terminology has been abandoned largely because the focus of ethical debate has changed from the *political* to the *economic* questions—from questions of community governance to questions of resource management. In short, the United States has moved from an era of *political philosophy* to an era of *business management,* where the entire nation is seen as a collective resource to be managed by those with authority over it. However, if the more political terms are applied, the roles of Epstein and Echeverria may be seen in this way: Echeverria is the conservative businessman, conserving resources and letting nature take its course, while Epstein is the defender of the strategy of instant consumption.

If you were the judge who had to decide the *Lucas* case, how would you rule? Do you believe that Lucas is entitled to compensation, as argued by Epstein, or that there was no instance of compensable taking involved in the legislation, as argued by Echeverria? Does your response reflect the conservative or the liberal position?

SUGGESTED READINGS

Robert M. Andersen, "Technology, Pollution Control, and EPA Access to Commercial Property: A Constitutional and Policy Framework," *Boston College Environmental Affairs Law Review* (Fall 1989).

Rogene Buchholz, *Principles of Environmental Management: The Greening of Business* (Prentice Hall, 1993).

John Campbell and Leon N. Lindberg, "Property Rights and the Organization of Economic Activity by the State," *American Sociological Review* (October 1990).

Rachel Carson, *The Edge of the Sea* (Houghton Mifflin, 1955).

Arthur Chan, "The Changing View of Property Rights in Natural Resources Management," *American Journal of Economics and Sociology* (April 1989).

G. Tyler Miller, *Living in the Environment,* 7th ed. (Wadsworth, 1992).

David E. Mills, "Zoning Rights and Land Development Timing," *Land Economics* (August 1990).

ISSUE 15

Is Incineration a Cost-Efficient Way to Dispose of Solid Waste?

YES: John Shortsleeve and Robert Roche, from "Analyzing the Integrated Approach," *Waste Age* (March 1990)

NO: Neil Seldman, from "Waste Management: Mass Burn Is Dying," *Environment* (September 1989)

ISSUE SUMMARY

YES: Incineration industry executives John Shortsleeve and Robert Roche argue that an integrated system that incinerates the residue from a municipal waste recycling and composting operation is the best disposal option.

NO: Neil Seldman, a waste disposal consultant, claims that intensive recycling and composting can do the job without the use of costly and hazardous mass incineration technology.

How do we get rid of our garbage? In the past, the most accepted way was to dump it out in back of the house, the farm, or the factory. If you traveled through the quaint farming areas of New England past, you would generally have seen an unsightly area just out of sight of each house that contained masses of rusting cans, a refrigerator, mattresses with shreds of cloth still clinging to the rusting springs, and a sink or two. A later and more civilized approach to waste centralized it in town or municipal landfills, although they were rarely lined to prevent leakage of waste into groundwater, and they were open to all on the basis of equal opportunity.

But landfills lost popularity in the more crowded areas of developed nations as population pressure overran the dumps and as the rats and the stench spread to the surrounding houses. Incineration began as the custom of setting fire to the dumps now and again. Later, municipal incinerators put the fire into a pit, under a roof, and within four walls, and topped it with a chimney; incineration therefore qualified as civilized. By the third quarter of the twentieth century, American cities were incinerating much of their garbage, and most new apartment complexes were building incinerators directly into their basements and garbage chutes into every floor.

The new environmental regulations of the 1970s and 1980s put a stop to the air-polluting habits of the incinerators and led to the closing of many of the older ones. In the absence of large amounts of money (or inexpensive alternatives), most municipalities turned to more intensively cultivated landfills for the waste. But space is running out on this solution; towns and small cities across the United States are closing their landfills as they become full and shipping their trash miles away for disposal. Complicating the dumping problem is the phenomenon known as NIMBY—"Not in My Backyard." NIMBY reflects the predictable reactions of individuals and communities to the proposed nearby placement of anything at all that might be construed as unpleasant or unhealthy (power lines, recycling centers, and houses or shelters for the disadvantaged or disabled, for example). These reactions include utilizing lawsuits and environmental regulations to drag out the siting process and even to prevent building altogether. NIMBY is especially evident when new landfills, which are undeniably smelly, noisy, unsightly, and infested with vermin, are proposed.

At this juncture, a move to revive incineration, this time in a more environmentally acceptable form, has begun to receive favorable attention. The situation is ideal for the entrepreneur: A market exists—indeed, a market desperate for a solution to a problem both real and perceived; money is available; and a host of new technologies for incineration, each one begging to be put to work in a city, are available for immediate use.

One major drawback is that we will never get away from some air pollution with any incineration alternative. If air pollution worries us enough, we may try to avoid it by emphasizing waste reduction (nonuse of plastic wrapping, for example), reusing products (such as paper bags), and recycling (turning glass, aluminum, steel, and certain types of plastic containers over to the town for remanufacturing processes, for example). Will these options sufficiently take care of waste? Neil Seldman is of the opinion that they will; John Shortsleeve and Robert Roche, however, believe that incineration will be a necessary part of all total waste disposal solutions.

Ask yourself, as you read these selections, what value we put on convenience of waste disposal solutions and what value we put on environmental conservation. Should the potential profitability of one waste disposal solution over another sway the decision about which method should be used?

YES

John Shortsleeve and
Robert Roche

ANALYZING THE INTEGRATED APPROACH

As solid waste managers increasingly include recycling and composting in their plans, waste-to-energy companies become more aware of the commercial possibilities of these approaches *and* of the synergy when combined with burning and landfilling in an integrated solid waste program.

Unfortunately, on a national level, the U.S. has not yet adopted an integrated program. While most Western European nations recycle, compost, and burn 80% of their waste (landfilling only 20%), the U.S. figures are reversed. We recover only 20% of our annual 165 million tons of refuse, and landfill 80%.

Legislators and policy makers in Washington, D.C. are currently debating whether or not to mandate a specified level of recycling as a matter of federal law. The current markup of the clean air act requires states to certify that they have a program in place to achieve 25% recycling by 1994 (Senate Bill 196). We think this type of legislation makes sense.

Our reliance on landfilling can't last much longer. Since 1979, the number of operating landfills has plummeted by 72%. EPA projects that in five years, the number of landfills will be slashed again by more than half. By the year 1994, says the agency, only 2,275 landfills will remain of the 19,500 that were operating in 1979. Even now, in most regions, it is a near political impossibility to site a new landfill or expand an old one.

A more promising approach to the problem of MSW [municipal solid waste] disposal is "integrated resource recovery,"—a coordinated mix of recycling, composting, and waste-to-energy. Of the 20% of our waste stream not going to landfills, half (or 10% of the total) is being recycled already.

Thus far, however, recycling, composting, and waste-to-energy have evolved in the U.S. as separate technologies.

COMPARING INTEGRATED VS. MASS-BURN

Foster Wheeler has developed an approach that lets us look at the economic interaction of these three technologies when integrated under unified management. This approach also lets us compare integrated resource recovery with conventional mass-burning, relative to construction and operating costs, and environmental impact.

For this article, we modeled two facilities, each designed to take in 1,000 tpd of refuse. One would burn all 1,000 tons. The other, using the integrated approach, would burn just 650 tons a day, recycling and composting the rest.

In the waste stream going to the integrated facility, all yard waste would be composted, and all PET (polyethylene terephthalate) beverage bottles, and high-density polyethylene (HDPE) milk and water bottles would be recycled. Seventy-five percent of the glass, and about half of the newspaper, cardboard, ferrous metals, and aluminum, would be recycled also.

Smaller Boiler, Richer Fuel

The most obvious effect of the integrated approach would be to reduce boiler size. In our hypothetical case, a 35% reduction in the amount of waste burned would reduce boiler size by 26%—and construction costs by 16%. While a 16% reduction in cost may be less than hoped for, it more than covers the added cost of building the recycling and composting facilities.

But perhaps the most surprising result of the integrated approach is that, although fuel is cut by 35%, energy output (and earnings) decline by only 26%. That's because the waste that remains after recycling has a higher energy content. Table 1 shows how reducing inorganic noncombustibles increases carbon content and triggers other changes to produce a more uniform fuel having 13% more energy per pound.

Table 1

Btu Content Of Waste Before and After Recycling/Composting

Component	Before (lbs/100 lbs)	After (lbs/100 lbs)
Moisture	26.41%	24.16%
Inorganic	20.65%	16.31%
Carbon	27.62%	31.06%
Hydrogen	3.73%	4.25%
Oxygen	20.40%	22.74%
Nitrogen	.59%	.66%
Chlorine	.48%	.67%
Sulfur	.12%	.15%
% Weight	100.00%	65.34%
Btu/lb	4,880	5,539

Note: The net effect of recycling and composting is to increase energy content of waste in the IRR burn unit by 13.5%.

Data source: Foster Wheeler Power Systems, Inc.

Easier on Boilers

Recycling removes or reduces waste elements that can damage boilers and interrupt their operation. One such component is chlorine, which in many municipal waste streams comes largely from waste paper and plastic. A U.S. Department of Commerce study of Baltimore County waste showed that 86% of the chlorine came from these two sources.

Chlorine forms chlorides that corrode metal tubes in the walls and superheater sections of the boiler. Recycling a significant amount of newspaper, cardboard, and plastic should reduce chlorine—and chloride attack.

Glass is another problem for boilers. Ash samples taken from waste-to-energy facilities typically contain 25% silica, the primary component of glass. If the temperature at which ash fuses into a coherent solid is at or below temperatures in the lower furnace, the ash can fuse onto the boiler walls, forming "slag." High silica content lowers ash fusion temperature. So, by removing glass from fuel, the silica fraction in the ash will decrease, the fusion temperature of the ash should rise, and the slagging phenomenon should be reduced. That should simplify maintenance, reduce hazards for boiler maintenance workers, and increase boiler efficiency.

Aluminum, also a worry, melts at 1,200 degrees Fahrenheit, a temperature far below those maintained in waste-to-energy boilers. Unless extracted from waste, the metal clogs boiler air circulation holes, causing uneven burning which reduces efficiency.

Easier on the Environment

An important result of integrated resource recovery, economically and environmentally, is reduction of ash and other landfill material. A computer comparison of our models shows that the amount going to a landfill from the integrated complex (178 tpd) is 39% less than the 290 tpd landfilled from the mass-burn unit.

Bypass waste, too, is less of a problem for the integrated complex. Nearly 50% more waste is processed in the summer and fall due to yard waste. Where yard waste is composted, deliveries of waste to the energy recovery facility are more uniform in amount throughout the year. Emergency storage capacity can be designed for a more predictable volume, reducing the likelihood of overflow (and the need to bypass during emergency shut-downs).

Getting the Lead Out

Spent batteries are a major source of heavy metals in the environment. Although automobile batteries have been recycled with commercial success since before World War II—and 80% are recycled today—they still add much lead to the waste stream. Recent marketing changes have made the problem worse by limiting their return to their place of purchase.

But because the market for spent auto batteries has been successful for so long, few states have thought it necessary to mandate recycling. This is changing, however.

In Connecticut, recycling of car batteries will be compulsory by January, 1991; other states are considering similar legislation. EPA's proposed standards for new and existing waste-to-energy plants would require removal of all lead-acid batteries from the waste stream before combustion.

EPA's standards would mandate some sort of program targeting removal of household batteries from the waste stream. The Hearing Aid Association and the American Watch Institute have mounted vigorous recycling programs in support of the market for spent "button" batteries. There is less of a market for spent nickel-cadmium batteries since most are found in small, cordless appliances not designed for battery extraction. According to the National Electrical Manufacturers Association, appliance manufacturers are now designing appliances from which batteries may be easily removed for recycling.

There is no market at all, to our knowledge, for used alkaline and zinc carbon dry cells, because, as yet, no commercially viable way exists to process them. All dry cells—except the lithium type—contain small amounts of mercury.

In the absence of commercial recycling, battery manufacturers continue

Table 2

Cost Comparisons

	IRR	Mass Burn
Thruput in Tons	300,000 (Burning: 196,000) (Recycling: 59,000) (Composting: 45,000)	300,000
Capital Cost	$102.5 m.	$110.5 m.
Operating Cost	$9.5 m.	$8.2 m.
Annual Revenue	$9.9 m.	$9.2 m.
Annual Landfill Costs	$2.7 m.	$4.3m.
Net Tipping Fee	$47.36/ton	$55.02/ton

Data source: Foster Wheeler Power Systems, Inc.

to reduce the amount of mercury used, while searching for nontoxic substitutes.

DISPOSAL ECONOMICS IMPROVED

Table 2 summarizes the capital cost, operating costs, and annual revenues of the 1,000-tpd mass-burn and integrated models. Both handle roughly 300,000 tons of waste per year and pay the same price for electricity, water, sewer use, and bypass and residue disposal. Both models assume that:

• electricity sells for six cents per kilowatt hour (.06/kWh);

• ash disposal costs $50/ton; and

• the state in which the facility operates does not have a beverage container redemption law or "bottle bill." (Since bottle-bill laws provide incentives for the return of aluminum cans to stores by consumers, the lack of such a law means more aluminum in the waste stream, from which it may be extracted to become a revenue.)

From the perspective of disposal economics alone, the cost advantage lies with the integrated model. Still, in some communities, the cost disadvantage of separate collection could easily outweigh cost-of-disposal advantages. The most sensitive variables are the amount of aluminum recovered and the cost of ash disposal.

Integrated resource recovery is more attractive economically wherever aluminum recovery can be maximized and residue disposal costs are high. In our models, by varying these assumptions within a reasonable range, the economic advantage of the integrated approach, in disposal costs only, ranges from a high of $11/ton to $0/ton.

Because it promises to benefit everyone in so many ways, and has already shown that it can keep its promises, integrated resource recovery is an idea whose time has come.

NO

Neil Seldman

WASTE MANAGEMENT: MASS BURN IS DYING

Public standards for solid waste management have been changing very rapidly. What was acceptable as recently as 1985 no longer meets with public approval. Furthermore, the new popular standards are being incorporated in state and federal regulations. This rapid change results from the fact that mass incineration technology, the solution proposed by federal and state agencies to the landfill disposal crisis, has proven to be technologically, environmentally, and financially unacceptable to concerned citizens, whose organizations now have a tight grip on local decisionmaking. After a mass incineration plan was unanimously rejected by the Prince George's County (Maryland) Council in favor of a comprehensive recycling and composting program, the *Washington Post* observed that citizens are involved, mobilized, and here to stay in the local political process. Roland Luedtke, the former mayor of Lincoln, Nebraska, put it more succinctly: "Garbage is an issue that can unseat an incumbent mayor."

Through the 1970s and the first half of the 1980s, mass incineration (burning garbage as is) was the technology of choice for most local planners. It was a convenient solution to the shortage of landfill space. Incinerators required essentially no change in the delivery system: Waste was simply delivered to an incinerator instead of to a landfill. Of course, the costs were much higher, but there appeared to be no alternative. The U.S. Environmental Protection Agency (EPA) and the U.S. Department of Energy (DOE) provided a decade of support worth perhaps $1 billion for planning, research, demonstration, and, finally, commercialization of incinerators. When the plants were unable to find steam customers, the 1979 Public Utilities Regulatory Policies Act (PURPA) provided a guaranteed market for electricity sales instead, despite the high cost of generating electricity from garbage. When incinerator ash was routinely found to be hazardous, it was exempted from state and federal hazardous waste laws. Also in 1979, DOE began a $300 million support program for plant construction. Program planners projected that, by 1992, they would be feeding 70 percent of the nation's waste into boilers. Recycling was considered merely a footnote. Don Walter, the head of the DOE Commercialization of Waste to Energy Program, glibly stated that he did not care

From Neil Seldman, "Waste Management: Mass Burn Is Dying," *Environment* (September 1989). Copyright © 1989 by The Helen Dwight Reid Educational Foundation. Reprinted by permission of Heldref Publications, 1319 Eighteenth St., NW, Washington, DC 20036-1802.

if recycling saved more energy than was generated by incineration. "My job is to create energy from garbage, and that is it." Through 1979, the federal government spent only about $1 million on recycling. (After 1979, all solid waste program funds were transferred to hazardous waste programs.)

Today, about 10 percent of the country's municipal solid waste is incinerated and the same percentage is recycled. EPA programming for recycling is only now being planned.

Since 1985, some 40 mass burn plants, valued at about $4 billion, have been canceled, most before reaching the construction stage. In 1987, for the first time, more plant capacity was canceled than was ordered. Only 11 plants were ordered in 1988. Major cities such as Seattle, Philadelphia, Los Angeles, San Diego, and Portland, Oregon, have canceled plants, as have smaller cities such as Chattanooga, Tennessee; Lowell, Massachusetts; Saratoga, New York; and Gainesville, Florida. Of the 100 plants that remain in the planning stage, most face very stiff opposition and probably will not be built. Very few large incinerators (processing 1,000 tons or more of garbage per day) will be built. The most dramatic cancellation occurred in Austin, Texas, where the city had spent $23 million on a plant in construction. But when two businessmen were elected to the city council in early 1988, they voted with the environmentalists against the plant. The new council members foresaw a $150 million savings over a 20-year period if they invested in recycling. Florida cities in Broward and Pasco Counties have also pulled out of mass burn projects for financial reasons. The costs, it was concluded, would require steep property tax increases. Many jurisdictions fear re-

peating the experience of Warren County, New Jersey. A plant that was supposed to cost $35 per ton to operate came on line in 1988. By the end of the year, the cost was $98 per ton, and it is expected to rise to $140 by the end of 1989 because the ash was found to be hazardous and has to be shipped to Buffalo, New York. Now the county must build a $30 million ash landfill. In addition, the county was fined by the state for failing to meet ash regulations and continues to pay $59,000 per week to subsidize the plant.

Mass burn plants were advertised as a way to stabilize disposal costs. The record hardly bears out such a claim. In fact, the technology is so uncertain that each year reveals new difficulties. Before 1985, bag houses and scrubbers were not required; now they are. The need for monofills (landfills for only one type of waste) for toxic ash was not anticipated, but they also are now required. EPA recently ordered a scrubber called Thermal DeNox to be installed in plants to control oxides of nitrogen emissions.

* * *

Now, based on a grassroots appeal from citizens in Spokane, Washington, a whole new set of criteria is being established for mass burn plants. The EPA office for Region 10 (Alaska, Idaho, Oregon, and Washington) has recommended to the national EPA office in Washington, D.C., that the mass burn permit given to Spokane be remanded because the plan for mass burn does not include comprehensive source reduction, recycling, and mechanical processing prior to incineration. Because these approaches are cost effective, commercially available, and known to reduce pollution, federal Best Available Control Technology (BACT) standards require that they be implemented before an air permit can be issued. Since June, the same arguments are being made in support of new Source Performance standards, which must be issued by EPA for national guidelines. In essence, mass burn is about to be declared unpermittable.

This development has not been lost on the industry. Already Westinghouse, Wheelabrator, and Waste Management, Inc., have acquired recycling and processing technologies to meet the new standards that have, in effect, been dictated by recycling and grassroots citizen groups. Further, the processing industry is now investing in ways to recover paper fiber for recycling instead of using it as a refuse-derived fuel. These developments seem to have caught the national environmental groups off guard. They never imagined that grassroots groups on their own could change federal policy. Many environmental organizations would have settled for less recycling and would have forgone requirements for mechanical processing.

What is the alternative to mass burn? The primary alternative is recycling that includes composting. Mechanical processing and some burning in small specialty boilers or existing coal-fired plants may be required. Depending upon source reduction activity, land-filling of 10 to 20 percent of the waste stream will still be necessary. Several key cities have already started implementation. Seattle has set a goal of 65 percent recycling/source reduction by 1992 and has already achieved half this goal. Philadelphia set a 50 percent goal, and Washington, D.C., a 45 percent goal. These recycling plans replace mass incineration; they are not simply afterthoughts to a mass burn system.

Throughout the United States, recycling is at the takeoff stage. This progress stems from the infinite patience and painstaking efforts of citizen groups. Cliff Humphrey, a recycling pioneer and organizer of the first environmental action organizations in the country, provides some insight:

> We knew early on [in 1968] that the tonnage was really in the commercial waste stream. But the houses were where the votes were. Even then we had to start with drop-off sites. This was a necessary first step, even though it was inefficient compared to curbside collection. It was the way that you established recycling values in the community.

The investment in time and effort has paid off. When Humphrey began his recycling odyssey in 1968, the word recycling was unfamiliar to the U.S. public. Today, it is the law of the land.

What are the mechanics of the new recycling paradigm that is replacing the burn and bury pattern of solid waste management? There are five key factors:

MANDATORY RECYCLING

While this may not be absolutely required, it certainly helps. When accompanied by proper education, mandatory recycling programs throughout the country have a 90 percent participation rate. Islip, New York, presents an interesting case study. Islip had a mandatory ordinance but never enforced it. Consequently, participation was at 25 percent. After the embarrassment of the garbage barge, the town's administration focused its attention on recycling. Now, according to Town supervisor Frank Jones, "We can't find a household that does not recycle."

ECONOMIC INCENTIVES TO HAULERS AND HOUSEHOLDS

In Seattle, the city pays haulers $48 per ton for recycled materials. This represents a shared savings payment, as the city would pay $96 per ton for new landfill space. Seattle households pay for garbage disposal by the bag. After the first bag, fees increase steeply, but collection of recyclables is free. In Perkasie, Pennsylvania, a similar system resulted in a 61 percent reduction in the amount of garbage going to landfills—49 percent through recycling and 13 percent through source reduction.

RECYCLING LITERACY

In-school education will be far more effective in the long run than general public-awareness raising. Children in daycare and elementary schools bring recycling home with them. Like reading and writing, once recycling is taught, it is never forgotten. Public schools must make sure that all graduates know why and how to recycle. This effort will make students better and less costly future citizens of the community. Thanks to the efforts of early environmental educators, a whole catalogue of lesson plans and curricula is available to teachers.

GOVERNMENT PROCUREMENT

If recycling programs are to succeed, local, state, and federal governments must start buying products made with recycled materials. Industry should be encouraged to do the same, perhaps with tax breaks in certain circumstances. Since 1976, EPA has been working on establishing government procurement guidelines, which are not yet mandatory. To sustain markets for recycled materials, EPA must act quickly. Such action would benefit trade as well as the environment because using recycled materials would make U.S. industry more competitive with other countries, which buy our exported recycled materials to outperform U.S. companies in the marketplace. Perhaps the U.S. Department of Commerce, and not EPA, should focus on procurement programs.

ECONOMIC INCENTIVES TO MANUFACTURERS

In most cases, all that is needed is a below-market rate loan to encourage manufacturers to locate in a given area and create markets for locally recovered materials. In this "everyone wins" scenario, there are tremendous payoffs for both public and private sectors. Recycled glass is worth $35 per ton as a raw material but from $4,000 to $7,000 as a finished glass product. Moreover, scrap-based manufacturing creates jobs and new skills, encourages investment, and enlarges the manufacturing taxbase of the local economy. The "Clean Michigan" program is a model for this policy, the program's low funding level notwithstanding. This five-year-old program provides grants to nonprofit groups, local governments, and private firms for planning, implementing, and maintaining recycling and market development projects. Along similar lines, the state of Minnesota lured a tire processor to locate there with an innovative loan package. As garbage becomes a larger and larger burden on local economies, the need to use economic development funds to attract users of recycled materials becomes more obvious.

* * *

In many jurisdictions, promoters of mass burn have conceded 25 percent of the waste stream to recycling as a tactic to guarantee the remaining 75 percent to incinerators. While mass incineration advocates begrudgingly admit that 25 percent recycling may be possible, many cities and towns are moving beyond this arbitrary boundary, whose actual function is to limit the demonstrated success of recycling.

Economic realities and fears of environmental catastrophe have mobilized citizens on the garbage issue. Michigan is an excellent example. That state has three mass burn plants, representing a billion dollar commitment, all of which stand idle because there is no place to dispose the hazardous ash they produce. The state legislature is rushing through a law to exempt the ash from existing hazardous waste regulations so that the plants can be put back in use and others can be built. Michigan citizens are fighting for a far more balanced program that would include recycling, composting, and mechanical processing, as well as landfills, to relieve the state of the capital and operating costs of these mass burn plants. A recent study of Michigan recycling programs revealed that collection of curbside recyclables costs $9.61 per load as compared with $37.33 per load for regular garbage collection.

In addition to its own disposal problem, Michigan faces an influx of waste from the eastern states of Connecticut, New York, and New Jersey, which cannot find local landfills for their mass burn residues. Because Ohio, Illinois, and Indiana are stiffening landfill regulations while Michigan is lowering barriers, the eastern ash will soon be heading by rail for Michigan's private landfills, which cannot bar out-of-state waste: If Michigan exempts its own ash from hazardous waste regulation, it must do the same for imported ash.

Progress in recycling at the local level in the United States has international as well as national implications. As industrial energy use is reduced and as virgin ore and fiber is replaced with recycled materials, the U.S. contribution to global pollution should decline. Moreover, as U.S. recycling increases, imports of Third World raw materials should decrease, enabling Third World countries to use their own raw materials for manufactured products instead of buying finished products at high prices from the industrialized nations. Finally, if U. S. cities generated far less toxic ash, they would not need to ship these wastes to Third World countries. Recycling involves acting locally. It impacts globally.

POSTSCRIPT

Is Incineration a Cost-Efficient Way to Dispose of Solid Waste?

Nothing happens without waste. To run a coal-fired plant, one must deal with slag and polluting smoke; to run a nuclear plant, one must deal with nuclear waste and the eventual decommissioning (shutdown) of the plant itself; to run an incineration plant, one must install scrubbers and dispose of the ash that the scrubbers leave behind—by some estimates, this ash equals up to 25 percent of the landfill volume of the original waste.

What shall we do with incinerator smoke? Scrub it with chemicals so the the air will be clean? What shall we do with the ash? Put it in the landfills again, or wait for a better idea?

The debate here concerns the cost efficiency of various waste disposal methods. However, is it appropriate to be thinking in terms of dollars and cents where the problem of how garbage should be disposed of is concerned? Should we develop the safest and most effective method for waste disposal regardless of the costs? Or is the disposal of solid waste simply another industry, one in which the job goes to the lowest bidder?

In the near future, a major opportunity will emerge from the problems of waste disposal. Individual ingenuity is running out, and very few of us have backyards large enough to bury our own waste, let alone the town's. We shall have to come up with better solutions or smother in our own waste. Incineration, carefully monitored, may be among those solutions.

SUGGESTED READINGS

"Europe Adopts Common Standards for Environment," *Personnel* (January 1991).

Robert McGough, "Ogden: Selling the Sizzle in Garbage," *Financial World* (May 15, 1990).

Michael Satchell, "Poisoning the Border," *US News and World Report* (May 6, 1991).

Stratford P. Sherman, "Trashing a $150 Billion Business," *Fortune* (August 28, 1989).

Erling Skorpen, "Images of the Environment in Corporate America," *Journal of Business Ethics* (September 1991).

Ann M. Thayer, "Degradable Plastics Generate Controversy in Solid Waste Issues," *Chemical and Engineering News* (June 25, 1990).

Peter Wilsher, "The Feeling Grows That Going Green is Good for Business," *Management Today* (October 1991).

PART 5

Operating in the International Arena

What do we want, or expect, of our business partners abroad? This section takes on the ethical problems that arise when we find ourselves doing business with people who do not act the way we expect business associates—customers, colleagues, and industrialists—to act, given the written or unwritten rules by which our business is usually conducted. The debates in this section question some common assumptions about business and its dealings. For example, if a customer buys a perfectly good product from a reputable dealer, it is often assumed that it is none of the manufacturer's concern whether the customer should or should not have done so. Likewise, most people view the payment of any bribe, no matter whom it is paid to, as a forbidden act, punishable by law. Finally, it is generally held that all customers and clients want and need to have access to the highest technology available.

- Did Nestlé Act Irresponsibly in Marketing Infant Formula to the
  Third World?

- Is Bribery Ever Justified?

- Should the Less Developed Countries Be
  Encouraged to Develop High Technology?

ISSUE 16

Did Nestlé Act Irresponsibly in Marketing Infant Formula to the Third World?

YES: Doug Clement, from "Infant Formula Malnutrition: Threat to the Third World," *The Christian Century* (March 1, 1978)

NO: Maggie McComas, Geoffrey Fookes, and George Taucher, from "The Dilemma of Third World Nutrition: Nestlé and the Role of Infant Formula," *Paper prepared for Nestlé, S.A.* (1985)

ISSUE SUMMARY

YES: Doug Clement, formerly the coordinator of the National Infant Formula Action (INFACT) coalition, argues that Nestlé has caused the deaths of countless infants by marketing infant formula to the Third World. INFACT brought this issue to world attention and called for the boycott of Nestlé products to protest the formula promotions.

NO: Maggie McComas, a public affairs analyst, Geoffrey Fookes, vice president of Nestlé Nutrition, and George Taucher, a professor of business administration, present Nestlé's response to its attackers and the company's view of its present and future role in protecting infant nutrition in the Third World.

The Nestlé Company has been involved in infant nutrition since 1987. It has always been known for producing high-quality products. In late 1973, however, a book appeared on the market entitled *Nestlé Kills Babies*, which described what some felt were questionable business operations in certain developing nations. Here were the makings of a public relations disaster. What had gone wrong?

American birthrates and Nestlé's market for infant formula had expanded comfortably through the 1950s and 1960s. Toward the end of the 1960s, American birthrates began to decline, so Nestlé went farther afield in search of markets. (Note: the branch of the Nestlé company that was actually involved in the Third World infant formula dispute was based in Switzerland and is independent of the American branch.) Birthrates are highest in developing nations, so Nestlé took its promotional campaign to several Third World countries. As it happened, the company's employees were able to accomplish some social good while making a profit. Not only did their product have the potential to enhance the nutrition of sparse diets, but the sales representatives that were sent to distribute product samples in the maternity hospitals volunteered to teach new mothers how to bathe and care for their babies. They were called "mothercraft nurses," and they were a help to overworked medical and nursing staffs. In addition to issuing samples in the hospitals, Nestlé employed the usual promotional tools to move the infant formula—broadcasts, billboards, and leaflets—all of which associated its product with fat, happy babies.

Then babies started to get sick, and when their mothers brought them to their pediatricians, the pediatricians noticed a correlation: many of the sick babies—too many of them—were on infant formula instead of mother's milk. An ominous pattern appeared in the poverty-level formula users: impressed by the convenience of formula feeding, as taught by the mothercraft nurses in the hospitals, new mothers would opt not to nurse their babies. Whether or not these mothers had their milk supplies chemically stopped, their milk would dry up after a short period of nonuse. Once home from the hospital, they would discover just how much of the expensive formula they would have to buy, especially as the baby's appetite grew, and they would try to save money by stretching the formula—using less than instructions called for and increasing the amount of water. Worse, the water was often polluted. The instructions on the package strictly warned mothers to boil the water, but many of them could not read. Deprived of the antibodies found naturally in mother's milk, the babies were more susceptible to waterborne diseases; deprived of sufficient nutrition as the formula was stretched thinner and thinner, the babies began to starve.

Who is at fault in this? Nestlé has a proven product, legally sold, readily available, moderately priced for the middle-class household, with clear directions for use. Mothers systematically do not follow the directions, do not use enough formula, and mix it with polluted water, and the babies get sick. How can it be said that "Nestlé kills babies"?

Ask yourself, as you read these selections, which comes first, maintaining the freedom to choose on the market or protecting the health of the infant? Also ask: Who should decide which comes first? How shall we assign liability and blame in cases where people get hurt by perfectly good products? To what extent must business modify its activities because of the presumed ignorance of its audience? And finally, should marketing techniques that have been developed in and for highly industrialized Western societies be modified in consideration of the cultural differences of Third World nations? Or is that a form of paternalism that can lead to racial stereotyping and oppression?

YES

Doug Clement

INFANT FORMULA MALNUTRITION: THREAT TO THE THIRD WORLD

CARACAS, VENEZUELA, July 1977—In the emergency room of the Hospital de Niños lie 52 infants. All of them suffer from gastroenteritis, a serious inflammation of the stomach and intestines. Many suffer from pneumonia as well. According to the doctor in charge, roughly 10,000 Venezuelan infants die each year from gastroenteritis and pneumonia. The doctor explains that these 52 babies—like the many who preceded them and those who will follow—have one thing in common: they have all been bottle-fed with artificial milk formulas. Surveying the room with a weary frustration, he adds: "A totally breast-fed baby just does not get sick like this."

THE RISKS OF BOTTLE-FEEDING

It is an episode that recurs increasingly throughout the developing world: bottle-fed infants turn up in clinics and hospitals, malnourished, dying of gastroenteritis, dehydration and respiratory illnesses. Few scenes can more vividly depict the outcome of what one prominent physician, R. G. Hendrickse, has called "probably the most significant change in human behavior in recorded history": the move from breast to artificial feeding of infants.

In most of the world, breast-feeding is on the decline. In 1951, roughly three out of every four babies in low-income Singapore families were being breast-fed at the age of three months. Twenty years later only 5 percent were still at the breast at three months. In the Philippines, 31 percent fewer mothers nursed their babies in 1968 than in 1960. Such trends are in contrast with the recent increases in breast-feeding rates in western Europe and the United States. But it is in the Third World, where breast-feeding rates are declining rapidly, that bottle-feeding is so dangerous.

Artificial milk formulas can be used safely only if a number of conditions are satisfied. For proper use, a family must have:

1. *Sufficient income* to purchase the amount of formula required for adequate infant nutrition. But the cost of bottle-feeding in Egypt and Pakistan exceeds 40 percent of the minimum wage, if the baby is three months old; for a

From Doug Clement, "Infant Formula Malnutrition: Threat to the Third World," *The Christian Century* (March 1, 1978). Copyright © 1978 by The Christian Century Foundation. Reprinted by permission.

six-month-old, almost two-thirds of the family's income would have to go to formula purchases.

2. *Reasonable access to clean water* that can be mixed with the formula and used to wash bottles, nipples and other equipment. In Indonesia, however, only 10 percent of all families have "reasonable" access to "safe" water, as defined by the U.N.

3. *The ability to read* and follow the fairly complex instructions for formula preparation. Barely 16 percent of women in Haiti are literate, and then usually in Creole or French. On the shelves of many Haitian grocery stores are formula cans with instructions in English and Spanish only.

4. *Access to refrigeration facilities* for storage of unused formula mixture. But fewer than 54 percent of all Brazilian families have electricity, let alone refrigerators. In rural areas of Brazil, only 11 percent of the people have electricity.

Using United Nations data for a large number of developing countries, one recent statistical study estimated that since *all* four conditions must be met before infant formulas can be properly used, only 20 percent of the people of these countries can safely feed artificial milks to their infants.

Breast-feeding, on the other hand, is a physiological possibility for well over 95 percent of all mothers. Breast milk is sterile and inexpensive, and requires no time-consuming preparation. Moreover, it contains antibodies that protect infants against a wide range of common diseases. So bottle-feeding not only presents high risks; it also replaces a virtually perfect and readily available food. Developing countries cannot afford to lose such a resource.

PROMOTING THE PRODUCT

Yet it is in these countries that the multinational corporate producers of infant formulas have begun to sell their wares. Nestlé, Bristol-Myers, Abbott Laboratories, American Home Products, Borden, Carnation and others have realized that the high birth rates of the Third World offer a profitable alternative to the stagnating baby-food markets of the industrialized countries.

Mass-media advertising is one way that these formula producers create a market for infant formula in the developing countries. Huge advertisements appear on the sides of panel trucks in Nigeria or station wagons in Thailand. In Barbados, advertisements for Bristol-Myers's "Enfamil" were on the back covers of the 1975 and 1976 telephone books. Some companies hold "baby shows," awarding large supplies of free formula to the cutest, healthiest babies, who are then used in future promotion efforts. In the maternity wards of Philippine hospitals there are full-color calendars and posters depicting bright, healthy babies next to large cans of Nestlé's "Lactogen" and "Pelargon" formulas. And in Uruguay, newspaper ads display a new Nestlé formula: "Eledon."

Even illiterate and rural populations can be reached by the spoken word, so radio, too, has become an extensive advertising medium for formula marketers in the Third World. In Kenya, for example, infant formula ads made up almost 13 percent of all Swahili radio advertising in 1973; nine-tenths of this advertising was for Nestlé's Lactogen. In Malaysia, where the poor and rural tend to listen to the radio while the relatively rich and urban watch television, Nestlé ran three and a half times as many formula ads on radio as on TV in 1976.

"Mothercraft nurses," hired by the companies to talk to new mothers about infant care and feeding, are perhaps an even more effective influence in persuading mothers to bottle-feed. The mothercraft nurses bring cans of their company's formula when they visit mothers on the maternity wards or in their homes, and often leave samples behind. In their crisp white uniforms, the nurses are seen as medical authorities, and their explicit endorsement of bottle-feeding is a powerful reinforcement of the media message.

Such advertising persuades Third World women that formula is the modern, healthy and Western way to feed babies. Bottle-feeding becomes a status symbol; breast-feeding, a vulgar tradition. In addition, these promotion techniques plant doubts in mothers' minds about their ability to breast-feed. A typical Nestlé radio advertisement tells listeners: "When mother's milk is not enough, baby needs a special milk... Lactogen Full Protein." That message reinforces the unproven notion that breast-feeding will not be sufficient. Furthermore, such words can become a self-fulfilling prophecy. By stimulating doubts about breast-feeding ability, the sales pitches create anxiety. Doctors have long recognized that anxiety and lack of confidence strongly inhibit the "let-down reflex" which allows milk to flow successfully. Thus, unsuccessful lactation and a "need" for formula.

By playing upon fear—fear of losing status by appearing "primitive," fear of maternal inadequacy, or fear of not feeding one's baby the "scientific" and healthy way—the marketing efforts of formula corporations have contributed to, if not created, the drastic decline in breast-feeding rates in the Third World.

When this large-scale increase in bottle-feeding is coupled with the inability to bottle-feed safely, the inevitable consequence is increased infant malnutrition and disease. In a tragic attempt to save money, poor mothers "stretch" the formula by adding too much water, or by mixing in cornstarch and rice powder. In a 1969 Barbados survey, 82 percent of the mothers who were fully bottle-feeding their babies were found to be making four-day formula supplies last anywhere from five days to three weeks. In addition, without clean water and refrigeration, baby bottles and formula become perfect breeding grounds for bacteria; researchers in rural Chile found that almost 80 percent of the bottles examined showed high bacterial contamination.

The result of this overdilution and contamination is disease and often death. A study of three Arab villages revealed that while only .5 percent of totally breast-fed infants were hospitalized for gastroenteritis, almost 25 percent of the bottle-fed babies had to be treated for that disease. In 13 Latin American countries, a 1972 study conducted by the Pan American Health Organization found that whereas diarrheal diseases were responsible for roughly 52 percent of the deaths of bottle-fed infants, they accounted for only 32 percent of the deaths occurring to breast-fed babies. Researchers in Chile discovered that death rates for bottle-fed infants were three times as high as those for completely breast-fed children. Countless other studies reveal the same tragic relationship.

ADDRESSING THE ISSUE

These problems have not gone unnoticed. During the early 1970s, a few nutritionists and physicians began to warn against the use of formulas. In 1972, the Protein-Calorie Advisory Group (PAG) of the United Nations issued a statement which stressed "the critical importance of breast-feeding under the sociocultural and economic conditions that prevail in many developing countries."

Several European social-justice groups became involved in the issue, and in 1974 Mike Muller, a British journalist, published *The Baby Killer*, an important exposé of the formula problem. The issue got front-page headlines throughout Europe when Nestlé sued a Swiss action group in 1974 for translating *The Baby Killer* into German and retitling it *Nestlé Kills Babies*.

For two years the Nestlé lawsuit received a great deal of European media coverage as testimony was given and evidence gathered about the harmful effect of bottle-feeding. But because it could not be proved that Nestlé had *directly* killed babies, in June 1976 the judge found the Swiss group guilty on one count of libel (of the four originally filed by Nestlé), served its members with minimal fines and, stating that "this verdict is not an acquittal of Nestlé," called on the company to fundamentally rethink its promotion practices.

Infant-formula malnutrition became an American issue through the work of concerned church groups. In late 1974 the Interfaith Center on Corporate Responsibility (ICCR), a National Council of Churches agency which coordinates the stockholder actions for 14 Protestant denominations and more than 140 Roman Catholic orders, raised the issue of formula abuse with several U.S. formula manufacturers. Meetings with corporate management and stockholder resolutions were the major strategies used by ICCR over the next two years in its efforts to uncover information about the companies' role in the problem and to press for changes in formula promotion practices.

BRISTOL-MYERS SUED BY NUNS

Negotiations with Bristol-Myers provide a most interesting example of ICCR's work. In 1975 a stockholder resolution was filed with Bristol-Myers by members of ICCR. The resolution asked for complete and accurate information on the company's formula sales and promotion practices. In response, Bristol-Myers's public relations department issued a 20-page report which medical authorities and church representatives found to include little specific information and a number of inaccuracies.

In 1976 another resolution was filed, asking again for a complete and accurate report on Bristol-Myers formula activities. To the surprise of ICCR members, the inaccuracies of the 1975 report were repeated in the management's proxy statement in opposition to the new resolution. Moreover, this statement was provided as "proof" that the 1975 report had been "totally responsive" to previous requests for information. Believing that the Bristol-Myers statements violated a Securities and Exchange Commission (SEC) law which prohibits misstatements in proxy materials, one ICCR member, the Sisters of the Precious Blood, filed suit against Bristol-Myers in April 1976.

The Bristol-Myers lawsuit began to generate the same kind of attention in America that the Nestlé lawsuit had in

Europe. ICCR and the Sisters gathered massive amounts of evidence from 18 countries, with the help of an international community of concerned doctors, nutritionists and church-related investigators. Over 40 affidavits documented the problems caused by the promotion and sale of Bristol-Myers infant formulas.

But in May 1977 the judge handed down his decision in favor of Bristol-Myers. Surprisingly, he based his decision not on whether Bristol-Myers had made "misstatements" in its proxy statement but on the question of how such alleged lies might have affected stockholders. He decided that while the Sisters may possibly have proved that Bristol-Myers's proxy statement did contain misstatements (that the company does, in fact, sell its formulas to people who do not have the means to use them safely), the Sisters had *not* shown that they, as shareholders, had been caused "irreparable harm" by such misstatements.

The Sisters decided to appeal the decision immediately, stating that the ruling "does not address the merits of the case and makes a mockery of Securities and Exchange Commission laws requiring truth in corporate proxy statements." Other church and institutional investors agreed to file friend-of-the-court briefs for the appeal, and the SEC submitted its own brief in support of the Sisters' demand for stockholder rights.

Under pressure from the appellate court, however, the Sisters and Bristol-Myers again entered into negotiations. Early this year a settlement was reached when Bristol-Myers agreed to publish a report to stockholders including some of the Sisters' evidence from Third World countries as well as company statements on planned policy changes. The changes in Bristol-Myers's promotion practices included the prohibition of *all* direct consumer-oriented advertising, including posters, calendars and name tags in hospitals, and a stop to milk nurses in Jamaica where they had violated government regulations. The settlement is viewed as an important landmark in the infant-formula controversy, but further restrictions on promotion will be necessary, according to ICCR staff.

During this same time period, U.S. congressional representatives were beginning to consider hearings and legislation on the infant-formula issue. Representative Michael Harrington (D., Mass.) introduced a resolution in August 1976 calling for an investigation of the problem. By the following summer, Congress had passed a bill encouraging the president—through the Agency for International Development—to carry out an extensive infant and maternal nutrition program in partnership with the developing nations, with special emphasis on breast-feeding. In early 1978, Senator Frank Church's foreign economic policy subcommittee and Senator Edward Kennedy's antitrust and monopoly subcommittee considered holding hearings on the infant-formula industry.

Concerned about the infant-formula problem and seeking solutions to it, a number of church and secular groups from around the country have recently joined together in the Infant Formula Action (INFACT) coalition. On July 4, 1977, the Minnesota chapter of INFACT called for a national boycott of Nestlé products, believing that a boycott is the most effective way to put pressure on a Swiss-based company in which few Americans hold stock. At a National INFACT conference in November, INFACT representatives from around the country agreed that the boycott would become a major INFACT strategy. A national office was established in Minneapolis to coordinate local and regional boycott efforts. INFACT members also agreed to support shareholder, legislative and research efforts dealing with the infant-formula problem. With the advent of the Nestlé boycott, the infant-formula controversy has stirred more action at the local level. And as the National Council of Churches debates whether or not to endorse the boycott, church leaders note that this is the first issue in a long time that has generated such a high level of concern among the people in the pews.

THE PRODUCERS FIGHT BACK

Such intense criticism has evoked a variety of responses from the various formula producers, but a few basic principles usually underlie a company's reaction to criticism about formula sales:

1. Although they will agree that breast milk is best, they say there is a sizable need for infant formulas—above and beyond the 1-to-5 percent of mothers who are physically unable to breast-feed. Nestlé and American Home Products, for example, claim that many mothers run out of sufficient amounts of breast milk after a few months and that formula is then needed as a "supplement."

2. While admitting that formula abuse may occur in some areas, they claim that their products are not responsible. First of all, their formulas are of high quality: scientifically designed and prepared under the most stringent sanitary conditions. They also stress that they cannot be held responsible for the poverty, illiteracy and poor sanitary conditions of the Third World. And, of course, their products are said to be responsibly promoted and sold only to people who can use them safely. Each company claims that its competitors are responsible for product abuses.

3. They may make some changes in company policy, usually restricting mass-media advertising or milk-nurse activity.

4. If they were to restrict their formula promotion greatly, and give out information about their marketing overseas, they claim, they would lose their competitive position, and smaller, less ethical companies with lower-quality products would take over the market.

Critics don't take issue with the claim that the products—while inferior to breast milk—are usually of high quality. But they do disagree with the unproven theory that breast milk is not sufficient for the first four to six months of life; the great body of medical research supports the opposite conclusion.

Furthermore, they disagree with the notion that a company should not be held responsible for the social consequences of its corporate practices. While it is not held that the companies have necessarily created the poverty that exists, critics do believe that formulas should not be advertised and sold where existing socioeconomic conditions make safe formula use impossible. The promotion of formulas—whether through the mass media or the hospital system—will inevitably lead to formula misuse in such an environment. It is the ethical responsibility of the companies, in cooperation with local health workers and government agencies, to ensure that formulas are used only in cases of clear-cut medical need and/or when it is certain that the formulas can be used safely.

SUPERFICIAL CHANGES

Critics also believe that policy changes made to date by most companies have been largely superficial. It is important to end mass-media advertising, but this is just the visible tip of the promotional iceberg. A halt to promotion through the health system is equally important. Formula companies are now distributing their products through hospitals in developing countries, offering free medical equipment and other inducements to persuade doctors and administrators that they should give mothers free samples of the company's formula. Until this promotion strategy is halted, a company has not made an adequate response to the problem.

Restrictions on milk-nurse activity have been minimal. Nestlé, for instance, has taken its milk nurses out of white uniforms, only to put them into blue ones. Abbott Labs has gone so far as to take theirs out of uniform and to call them "company representatives," but the nurses still promote formula in the same deadly efficient manner.

Moreover, critics point out, there is little assurance that the new policies, weak as they are, are being enforced. Nestlé says that it has never done mass-media advertising in Latin America, but as recently as December 1977, Uruguayan newspapers published ads for "Eledon," a Nestlé formula. Bristol-Myers claims that its milk nurses operate only with the express permission of local health authorities, but during summer 1977, a Bristol-Myers nurse was found on the maternity ward of Jamaica's largest public hospital. Jamaica's Ministry of Health has long prohibited such visits.

Finally, in response to the industry argument that regulating the big companies will simply encourage the smaller ones, critics argue that only the large companies can afford the massive promotion campaigns that are so persuasive. Small companies which ride the crest of this promotional wave will find their markets considerably smaller when promotion is halted. Also, criticism of the well-known formula sellers has alerted Third World governments to the problem and led to local efforts to solve it.

Papua New Guinea, for example, has passed a law requiring a doctor's prescription in order to buy any sort of formula-feeding equipment. Guinea-Bissau has enacted a similar law. Algeria has prohibited advertising of processed baby milk, and all infant-formula trade is now under federal control. In Singapore and Malaysia, consumer groups and health professionals have begun breast-feeding campaigns, giving American and European activists credit for raising their awareness of the problem and making possible the initiation of the campaigns. In the Caribbean, significant regional efforts have been under way since 1974 to restrict bottle-feeding and encourage breast-feeding.

THE U.S. MARKET

It is ironic that the U.S. church and secular activists, who have been quite successful in illuminating the formula-abuse problem in the Third World, have devoted so little attention to the same problem at home. While extensive research on abuse problems among the American poor has just begun, there have been several reports of infant-formula malnutrition on native American reservations, in migrant labor camps, and in inner-city areas.

But restricting corporate promotion will be difficult here as well. American formula producers have a strong interest in maintaining a large domestic market, and formula promotion may be even more intense here than in the Third World. Less mass-media advertising is done, but the companies control the market more tightly and are better integrated into the health system. Abbott and Bristol-Myers together hold roughly 85 percent of the U.S. formula market. American Home Products accounts for another 10.5 percent of domestic formula sales.

These "Big Three" companies send salespeople to hospitals on a regular and frequent basis—according to one recent survey, three out of four hospitals received visits *at least* once a month. Over four-fifths of hospitals in the survey were given free formula by the companies. Doctors often get free supplies of a company's formula for their own children, presumably to persuade them to recommend that brand to their patients. In the words of one Bristol-Myers spokesperson, "If the pediatrician doesn't recommend us, we don't get the business."

The formula corporations offer hospitals substantial inducements to ensure that their formulas are distributed on maternity wards. Money for medical conferences, research grants, planning assistance for nursery additions, supplies of medical equipment and other gifts are commonly given to persuade hospitals to use a certain brand of formula. Hospitals are the perfect place to create infant-formula consumers, and the companies don't want to miss that opportunity. (It is also significant that the directors of several major formula companies hold influential positions at large hospitals and medical schools.)

The result of this heavy promotion? Over three-quarters of the hospitals in a 1976 survey reported that they gave new mothers "gift paks" of formula when they left for home. Coincidentally, perhaps an equal proportion of American women bottle-fed their infants that year. Formula promotion by the Big Three companies has also been a major factor in the very common hospital practice of placing babies on bottles from the moment of birth on, rather than encouraging breast-feeding. Often mothers who want to breast-feed encounter strong resistance in U.S. hospitals, especially in those that serve low-income families.

Government/industry ties also seem to be rather close. A number of formula-industry employees have taken government jobs, and government programs often reflect this influence. Lobbying reinforces further the pro-industry bias. The federal Women, Infants and Children (WIC) low-cost food program, for instance, has for several years supplied infant formulas to eligible mothers. According to one doctor:

> The formula companies lobbied WIC through Congress. Ross [Abbott Labs' formula subsidiary] gave a big breakfast in Washington, D.C., invited all congressmen and their aides, and showed their film *Prescription: Food....* WIC coupons specify three formulas by name: Similac, SMA, and Enfamil.

The specified formulas are the major sellers of the Big Three.

While such intense pressure to use formulas can be viewed as a restriction of choice for American women, and one that may lead to higher rates of infant disease, the outcome is still less tragic than it is in the Third World where formula use often results in death. What is perhaps most significant about this integration of formula industry, health system and government programs in the United States is that it provides a model for future marketing efforts in the Third World.

Following the U.S. model, formula companies in developing countries use every means available to persuade doctors and hospitals to use their formulas. Abbott Labs—because it is a pharmaceutical company and knows how to sell its products via health systems—has been able to stop its direct advertising of formulas in Third World countries, and can now criticize other companies for persisting in such practices. Meanwhile, Abbott promotes heavily through the hospitals and pediatricians.

Bristol-Myers has also learned this route. Its Venezuelan formula subsidiary is reported to have paid from $5,000 to $7,000 for medical school graduation parties. And on a Philippine banana plantation, the nursery of the workers clinic has been almost totally furnished by Bristol-Myers; according to a nurse there, every baby born in that clinic is formula-fed from the hour of birth. Unfortunately, none of the plantation workers have refrigerators or running water in their homes, and formula purchases cost roughly 20 percent of the entire family's income.

AN ONGOING STRUGGLE

The problem of infant-formula malnutrition will not be an easy one to solve. Companies will resist any efforts that threaten what appears to be a lucrative market (Brazilian figures indicate a 72 percent profit margin on infant-formula sales at the retail level), and their financial resources present a major obstacle to the efforts of concerned groups.

Some companies have—under sustained pressure from critics—marginally improved their promotion and sales policies, but further changes will be harder to bring about as the squeeze on profits begins. The companies will continue to explain that their promotion of infant formulas is just one factor among many in the decline of breast-feeding in the Third World. They will insist that they are satisfying a need, not creating one. But as long as the use of their formulas continues to fill emergency rooms like that of Hospital de Niños, the struggle of the churches, governments, health organizations and social-action groups must not end.

NO

Maggie McComas, Geoffrey Fookes, and George Taucher

THE DILEMMA OF THIRD WORLD NUTRITION

NESTLÉ AND THE ROLE OF INFANT FORMULA

More than 10 years ago, Nestlé became embroiled in an emotional controversy over infant feeding in the Third World. As the debate became ever more intense and an activist-led campaign held up to scrutiny the marketing practices of the infant formula industry as a whole, Nestlé remained the focus of the most vocal of critics, who for several years solicited support for a consumer boycott of the company's products in the United States.

This debate took a different, more positive, turn in May 1981, when the World Health Organization (WHO) adopted guidelines for the marketing of infant formula. This framework is now being translated into concrete measures by the national governments of some of the countries affected. At the same time, Nestlé has on its own initiative begun to apply the code in all Third World countries except where national measures are even more restrictive.

The account that follows traces the evolution of this controversy and analyzes the issues raised, the techniques employed by the critics, and Nestlé's response to both the real issues and the public debate. It is the work of a team composed of an independent business journalist, a professor of business administration and a Nestlé executive. They were asked to examine the history of the controversy in depth, being as frank and objective as possible.

The aim of this exercise is not simply to ruminate on management's past actions or provide a defense of them. The objective, rather, is to make it possible for those with an interest in the social, economic and political aspects of the controversy to review the path of events that led Nestlé to its current policy on infant formula marketing—and to judge for themselves whether the company is serving the best interest of consumers.

From a report prepared for Nestlé, S.A., in 1982 by Maggie McComas, Geoffrey Fookes, and George Taucher. Reviewed for medical accuracy by Professor Frank T. Falkner, M.D., F.R.C.P. Additional material added in 1985 by Richard Worsnop. Reprinted by permission of The Nestlé Company. Notes omitted.

THE ISSUES AT STAKE

For as long as mothers have been feeding their babies, the need for breast-milk substitutes has existed. There have always been mothers who cannot or will not breast-feed their babies, or who cannot fully satisfy their babies' needs from the breast alone. Too, other physiological factors—disease, undernourishment of the mother, death in childbirth—as well as economic, social, historical and cultural factors, account for the need for breast-milk substitutes. Work outside the home, for example, whether it be the case of the Third World mother who goes off daily to the fields or the Western office employee, may rule out the possibility of regular breast feeding. Moreover, even breast-fed babies often need supplementary foods in order to achieve optimal growth during the first few months of life.

The quality of most commercially produced infant formula has seldom been in question throughout the public controversy which began unfolding in the early 1970s. Rather, it was the way in which these products were marketed and used throughout the Third World that advocacy groups attacked. They based a worldwide campaign against the industry on claims that companies such as Nestlé were aggressively promoting the infant formula in the Third World. As a result, they said, mothers were encouraged unnecessarily to give up breast feeding, and the product was often used in settings where it could not possibly be prepared or administered hygienically. The consequence of all this, continued the critics' argument, was grave harm to some 10 million babies annually, the effect of companies' marketing practices being disease, malnutrition and even death.

ORIGINS OF THE CONTROVERSY

Among the international organizations concerned with the study and, insofar as it is possible, the improvement of worldwide nutrition, one of the most active during the 1960s was the United Nations Protein-Calorie Advisory Group (PAG). Until its dissolution in 1977, its job was to assure the coordination of nutrition research and aid programs carried out by UN agencies such as the World Health Organization (WHO), the Food and Agriculture Organization (FAO) and the UN Children's Fund (UNICEF).

The Bogotá Meeting

In December 1969, a working group organized by PAG began to study the question of nutrition *in utero*, i.e. in the unborn child, and also during the first few months of life. The group outlined a preliminary action program addressed to the governments of UN member states, to health professionals, and to representatives of the infant food industry. As a result, a cross-sectoral meeting of minds on the subject of infant nutrition was held at Bogotá, Colombia, in November 1970. The participants, who included experts from academia, governments and industry, represented an impressive storehouse of expertise on problems of nutrition, especially those relative to Latin America and the Caribbean. PAG officials, fully appreciating the great diversity among the regions and countries that make up the Third World, thought it wise to limit this first discussion to a particulargeographical region.

They outlined four general topics and objectives:

- emphasis of the importance of prolonged breast feeding;
- tentative guidelines for the marketing of breast-milk substitutes;
- support of the development of low-cost protein-rich weaning foods; and
- other possibilities for public health and industry "joint action."

Underlying the discussion was the concern of many health specialists over the evidence of a worldwide decline in breast feeding. While the factors causing this trend could not be precisely identified, there was natural suspicion over the obvious presence of commercial infant formula in areas where such a decline had taken place. So, these health experts sought to secure the industry's cooperation in assuring that aggressive marketing of breast-milk substitutes and possible consequent exacerbation of the trend would be avoided. Yet even as these seeds of doubt were being sown, many of the experts acknowledged that the infant formula industry did indeed have a positive impact on infant nutrition in Third World settings.

This generally positive view of the potential benefits of infant formula use in developing countries was not held by all the participants, however. The most determined, and the most vocal, among the doubters was Dr. Derrick B. Jelliffe, a PAG consulting expert who was at the time Director of the Caribbean Food and Nutrition Institute. He claimed that industry marketing practices were the *major factor* contributing to the decline in breast feeding and the parallel growth in the consumption of products that, given the poor hygienic conditions prevalent in most developing countries, contributed to infant disease, malnutrition and death. This was

the first time that a prominent health professional claimed a direct link between infant mortality trends and the promotion and consumption of infant formula. His thesis was expressed in a dramatic fashion, offering few reservations and no apologies. Not surprisingly, it provoked a lively debate that soon went beyond the confines of the PAG meeting, to be fueled for several years after by the absence of scientific data that might have definitively answered the charges that Jelliffe made.

The Debate Goes Public

In July 1973,... Dr. Jelliffe spoke in despairing terms of the PAG's efforts over the past three years. "I don't think we shall get far with this," he told an audience of health professionals, "and some other group may have to take a more aggressive, Nader-like stance in this regard."[1]

It did not take long for the "Nader-like" stance to manifest itself, and it did so within consumer advocacy groups and organizations concerned with Third World development policies. These critics of industry practices for the most part had no experience in infant nutrition. Rather, they were simply quintessential advocates, defending the interests of others, the others in this case being continents away. In any event, these critics ushered the debate into a new phase quite different from what had gone before, as cooperation gave way to confrontation.

The critics fired the first volley in the pages of the *New Internationalist*, a British publication produced under the sponsorship of three UK-based charity organizations, Oxfam, Christian Aid and Third World First. The magazine's

August 1973 issue featured a question-and-answer interview with two UK child-health specialists experienced in Third World nutrition issues. This report constituted an even harsher critique than that Dr. Jelliffe had issued. It was sprinkled with assumptions about how and why infant formula was used and went on to make many damaging claims about corporate marketing practices, citing Nestlé's in particular. Among the charges, soon to be disputed or refuted, were those that Nestlé had modified its advertising in only one African country and, in that case, only under pressure from government authorities; that infant formula producers had not attempted to develop simplified feeding instructions for illiterate mothers; that supplies of substandard infant formula were often shipped to developing countries; and that company nurses sold infant formula to new mothers even as they lay in the beds of maternity hospitals.[2]

The report lacked substantiation of these claims, ignoring even the existing scientific data on Third World nutrition which, though woefully inadequate, might have given it greater credibility. Instead, the interviews were composed primarily of anecdotes that could be neither confirmed nor denied. What troubled Nestlé management in particular was the implication that certain practices pursued within the industry were those followed by Nestlé. More distressing still was the outright misrepresentation of the company's actual marketing policies. Then there was the magazine's cover, featuring a photograph of an infant's grave, atop it the empty feeding bottle and a crumpled container of Lactogen, a Nestlé product.

In late 1973, Mike Muller, a free-lance journalist on assignment for War on Want, another British charity organization, turned up on Nestlé's doorstep. Management devoted two days to interviews with Muller, who pursued a constructive, if often tough, line of questioning. Nestlé was left with the impression that both sides would benefit from the results of the discussion, yet that was not to be so. Within a few weeks, Muller's account was published and released with the flourish of a London press conference that befitted the report's sensational title *The Baby Killer*.

Skillfully written in a thrust-and-parry style, the report gave the infant formula industry some credit for its good intentions in making available a needed product. But this faint accolade was more than offset by very harsh criticism of corporate marketing practices. An introductory disclaimer pointed out that "the object of this report is not to prove that baby milks kill babies... not to prove that the baby food industry is exclusively responsible for this trend away from breast feeding."[3] Still, *The Baby Killer* glossed over all the socio-economic constraints on breast feeding that had been an important part of the debate, concentrating instead almost exclusively on the presumed impact of marketing and promotion. The report also ignored what both nutritionists and the industry knew to be the reality of infant feeding in developing countries, namely that breast-milk substitutes were seldom used as total replacements for mother's milk, but rather as supplements in a program of "mixed feeding," and that locally produced substitutes were even more commonly used than commercial infant formula.

Of the greatest concern to Nestlé management were the out-of-context quotes that misrepresented the company's policies and attitudes to an even greater extent than had the outright errors of the *New Internationalist* report. Nestlé had made the mistake of assuming that in telling its story to this journalist, the public would finally see the full picture. That was hardly the case. Among the glaring omissions from the published report, felt Nestlé managers, were their painstaking explanations of the advantages of a "full-protein" formula the company had developed, a product designed to offer a margin of safety that would ensure the product's nutritional value in cases where a mother might be tempted to over-dilute it in preparation. Yet *The Baby Killer* presented this development as simply another commercial gimmick to build market share. Another contribution, acidified milk, a product that is less susceptible than other formulas to bacterial contamination in tropical areas, was not mentioned at all. And more damaging still was the recitation of "unethical and immoral" promotion practices, which, the report seemed to imply, could be attributed to Nestlé. Yet the practices in question had only been *described* to the journalist by Nestlé, which had in fact been referring to its competitors' practices.

In proposing solutions to the perceived problem, the author asked for nothing less than the elimination of "all promotion" to both consumers and the health profession. Even at this early stage of the campaign, it was obvious that such critics defined "promotion" so as to encompass educational materials essential to ensuring proper feeding practices. In addition, War on Want suggested that a "more broadly based campaign involving many national organizations" could have an effect on "intransigent" corporate policies.

These terms were so harsh and dictatorial that Nestlé knew it would have a hard time continuing the dialogue with organizations such as War on Want. Yet management had to face the fact that as long as the suspicions about infant formula's relationship to infant disease and malnutrition could not be definitively cast aside, it would do well to follow even more strictly the guidelines of PAG Statement 23, ensuring that its promotional campaigns provided truly useful information and did not discourage mothers from breast feeding.

So, after an internal review of marketing practices then in effect in developing-country markets, management imposed more stringent control over the distribution of product samples, elimination of direct contact between company representatives and new mothers, and the suspension of advertising that did not meet the full approval of public authorities. Meanwhile, an extensive review of the body of scientific literature on infant malnutrition and feeding patterns in developing countries was undertaken.

Even as this policy review was in progress, however, the company found itself facing a new challenge, this one in its own backyard. *The Baby Killer* had been translated into German by a Swiss activist group, and this time the errors and flaws that had characterized the original tract were greatly exaggerated. All the allegations of too-aggressive promotion and the unproven thesis that commercial formula contributed to malnutrition were now boiled down to libelous simplicity in book's title: *Nestlé Kills Babies*.

LIBEL PROCEEDINGS IN BERN

The original version of *The Baby Killer* had directly misrepresented some of Nestlé's policies. Still, it had underscored some very real problems of which industry was aware. The German-language translation, however, went considerably further in claiming infant formula to be the direct cause of infant deaths. Moreover, the title, *Nestlé Kills Babies (Nestlé tötet Babys)* cast one firm, Nestlé, as the sole perpetrator of the alleged crime.

Legal Action

Management was caught completely off guard by the publication of *Nestlé tötet Babys*. The booklet's existence came to the company's attention concurrently with its release to the press and general public in early June 1974. This time, there was no question of pursuing a rebuttal through a letter to the editor. Nor could the company simply turn a deaf ear, for Nestlé's employees and shareholders were in effect being slandered. These constituencies, along with the wider public audience, deserved a response that matched the accusations. In management's view, legal action seemed the best, perhaps the only, recourse.

Formation of ICIFI

Away from the heat of Nestlé's legal challenge, the infant foods industry as a whole had not abandoned efforts to act upon the mandate spelled out in PAG Statement 23, the result of an intense cooperative effort among industry, governments, and health professionals. Following the release of this document in late 1973, the next PAG-sponsored meeting was held in Singapore in November 1974, and it was here that company executives first discussed the possibility of forming an industry council whose principal concern would be companies' marketing practices in developing countries. In late 1975 the International Council of Infant Food Industries (ICIFI) was formally organized in Zurich, Switzerland, bringing together eight of the largest infant formula producers, companies based in the US, Europe and Japan, Nestlé among them. One of their first actions was to develop a code of conduct embodying the principles of PAG Statement 23.

DEVELOPING INTERNATIONAL RECOMMENDATIONS

The October 1979 conference on infant feeding, sponsored jointly by WHO and UNICEF, represented the convergence of several different forces. The industry wished to shift the discussion on infant formula marketing back to the sphere of relevant government authorities, health professionals and industry experts, where the responsibility for resolving the issues lay. As for WHO, this new project meshed neatly with its ongoing programs of promoting better health for mothers and children and improving public hygiene in developing countries.

Industry was hoping that WHO's assumption of leadership would depoliticize the controversy. Yet despite the organization's strong scientific orientation and generally high degree of professionalism, international political sensitivities have tended to surface whenever the 150 member countries' delegations have convened. And each of these countries in turn must take into account internal political considerations as policymakers attempt to implement internationally agreed upon policies. This is particularly challenging in the case of the developing countries, whose obviously limited national resources must be carefully allocated to meet the several objectives that are collectively defined as the "national interest." As a practical matter, the health ministers of such countries, once they have unpacked their bags following the annual gathering of delegates at the World Health Assembly, often must vie with other public officials for limited financial and physical resources in order to implement commitments made within WHO.

In Search of Consensus

As the date for the meeting approached, corporate executives were disturbed to learn that instead of the 30 or so nutrition and industry experts anticipated, more than 150 participants, including the more vocal critics of the industry such as INFACT, ADW and War on Want, had signed up. Industry's hopes for the meeting were further deflated when it was discovered that only one background document (prepared by WHO and UNICEF) was to be circulated, and that this paper repeated essentially the same assumptions and conclusions that had long been the basis of the activist campaign. In addition, the paper's sparse review of the "current knowledge" of infant feeding was criticized not only by industrialists, but also by such a credible source as The Lancet, a leading UK medical journal.[4]

Although the meeting's conclusions were labeled a "consensus," this was something of a misnomer, given that strong differences over precisely what should be considered "appropriate" marketing practices still existed. Nestlé, however, was, on the whole, satisfied with the outcome. For one thing, many of the marketing reforms suggested in the consensus document echoed policy changes that the company had already put into effect. In addition, the meeting's concluding commitment to develop a more formal marketing code for developing countries was obviously compatible with the initiatives undertaken by the ICIFI group of companies.

NESTLÉ'S RESPONSE TO THE ISSUES

Nestlé's policy of replying quietly to its critics—when it has chosen to make any sort of reply—has puzzled many who have followed the development of the infant formula controversy. The company's approach to handling the issue is less of a mystery, however, when one examines in some detail its particular corporate culture and commercial orientation. First among these elements is Nestlé's high product quality standards, which helped the firm sail through the wave of consumer advocacy in the 1960s and 1970s largely unscathed. Nestlé's long-standing policy has been to modify a product or its accompanying marketing "package" to meet changing consumer needs or to provide a higher level of quality and safety whenever technological breakthroughs have made it possible and feasible to do so.

Because of this high level of consumer protection reflected in its product and marketing policies, Nestlé was seldom in the position of having to answer to public criticism. And management was always more concerned with responding to an identified problem in a substantive way than in publicizing the fact that such efforts had been undertaken. Thus company managers responsible for press and public relations were accustomed to handling inquiries that were modest in volume and generally uncontroversial in nature. As questions over infant formula marketing developed into an intense debate, however, it became evident that what the company *said* about the issue was as important a factor in resolving the controversy as what it actually *did* to assure that the product was used in the proper manner only by those who needed it. Thus it was particularly ironic when, at the height of the US campaign, Nestlé was accused of devoting its resources to a "massive public relations campaign" to discourage support of the boycott. This simply was not the case. If anything, the company had done too little, too late in the way of public relations, failing to inform the public at large of the steps it had taken over the years to ensure that infant formula was being made available on a selective basis and that Third World consumers were being educated as to its proper use.

Contribution to Nutrition Research

Determining the consumer's needs and how these can be met most effectively is usually accomplished through traditional, commercially oriented marketing research. In the case of infant formula, however, particularly as its use applies to Third World consumers, a more scientific approach is in order, and such research could logically be expected to be the responsibility of academic or other non-commercial institutes. The severe vacuum of knowledge about Third World nutrition and infant feeding, however, underscored by the activists' practice of advertising the very limited data that appeared to support their claims, finally led Nestlé to support new basic research in infant nutrition. In doing so, the company sought to establish a research base that would help determine, once and for all, whether there was any validity to the activists' claims that:

- only 2% of mothers are physiologically incapable of breast feeding;
- less than 6% of mothers are unable to breast-feed because of work outside the home;
- even a malnourished mother can "adequately feed" her child for at least the first four months of life.

If all that were true, Nestlé would have to rethink not only specific marketing practices but also the more important strategic question of whether infant formula is really needed. For that reason, Nestlé undertook a review of the existing scientific literature on the subject of infant feeding shortly after it sued the Swiss activists for libel and then, once the information gaps were identified, developed a research program aimed at identifying who uses infant formula, how and why it is used, and the effects of infant formula feeding on infant health. In 1979 this general program began to acquire some substance as Nestlé commissioned an independent research institute to investigate such questions within the controlled scope of three developing countries, Kenya, Malaysia and Mexico, focusing on a sample population of some 6,000 mothers. Completed in 1981, this research showed that in the countries surveyed:

- more than half of the mothers introduced supplementary foods before their infants were four months old, regardless of whether commercially produced infant formula was available;
- many of the foods being used as breast-milk substitutes and supplements were not normally recommended for this purpose; and
- infant feeding patterns in general varied enormously among the countries

studied, further evidence that generalizations about nutrition and feeding habits, and even "appropriate" marketing practices, could not be applied to the Third World as a whole.

Nestlé is also sponsoring other research on the use of infant formula. One study currently under way is designed to determine how long breast feeding alone will satisfy an infant's nutritional requirements for normal growth. This research, conducted in the setting of a Third world community, will deal with the issue of mixed feeding and the timing of the introduction of breast-milk supplements. Finally, Nestlé has underwritten an extensive critical review of major scientific literature on infant feeding and nutrition. Prepared under the supervision of an internationally recognized expert, this review is now available to other researchers, industrialists and lay groups with a serious interest in the subject.[5]

Product and Marketing Policies

Amidst all the clamor over infant formula marketing, Nestlé has seldom had the opportunity to demonstrate to the public that its product and marketing policies have indeed undergone substantive modification over the years. Activist demands that industry promotion be designed so as to encourage breast feeding, for example, ignore the fact that Nestlé, for one, has followed such a policy ever since it first began making products for infant feeding. More than a hundred years ago, for example, a Nestlé guidebook for new mothers put it this way: "during the first months, the mother's milk will always be the most natural nutriment, and every mother able to do so should herself suckle her children."[6] Because Nestlé continued to uphold that principle over the years, the company felt that the accusation that it was actively discouraging breast feeding was simple libel.

The developing controversy over various marketing practices underscored the need to reconsider this evolution in feeding recommendations, however. Nestlé, for its part, decided to modify its promotional and educational materials at this point so as to place greater emphasis on breast feeding. Because of the scope and complexity of this task, the process of implementation that began in 1976 was gradual, though steady, and in taking this initiative, Nestlé was running a step ahead of the move toward international policy formulation. By the time the question of industry's role in emphasizing breast feeding was raised at the WHO/UNICEF sponsored meeting in 1979, Nestlé's new policy was in effect.

Nestlé has undertaken other substantive changes in its marketing practices over the years, including the use of mass media, the role of medical representative and qualified mothercraft personnel, and the provision of samples. In 1978, for example, Nestlé decided to end all use of mass media for advertising infant formula in Third World markets, even though such messages had already undergone considerable modification to make them much more educational and less commercial in tone and content. Virtually overnight, useful nutrition education information that had not merely been tolerated, but explicitly approved, disappeared from the scene.

LOOKING AHEAD

Over recent months, several developments have signaled the end of the controversy over infant formula marketing and the start of progress in resolving the dilemma of Third World nutrition. First has been the development of the International Code of Marketing of Breast-milk Substitutes and its adoption by most WHO member states in May 1981. Nestlé has fully embraced these guidelines, and the company is now engaged in consultations with WHO member governments that are implementing the code.

In addition, Nestlé has begun to implement the code's provisions in developing countries where governments do not plan to introduce national measures. Early in 1982, the company issued to its personnel in these countries, as well as to independent agents and distributors who play a role in Nestlé's distribution system, new marketing guidelines substantially reflecting the code's provisions. Nestlé has also taken steps to ensure compliance with the code, whether implemented through national measures or upon the company's own initiative, by forming the Nestlé Infant Formula Audit Commission, a panel of prominent medical experts, clergymen, civic leaders and experts on international policy issues. Headed by Edmund Muskie, former Secretary of State and Democratic Senator from Maine, the Commission is monitoring Nestlé's performance as measured against the code, investigating complaints and allegations concerning marketing practices now considered inappropriate in Third World markets.

One of the commission's first moves was to step into its role of monitoring Nestlé's compliance with the WHO code as interpreted either through national measures (where they existed) or, alternatively, through the company's own guidelines. Members of the commission contacted approximately 100 individuals and organizations long identified with the controversy, providing copies of the company's marketing guidelines, background material on commission and—most important—forms to be used in the documentation of reported violations of the guidelines, designed to enable the commission to pursue an investigation in each such case.

Next, the commission met with representatives of WHO and UNICEF, as well as with members of various church organizations and consumer advocacy groups, soliciting their views of the company's new instructions to its marketing personnel. The response was somewhat critical, but, in general, constructively so. As a consequence, the commission set to work proposing changes in the guidelines that would respond to two areas of criticism: first, that arising from a general misunderstanding about the role of the company's own guidelines, and second, those more substantive points in the Nestlé instructions which did indeed require some adjustment in order to better conform to the WHO code.

By the time the full commission met and issued its first quarterly report in September 1982, these suggested changes had been incorporated into the company's marketing guidelines. Said Senator Muskie in the report, "In the experience of the commission, Nestlé has demonstrated a willingness to respond positively to the imperative of change in its marketing practices."[7]

As they now stand, Nestlé's marketing policy and specific instructions to personnel include the following significant points:

• elimination of baby pictures on all product labels;
• elimination of mothercraft-nurse function;

• provision of free or reduced-cost supplies of infant formula only for children who cannot be breast-fed, and in those cases, only through health workers;

• elimination of advertising and promotion of infant formula, including "generic" promotion in which brand names are not mentioned;

• discouragement of point-of-sale infant formula promotion by retailers;

• elimination of all gifts related to product promotion, regardless of their significance in terms of value; and

• prohibition of Nestlé-initiated contact between company personnel and mothers.

Finally, the commission simplified the complaint form to be used as the basis for investigating reported violations, in response to those concerned over the original form's length and complexity.

Also at this time, new research on infant nutrition and feeding supported by Nestlé and other companies of the ICIFI group, as well as that undertaken by international organizations such as WHO, has begun to yield results that should provide the framework against which questions of infant formula marketing need to be placed. Finally, many members of the scientific community and public figures, the very people whose support of Nestlé's adversaries was earlier so crucial to their campaign, have begun to doubt the motivations of some of the critics and to be more outspoken in their criticism of the arguments and tactics employed by the activists. This attitude puts a new burden on the advocates, who have claimed to have at heart only the best interest of Third World consumers. As a leading medical journal recently observed, "Let's hope that the people who organized this campaign to condemn the baby food companies

will now turn their attention to actually doing something about the major causes of infant mortality."[8]

In a similar vein, the *Washington Post*, the newspaper which had sharply rebuked Nestlé in its editorial columns at the height of the activist campaign, has had second thoughts on the issue. In an editorial published in late 1982, the *Post* said: "There is concern, however, among health professionals and researchers—including the American Academy of Pediatrics—that the role of infant formula as a threat to infants in developing nations has been blown out of proportion.... Upon closer inspection, the data linking formula marketing and infant mortality turn out to be sketchy at best."[9]

In other sectors, these words have been echoed by positive actions that indicate a new recognition of Nestlé's commitment to follow both the letter and spirit of the WHO code. In September 1982, for example, the United Methodist Church concluded an in-depth, two-year study of the infant formula issue and resolved, by a two-to-one vote, not to boycott the company, calling upon any Methodist organizations in disagreement to establish reasons for their position by April 1983. Also, in early 1983 the American Federation of Teachers, which had backed the boycott campaign for several years, decided to end its support.

This is the time to replace futile confrontation with a renewed effort to improve infant health in the Third World. The infant formula industry has never denied the role of constructive criticism, but unsubstantiated reports of corporate misconduct are quite another thing. Nestlé now welcomes responsible advocates and professional organizations who choose to assist in the implementation and continued monitoring of compliance with the WHO code.

The fact that a company staked its reputation, as Nestlé did, upon the preservation of what is only a small part—2.5%—of its total business, flies in the face of the critics' claims that Nestlé's marketing policies are based on nothing more than the profit motive. Had it been predicted that Nestlé would spend 10 long years defending its name and actions, the company might have been well advised some time ago to give up the infant formula business altogether. By this time, surely, it could have filled the commercial gap with sales of another product, one lacking the potential for controversy—but also, no doubt, lacking the potential to fill such a vital need an infant formula does. And that is precisely the point. Nestlé has spent time and effort defending its infant formula marketing policy for the Third World not out of any attachment to particular marketing practices per se, but because the needs of these very special consumers give them far greater weight on the scale of corporate priorities than mere sales figures can indicate.

The dilemma of infant formula marketing in the Third World was apparent to Nestlé well before the activist campaign came into full bloom: The more disadvantaged the circumstances of the population, the greater the need for the product, yet the greater the hazards in preparing and administering it.

Having taken the initiative of complying with the WHO code through the development and application of its own set of instructions, Nestlé now hopes that the international guidelines will be implemented in such a way that those truly in need are not deprived of either the product or the marketing support services of information and education that are crucial to ensuring its proper use. Yet there is a greater task in improving Third World nutrition, and this is to break the vicious circle of poverty, lack of education, and insufficient health services that together contribute to disease and malnutrition. This will require a much more intensive commitment of resources not only by industry, but also by the international health and development agencies, and individual governments.

REFERENCES

1. Jelliffe, D. B., remarks at Ciba Foundation symposium, "Human Rights in Health," London, July 4–6, 1973.

2. Geach, Hugh, "The Baby Food Tragedy," *New Internationalist*, No. 6, August 1973, pp. 8–12, 23.

3. Muller, Mike, *The Baby Killer*, War on Want, March 1974.

4. "Uneasy Prelude to Meeting on Infant Feeding," *The Lancet*, Vol. II, Sept. 28, 1979, pp. 680–81.

5. Ashworth, A., et al., *Infant and Young Child Feeding—A Selected Annotated Bibliography. Early Human Development*, 1982, 6. (Supplement.)

6. Translated from the German, *Ueber die Ernärurg der Kinder*, 1871.

7. Muskie, Edmund, "First Quarterly Report—Nestlé Infant Formula Audit Commission," Oct. 14, 1982, p. 4.

8. "Does a Vote of 118 to 1 Mean the USA Was Wrong?" *Pediatrics*, Vol. 68, No. 3, September 1981, p. 431.

9. "Revisiting the Formula Fight," *The Washington Post*, Nov. 5, 1982.

POSTSCRIPT

Did Nestlé Act Irresponsibly in Marketing Infant Formula to the Third World?

These are not simple questions, and there are no simple answers. To protect Third World mothers from buying a product that may make life easier for them seems perverse; to ignore the deaths of infants seems callous. Faced with a conflict between the freedom of the mother and the welfare of the child, it seems in poor taste to mention the interest of the company in making a profit and the interest of the country in establishing a favorable balance of trade. Yet these, too, are valid objectives.

Some feel that the promotional devices that Nestlé used were at fault. These devices were not necessarily deceptive or coercive by American standards, but to mothers in developing nations, the promotions had different significance. The mothercraft nurses were, to these mothers, real nurses wielding medical authority. The signs that showed fat babies beside bottles of formula were taken as guarantees that using the formula yields healthy babies. The fact that powerful, professional, and rich Westerners stood behind a course of action was overwhelmingly persuasive and often left Third World mothers with little real choice.

The infant formula issue is a paradigm case for multinational issues. To what extent shall merchants of any country promote products as they like? Is it America's right or duty to decide what is beneficial for others?

SUGGESTED READINGS

William Aiken and Hugh LaFollette, eds., *World Hunger and Moral Obligations* (Prentice Hall, 1977).

Alex M. Freedman, "Nestlé Ad Claims for Baby Formula Probed in Three States," *The Wall Street Journal* (March 2, 1989).

John Marcom, Jr., "Feed the World," *Forbes* (October 1, 1990).

Barbara Presley Noble, "Price-Fixing and Other Charges Roil a Once-Placid Market," *The New York Times* (July 28, 1991).

James E. Post, "The International Infant Formula Industry," in *Marketing and Promotion of Infant Formula in the Developing Nations*, a report prepared for the Subcommittee on Health and Scientific Research, Committee on Human Resources, U.S. Senate (1978).

Leslie Savan, "Forget the Dead Babies: Nestlé's PR Firm Spins Feel-Good Line," *Village Voice* (May 2, 1989).

ISSUE 17

Is Bribery Ever Justified?

YES: Michael Philips, from "Bribery," *Ethics* (July 1984)

NO: Thomas L. Carson, from "Bribery and Implicit Agreements: A Reply to Philips," *Journal of Business Ethics* (vol. 6, 1987)

ISSUE SUMMARY

YES: Professor of philosophy Michael Philips argues that not every payment that seems to be a bribe is, in fact, a bribe. He claims that although it is often difficult to distinguish a true bribe from other payments, there may be no *prima facie* reason to refuse the offer of a bribe.

NO: Professor of philosophy Thomas L. Carson argues that every acceptance of a bribe involves the violation of an implicit or explicit promise or understanding connected with one's office and that Philips has failed to show that acceptance of a bribe can sometimes be morally permissible.

A *bribe* is a payment made to someone in order to influence the payee to do something that the payer wants him or her to do. But that does not include every fee for service, such as the payment one makes to induce the plumber to fix the bathtub drain. If a payment is to be called a "bribe," there must be something wrong or illegitimate about the payment; at the least, the payee must accept the bribe and perform the service so obtained secretly and/or for wrong or illegitimate sorts of reasons. *Bribe,* then, is a term that does not stand alone: it always designates a payment, but it also carries normative content that simultaneously condemns the payment. The grounds for the condemnation come from the social context of the payment: the payment is against the law, the service demanded violates the rules or professional ethics of the payee, or the payee is in some position of judgment, and American culture presupposes objectivity of the judge that is incompatible with receiving money from one of the parties judged.

But then it would follow that what counts as a bribe in one social context would not count as a bribe in another. More to the point, there are times when what American law calls a bribe is not a bribe in the countries where America tries to do business.

Among the bribery scandals that shocked the United States during the mid-1970s, the Lockheed case stands out as showing both the seriousness of the problem for normal business dealings (in, for instance, the amount that changed hands over the course of the deal) and the fuzziness of the rules that

American businesses must conform to. In 1972, the president of Lockheed was A. Carl Kotchian, who, in the course of his job, was sent to Japan to sell Lockheed's new TriStar passenger plane to a Japanese airline. Kotchian found himself kept entirely uninformed by his Japanese partners, who surfaced at odd intervals with demands for odd amounts of money, the large payments all apparently bound for the office of the prime minister; he was told that all this was standard practice and that the fees were the accepted level of payment. In the months that dragged by, while the "negotiations" continued, Kotchian was constantly warned that nonpayment would lose the sale of Lockheed's TriStar planes to the national Japanese airline; he was assured that each payment would be the last one that was necessary; and he was haunted by the vision of much of Lockheed's workforce laid off if the deal somehow, through his fault, fell through. The maddening part of the deal, as for many such transactions, was that as far as Kotchian knew, the TriStar was the best plane for the purpose for which the airline wanted it and in a fair competition would have been the plane adopted. But the fair competition was not the method of choice for that Japanese government.

In the end, the story came out; Lockheed was condemned as an immoral company, and Kotchian took the heat for bribery. In a revealing piece, Kotchian wrote up his Japanese experiences for the *Saturday Review* (July 9, 1977). The case, as he wrote it, illustrates the difficulty of doing business in a country where cultural expectations, government regulations, and business practices are entirely different from those of the United States. If it is of any comfort, the Japanese officials were also punished for their role in the affair.

In the following selections, Michael Philips concludes that many instances that are called bribery are no such thing and that it is often difficult to distinguish bribery from extortion or even from legitimate practices. Thomas L. Carson responds that any acceptance of payment in which the payee is expected to violate a "tacit agreement" is bribery and is always morally wrong.

Ask yourself, as you read these selections, why some payments are called "bribes" and others are not. Bribery and extortion are wrong, but how are they wrong? What would the plumber have to say to make his agreement to fix the drain in return for payment a case of extortion rather than a fee for service? What would the person paying for the service have to say to make that payment a bribe? How do our expectations of those who hold an office in American society help to define what counts as a bribe? The problems become especially acute when we try to do business abroad. Should the United States be in the business of telling the officers of multinationals how to behave in foreign business, thereby telling foreign countries how to run their business transactions? Or should businesspeople be required to conform their behavior to that of the country in which they are doing business?

YES

Michael Philips

BRIBERY

Although disclosures of bribery have elicited considerable public indignation over the last decade, popular discussions of the morality of bribery have tended largely to be unilluminating. One reason for this is that little care has been taken to distinguish bribes from an assortment of related practices with which they are easily confused. Before we can be in a position to determine what to do about the problem of bribery, we need to be clearer about what count and ought to count as bribes. Unfortunately, there is as yet very little philosophical literature on this topic.[1] In this essay I shall remedy this defect by presenting an account of the concept of bribery and by employing that account to clarify matters in three areas in which there is public controversy and confusion.

At least some confusion in discussions of bribery arises from a failure adequately to appreciate the distinction between bribery and extortion. This is true, for example, of accounts of the notorious case of Lockheed in Japan. I shall attempt to show that the morality of this and similar transactions is better assessed if we are clear on that distinction.

A second problem area arises out of the fact of cultural variability. As is generally recognized, the conduct of business, government, and the professions differs from culture to culture. In some places transactions that many Americans would consider bribes are not only expected behavior but accepted practice as well. That is, they are condoned by the system of rule governing the conduct of the relevant parties. Are they bribes? Are only some of them bribes? If so, which?

A third problem arises out of the general difficulty of distinguishing between bribes, on the one hand, and gifts and rewards, on the other. Suppose that a manufacturer of dresses keeps a buyer for a catalog company happy by supplying him with any tickets to expensive shows and athletic events that he requests. Are these bribes? Or suppose that a special interest group rewards public administrators who rule in its favor with vacations, automobiles, and jewelry. May we correctly speak of bribery here?

I

To answer such questions we need to say more precisely what bribes are. A bribe is a payment (or promise of payment) for a service. Typically, this payment is made to an official in exchange for her violating some official duty or responsibility. And typically she does this by failing deliberately to make a decision on its merits. This does not necessarily mean that a bribed official will make an improper decision; a judge who is paid to show favoritism may do so and yet, coincidentally, make the correct legal decision (i.e., the bribe offerer may in fact have the law on her side). The violation of duty consists in deciding a case for the wrong sorts of reasons.

Although the most typical and important cases of bribery concern political officials and civil servants, one need not be a political official or a civil servant to be bribed. Indeed, one need not be an official of any sort. Thus, a mortician may be bribed to bury a bodyless casket, and a baseball player may be bribed to strike out each time he bats. Still, baseball players and morticians are members of organizations and have duties and responsibilities by virtue of the positions they occupy in these organizations. It is tempting, then, to define a bribe as a payment made to a member of an organization in exchange for the violation of some positional duty or responsibility. This temptation is strengthened by our recognition that we cannot be bribed to violate a duty we have simply by virtue of being a moral agent. (Hired killers, e.g., are not bribed to violate their duty not to kill.) And it is further strengthened when we recognize that we may be paid to violate duties we have by virtue of a nonorganizationally based status without being bribed. (I am not bribed if—as a nonhandicapped person—I accept payment to park in a space reserved for the handicapped; nor am I bribed if—as a pet owner—I accept payment illegally to allow my dog to run free on the city streets.)

Still, it is too strong to say that occupying a position in an organization is a necessary condition of being bribed. We may also speak of bribing a boxer to throw a fight or of bribing a runner to lose a race. These cases, however, are importantly like the cases already described. Roughly, both the boxer and the runner are paid to do something they ought not to do given what they are. What they are, in these cases, are participants in certain practices. What they are paid to do is to act in a manner dictated by some person or organization rather than to act according to the understandings constitutive of their practices. Civil servants, business executives, morticians, and baseball players, of course, are also participants in practices. And their responsibilities, as such, are defined by the rules and understandings governing the organizations to which they belong. At this point, then, we are in a position to state a provisional definition of bribery. Thus, P accepts a bribe from R if and only if P agrees for payment to act in a manner dictated by R rather than doing what is required of him as a participant in his practice.[2]

One advantage of this account is that it enables us to deal with certain difficult cases. Suppose that a high-ranking officer at the Pentagon is paid by a Soviet agent to pass on defense secrets. The first few times he does this we would not hesitate to say that he is bribed. But suppose that he is paid a salary to do this and that the arrangement lasts for a number of years. At this point talk of bribery appears less appropriate. But why should something that has the character of a bribe if done once or twice (or, perhaps, on a piecework basis) cease to have that character if done more often (or, perhaps, on a salaried basis)? In my account the explanation is that the frequency or basis of payment may incline us differently to identify the practice in question. Thus, if an American officer works for the Soviet Union long enough, we begin to think of him as a Soviet spy. In any case, to the extent to which we regard his practice as spying we are inclined to think of the payments in question as payments of a salary as opposed to so many bribes. A similar analysis holds in the case of industrial spies, undercover agents recruited from within organizations, and so forth.[3] We do not think of them as bribed because we do not think of them as full-fledged practitioners of the practices in which they appear to engage.

This practice conception is further supported by the fact that a person may satisfy my account of bribery on a long-term and regularized basis and still be said to be a recipient of bribes. This is so where his continued and regularized acceptance of payments does not warrant any change in our understanding of the practices in which he participates. Thus, we do not think of a judge who routinely accepts payments for favors from organized crime as participating in some practice other than judging, even if he sits almost exclusively on such cases. This may be arbitrary: perhaps we ought rather think of him as an agent of a criminal organization (a paid saboteur of the legal system) and treat him accordingly. My point, however, is that because we do not think of him in this way—because we continue to think of him as a judge— we regard each fresh occurrence as an instance of bribery.

At least two additional important features of bribery deserve mention.

The first is a consequence of the fact that bribes are payments. For, like other kinds of payments (e.g., rent), bribes presuppose agreements of a certain kind.[4] That is, it must be understood by both parties that the payment in question is exchanged, or is to be exchanged, for the relevant conduct. In the most typical and important cases, the bribed party is an official and the conduct in question is the violation of some official duty. In these cases we may say simply that an official P is bribed by R when she accepts payment or the promise of payment for agreeing to violate a positional duty to act on R's behalf. This agreement requirement is of great importance. As I shall argue in Section IV, without it we cannot properly distinguish between bribes and gifts or rewards.

Such agreements need not be explicit. If I am stopped by a policeman for speeding and hand him a fifty-dollar bill along with my driver's license, and he accepts the fifty-dollar bill, it is arguable that we have entered into such an agreement despite what we might say about contributions to the Police Benevolence Association. As I shall argue, some of the difficulties we have in determining what transactions to count as bribes may stem from unclarity concerning the conditions under which we are entitled to say an agreement has been made.

It is a consequence of this account that someone may be bribed despite the fact that she subsequently decides not to perform the service she has agreed to perform. Indeed, we must say this even if she has never been paid but has been only promised payment, or even if she has been paid but returns this payment after she decides not to abide by her part of the agreement. I see nothing strange about this. After all, if one accepts a bribe it seems natural to say that one has been bribed. Still, I have no strong objection to distinguishing between accepting a bribe and being bribed, where a necessary condition of the latter is that one carries out one's part of the bribery agreement. As far as I can see, no important moral question turns on this choice of language.

A final interesting feature of bribery emerges when we reflect on the claim that offering and accepting bribes is prima facie wrong. I will begin with the case of officials. The claim that it is prima facie wrong for someone in an official position to accept a bribe is plausible only if persons in official capacities have prima facie obligations to discharge their official duties. The most plausible argument for this claim is grounded in a social contract model of organizations. By accepting a position in an organization, it might be argued, one tacitly agrees to abide by the rules of that organization. To be bribed is to violate that agreement—it is to break a promise—and is, therefore, prima facie wrong.[5] While I concede that this argument has merit in a context of just and voluntary institutions, it seems questionable in a context of morally corrupt institutions (e.g., Nazi Germany or contemporary El Salvador). And even were it technically valid for those contexts, its conclusion would nonetheless be a misleading half-truth.

II

I now turn to the first of three problem areas I shall address in this paper, namely, the problem of distinguishing between bribery and extortion. Compare the following cases:

a) Executive P hopes to sell an airplane to the national airline of country C. The deal requires the approval of minister R. P knows that R can make a better deal elsewhere and that R knows this as well. P's researchers have discovered that R has a reputation for honesty but that R is in serious financial difficulties. Accordingly P offers R a large sum of money to buy from him. R accepts and abides by the agreement.

b) The same as *a* except that P knows that he is offering the best deal R can get, and R knows this too. Nonetheless, P is informed by reliable sources that R will not deal with P unless P offers to pay him a considerabe sum of money. P complies, and R completes the deal.

According to my analysis *a* is bribery and *b* is not.

The difference between *a* and *b* is clear enough. In *a* P pays R to violate R's duty (in this case, to make the best deal that R can). In *b* P does no such thing. Instead, he pays R to do what is required of R by his institutional commitments in any case. Moreover, he does so in response to R's threat to violate those commitments in a manner that jeopardizes P's interests. Accordingly, *b* resembles extortion more than it does bribery. For, roughly speaking, R extorts P if R threatens P with a penalty in case P fails to give R something to which R has no rightful claim.

If this is true it may be that American corporate executives accused of bribing foreign officials are sometimes more like victims of extortion than offerers of bribes. For in at least some cases they are required to make payments to assure that an official does what he is supposed to do in any case. This is especially true in the case of inspectors of various kinds and in relation to government officials who must approve transactions between American and local companies. An inspector who refuses to approve a shipment that is up to standards unless he is paid off is like a bandit who demands tribute on all goods passing through his territory.

It does not follow that it is morally correct for American companies to pay off such corrupt officials. There are cases in which it is morally wrong to surrender to the demands of bandits and other extortionists. But it is clear that the moral questions that arise here are different sorts of questions than those that arise in relation to bribery. The moral relations between the relevant parties differ. The bribery agreement is not by its nature an agreement between victims and victimizers. The extortion agreement is. Moral justifications and excuses for complying with the demands of an extortionist are easier to come by than moral justifications and excuses for offering bribes.

Of course, the distinction in question is often easier to draw in theory than in practice. An inspector who demands a payoff to authorize a shipment is likely to fortify his demand by insisting that the product does not meet standards. In some cases it may be difficult to know whether or not he is lying (e.g., whether the shipment has been contaminated in transit). And given the high cost of delays, a company may decide that it is too expensive to take the time to find out. In this case, a company may decide to pay off without knowing whether it is agreeing to pay a bribe or surrendering to extortion. Since the morality of its decisions may well turn on what it is in fact doing in such cases, a company that does not take the time to find out acts in a morally irresponsible manner (unless, of course, it is in a position to defend both courses of action).

What sorts of justifications can a company present for offering bribes? It is beyond the scope of this paper to provide a detailed discussion of this question. However, I have already mentioned a number of considerations that count as moral reasons against bribery in a variety of contexts. To begin with in reasonably just contexts, officials ordinarily are obligated to discharge the duties of their offices. In these cases bribe offers are normally attempts to induce officials to violate duties. Moreover, if accepted, a bribe offer may make it more likely that that official will violate future duties. Accordingly, it may contribute to the corruption of an official. In addition, the intent of a bribe offer is often to secure an unfair advantage or an undeserved privilege. Where this is the case, it too counts as a reason against bribery. To determine whether a bribe offer is wrong in any particular case, then, we must decide: (1) whether these reasons obtain in that case; (2) if they obtain, how much weight we ought to attach to them; and (3) how much weight we ought to attach to countervailing considerations. (Suppose, e.g., that it is necessary to bribe an official in order to meet an important contractual obligation.) It is worth remarking in this regard that, where officials routinely take bribes, the presumption against corrupting officials normally will not apply. Similarly, to the extent that bribery is an accepted weapon in the arsenal of all competitors, bribe offers cannot be construed as attempts to achieve an unfair advantage over one's competitors.

III

It is sometimes suggested that an environment may be so corrupt that no payments count as bribes. These are circumstances in which the level of official compliance to duty is very low, and payoffs are so widespread that they are virtually institutionalized. Suppose, for example, that the laws of country N impose very high duties on a variety of products but that it is common practice in N for importers and exporters to pay customs officials to overlook certain goods and/or to underestimate their number or value. Suppose, moreover, that the existence of this practice is common knowledge but that no effort is made to stop it by law enforcement officials at any level;[6] indeed, that any attempts to stop it would be met by widespread social disapproval. One might even imagine that customs officials receive no salary in N but earn their entire livelihood in this way. One might further imagine that customs officials are expected to return a certain amount of money to the government every month and are fired from their jobs for failure to do so. Finally, one might suppose that the cumulative advantages and disadvantages of this way of doing things is such that the economy of N is about as strong as it would be under a more rule-bound alternative. Are these officials bribed?

In my analysis, the answer to this question depends on how we understand the duties of the customs officer. If the official job description for the customs officer in N (and the written laws of N) is like those of most countries, the customs officer violates his official duties according to these codes by allowing goods to leave the country without collecting the full duty. The question, however, is how seriously we are to take these written codes. Where social and political practice routinely violates them, nothing is done about it, and few members of the legal and nonlegal community believe that anything ought to be done about it, it is arguable that these codes are dead letters. If we find this to be true of the codes

governing the duties of the customs officials in country N, we have good reason for saying that the real obligations of these officials do not require that they impose the duties described in those written codes (but only that they return a certain sum of the money they collect to the central government each month). Anything collected in excess of that amount they are entitled to keep as salary (recall that they are officially unpaid). In reality we might say that duties on exports in country N are not fixed but negotiable.

Of course if we decide that the written law of N is the law of N, we must describe the situation otherwise. In that case, the official obligations of the customs officials are as they are described, and the system in N must be characterized as one of rampant bribery condoned both by government and by popular opinion. It seems to me that the philosophy of law on which this account rests is implausible. However, there is no need to argue this to defend my analysis of this case. My position is simply that whether or not we describe what goes on here as bribery depends on what we take the real legal responsibilities of the customs official to be. To the extent that we are inclined to identify his duties with the written law we will be inclined to speak of bribery here. To the extent that we are unwilling so to identify his duties we will not.[7]

IV

Let us now consider the problem of distinguishing bribes from rewards and gifts. The problem arises because gifts are often used in business and government to facilitate transactions. And to the degree to which a business person, professional person, or government official is influenced in her decision by gifts, it is tempting to conclude that she is violating her duties. In such cases we are tempted to speak of these gifts as bribes.

If I am correct, however, this temptation should be resisted. A bribe, after all, presupposes an agreement. A gift may be made with the intention of inducing an official to show favoritism to the giver, but unless acceptance of what is transferred can be construed as an agreement to show favoritism, what is transferred is not a bribe.

In some cases, of course, the acceptance of what is offered can be so construed. Again, if I offer fifty dollars to a policeman who has stopped me for speeding, he has a right to construe my act as one of offering a bribe, and I have a right to construe his acceptance in the corresponding manner. If I regularly treat the neighborhood policeman to a free lunch at my diner and he regularly neglects to ticket my illegally parked car, we have reason to say the same. Agreements need not be explicit. My point is just that to the degree that it is inappropriate to speak of agreements, it is also inappropriate to speak of bribes.

It follows from this that, if I present an official with an expensive item to induce him to show favoritism on my behalf, in violation of his duty, I have not necessarily bribed him. It does not follow from this, however, that I have done nothing wrong. So long as you are morally obligated to perform your official duty, normally it will be wrong of me to induce you to do otherwise by presenting you with some expensive item. Moreover, if you have any reason to believe that accepting what I offer will induce you not to do your duty, you have done something wrong by accepting my gift. To prevent such wrongs we have laws prohibiting persons whose interests are closely tied to the decisions of public officials from offering gifts to these officials. And we have laws forbidding officials to accept such gifts.

It might be objected that this account is too lenient. Specifically, it might be argued that wherever P presents Q with something of value to induce Q to violate Q's official duties P has offered a bribe.

But this is surely a mistake. It suggests, among other things, that an official is bribed so long as she accepts what is offered with this intent. Yet an official may accept such a gift innocently, believing that it is what it purports to be, namely, a token of friendship or goodwill. And she may do so with justifiable confidence that doing so will not in any way affect the discharge of her duty.

It may be replied that officials are bribed by such inducements only when they are in fact induced to do what is desired of them. But again, it may be the case that an official accepts what is offered innocently, believing it to be a gift, and that she believes falsely that it will not affect her conduct. In this case she has exercised bad judgment, but she has not been bribed. Indeed, it seems to me that it is improper to say that she accepts a bribe even when she recognizes the intent of the inducement and believes that accepting it is likely to influence her. There is a distinction between accepting a drink with the understanding that one is agreeing to be seduced and accepting a drink with the knowledge that so doing will make one's seduction more likely. To be bribed is to be bought, not merely to be influenced to do something.

From a moral point of view, whenever failure to perform one's official duties is wrong it may be as bad to accept a gift that one knows will influence one in the conduct of one's duty as it is to accept a bribe.

And clearly we are entitled morally to criticize those who offer and accept such inducements. Moreover, we are right to attempt to prevent this sort of thing by legally restricting the conditions under which persons may offer gifts to officials and the conditions under which officials may accept such gifts. Nonetheless, such gifts ought not to be confused with bribes. If P accepts a gift from R and does not show the desired favoritism, R may complain of P's ingratitude but not of P's dishonesty (unless, of course, P led him on in some way). If P accepts a bribe from R and does not show the desired favoritism, P has been dishonest (perhaps twice).

This point is not without practical importance. People who work in the same organization or in the same profession often form friendships despite the fact that some of them are in a position to make decisions that affect the interests of others. Here, as everywhere, friendships are developed and maintained in part by exchanges of favors, gifts, meals, and so forth. Were we to take seriously the inducement theory of bribery, however, this dimension of collegial and organizational existence would be threatened. In that case, if P's position is such that he must make decisions affecting R, any gifts, favors, et cetera from R to P should be regarded with at least some suspicion. To guard against the accusation that he has been bribed by R, P must be in a position to offer reasons for believing that R's intent in inviting him to dinner was not to induce him to show favoritism. And for R to be certain that he is not offering P a bribe in this case, R must be certain that his intentions are pure. All of this would require such vigilance in relation to one's own motives and the motives of others that friendships in collegial and organizational settings would be more difficult to sustain than they are at present.

Since decision makers are required to show impartiality they must in any case be careful not to accept gifts and favors that will influence them to show favoritism. Moreover, if they are required by their position to assess the moral character of those affected by their decisions, they may be required to assess the intent with which such gifts or favors are offered. Most officials, however, are not required to assess character in this way. In order to avoid doing wrong by accepting gifts and favors they need only be justly confident of their own continued impartiality. Thus, they are ordinarily entitled to ignore questions of intent unless there is some special reason to do otherwise. If the intent to influence were sufficient for a bribe, however, they would not be at liberty to bestow the benefit of the doubt in this way.

Again, there are cases in which impartiality is so important that decision makers should be prohibited both from accepting gifts or favors from any persons likely to be directly affected by their decisions and from forming friendships with such persons. And they should disqualify themselves when they are asked to make a decision that affects either a friend or someone from whom they have accepted gifts or favors in the reasonably recent past. Judges are a case in point. In other cases, however, institutions and professions should be willing to risk some loss in impartiality in order to enjoy the benefits of friendship and mutual aid. For these are essential to the functioning of some organizations and to the well-being of the people within them. Consider, for example, universities. The practical disadvantage of the inducement account is that it may require us to be unnecessarily suspicious of certain exchanges constitutive of mutual aid and friendship (at least if we take it seriously).

V

An interesting related problem arises in cultures in which a more formal exchange of gifts may be partly constitutive of a special relationship between persons, namely, something like friendship. In such cultures, so long as certain other conditions are satisfied, to make such exchanges is to enter into a system of reciprocal rights and duties. Among these duties may be the duty to show favoritism toward "friends," even when one acts in an official capacity. Moreover, the giver may be expected to show gratitude for each occasion of favoritism by further gift giving. On the face of it, this certainly looks like bribery. Is that description warranted?

To begin with, we need to distinguish between cases in which the special relationships in question are genuine and cases in which they are not. In the latter case certain ritual or ceremonial forms may be used to dress up what each party regards as a business transaction of the standard Western variety in a manner that provides an excuse for bribery. I shall say more about this presently. But let me begin with the first case.

Where the relationships in question are genuine and the laws of the relevant society are such that the official duties of the relevant official do not prohibit favoritism, this practice of gift giving cannot be called bribery. For in this case there is no question of the violation of duty. All that can be said here is that such societies condone different ways of doing business than we do. Specifically, they do not mark off a sphere of business and/or bureaucratic activity in which persons are supposed to meet as "abstract individuals," that is, in which they are required to ignore their social and familial ties. Their obligations, rather, are importantly determined by such ties even in the conduct of business and governmental affairs. Favoritism is shown, then, not in order to carry out one's part of a bargain but, rather, to discharge an obligation of kinship or loyalty. Failure to show favoritism would entitle one's kinsman or friend to complain not that one reneged on an agreement but, rather, that one had wronged him as an ally or a kinsman.

This is not to say that one cannot bribe an official in such a society. One does this here, as elsewhere, by entering into an agreement with him such that he violates his official duties for payment. The point is just that favoritism shown to friends and kinsmen is not necessarily a violation of duty in such societies. Indeed, one might be bribed not to show favoritism.

The official duties of an official, of course, may not be clear. Thus, the written law may prohibit favoritism to kin and ally, though this is widely practiced and condoned and infrequently prosecuted. This may occur when a society is in a transitional state from feudalism or tribalism to a Western-style industrial society, but it may also occur in an industrial society with different traditions than our own. To the extent that it is unclear what the official duties of officials are in such cases it will also be difficult to say what count as bribes. Indeed, even if we decide that an official does violate his duty by showing favoritism to kin and allies who reciprocate with gifts, we may not be justified in speaking of bribery here. For the official may not be acting as he does in order to fulfill his part of an agreement. Rather, he may be acting to fulfill some obligation of kinship or loyalty. Again, his failure so to act may not entitle his kinsmen or allies to complain that he had welched on a deal; rather, it would entitle them to complain that he wronged them as kinsmen or allies.

Of course, all this is so only when the relationships in question are genuine. In some cases, however, the rhetoric and ceremonial forms of a traditional culture may be used to camouflage what are in fact business relations of the standard Western variety. To the extent that this is so, the favoritism in question may in fact be bribery in ethnic dress. The relationships in question are not genuine when they are not entered into in good faith. It is clear, moreover, that when American executives present expensive gifts to foreign businessmen or foreign government officials they do so for business reasons. That is, they have no intention of entering into a system of reciprocal rights and duties that may obligate them in the future to act contrary to their long-term interest. Rather, they perform the required ceremonies knowing that they will continue to base their decisions on business reasons. Their intention is to buy favoritism. And the foreign officials and companies with whom they do business are typically aware of this. This being the case, the invitations of the form "First we become friends, then we do business" cannot plausibly be construed as invitations to participate in some traditional way of life. Typically, both parties recognize that what is requested here is a bribe made in an appropriate ceremonial way.

VI

On the basis of this analysis it seems clear that American officials are not always guilty of bribery when they pay off foreign officials. In some cases they are victims of extortion; in other cases, the context may be such that the action purchased from the relevant official does not count as a violation of his duty. The fact that American executives engaged in international commerce are innocent of some of the charges that have been made against them, however, does not imply that those who have made them are mistaken in their assessment of the character of these executives. One's character, after all, is a matter of what one is disposed to do. If these executives are willing to engage in bribery whenever this is necessary to promote their perceived long-term business interests, whatever the morality of the situation, it follows (at very least) that they are amoral.

NOTES

1. At the time this paper was written there were no references to bribes or bribery in the *Philosopher's Index*. Since that time one paper has been indexed—Arnold Berleant's "Multinationals, Local Practice, and the Problems of Ethical Consistency" (*Journal of Business Ethics* I [August 1982]: 185–93)—but, as the title of this short paper suggests, Berleant is not primarily concerned with providing an analysis of the concept of bribery. However, three presentations on the topic of bribery were made at the 1983 "Conference for Business Ethics" (organized by the Society for Business Ethics at DePaul University, July 25–26) and have subsequently been accepted for publication. These are: Kendall D'Andrade's "Bribery" (...in a special issue of the *Journal of Business Ethics*, devoted to the DePaul conference, 1984); John Danley's "Toward a Theory of Bribery" (...in the *Journal of Business and Professional Ethics*, 1984); and Tom Carson's "Bribery, Extortion and the Foreign Corrupt Practices Act" (...in *Philosophy and Public Affairs*, Summer 1984). Where my position on substantive questions differs significantly from D'Andrade's, Carson's, or Danley's, I shall discuss this in the notes.

2. Danley defines "bribing" as "offering or giving something of value with a corrupt intent to induce or influence an action of someone in a public or official capacity." Carson defines a bribe as a payment to someone "in exchange for special con-

sideration that is incompatible with the duties of his position." Both go on to discuss bribery as if it were restricted to officials of organizations. Since these are the most typical and important cases of bribery, their focus is understandable. But it does have at least one unfortunate consequence. For it leads both Danley and Carson to think that the question of whether it is prima facie wrong to offer or accept bribes reduces to the question of whether officials have obligations to satisfy their positional duties. Danley argues that they do not if the institutions they serve are illegitimate. Carson argues that they do on the ground that they have made a tacit agreement with their institution to discharge those duties (accepting a bribe, for Carson, is an instance of promise breaking). Whatever the merits of their arguments concerning the responsibilities of officials, both approach the question of the prima facie morality of bribery too narrowly. For different issues seem to arise when we consider bribery outside the realm of officialdom. Clearly it is more difficult for Carson to make his tacit consent argument in relation to the bribed athlete. For it is not clear that a runner who enters a race tacitly agrees to win it (if so, he would be breaking a promise by running to prepare for future races or by entering to set the pace for someone else). Nor is it clear that a boxer who accepts payment not to knock out his opponent in the early rounds violates a tacit agreement to attempt a knockout at his earliest convenience. Danley must expand his account to accommodate such cases as well. For it is not clear what it means to say that a practice such as running or boxing is legitimate.

3. Such cases present a problem for the accounts of both Danley and Carson. At the very least they must expand their accounts of positional duties such that we can distinguish between a bribe, on the one hand, and a salary paid to a spy recruited from within an organization, on the other.

4. Carson fails to recognize the significance of this feature of bribery. This view of bribery, moreover, is inconsistent with Danley's account. Danley understands a bribe as an attempt to induce or influence someone. In this matter he appears to have most dictionaries on his side (including the OED). However, as I argue in more detail in Sec. IV he is mistaken.

5. This is Carson's argument.

6. In D'Andrade's account bribes are necessarily secret, so these could not count as bribes.

7. A corresponding point holds in relation to bribery outside the realm of officialdom. Consider the case of professional wrestling. Most of us believe that the outcome of professional wrestling matches is determined in advance. Are the losers bribed? (To simplify matters let us assume that they are paid a bit of extra money for losing.) The answer here depends on how we understand their practice. If we take them to be participating in a wrestling competition, we must say that they are bribed. In that case, by failing to compete they violate an understanding constitutive of their practice. It is reasonably clear, however, that professional wrestlers are not engaged in an athletic competition. Rather, they are engaged in a dramatic performance. This being the case the losers are not bribed. They are merely doing what professional wrestlers are ordinarily paid to do, namely, to play out their part in an informal script.

NO

Thomas L. Carson

BRIBERY AND IMPLICIT AGREEMENTS: A REPLY TO PHILIPS

In a paper that appeared recently in *Ethics*, Michael Philips defends at some length an analysis of the concept of bribery.[1] He also attempts to give an account of the moral status of bribery. Philips attacks several views defended in my paper, "Bribery, Extortion and the 'Foreign Corrupt Practices Act,'" *Philosophy and Public Affairs*, Winter 1985, pp. 66–90. In my paper, I argue that accepting a bribe involves the violation of an implicit or explicit promise or understanding associated with one's office or role and that, therefore, accepting a bribe is always *prima facie* wrong. Philips offers two separate criticisms of this position. (1) He argues that in at least some cases of bribery the person who accepts the bribe does not thereby violate any agreements or understandings associated with any offices or positions that he holds. (2) He argues that in "morally corrupt contexts" there may be no *prima facie* duty to adhere to the agreements or understandings implicit in one's role or position. I shall offer replies to both of these criticisms, although I make some concessions to the first.

(1) Standard cases of bribery involve paying an official of an organization to do things contrary to the obligations of his office or position. The following examples all fit this model of bribery: (1) paying a judge or juror to decide in one's favor, (2) paying a policeman not to give one a traffic ticket, and (3) paying a government official not to report violations of health and safety standards. Philips concedes that in cases in which a bribe is paid to an official it is plausible to suppose that the official's acceptance of the bribe constitutes the violation of a "tacit agreement."[2] However, he claims that there are cases of bribery in which the person being bribed is self-employed and in which his acceptance of the bribe cannot be said to constitute the violation of an agreement or understanding between himself and some other party. (Philips seems to imply that in such cases there is no identifiable party *with whom* one can be said to have made an agreement.) Philips gives the example of bribing a self-employed professional athlete. In such cases, he claims, the acceptance of the bribe cannot be said to constitute the violation of a tacit agreement.

From Thomas L. Carson, "Bribery and Implicit Agreements: A Reply to Philips," *Journal of Business Ethics*, vol. 6 (1987), pp. 123–125. Copyright © 1987 by D. Reidel Publishing Co., Dordrecht, Holland, and Boston, U.S.A. Reprinted by permission of Kluwer Academic Publishers.

Clearly it is more difficult for Carson to make his tacit consent argument in relation to the bribed athlete. For it is not clear that a runner who enters a race tacitly agrees to win it (if so, he would be breaking a promise by running to prepare for future races or by entering to set the pace for someone else). Nor is it clear that a boxer who accepts payment not to knock out his opponent in the early rounds violates a tacit agreement to attempt a knock-out at his earliest convenience.[3]

But, Philips to the contrary, athletes, even self-employed athletes who are not members of teams or any other organizations, compete in *public competition* (as opposed to private matches or exhibition matches) on the understanding that they will do their best to win. This understanding constitutes an implicit promise or agreement between the athlete and (i) the sponsors or promoters of the competition, (ii) the spectators, fans, gamblers, and others who follow the competition (they take an interest in the competition only on the assumption that it is serious competition in which each athlete does his best to win), and (iii) his fellow competitors. The runner who enters a public competition tacitly agrees to do his best to win. To run the race with only the intention to 'warm up' for a future race is to violate an implicit agreement. Running so as to 'pace' a teammate violates no understanding, provided that one is competing as a member of a team. In such cases, we can say that one competes on the understanding that one will do the best one can to promote the victory of one's team. The boxer who accepts a bribe not to knock his opponent out in the early rounds violates a tacit agreement to try his best to win. For him to forego early opportunities to knock his opponent out is for him to fail to do his

best to win. An athlete who participates in public competition tacitly agrees to do his best to win, short of injuring himself or others or breaking the rules of the sport. The promoters and/or sponsors of the competition, the spectators, and his fellow athletes all act on the assumption that the athletes will do their best to win. Of course, the fact that others *expect* one to do something does not suffice to show that one has consented or agreed to do it. However, there are other features in addition to the mere expectation that the athlete will do his best to win, which permit us to conclude that a tacit agreement exists in this case. The athlete knows that the others expect that he will do his best to win. Further, he knows that they play their roles in this competition only on the basis of this expectation. They would not do what they are doing (or even take an interest in the competition) if they came to believe that the athletes were not attempting to win.

Philips briefly mentions a somewhat different example that poses serious problems for my position. The case that he mentions is one in which a slave is bribed to lose a boxing match promoted by his master.[4] I find it a bit odd to refer to this as a bribe and am tempted to conclude that a necessary condition of bribery is that the person who receives the bribe accepts the payment in exchange for actions contrary to the duties associated with a position or role that he has accepted voluntarily. However, there are other cases of paying individuals to violate duties attached to positions or roles that they have not accepted voluntarily which we would not be hesitant to describe as bribes. Ordinary usage would allow that it makes sense to speak of bribing a conscripted soldier, even though he has not voluntarily accepted the duties attached to his position. Understandings or agreements entered into by slaves with their masters (or conscript soldiers with the armies of which they are a part) are not voluntary and thus do not create *prima facie* duties in virtue of implicit promises. (Perhaps some conscript soldiers do have a *prima facie* duty to fulfill the obligations of their positions, but these are not duties that they have in virtue of any promises or agreements.) I must, therefore, concede that in such cases the person accepting the bribe has not entered into any agreements or understandings of the sort that could generate a *prima facie* duty not to accept the bribe. However, it is well to note that my account still holds for the vast majority of cases of bribery. In almost all ordinary cases of bribery, the person who accepts the bribe violates duties associated with roles or positions that he has voluntarily assumed. The only exceptions are bribery of conscripted soldiers, some prostitutes, and others held as virtual slaves. The vast majority of us freely choose the roles and offices that we occupy.

(2) Philips argues that, even in those cases of bribery in which the recipient of the bribe is a member of an organization and can be plausibly said to be taking the bribe in violation of some implicit agreement or understanding, this understanding does not necessarily generate a *prima facie* duty not to accept the bribe.

> By accepting a position in an organization, it might be argued, one tacitly agrees to abide by the rules of that organization. To be bribed is to violate that agreement—it is to break a promise—and is, therefore, *prima facie* wrong. While I concede that this argument has merit in the context of just and voluntary institutions, it seems questionable in a context of morally corrupt institutions (e.g., Nazi Germany or contemporary El Salvador). And even were it technically valid for those contexts, its conclusion would nonetheless be a misleading half-truth.... Thus, for example, it does not seem to me that, if I join the Mafia with the intention of subverting its operations and bringing its members to justice, I have thereby undertaken a *prima facie* obligation to abide by the code of that organization. Of course, one could say this and add that the obligation in question is typically overridden by other moral considerations. But this seems to me an *ad hoc* move to defend a position. We use the expression "*prima facie* duty" to point to a moral presumption for or against a certain type of action. And surely it is strange to insist that there is a moral presumption, in the present case, in favor of carrying out the commands of one's Don.[5]

I fail to see the force of this argument. Philips thinks it 'dangerous' to suppose that we have a *prima facie* duty to keep all implicit agreements, lest we fail to see that it would be wrong to fulfill our institutional duties in many morally corrupt situations (see Philips' footnote 7). But surely this is not a convincing argument. In general, it is not a valid argument to claim that since it is very clear that *S* ought to do *x* (all things considered), it cannot, in any sense, be his *prima facie* duty not to do *x*. Conflicts of duties aren't necessarily cases in which it is difficult to determine what one ought to do, all things considered. Nor is it an "*ad hoc* move" to say that *prima facie* duties can be overridden by other more important duties. The concept of a *prima facie* duty is derived from Ross. Ross is perfectly prepared to allow that some *prima facie* duties create only a very *weak moral presumption* for certain kinds of acts. He would have no hesitancy to say that implicit promises in the context of morally corrupt institutions create *prima facie* duties—albeit duties that can sometimes be easily overridden by other considerations. If we accept Ross' view that breaking promises (or breaking voluntary promises) is *prima facie* wrong, then we should have no reluctance to say that it is always *prima facie* wrong to accept bribes to do things that are contrary to implicit agreements or understandings into which one has entered *voluntarily.*

NOTES

1. Michael Philips, 'Bribery', *Ethics* 94 (July 1984), pp. 621–636.
2. Philips, p. 623, n.2.
3. Philips, p. 623, n.2.
4. Philips, p. 625.
5. Philips, p. 627. Philips attributes this argument to me in his footnote [5].

POSTSCRIPT

Is Bribery Ever Justified?

There are many points of view with regard to bribery. Where do you stand? Should the view of the moralists prevail, which insists on fair salaries, fair competition, and never a need to slip a payment into the outstretched hand of the customs official, dock supervisor, maitre d', purveyor of licenses, or rubber-stamper of documents? Is there a need to define with more precision what constitutes a bribe rather than a fee, license, reward, or gift?

Should governments regulate business operations more or less? Or should government remove itself from the position of regulating such payments? What group or agency should oversee any accusations or disputes regarding bribes, fees, and licenses? Should such disputes be the jurisdiction of the nation in which the transaction takes place or that of the nation of incorporation for the multinational? Or should a world court, UN committee, or some other international agency decide the issue?

There are further ethical dimensions that need to be kept in mind while considering this issue. First, we ought to have compassion for the poor. In many countries the bureaucracy is made up of low-status, poorly paid individuals that simply cannot survive without charging a "fee" to complete the paperwork and official procedures that a company needs to operate in those countries. What virtue is there in refusing to pay these usually inconsequential fees? Second, there is the troublesome status of hypocrisy. Sometimes a corporation operating in a corrupt atmosphere will hire a local "agent" who "takes care of the paperwork" and pays all the "fees." This agent is given a salary or consultant's fee for doing this task. The corporate officers probably know that the agent's "job" is to pay out bribes in their name; are *they* guilty of bribery?

SUGGESTED READINGS

David Bulton, *The Grease Machine* (Harper & Row, 1978).

Kendall D'Andrade, Jr., "Bribery," *Journal of Business Ethics* (August 1985)

Jeffrey A. Fadiman, "A Business Traveler's Guide to Gifts and Bribes," *Harvard Business Review* (July–August 1986).

John B. Matthews and Kenneth E. Goodpaster, *Policies and Persons: A Casebook in Business Ethics*, 2d ed. (McGraw-Hill, 1991).

John Tsalikis and Osita Nwachukwu, "A Comparison of Nigerian to American Views of Bribery and Extortion in International Commerce," *Journal of Business Ethics* (February 1991).

Scott Turow, "What's Wrong With Bribery?" *Journal of Business Ethics* (August 1985).

ISSUE 18

Should the Less Developed Countries Be Encouraged to Develop High Technology?

YES: Alvin Toffler, from "Toffler's Next Shock," *World Monitor* (November 1990)

NO: E. F. Schumacher, from *Small Is Beautiful: Economics as If People Mattered* (Harper & Row, 1973)

ISSUE SUMMARY

YES: Social commentator Alvin Toffler argues that if the less developed countries (LDCs) fail to catch up with the United States and Europe in the development of computer and other technology, they will be totally left out of the activity and rewards of the world in the twenty-first century.

NO: Economist E. F. Schumacher argues that there is a level of appropriate technology for the less developed countries that is more in accord with human effort, appreciation, rhythm, and spirituality than the machine-driven civilization of the West and that the LDCs would be well advised to stay with it.

How, on what scale, and at what speed should human enterprise be carried out? What goods should be made? How fast should goods be made and delivered? How much should they cost? What sorts of tools and machines should be used in their manufacture?

According to the free market, the answers to all those questions lie, in fact, in the impersonal workings of the free marketplace exchange, which guides individuals to promote the public interest, even as they pursue their own self-interests. What goods should we make? The goods that will sell at prices that make them profitable to make. In fact, if we make goods that do not sell, we shall go out of business and stop making goods altogether; if we make goods that sell profitably, we will have the resources to make more; and if we decide for some reason not to make a particular profitable good, someone else will. So only certain goods will be made. How fast should goods be made and delivered? As fast as possible, and only the fastest makers will remain in business. The goods should be sold at prices that the market will bear. And the tools used should be those that permit manufacture at the lowest possible cost.

In short, the effect of the free market is to take the vast majority of questions about the conduct of human economic life out of reach of human decision and consign them to the inevitable workings of the so-called iron laws of a market economy. There is no point in protesting against these laws nor in attempting to modify their results, for the market will simply flow around objections (through devices like the black market) and reestablish a balance of supply and demand somewhere else.

Two questions arise immediately: First, how is this conclusion to be reconciled with the dozens of restraints on free market activity that we recognize already? And second, if we accept certain restraints in the name of human life and dignity, should we reexamine these iron laws and see if we might want to apply others? Which do we value more, human life or the iron law that claims to be able to limit it? Recall, we are not talking about the laws of gravity or magnetism but about human work, leisure, and life, and the human decisions that shape these.

How are these iron laws to be reconciled with the restraints that we already recognize? For thousands of years, for example, ownership of persons (as slaves and as serfs) was highly profitable and legally recognized in every society in the world. Now it is not. Did iron laws change? The answer is no. It would still be profitable to sell oneself or one's children into slavery, but we have decided that economics matters less than human dignity on this subject, and so we do not permit slavery.

With this in mind, is it possible to adopt other restraints on the market, restraints that are designed to make human life more human? Can we start our economic thinking with a human being and radiate out from there?

The market-centered and human-centered views of work face off directly in the selections that follow. Alvin Toffler asks where the is market going and concludes (in fact, insists) that wherever it goes, humans must follow. He maintains that the consequences of being left behind in the global race to high-technology production are too awful to contemplate. E. F. Schumacher, in contrast, asks what humans really need and concludes that high technology is not vital to the survival and happiness of people.

Ask yourself, as you read the following selections, to what extent we are bound by the iron laws of the market. Would it be possible to order our economy for human fulfillment rather than for maximum liquidity and profit? What would we lose? What would we gain?

YES   Alvin Toffler

TOFFLER'S NEXT SHOCK

One of the greatest power imbalances on earth today divides the rich countries from the poor. That unequal distribution of power, which affects the lives of billions of us, will soon be transformed as a new system of wealth creation spreads.

Since the end of World War II the world has been split between capitalist and communist, North and South. Today as these old divisions fade in significance, a new one arises.

For from now on the world will be split between the fast and the slow.

To be fast or slow is not simply a matter of metaphor. Whole economies are either fast or slow. Primitive organisms have slow neural systems. The more evolved human nervous system processes signals faster. The same is true of primitive and advanced economies. Historically, power has shifted from the slow to the fast—whether we speak of species *or* nations.

In fast economies advanced technology speeds production. But this is the least of it. Their pace is determined by the speed of transactions, the time needed to take decisions (especially about investment), the speed with which new ideas are created in laboratories, the rate at which they are brought to market, the velocity of capital flows, and above all the speed with which data, information, and knowledge pulse through the economic system. Fast economies generate wealth—and power—faster than slow ones.

By contrast, in peasant societies economic processes move at a glacial pace. Tradition, ritual, and ignorance limit socially acceptable choices. Communications are primitive, transport restricted. Before the market system arose as an instrument for making investment choices, tradition governed technological decisions. Tradition, in turn, relied on "rules or taboos to preserve productive techniques that were proven workable over the slow course of biological or cultural evolution," according to economist Don Lavoie.

With most people living at the bare edge of subsistence, experiment was dangerous, innovators were suppressed, and advances in the methods of wealth creation came so slowly they were barely perceptible from lifetime to lifetime. Moments of innovation were followed by what seemed like centuries of stagnation.

The historical explosion we now call the industrial revolution stepped up the economic metabolism. Roads and communications improved. Profit-motivated entrepreneurs actively searched for innovations. Brute force technologies were introduced. Society had a larger surplus to fall back on, reducing the social risks of experimentation. "With technological experimentation now so much less costly," Lavoie points out, "productive methods [could] change much more rapidly."

All this, however, merely set the stage for today's super-fast symbolic economy.

The bar code on the box of Cheerios, the computer in the Federal Express truck, the scanner at the Safeway checkout counter, the bank's automatic teller, the spread of extra-intelligent data networks across the planet, the remotely operated robot, the informationalization of capital—are all preliminary steps in the formation of a 21st-century economy that will operate at nearly real-time speeds.

In due course, the entire wealth-creation cycle will be monitored *as it happens.* Continual feedback will stream in from sensors built into intelligent technology, from optical scanners in stores, and from transmitters in trucks, planes, and ships that send signals to satellites so managers can track the changing location of every vehicle at every moment. This information will be combined with the results of continuous polling of people, and information from a thousand other sources.

The acceleration effect, by making each unit of saved time *more* valuable than the last unit, thus creates a positive feed-back loop that accelerates the acceleration.

The consequences of this, in turn, will be not merely evolutionary, but revolutionary, because real-time work, manage-ment, and finance will be radically different from even today's most advanced methods.

Even now, however, well before real-time operations are achieved, time itself has become an increasingly critical factor of production. As a result, knowledge is used to shrink time intervals.

This quickening of economic neural responses in the high technology nations holds still-unnoticed consequences for low-technology or no-technology economies.

For the more valuable time becomes, the less valuable the traditional factors of production like raw materials and labor. And that, for the most part, is what these countries sell.

REV UP OR DROP OUT

The acceleration effect will transform all present strategies for economic development.

The new system for making wealth consists of an expanding, global network of markets, banks, production centers, and laboratories in instant communication with one another, constantly exchanging huge—and ever increasing—flows of data, information, and knowledge.

This is the "fast" economy of tomorrow. It is this accelerative, dynamic new wealth-machine that is the source of economic advance. As such it is the source of great power as well. To be de-coupled from it is to be excluded from the future.

Yet that is the fate facing many of today's "LDCs" or "less developed countries." (The term "less developed" is an arrogant misnomer, since many LDCs are highly developed culturally and in other ways. A more appropriate term would be "less economically developed," which is the sense in which it will be used here.)

As the world's main system for producing wealth revs up, countries that wish to sell will have to operate at the pace of those in a position to buy. This means that slow economies will have to speed up their neural responses, lose contracts and investments, or drop out of the race entirely.

The earliest signs of this development are already detectable.

The United States in the 1980s spent $125 billion a year on clothing. Half of that came from cheap labor factories dotted around the world from Haiti to Hong Kong. Tomorrow much of this work will return to the US. The reason is speed.

Of course, shifting taxes, tariffs, currency ratios, and other factors still influence businesses when overseas investment or purchasing decisions are made. But far more fundamental in the long run are changes in the structure of cost. These changes, part of the transition to the new wealth-creation system, are already sending runaway factories and contracts home again to the US, Japan, and Europe.

The Tandy Corporation, a major manufacturer and retailer of electronic products, not long ago brought its "Tandy Color Computer" production back from South Korea to Texas. While the Asian plant was automated, the Texas plant operated on an "absolutely continuous flow" basis and had more sophisticated test equipment. In Virginia, Tandy set up a no-human-hands automated plant to turn out 5,000 speaker enclosures a day. These supply Japanese manufacturers who previously had them made with low-cost labor in the Caribbean.

The computer industry is, of course, extremely fast-paced. But even in a slower industry, the Arrow Co., one of the biggest US shirtmakers, recently transferred 20% of its production back to the US after 15 years of off-shore sourcing. Frederick Atkins Inc., a buyer for US department stores, has increased domestic purchases from 5% to 40% in three years.

These shifts can be traced, at least in part, to the rising importance of time in economics.

DELIVERY DELAYED IS DELIVERY DENIED

"The new technology," reports Forbes magazine, "is giving domestic apparel makers an important advantage over their Asian competitors. Because of fickle fashion trends and the practice of changing styles as often as six times a year, retailers want to be able to keep inventories low. This calls for quick response from apparel makers that can offer fast turnaround on smaller lots in all styles, sizes, and colors. Asian suppliers, half a world away, typically require orders three months or more in advance."

By contrast, Italy's Benetton Group delivers mid-season reorders within two to three weeks. Because of its electronic network, Haggar Apparel in Dallas is now able to restock its 2,500 customers with slacks every three days, instead of the seven weeks it once needed.

Compare this with the situation facing manufacturers in China who happen to need steel.

In 1988 China suffered the worst steel shortages in memory. Yet, with fabricators crying out for supplies, 40% of the country's total annual output remained padlocked in the warehouses of the China Storage and Transportation General Corporation (CSTGC). Why? Because this enterprise—incredible as it may seem to the citizens of fast economies—makes deliveries only twice a year.

The fact that steel prices were skyrocketing, that the shortages were creating a black market, that fraud was widespread, and that companies needing the steel faced crisis and bankruptcy meant nothing to the managers of CSTGC. The organization was simply not geared to making more frequent deliveries. While this is no doubt an extreme example, it is not isolated. A "great wall" separates the fast from the slow, and that wall is rising higher with each passing day.

It is this cultural and technological great wall that explains, in part, the high rate of failures in joint projects between fast and slow countries.

Many deals collapse when a slow-country supplier fails to meet promised deadlines. The different pace of economic life in the two worlds makes for cross-cultural static. Officials in the slow country typically do not appreciate how important time is to the partner from the fast country—or why it matters so much. Demands for speed seem unreasonable, arrogant. Yet for the fast-country partner, nothing is more important. Delivery delayed is almost as bad as delivery denied.

The increasing costs of unreliability, of endless negotiation, of inadequate tracking and monitoring, and of late responses to demands for up-to-the-instant information further diminish the competitive edge of low-wage muscle work in the slow economies.

So do expenses arising from delays, lags, irregularities, bureaucratic stalling, and slow decisionmaking—not to mention the corrupt payments often required to speed things up.

In the advanced economies the speed of decision is becoming a critical consideration. Some executives refer to the inventory of "decisions in process" or "DIP" as an important cost, similar to "work in progress." They are trying to replace sequential decisionmaking with "parallel processing," which breaks with bureaucracy. They speak of "speed to market," "quick response," "fast cycle time," and "time-based competition."

The increased precision of timing required by systems like "just-in-time delivery" means that the seller must meet far more rigid and restrictive schedule requirements than before, so that it is easier than ever to slip up.

In turn, as buyers demand more frequent and timely deliveries from overseas, the slow-country suppliers are compelled to maintain larger inventories or buffer stocks at their own expense—with the risk that the stored parts will rapidly become obsolete or unsalable.

The new economic imperative is clear: Overseas suppliers from developing countries will either advance their own technologies to meet the world speed standards, or they will be brutally cut off from their markets—casualties of the acceleration effect.

The likelihood that many of the world's poorest countries will be isolated from the dynamic global economy and left to stagnate is enhanced by three other powerful factors that stem, directly or indirectly, from the arrival of a new system of wealth creation on the earth.

STRATEGIC REAL ESTATE

One way to think about the economic power or powerlessness of the LDCs is to ask what they have to sell to the rest of the world. We can begin with a scarce resource that only a few countries at any given moment can offer the rest of the world: strategic location.

Economists don't normally consider militarily strategic real estate a salable resource, but for many LDCs that is precisely what it has been.

Countries seeking military and political power are frequently prepared to pay for it. Like Cuba, many LDCs now have sold, leased, or lent their location or facilities to the Soviet Union, the US, or others for military, political, and intelligence purposes....

For almost half a century, the Cold War has meant that even the poorest country (assuming it was strategically located) had something to sell to the highest bidder. Some, like Egypt, managed to sell their favors first to one superpower, then to the other.

But while the relaxation of US-Soviet tensions may be good news for the world, it is decidedly bad news for places like the Philippines, Vietnam, Cuba, or Nicaragua, each of which has successfully peddled access to its strategic geography....

Moreover, as logistic capabilities rise, as aircraft and missile range increases, as submarines proliferate, and as military airlift operations quicken, the need for overseas bases, repair facilities, and prepositioned supplies declines.

LDCs must, therefore, anticipate the end of the seller's market for such strategic locations. Unless replaced by other forms of international support, this will choke off billions of dollars of "foreign aid" and "military assistance" funds that have until now flowed into certain LDCs....

Even if the great powers of the future (whoever they may be) do continue to locate bases, set up satellite listening posts, or build airfields and submarine facilities on foreign soil, the "leases" will be for shorter times. Today's accelerating changes make all alliances more tenuous and temporary, discouraging the great powers from making long-term investments in fixed locations.

Wars, threats, insurrections will arise at unexpected places. Thus the military of the great powers will increasingly stress mobile, rapid deployment forces, the projection of naval power, and space operations rather than fixed installations. All this will further drive down the bargaining power of countries with locations to let or lease.

Finally, the rise of Japanese military power in the Pacific may well lead the Philippines and other Southeast Asian countries to *welcome* US or other forces as a counterbalance to a perceived Japanese threat. Carried far enough, this implies even a willingness to *pay* for protection, instead of charging for allowing it.

UPSETTING THE LDC POWER BALANCE

New outbreaks of regional war or internal violence on many continents will keep the arms business booming. But whatever happens, it will be harder to extract benefits from the US [with the collapse of the Soviet challenge]. This will upset the delicate power balance among LDCs—as between India and Pakistan, for instance, or Nicaragua and its neighbors—and will trigger potentially violent power shifts *within* the LDCs as well, especially among the elites closely (and sometimes corruptly) linked to aid programs, military procurement, and intelligence operations.

In short, the heyday of the Cold War is over. Far more complex power shifts lie ahead. And the market for strategic locations in the LDCs will never be the same.

A second blow awaits countries that base their development plans on the export of bulk raw materials such as copper or bauxite.

Here, too, power-shifting changes are just around the corner.

Mass production required vast amounts of a small number of resources. By contrast, as de-massified manufacturing methods spread, they will need many more different resources—in much smaller quantities.

Furthermore, the faster metabolism of the new global production system also means that resources regarded as crucial today may be worthless tomorrow— along with all the extractive industries, railroad sidings, mines, harbor facilities, and other installations built to move these resources. Conversely, today's useless junk could suddenly acquire great value.

Oil itself was regarded as useless until new technologies, and especially the internal combustion engine, made it vital. Titanium was a largely useless white powder until it became valuable in aircraft and submarine production. But the rate at which new technologies arrived was slow. That, of course, is no longer true.

Superconductivity, to choose a single example, will eventually reduce the need for energy by cutting transmission losses and, at the same time, will require new raw materials for its use. New anti-pollution devices for automobiles no longer depend on platinum. New pharmaceuticals may call for organic substances that today are either unknown or unvalued. In turn, this could change poverty-stricken countries into

important suppliers—while undercutting today's big-bulk exporters.

What's more, in the words of Umberto Colombo, chairman of the European Community's Committee on Science and Technology, "in the advanced and affluent societies, each successive increment in per capita income is linked to an ever-smaller rise in quantities of raw materials and energy used." Colombo cites figures from the International Monetary Fund showing that "Japan... in 1984 consumed only 60% of the raw materials required for the same volume of industrial output in 1973."

DOING MORE WITH LESS

Advancing knowledge permits us to do more with less. As it does so, it shifts power away from the bulk producers.

Beyond this development, fast-expanding scientific knowledge increases the ability to create substitutes for imported resources. Indeed, the advanced economies may soon be able to create whole arrays of new customized materials such as "nano-composites" virtually from scratch. The smarter the high-tech nations become about micro-manipulating matter, the less dependent they become on imports of bulk raw materials from abroad.

The new wealth system is too protean, too fast-moving to be shackled to a few "vital" materials. Power will therefore flow from bulk raw material producers to those who control "eyedropper" quantities of temporarily crucial substances, and from them to those who control the knowledge necessary to create totally new resources.

All this would be bad enough. But a third jolting blow is likely to hit the LDCs even harder and change power relations among and within them.

Ever since the smoky dawn of the industrial era, manufacturers have pursued the golden grail of cheap labor. After World War II the hunt for foreign sources of cheap labor became a stampede. Many developing countries bet their entire economic future on the theory that selling labor cheap would lead to modernization.

Some, like the "four tigers" of East Asia—South Korea, Taiwan, Hong Kong, and Singapore—even won their bet. They were helped along by a strong work ethic and by cultural and other unique factors, including the fact that the "containment" of China for a quarter century and two bitter wars, the Korean conflict in the '50s and Vietnam in the '60s and early '70s, pumped billions of dollars into the region.

Because of the Asian tigers' success, it is now almost universally believed that shifting from the export of agricultural products or raw materials to the export of goods manufactured by cheap labor is the path to development. Yet nothing could be further from the long-range truth.

There is n· ·˄ bt that the cheap labor game is still being played all over the world. Even now Japan is transferring plants and contracts from Taiwan and Hong Kong, where wages have risen, to Thailand, the Philippines, and China where wages are still one-tenth those in Japan. No doubt many opportunities still exist for rich countries to locate pools of cheap labor in the LDCs.

But, like leasing military bases or shipping ore, the sale of cheap labor is also reaching its outer limits.

The reason for this is simple: Under the newly emerging system of wealth creation, cheap labor is increasingly expensive.

As the new system spreads, labor costs themselves become a smaller fraction of total costs of production. In some industries today, labor costs represent only 10% of the total costs of production. A 1% saving of a 10% cost factor is only 1/10th of 1%.

By contrast, better technology, faster and better information flows, decreased inventory, or streamlined organization can yield savings far beyond any that can be squeezed out of hourly workers.

This is why it may be more profitable to run an advanced facility in Japan or the US, with a handful of highly educated, highly paid employees than a backward factory in China or Brazil that depends on masses of badly educated, low-wage workers.

Cheap labor, in the words of Umberto Colombo, "is no longer enough to ensure market advantage to developing countries."

HYPER-SPEEDS

Looming on the horizon, therefore, is a dangerous de-coupling of the fast economies from the slow, an event that would spark enormous power shifts throughout the so-called South—with big impacts on the planet as a whole.

The new wealth creation system holds the possibility of a far better future for vast populations who are now among the planet's poor. Unless the leaders of the LDCs anticipate these changes, however, they will condemn their people to perpetuated misery—and themselves to impotence.

For even as Chinese manufacturers wait for their steel, and traditional economies around the world crawl slowly through their paces, the United States, Japan, [and] Europe... are pressing forward with plans to build hypersonic jets capable of moving 250 tons of people and cargo at Mach 5, meaning that cities like New York, Sydney, London, or Los Angeles will be two-and-a-half hours from Tokyo.

Jiro Tokuyama, former director of research for Nomura Securities and now a senior adviser to the Mitsui Research Institute, heads a 15-nation study of what are called the "Three T's"—telecommunications, transportation, and tourism. Sponsored by the Pacific Economic Community Commission, the study focuses on three key factors likely to accelerate the pace of economic processes in the region still further.

According to Tokuyama, Pacific air passenger traffic is likely to reach 134 million... at the turn of the century. The Society of Japanese Aerospace Companies, Tokuyama adds, estimates that 500 to 1,000 hypersonic jets must be built. Many of these will ply Pacific routes, speeding further the economic development of the region and promoting faster telecommunications as well. In a paper prepared for the Three T's study, Tokuyama spells out the commercial, social, and political implications of this development.

He also describes a proposal by Taisei, the Japanese construction firm, to build an artificial island five kilometers (three miles) in length to serve as a "VAA" or "value-added airport" capable of handling hypersonics and providing an international conference center, shops, and other facilities to be linked by high-speed linear trains to a densely populated area.

AIRPORT ASSEMBLY LINES

In Texas, meanwhile, billionaire H. Ross Perot is building an airport to be surrounded by advanced manufacturing facilities. As conceived by him, planes would roar in day and night bearing components for overnight processing or assembly in facilities at the airport. The next morning the jets would carry them to all parts of the world.

Simultaneously, on the telecommunications front, the advanced economies are investing billions in the electronic infrastructure essential to operations in the super-fast economy.

The spread of extra-intelligent nets is moving swiftly, and there are now proposals afoot to create special higher-speed fiber optic networks linking supercomputers all across the US with thousands of laboratories and research groups. (Existing networks, which move 1.5 million bits of information a second, are regarded as too slow. The proposed new nets would send 3 billion bits per second—i.e. three "gigabits"—streaming across the country.)

The new network is needed, say its advocates, because the existing slower nets are already choked and overloaded. They argue that the project merits government backing because it would help the US keep ahead of Europe and Japan in a field it now leads.

This, however, is only a special case of a more general clamor. In the words of Mitch Kapor, a founder of Lotus Development Corp., the software giant, "We need to build a national infrastructure that will be the information equivalent of the national highway-building of the '50s and '60s. "An even more appropriate analogy would compare today's computerized telecom infrastructures with the rail and road networks needed at the beginning of the industrial revolution.

What is happening, therefore, is the emergence of an electronic neural system for the economy—without which any nation, no matter how many smokestacks it has, will be doomed to backwardness.

For the LDCs, as for the rest of the world, power stems from the holster, the wallet, and the book—or, nowadays, the computer. Unless we want an anarchic world—with billions of poverty-stricken people, unstable governments led by unstable leaders, each with a finger on the missile launcher or chemical or bacteriological triggers—we need global strategies for preventing the de-coupling of fast and slow economies that looms before us.

A study of "Intelligence Requirements for the 1990s" made by US academic experts, warns that in the years immediately ahead the LDCs will acquire sophisticated new arms—enormous firepower will be added to their already formidable arsenals. Why?

As the LDCs' economic power diminishes, their rulers face political opposition and instability. Under the circumstances, they are likely to do what rulers have done since the origins of the state—reach for the most primitive form of power: military force.

But the most acute shortage facing LDCs is the shortage of economically relevant knowledge. The 21st-century path to economic development and power is no longer through the exploitation of raw materials and human muscle, but, as we've seen, through application of the human mind.

KNOWLEDGE IS WEALTH

Development strategies make no sense, therefore, unless they take full account of the new role of knowledge in wealth creation, and of the accelerative imperative that goes hand in hand with it.

With knowledge (which in our definition includes such things as imagination, values, images, and motivation, along with formal technical skills) increasingly central to the economy, the Brazils and Nigerias, the Bangladeshes and Haitis, must consider how they might best acquire or generate this resource.

It is clear that every wretched child in northeast Brazil or anywhere else in the world who remains ignorant or intellectually underdeveloped because of malnutrition represents a permanent drain on the future. Revolutionary new forms of education will be needed, ones that are not based on the old factory model.

Acquiring knowledge from elsewhere will also be necessary. This may take unconventional—and sometimes even illicit—forms. Stealing technological secrets is already a booming business around the world. We must expect shrewd LDCs to join the hunt.

Another way of obtaining wealthmaking know-how is to organize a brain drain. This can be done on a small scale by bribing or attracting teams of researchers. But some clever countries will figure out that, around the world, there are certain dynamic minorities—often persecuted groups—that can energize a host economy if given the chance. The overseas Chinese in Southeast Asia, Indians in East Africa, Syrians in West Africa, Palestinians in parts of the Mideast, Jews in America, and Japanese in Brazil have all played this role at one time or another.

Transplanted into a different culture, each has brought not merely energy, drive, and commercial or technical acumen, but a pro-knowledge attitude—a ravenous hunger for the latest information, new ideas, skills. These groups have provided a kind of hybrid economic vigor. They work hard, they innovate, they educate their children, and, even if they get rich in the process, they stimulate and accelerate the reflexes of the host economy.

We will no doubt see various LDCs searching out such groups and inviting them to settle within their borders, in the hopes of injecting a needed adrenalin into the economy. (During World War II the Japanese military actually drafted a plan to bring large numbers of persecuted European Jews to Manchuria, then called Manchukuo, for this purpose. However, the "Fugu Plan," as it was known, was never implemented.)

NEGLECTED MEDIA

Smart governments will also encourage the spread of nongovernmental associations and organizations, since such groups accelerate the spread of economically useful information through newsletters, meetings, conferences, and foreign travel. Associations of merchants, plastics engineers, employers, programmers, trade unions, bankers, journalists, etc., serve as channels for rapid exchange of information about what does, and does not, work in their respective fields. They are an important, often neglected communications medium.

Governments serious about economic development will also have to recognize the new economic significance of free expression. Failure to permit the circulation of new ideas, including economic and political ideas, even if unflattering to the state, is almost always prima facie proof that the state is weak at its core, and that those in power regard staying there as more important than economic improve-

ment in the lives of their people. Governments committed to becoming part of the new world will systematically open the valves of public discussion.

Other governments will join "knowledge consortia"—partnerships with other countries or with global companies—to explore the far reaches of technology and science and, especially, the possibility of creating new materials.

Instead of pandering to obsolete nationalist notions, they will pursue the national interest passionately—but intelligently. Rather than refusing to pay royalties to foreign pharmaceutical companies on the lofty ground that health is above such grubby concerns, as Brazil has done, they will gladly pay the royalties—provided these funds stay inside the country for a fixed number of years, and are used to fund research projects carried out jointly with the local pharmaceutical firm's own experts.

Profits from products that originate in this joint research then can be divided between the host country and the multinational. In this way, the royalties pay for technology transfer—and for themselves. Effective nationalism thus replaces obsolete, self-destructive nationalism.

Similarly, intelligent governments will welcome the latest computers, regardless of who built them, rather than trying to build a local computer industry behind tariff walls that keep out not merely products—but advanced knowledge.

The computer industry is changing so fast on a world scale that no nation, not even the US or Japan, can keep up without help from the rest of the world.

FREEDOM FOR COMPUTERS

By barring certain outside computers and software, Brazil managed to build its own computer industry—but its products are backward compared with those available outside. This means that Brazilian banks, manufacturers, and other businesses have had to use technology that is inefficient compared with that of their foreign competitors. They compete with one hand tied behind them. Rather than gaining, the country loses.

Brazil violated the first rule of the new system of wealth creation: Do what you will with the slowly changing industries, but get out of the way of a fast-advancing industry. Especially one that processes the most important resource of all—Knowledge.

Other LDCs will avoid these errors. Some, we may speculate, will actually invest modestly in existing venture capital funds in the US, Europe, and Japan—on condition that their own technicians, scientists, and students accompany the capital and share in the know-how developed by the resulting startup firms. In this way, Brazilians—or Indonesians or Nigerians or Egyptians—might find themselves at the front edge of tomorrow's industries. Astutely managed, such a program could well pay for itself—or even make a profit.

Above all, the LDCs will take a completely fresh look at the role of agriculture, regarding it not necessarily as a "backward" sector, but as a sector that, potentially, with the help of computers, genetics, satellites, and other new technologies, could some day be more advanced, more progressive than all the smokestacks, steel mills, and mines in the world. Knowledge-based agriculture may be the cutting edge of economic advance tomorrow.

FARMING FOR MORE THAN FOOD

Moreover, agriculture will not limit itself to growing food—but will increasingly grow energy crops and feedstocks for new materials. These are but a few of the ideas likely to be tested in the years to come.

But none of these efforts will bear fruit if a country is cut off from participation in the fast-moving global economy and the telecommunications and commuter networks that support it.

The maldistribution of telecommunications in today's world is even more dramatic than the maldistribution of food. There are 600 million telephones in the world—with 450 million of them in only nine countries. The lopsided distribution of computers, databases, technical publications, research expenditures, tells us more about the future potential of nations than all the gross national product figures ground out by economists.

To plug into the new world economy, countries like China, Brazil, Mexico, Indonesia, India, as well as ... the East European nations must find the resources needed to install their own electronic infrastructures. These must go far beyond mere telephone services to include up-to-date, high-speed data systems capable of linking into the latest global networks.

The "gap" that must be closed is informational and electronic. It is a gap not between the North and the South, but between the slow and the fast.

NO

E. F. Schumacher

SMALL IS BEAUTIFUL

BUDDHIST ECONOMICS

'Right Livelihood' is one of the requirements of the Buddha's Noble Eight-fold Path. It is clear, therefore, that there must be such a thing as Buddhist economics.

Buddhist countries have often stated that they wish to remain faithful to their heritage. So Burma: "The New Burma sees no conflict between religious values and economic progress. Spiritual health and material wellbeing are not enemies: they are natural allies."[1] Or: "We can blend successfully the religious and spiritual values of our heritage with the benefits of modern technology."[2] Or: "We Burmans have a sacred duty to conform both our dreams and our acts to our faith. This we shall ever do."[3]

All the same, such countries invariably assume that they can model their economic development plans in accordance with modern economics, and they call upon modern economists from so-called advanced countries to advise them, to formulate the policies to be pursued, and to construct the grand design for development, the Five-Year Plan or whatever it may be called. No one seems to think that a Buddhist way of life would call for Buddhist economics, just as the modern materialist way of life has brought forth modern economics.

Economists themselves, like most specialists, normally suffer from a kind of metaphysical blindness, assuming that theirs is a science of absolute and invariable truths, without any presuppositions. Some go as far as to claim that economic laws are as free from 'metaphysics' or 'values' as the law of gravitation. We need not, however, get involved in arguments of methodology. Instead, let us take some fundamentals and see what they look like when viewed by a modern economist and a Buddhist economist.

There is universal agreement that a fundamental source of wealth is human labour. Now, the modern economist has been brought up to consider 'labour' or work as little more than a necessary evil. From the point of view of the employer, it is in any case simply an item of cost, to be reduced to a minimum if it cannot be eliminated altogether, say, by automation. From the point of view of the workman, it is a 'disutility'; to work is to make a sacrifice of one's leisure and comfort, and wages are a kind of compensation for the sacrifice. Hence the ideal from the point of view of the employer is to have output without employees, and the ideal from the point of view of the employee is to have income without employment.

The consequences of these attitudes both in theory and in practice are, of course, extremely far-reaching. If the ideal with regard to work is to get rid of it, every method that 'reduces the work load' is a good thing. The most potent method, short of automation, is the so-called 'division of labour' and the classical example is the pin factory eulogised in Adam Smith's *Wealth of Nations*.[4] Here it is not a matter of ordinary specialisation, which mankind has practised from time immemorial, but of dividing up every complete process of production into minute parts, so that the final product can be produced at great speed without anyone having had to contribute more than a totally insignificant and, in most cases, unskilled movement of his limbs.

The Buddhist point of view takes the function of work to be at least threefold: to give a man a chance to utilise and develop his faculties; to enable him to overcome his ego-centredness by joining with other people in a common task; and to bring forth the goods and services needed for a becoming existence. Again, the consequences that flow from this view are endless. To organise work in such a manner that it becomes meaningless, boring, stultifying, or nerve-racking for the worker would be little short of criminal; it would indicate a greater concern with goods than with people, an evil lack of compassion and a soul-destroying degree of attachment to the most primitive side of this worldly existence. Equally, to strive for leisure as an alternative to work would be considered a complete misunderstanding of one of the basic truths of human existence, namely that work and leisure are complementary parts of the same living process and cannot be separated without destroying the joy of work and the bliss of leisure.

From the Buddhist point of view, there are therefore two types of mechanisation which must be clearly distinguished: one that enhances a man's skill and power and one that turns the work of man over to a mechanical slave, leaving man in a position of having to serve the slave. How to tell the one from the other? "The craftsman himself," says Ananda Coomaraswamy, a man equally competent to talk about the modern west as the ancient east, "can always, if allowed to, draw the delicate distinction between the machine and the tool. The carpet loom is a tool, a contrivance for holding warp threads at a stretch for the pile to be woven round them by the craftsmen's fingers; but the power loom is a machine, and its significance as a destroyer of culture lies in the fact that it does the essentially human part of the work."[5] It is clear, therefore, that Buddhist economics must be very different from the economics of modern materialism, since the Buddhist sees the essence of civilisation not in a multiplication of wants but in the purification of human character. Character, at the same time, is formed primarily by a man's work. And work, properly conducted in conditions of human dignity and freedom, blesses those who do it and equally their products. The Indian philosopher and economist J. C. Kumarappa sums the matter up as follows:

"If the nature of the work is properly appreciated and applied, it will stand in the same relation to the higher faculties as food is to the physical body. It nourishes and enlivens the higher man and urges him to produce the best he is capable of. It directs his free will along the proper course and disciplines the animal in him into progressive channels. It furnishes an excellent background for man to display his scale of values and develop his personality."[6]

If a man has no chance of obtaining work he is in a desperate position, not simply because he lacks an income but because he lacks this nourishing and enlivening factor of disciplined work which nothing can replace. A modern economist may engage in highly sophisticated calculations on whether full employment 'pays' or whether it might be more 'economic' to run an economy at less than full employment so as to ensure a greater mobility of labour, a better stability of wages, and so forth. His fundamental criterion of success is simply the total quantity of goods produced during a given period of time. "If the marginal urgency of goods is low," says Professor Galbraith in *The Affluent Society*, "then so is the urgency of employing the last man or the last million men in the labour force."[7] And again: "If... we can afford some unemployment in the interest of stability—a proposition, incidentally, of impeccably conservative antecedents—then we can afford to give those who are unemployed the goods that enable them to sustain their accustomed standard of living."

From a Buddhist point of view, this is standing the truth on its head by considering goods as more important than people and consumption as more important than creative activity. It means shifting the emphasis from the worker to the product of work, that is, from the human to the subhuman, a surrender to the forces of evil....

While the materialist is mainly interested in goods, the Buddhist is mainly interested in liberation. But Buddhism is 'The Middle Way' and therefore in no way antagonistic to physical well-being. It is not wealth that stands in the way of liberation but the attachment to wealth; not the enjoyment of pleasurable things but the craving for them. The keynote of Buddhist economics, therefore, is simplicity and non-violence. From an economist's point of view, the marvel of the Buddhist way of life is the utter rationality of its pattern—amazingly small means leading to extraordinarily satisfactory results.

For the modern economist this is very difficult to understand. He is used to measuring the 'standard of living' by the amount of annual consumption, assuming all the time that a man who consumes more is 'better off' than a man who consumes less. A Buddhist economist would consider this approach excessively irrational: since consumption is merely a means to human well-being, the aim should be to obtain the maximum of well-being with the minimum of consumption. Thus, if the purpose of clothing is a certain amount of temperature comfort and an attractive appearance, the task is to attain this purpose with the smallest possible effort, that is, with the smallest annual destruction of cloth and with the help of designs that involve the smallest possible input of toil. The less toil there is, the more time and strength is left for artistic creativity. It would be highly uneconomic, for instance, to go in for complicated tailoring, like the modern west, when a much more beautiful effect can be achieved by the skilful draping of uncut material. It would be the height of folly to make material so that it should wear out quickly and the height of barbarity to make anything ugly, shabby or mean. What has just been said about clothing applies equally to all other human requirements. The ownership and the consumption of goods is a means to an end, and Buddhist economics is the systematic study of how to attain given ends with the minimum means.

Modern economics, on the other hand, considers consumption to be the sole end and purpose of all economic activity, taking the factors of production—land, labour, and capital—as the means. The former, in short, tries to maximise human satisfactions by the optimal pattern of consumption, while the latter tries to maximise consumption by the optimal pattern of productive effort. It is easy to see that the effort needed to sustain a way of life which seeks to attain the optimal pattern of consumption is likely to be much smaller than the effort needed to sustain a drive for maximum consumption. We need not be surprised, therefore, that the pressure and strain of living is very much less in, say, Burma than it is in the United States, in spite of the fact that the amount of labour-saving machinery used in the former country is only a minute fraction of the amount used in the latter.

Simplicity and non-violence are obviously closely related. The optimal pattern of consumption, producing a high degree of human satisfaction by means of a relatively low rate of consumption, allows people to live without great pressure and strain and to fulfil the primary injunction of Buddhist teaching: 'Cease to do evil; try to do good.' As physical resources are everywhere limited, people satisfying their needs by means of a modest use of resources are obviously less likely to be at each other's throats than people depending upon a high rate of use. Equally, people who live in highly self-sufficient local communities are less likely to get involved in large-scale violence than people whose existence depends on world-wide systems of trade.

From the point of view of Buddhist economics, therefore, production from local resources for local needs is the most rational way of economic life, while dependence on imports from afar and the consequent need to produce for export to unknown and distant peoples is highly uneconomic and justifiable only in exceptional cases, and on a small scale. Just as the modern economist would admit that a high rate of consumption of transport services between a man's home and his place of work signifies a misfortune and not a high standard of life, so the Buddhist economist would hold that to satisfy human wants from faraway sources rather than from sources nearby signifies failure rather than success. The former tends to take statistics showing an increase in the number of ton/miles per head of the population carried by a country's transport system as proof of economic progress, while to the latter—the Buddhist economist—the same statistics would indicate a highly undesirable deterioration in the *pattern* of consumption.

Another striking difference between modern economics and Buddhist economics arises over the use of natural resources. Bertrand de Jouvenel, the eminent French political philosopher, has characterised 'western man' in words which may be taken as a fair description of the modern economist:

"He tends to count nothing as an expenditure, other than human effort; he does not seem to mind how much mineral matter he wastes and, far worse, how much living matter he destroys. He does not seem to realise at all that human life is a dependent part of an ecosystem of many different forms of life. As the world is ruled from towns where men are cut off from any form of life other than human, the feeling of belonging to an ecosystem is not revived. This results in a harsh and improvident treatment of things upon which we ultimately depend, such as water and trees."[8]

The teaching of the Buddha, on the other hand, enjoins a reverent and non-violent attitude not only to all sentient beings but also, with great emphasis, to trees. Every follower of the Buddha ought to plant a tree every few years and look after it until it is safely established, and the Buddhist economist can demonstrate without difficulty that the universal observation of this rule would result in a high rate of genuine economic development independent of any foreign aid. Much of the economic decay of south-east Asia (as of many other parts of the world) is undoubtedly due to a heedless and shameful neglect of trees.

Modern economics does not distinguish between renewable and non-renewable materials, as its very method is to equalise and quantify everything by means of a money price. Thus, taking various alternative fuels, like coal, oil, wood, or water-power: the only difference between them recognised by modern economics is relative cost per equivalent unit. The cheapest is automatically the one to be preferred, as to do otherwise would be irrational and 'uneconomic'. From a Buddhist point of view, of course, this will not do; the essential difference between non-renewable fuels like coal and oil on the one hand and renewable fuels like wood and water-power on the other cannot be simply overlooked. Non-renewable goods must be used only if they are indispensable, and then only with the greatest care and the most meticulous concern for conservation. To use them heedlessly or extravagantly is an act of violence, and while complete non-violence may not be attainable on this earth, there is nonetheless an ineluctable duty on man to aim at the ideal of non-violence in all he does.

Just as a modern European economist would not consider it a great economic achievement if all European art treasures were sold to America at attractive prices, so the Buddhist economist would insist that a population basing its economic life on non-renewable fuels is living parasitically, on capital instead of income. Such a way of life could have no permanence and could therefore be justified only as a purely temporary expedient. As the world's resources of non-renewable fuels—coal, oil and natural gas—are exceedingly unevenly distributed over the globe and undoubtedly limited in quantity, it is clear that their exploitation at an ever-increasing rate is an act of violence against nature which must almost inevitably lead to violence between men.

This fact alone might give food for thought even to those people in Buddhist countries who care nothing for the religious and spiritual values of their heritage and ardently desire to embrace the materialism of modern economics at the fastest possible speed. Before they dismiss Buddhist economics as nothing better than a nostalgic dream, they might wish to consider whether the path of economic development outlined by modern economics is likely to lead them to places where they really want to be. Towards the end of his courageous book *The Challenge of Man's Future*, Professor Harrison Brown of the California Institute of Technology gives the following appraisal:

"Thus we see that, just as industrial society is fundamentally unstable and subject to reversion to agrarian existence, so within it the conditions which offer individual freedom are unstable in their ability to avoid the conditions which impose rigid organisation and totalitarian control. Indeed, when we examine all of the foreseeable difficulties which threaten the survival of industrial civilisation, it is difficult to see how the achievement of stability and the maintenance of individual liberty can be made compatible."[9]

Even if this were dismissed as a long-term view there is the immediate question of whether 'modernisation', as currently practised without regard to religious and spiritual values, is actually producing agreeable results. As far as the masses are concerned, the results appear to be disastrous—a collapse of the rural economy, a rising tide of unemployment in town and country, and the growth of a city proletariat without nourishment for either body or soul.

It is in the light of both immediate experience and long-term prospects that the study of Buddhist economics could be recommended even to those who believe that economic growth is more important than any spiritual or religious values. For it is not a question of choosing between 'modern growth' and 'traditional stagnation'. It is a question of finding the right path of development, the Middle Way between materialist heedlessness and traditionalist immobility, in short, of finding 'Right Livelihood'.

A QUESTION OF SIZE

... Let us now approach our subject from another angle and ask what is actually *needed*. In the affairs of men, there always appears to be a need for at least two things simultaneously, which, on the face of it, seem to be incompatible and to exclude one another. We always need both freedom and order. We need the freedom of lots and lots of small, autonomous units, and, at the same time, the orderliness of large-scale, possibly global, unity and coordination. When it comes to action, we obviously need small units, because action is a highly personal affair, and one cannot be in touch with more than a very limited number of persons at any one time. But when it comes to the world of ideas, to principles or to ethics, to the indivisibility of peace and also of ecology, we need to recognise the unity of mankind and base our actions upon this recognition. Or to put it differently, it is true that all men are brothers, but it is also true that in our active personal relationships we can, in fact, be brothers to only a few of them, and we are called upon to show more brotherliness to them than we could possibly show to the whole of mankind. We all know people who freely talk about the brotherhood of man while treating their neighbours as enemies, just as we also know people who have, in fact, excellent relations with all their neighbours while harbouring, at the same time, appalling prejudices about all human groups outside their particular circle.

What I wish to emphasise is the *duality* of the human requirement when it comes to the question of size: there is no *single* answer. For his different purposes man needs many different structures, both small ones and large ones, some exclusive and some comprehensive. Yet people find it most difficult to keep two seemingly opposite necessities of truth in their minds at the same time. They always tend to clamour for a final solution, as if in actual life there could ever be a final solution other than death. For constructive work, the principal task is always the restoration of some kind of balance. Today, we suffer from an almost universal idolatry of giantism. It is therefore necessary to insist on the virtues of smallness—where this applies. (If there were a prevailing idolatry of smallness, irrespective of subject or purpose, one would have to try and exercise influence in the opposite direction.)

The question of scale might be put in another way: what is needed in all these matters is to discriminate, to get things sorted out. For every activity there is a certain appropriate scale, and the more active and intimate the activity, the smaller the number of people that can take part, the greater is the number of such relationship arrangements that need to be established. Take teaching: one listens to all sorts of extraordinary debates about the superiority of the teaching machine over some other forms of teaching. Well, let us discriminate: what are we trying to teach? It then becomes immediately apparent that certain things can only be taught in a very intimate circle, whereas other things can obviously be taught *en masse*, via the air, via television, via teaching machines, and so on.

What scale is appropriate? It depends on what we are trying to do. The question of scale is extremely crucial today, in political, social and economic affairs just as in almost everything else. What, for instance, is the appropriate size of a city? And also, one might ask, what is the ap-

propriate size of a country? Now these are serious and difficult questions. It is not possible to programme a computer and get the answer. The really serious matters of life cannot be calculated. We cannot directly calculate what is right; but we jolly well know what is wrong! We can recognise right and wrong at the extremes, although we cannot normally judge them finely enough to say: 'This ought to be five per cent more; or that ought to be five per cent less.'

Take the question of size of a city. While one cannot judge these things with precision, I think it is fairly safe to say that the upper limit of what is desirable for the size of a city is probably something of the order of half a million inhabitants. It is quite clear that above such a size nothing is added to the virtue of the city. In places like London, or Tokyo, or New York, the millions do not add to the city's real value but merely create *enormous* problems and produce human degradation. So probably the order of magnitude of 500,000 inhabitants could be looked upon as the upper limit. The question of the lower limit of a real city is much more difficult to judge. The finest cities in history have been very small by twentieth-century standards. The instruments and institutions of city culture depend, no doubt, on a certain accumulation of wealth. But how much wealth has to be accumulated depends on the type of culture pursued. Philosophy, the arts and religion cost very, very little money. Other types of what claims to be 'high culture'—space research or ultra-modern physics—cost a lot of money, but are somewhat remote from the real needs of men.

I raise the question of the proper size of cities both for its own sake but also because it is, to my mind, the most relevant point when we come to consider the size of nations.

The idolatry of giantism that I have talked about is possibly one of the causes and certainly one of the effects of modern technology, particularly in matters of transport and communications. A highly developed transport and communications system has one immensely powerful effect: it makes people *footloose*.

Millions of people start moving about, deserting the rural areas and the smaller towns to follow the city lights, to go to the big city, causing a pathological growth. Take the country in which all this is perhaps most exemplified—the United States. Sociologists are studying the problem of 'megalopolis'. The word 'metropolis' is no longer big enough; hence 'megalopolis'. They freely talk about the polarisation of the population of the United States into three immense megalopolitan areas: one extending from Boston to Washington, a continuous built-up area, with sixty million people; one around Chicago, another sixty million; and one on the West Coast, from San Francisco to San Diego, again a continuous built-up area with sixty million people; the rest of the country being left practically empty; deserted provincial towns, and the land cultivated with vast tractors, combine harvesters, and immense amounts of chemicals.

If this is somebody's conception of the future of the United States, it is hardly a future worth having. But whether we like it or not, this is the result of people having become footloose; it is the result of that marvellous mobility of labour which economists treasure above all else.

Everything in this world has to have a *structure*, otherwise it is chaos. Before the advent of mass transport and mass communications, the structure was sim-ply there, because people were relatively immobile. People who wanted to move did so; witness the flood of saints from Ireland moving all over Europe. There were communications, there was mobility, but no footlooseness. Now, a great deal of structure has collapsed, and a country is like a big cargo ship in which the load is in no way secured. It tilts, and all the load slips over, and the ship founders.

One of the chief elements of structure for the whole of mankind is of course *the state*. And one of the chief elements or instruments of structuralisation (if I may use that term), is *frontiers*, national frontiers. Now previously, before this technological intervention, the relevance of frontiers was almost exclusively political and dynastic; frontiers were delimitations of political power, determining how many people you could raise for war. Economists fought against such frontiers becoming economic barriers— hence the ideology of free trade. But, then, people and things were not footloose; transport was expensive enough so that movements, both of people and of goods, were never more than marginal. Trade in the pre-industrial era was not a trade in essentials, but a trade in precious stones, precious metals, luxury goods, spices and—unhappily—slaves. The basic requirements of life had of course to be indigenously produced. And the movement of populations, except in periods of disaster, was confined to persons who had a very special reason to move, such as the Irish saints or the scholars of the University of Paris.

But now everything and everybody has become mobile. All structures are threatened, and all structures are *vulnerable* to an extent that they have never been before.

Economics, which Lord Keynes had hoped would settle down as a modest occupation similar to dentistry, suddenly becomes the most important subject of all. Economic policies absorb almost the entire attention of government, and at the same time become ever more impotent. The simplest things, which only fifty years ago one could do without difficulty, cannot get done any more. The richer a society, the more impossible it becomes to do worthwhile things without immediate pay-off. Economics has become such a thraldom that it absorbs almost the whole of foreign policy. People say, 'Ah yes, we don't like to go with these people, but we depend on them economically so we must humour them.' It tends to absorb the whole of ethics and to take precedence over all other human considerations. Now, quite clearly, this is a pathological development, which has, of course, many roots, but one of its clearly visible roots lies in the great achievements of modern technology in terms of transport and communications.

While people, with an easy-going kind of logic, believe that fast transport and instantaneous communications open up a new dimension of freedom (which they do in some rather trivial respects), they overlook the fact that these achievements also tend to destroy freedom, by making everything extremely vulnerable and extremely insecure, unless conscious policies are developed and conscious action is taken, to mitigate the destructive effects of these technological developments.

Now, these destructive effects are obviously most severe in *large* countries, because, as we have seen, frontiers produce 'structure', and it is a much bigger decision for someone to cross a frontier, to uproot himself from his native land and try and put down roots in another land, than to move within the frontiers of his country. The factor of footlooseness is, therefore, the more serious, the bigger the country. Its destructive effects can be traced both in the rich and in the poor countries. In the rich countries such as the United States of America, it produces, as already mentioned, 'megalopolis'. It also produces a rapidly increasing and ever more intractable problem of 'dropouts', of people, who, having become footloose, cannot find a place anywhere in society. Directly connected with this, it produces an appalling problem of crime, alienation, stress, social breakdown, right down to the level of the family. In the poor countries, again most severely in the largest ones, it produces mass migration into cities, mass unemployment, and, as vitality is drained out of the rural areas, the threat of famine. The result is a 'dual society' without any inner cohesion, subject to a maximum of political instability.

As an illustration, let me take the case of Peru. The capital city, Lima, situated on the Pacific coast, had a population of 175,000 in the early 1920s, just fifty years ago. Its population is now approaching three million. The once beautiful Spanish city is now infested by slums, surrounded by misery-belts that are crawling up the Andes. But this is not all. People are arriving from the rural areas at the rate of a thousand a day—and nobody knows what to do with them. The social or psychological structure of life in the hinterland has collapsed; people have become footloose and arrive in the capital city at the rate of a thousand a day to squat on some empty land, against the police who come to beat them out, to build their mud hovels and look for a job. *And nobody knows what to do about them.* Nobody knows how to stop the drift.

Imagine that in 1864 Bismarck had annexed the whole of Denmark instead of only a small part of it, and that nothing had happened since. The Danes would be an ethnic minority in Germany, perhaps struggling to maintain their language by becoming bilingual, the official language of course being German. Only by thoroughly Germanising themselves could they avoid becoming second-class citizens. There would be an irresistible drift of the most ambitious and enterprising Danes, thoroughly Germanised, to the mainland in the south, and what then would be the status of Copenhagen? That of a remote provincial city. Or imagine Belgium as part of France. What would be the status of Brussels? Again, that of an unimportant provincial city. I don't have to enlarge on it. Imagine now that Denmark a part of Germany, and Belgium a part of France, suddenly turned what is now charmingly called 'nats' wanting independence. There would be endless, heated arguments that these 'non-countries' could not be economically viable, that their desire for independence was, to quote a famous political commentator, 'adolescent emotionalism, political naivety, phoney economics, and sheer bare-faced opportunism'.

How can one talk about the economics of small independent countries? How can one discuss a problem that is a non-problem? There is no such thing as the viability of states or of nations, there is only a problem of viability of people: people, actual persons like you and me, are viable when they can stand on their own feet and earn their keep. You do not make non-viable people viable by putting large numbers of them into one huge community, and you do not make viable people non-viable by splitting a large community into a number of smaller, more intimate, more coherent and more manageable groups. All this is perfectly obvious and there is absolutely nothing to argue about. Some people ask: 'What happens when a country, composed of one rich province and several poor ones, falls apart because the rich province secedes?' Most probably the answer is: 'Nothing very much happens.' The rich will continue to be rich and the poor will continue to be poor. 'But if, before secession, the rich province had subsidised the poor, what happens then?' Well then, of course, the subsidy might stop. But the rich rarely subsidise the poor; more often they exploit them. They may not do so directly so much as through the terms of trade. They may obscure the situation a little by a certain redistribution of tax revenue or small-scale charity, but the last thing they want to do is to secede from the poor.

The normal case is quite different, namely that the poor provinces wish to separate from the rich, and that the rich want to hold on because they know that exploitation of the poor within one's own frontiers is infinitely easier than exploitation of the poor beyond them. Now if a poor province wishes to secede at the risk of losing some subsidies, what attitude should one take?

Not that we have to decide this, but what should be think about it? Is it not a wish to be applauded and respected? Do we not *want* people to stand on their own feet, as free and self-reliant men? So again this is a 'non-problem'. I would assert therefore that there is no problem of viability, as all experience shows. If a country wishes to export all over the world, and import from all over the world, it has never been held that it had to annex the whole world in order to do so.

What about the absolute necessity of having a large internal market? This again is an optical illusion if the meaning of 'large' is conceived in terms of political boundaries. Needless to say, a prosperous market is better than a poor one, but whether that market is outside the political boundaries or inside, makes on the whole very little difference. I am not aware, for instance, that Germany, in order to export a large number of Volkswagens to the United States, a very prosperous market, could only do so after annexing the United States. But it does make a lot of difference if a poor community or province finds itself politically tied to or ruled by a rich community or province. Why? Because, in a mobile, footloose society the law of disequilibrium is infinitely stronger than the so-called law of equilibrium. Nothing succeeds like success, and nothing stagnates like stagnation. The successful province drains the life out of the unsuccessful, and without protection against the strong, the weak have no chance; either they remain weak or they must migrate and join the strong; they cannot effectively help themselves.

A most important problem in the second half of the twentieth century is the geographical distribution of population, the question of 'regionalism'. But regionalism, not in the sense of combining a lot of states into free-trade systems, but in the opposite sense of developing all the regions within each country. This, in fact, is the most important subject on the agenda of all the larger countries today. And a lot of the nationalism of small nations today, and the desire for self-government and so-called independence, is simply a logical and rational response to the need for regional development. In the poor countries in particular there is no hope for the poor unless there is successful regional development, a development effort outside the capital city covering all the rural areas wherever people happen to be.

If this effort is not brought forth, their only choice is either to remain in their miserable condition where they are, or to migrate into the big city where their condition will be even more miserable. It is a strange phenomenon indeed that the conventional wisdom of present-day economics can do nothing to help the poor.

Invariably it proves that only such policies are viable as have in fact the result of making those already rich and powerful, richer and more powerful. It proves that industrial development only pays if it is as near as possible to the capital city or another very large town, and not in the rural areas. It proves that large projects are invariably more economic than small ones, and it proves that capital-intensive projects are invariably to be preferred as against labour-intensive ones. The economic calculus, as applied by present-day economics, forces the industrialist to eliminate the human factor because machines do not make mistakes which people do. Hence the enormous effort at automation and the drive for ever-larger units. This means that those who have nothing to sell but their labour remain in the weakest possible bargaining position. The conventional wisdom of what is now taught as economics by-passes the poor, the very people for whom development is really needed. The economics of giantism and automation is a left-over of nineteenth-century conditions and nineteenth-century thinking and it is totally incapable of solving any of the real problems of today. An entirely new system of thought is needed, a system based on attention to people, and not primarily attention to goods—(the goods will look after themselves!). It could be summed up in the phrase, 'production by the masses, rather than mass production'. What was impossible, however, in the nineteenth century, is possible now. And what was in fact—if not necessarily at least understandably—neglected in the nineteenth century is unbelievably urgent now. That is, the conscious utilisation of our enormous technological and scientific potential for the fight against misery and human degradation—a fight in intimate contact with actual people, with individuals, families, small groups, rather than states and other anonymous abstractions. And this presupposes a political and organisational structure that can provide this intimacy.

What is the meaning of democracy, freedom, human dignity, standard of living, self-realisation, fulfilment? Is it a matter of goods, or of people? Of course it is a matter of people. But people can be themselves only in small comprehensible groups. Therefore we must learn to think in terms of an articulated structure that can cope with a multiplicity of small-scale units. If economic thinking cannot grasp this it is useless. If it cannot get beyond its vast abstractions, the national income, the rate of growth, capital/output ratio, input-output analysis, labour mobility, capital accumulation; if it cannot get beyond all this and make contact with the human realities of poverty, frustration, alienation, despair, breakdown, crime, escapism, stress, congestion, ugliness, and spiritual death, then let us scrap economics and start afresh.

Are there not indeed enough 'signs of the times' to indicate that a new start is needed?

NOTES

1. *The New Burma* (Economic and Social Board, Government of the Union of Burma, 1954)
2. *Ibid*
3. *Ibid*
4. *Wealth of Nations* by Adam Smith
5. *Art and Swadeshi* by Ananda K. Coomaraswamy (Ganesh & Co., Madras)
6. *Economy of Permanence* by J. C. Kumarappa (Sarva-Seva Sangh Publication, Rajghat, Kashi, 4th edn., 1958)
7. *The Affluent Society* by John Kenneth Galbraith (Penguin Books Ltd., 1962)
8. *A Philosophy of Indian Economic Development* by Richard B. Gregg (Navajivan Publishing House, Ahmedabad, 1958)
9. *The Challenge of Man's Future* by Harrison Brown (The Viking Press, New York, 1954)

POSTSCRIPT

Should the Less Developed Countries Be Encouraged to Develop High Technology?

Historically, Toffler's view seems to be supported: no nation has consciously adopted low-technology alternative lifestyles and had them survive competition with the high-technology alternatives next door. Although small religious communities have managed to maintain low-technology alternatives for several generations, they are currently threatened and eroding. But Schumacher's point remains valid: a community's lifestyle *is* a matter of human choice. Although most humans will choose to live in an advanced consumer economy, it still remains a choice; people are free to choose alternative ways of living, including one absent of high technology.

What would you prefer to do for the rest of your life once you stop being a student? The following is a likely possibility. You would have a job that you can wake up looking forward to. You would have work that challenges your mind, your body, your talents, and your creativity; in short, work that will stretch you to become all that you can. You would work (at least occasionally) with others and share with them the effort, the thinking, and the joy of accomplishment that goes with the job. You would work in surroundings that you consider pleasant and supportive. You would produce something that is good, beautiful, and useful for human life and activity. The value of the product, of course, would return enough profit to allow you to survive, have a family, and live comfortably throughout your life. How does this last point connect with all the other points, or does it? Do people work to be paid, or do they work because that is one of the most human and fulfilling activities they can do? How does this scenario fit in with Toffler's view of the world? Schumacher's?

SUGGESTED READINGS

Harrison Brown, *The Challenge of Man's Future* (1954, Reprint, Westview, 1984).

E. F. Schumacher, *Small Is Beautiful: Economics as If People Mattered* (Harper & Row, 1973).

Philip Slater, *The Pursuit of Loneliness: American Culture at the Breaking Point* (Beacon Press, 1976).

Alvin Toffler, *Future Shock* (Random House, 1970).

CONTRIBUTORS
TO THIS VOLUME

EDITORS

LISA H. NEWTON is a professor of philosophy and the director of the Program in Applied Ethics at Fairfield University in Fairfield, Connecticut. She received a B.S. in philosophy, with honors, from Columbia University in 1962 and a Ph.D. from Columbia in 1967. She was an assistant professor of philosophy at Hofstra University in Hempstead, New York, from 1967 to 1969, and she began teaching at Fairfield University in 1969. Professor Newton's articles have appeared in *Ethics* and the *Journal of Business Ethics*, among other publications. She is a member of the American Philosophical Association, the Academy of Management, and the American Society of Law and Medicine. Professor Newton currently serves as president of the Society for Business Ethics.

MAUREEN M. FORD is an associate for the Program in Applied Ethics at Fairfield University in Fairfield, Connecticut. She received a B.S. in business management and applied ethics from Fairfield University. Active as a consultant to community agencies, Mrs. Ford is a former president of the YWCA in Bridgeport, Connecticut, and was for several years vice president–secretary for JHLF, Inc., a marketing and consulting firm in Westport, Connecticut.

AUTHORS

FREDRICK R. ABRAMS is the director of the Clinical Ethics Consultation Group in Englewood, Colorado.

GEORGE J. ANNAS is the Edward R. Utley Professor of Law and Medicine at Boston University's Schools of Medicine and Public Health in Boston, Massachusetts. He is also the director of Boston University's Law, Medicine, and Ethics Program and the chair of the Health Law Department. His publications include *Judging Medicine* (Humana Press, 1988) and *Standard of Care: The Law of American Bioethics* (Oxford University Press, 1993).

CYNTHIA A. BELTZ is a technology policy analyst at the American Enterprise Institute in Washington, D.C., a nonprofit public policy research institute. She recently testified before the U.S. House of Representatives Budget and Science Committees on American living standards and on the problems of high-technology targeting. She is the editor of *Financing Entrepreneurs* (AEI Press, 1994), and her articles on technology and trade policy have appeared in the *New York Times,* the *Los Angeles Times,* the *Journal of Commerce,* and *Reason.*

SISSELA BOK is a faculty member of the Center for Advanced Study in the Behavioral Sciences in Stanford, California, and a former associate professor of philosophy at Brandeis University in Waltham, Massachusetts. Her publications include *Lying: Moral Choice in Public and Private Life* (Random House, 1979), *Secrets: On the*

Ethics of Concealment and Revelation (Vintage Books, 1983), and *A Strategy for Peace: Human Values and the Threat of War* (Pantheon Books, 1989).

THOMAS L. CARSON is an associate professor of philosophy at the Loyola University of Chicago in Chicago, Illinois. He has written numerous articles on ethical theory and business ethics, and he is the author of *The Status of Morality* (Kluwer Academic Publishers, 1984).

DOUG CLEMENT is a former coordinator of the National Infant Formula Action Coalition (INFACT).

ROGER CRISP received a B.A. and a B.Phil. at Oxford University in Oxford, England. He has published several articles on practical ethics.

MARK DOWIE has received numerous journalism awards for his investigative reporting, including the National Magazine Award from the Columbia University School of Journalism for his article "Pinto Madness." His interests are in investigating and exposing business and government practices that are legal "but nonetheless reprehensible." He is a regular contributor to *American Health* magazine and the author of *We Have a Donor: The Bold New World of Organ Transplants* (St. Martin's Press, 1988).

JOHN ECHEVERRIA is a legal counsel to the National Audubon Society in New York City. A 1981 graduate of the Yale Law School and the Yale School of Forestry and Environmental Studies, he has also been a legal counsel and conservation director of American Rivers, Inc., and he has served as a law clerk to U.S. district judge Gerhard A. Gesell.

RICHARD EPSTEIN is the James Parker Hall Distinguished Service Professor of Law at the University of Chicago in Chicago, Illinois, where he has been teaching since 1972. He has been a member of the American Academy of Arts and Sciences since 1985 and a senior fellow of the Center for Clinical Medical Ethics at the University of Chicago Medical School since 1983. He has written numerous articles on a wide range of legal and interdisciplinary subjects, and he is the author of *Forbidden Grounds: The Case Against Employment Discrimination Laws* (Harvard University Press, 1992).

FARMERS FOR AN ORDERLY MARKET, a coalition of citrus growers from California and Arizona, including Sunkist Growers, Inc., was formed in April 1985 to defend the citrus marketing system of flow-to-market regulation, which was established by the Agricultural Marketing Agreement Act of 1937, and to counter arguments for free-enterprise deregulation being made in the press by dissatisfied citrus marketers.

HUGH M. FINNERAN (d. 1985) was the senior labor counsel for PPG Industries, Inc., a *Fortune* 500 company based in Pittsburgh, Pennsylvania, that manufactures paints, glass, printing inks, paper coatings, varnishes, and adhesives, as well as many other products.

GEOFFREY FOOKES is a vice president of Nestlé Nutrition. He has been intimately involved in the infant formula controversy from 1973 onward, having had extensive field experience in Third World infant formula marketing.

MARK GREEN is New York City's commissioner of Consumer Affairs. He has published 14 books on government, business, and law, including *There He Goes Again: Ronald Reagan's Reign of Error* (Pantheon Books, 1983), coauthored with Gail MacColl.

LaRUE TONE HOSMER is a professor of corporate strategies in the Graduate School of Business Administration at the University of Michigan in Ann Arbor, Michigan.

ROBERT A. LARMER is an associate professor of philosophy at the University of New Brunswick in Fredericton, New Brunswick, Canada. His research interests focus on the philosophy of religion, the philosophy of the mind, and on business ethics. He has written numerous articles in these fields, and he is the author of *Water Into Wine: An Investigation of the Concept of Miracle* (McGill-Queens University Press, 1988). He received a Ph.D. from the University of Ottawa.

DAVID R. LARSON is an associate professor in the Faculty of Religion at Loma Linda University in Loma Linda, California, and a codirector of the Loma Linda University Center for Christian Bioethics.

CAROLYN LOCHHEAD is a former reporter on the news staff for *Insight* magazine.

JOHN LUIK is a senior associate in the corporate values and ethics programs of the Niagara Institute in Niagara-on-the-Lake, Ontario, Canada. He has also served as an ethics consultant to a number of government institutions, professional organizations, and corporations. He received degrees in politics and philosophy from Oxford University, and he has held academic appointments at the University of Oxford, the University of Manitoba, and Brock University. In addition to the ethics of advertising, his research interests include business ethics, medical ethics, environmental ethics, political philosophy, and the philosophy of Immanuel Kant.

MAGGIE McCOMAS is a business writer and a public affairs analyst. She first developed an interest in the Third World infant formula controversy while conducting research for the study "Europe's Consumer Movement: Key Issues and Corporate Responses," published by Business International S.A. (Geneva).

JENNIFER MOORE is a former assistant professor of philosophy at the University of Delaware in Newark, Delaware. She has done teaching and research in business ethics and business law, and she is a coeditor, with W. Michael Hoffman, of *Business Ethics: Readings and Cases in Corporate Morality*, 2d ed. (McGraw-Hill, 1990).

JAMES NEAL has served as a lawyer in many mass disaster and product liability cases, including the Ford Pinto suit and *The Twilight Zone* movie accident trial.

JOHN O'TOOLE is the president of the American Association of Advertising Agencies in New York City. He has had a long career in advertising, and he remained with the firm of Foote, Cone & Belding Communications, Inc., for 31 years, serving 5 of those years as chair of the board.

FRANK A. OLSON is the chair of the board and the chief executive officer of the Hertz Corporation in Park Ridge, New Jersey, and a former John M. Olin Fellow of the Olin Papers/Olin Fellows Program at Fairfield University in Fairfield, Connecticut. He is also a director of the UAL Corporation, Becton Dickinson and Company, and Cooper Industries.

THE PHARMACEUTICAL MANUFACTURERS ASSOCIATION, founded in 1958 and located in Washington, D.C., is an association of 93 manufacturers of pharmaceutical and biological products that are distributed under their own labels. It encourages high standards for quality control and good manufacturing practices, research toward the development of new and better medical products, and the enactment of uniform and reasonable drug legislation for the protection of public health.

MICHAEL PHILIPS is a professor of philosophy at Portland State University in Portland, Oregon. A member of the Society for the Study of Business and Professional Ethics, he is a contributor to such publications as *Philosophical Studies*, the *Canadian Journal of Philosophy*, the *Journal of Business Ethics*, and *Ethics*.

ROBERT ROCHE is the manager of proposals at Foster Wheeler Power Systems, Inc.

E. F. SCHUMACHER (1911–1977) was a Rhodes Scholar in economics, an adviser to the British Control Commission in postwar Germany, and, for 20 years prior to 1971, the top economist and director of statistics for Britain's National Coal Board. He was also the founder and chairperson of the Intermediate Technology Development Group in London, England, which was founded to assist underdeveloped countries in establishing alternative growth plans that were feasible, not exploitative of the environment, and humane.

NEIL SELDMAN is the cofounder and president of the Institute for Local Self-Reliance in Washington, D.C., which advises city and state governments, citizen groups, and private industry on approaches to municipal and solid waste management that respect environmental quality and create economic development opportunities for minority youth, community organizations, and small businesses. He has also served on advisory panels for the Office of Technology Assessment. He is the coauthor, with Lawrence R. Martin, of *An Environmental Review of Incineration Technologies* (Institute for Local Self-Reliance, 1986).

JOHN SHORTSLEEVE is the vice president of marketing at Foster Wheeler Power Systems, Inc.

RICHARD A. SPINELLO is an associate dean of faculties and an adjunct assistant professor of philosophy at Boston College in Chestnut Hill, Massachusetts. He has written numerous articles on business ethics and ethical theory and on the social implications of new information retrieval technologies, and he is the author of a textbook on computer ethics entitled *Ethical Aspects of Information Technology* (Prentice Hall, 1994).

GEORGE TAUCHER is a professor of business administration at the International Management Development Institute in Lausanne, Switzerland, and a visiting fellow at the Oxford Management Center.

LESTER THUROW is a professor in the Sloan School of Management at the Massachusetts Institute of Technology in Cambridge, Massachusetts. He received M.A. degrees from Balliol College and Harvard University in 1960 and 1964, respectively, and he received a Ph.D. from Harvard University in 1964. He is the author of *Poverty and Discrimination* (Brookings Institution, 1969), for which he won the David A. Wells Prize from Harvard University, and of *Generating Inequality: The Distributional Mechanisms of the Economy* (Basic Books, 1975).

ALVIN TOFFLER is a social commentator whose writings on future trends in global industry, government, communications, and learning have had a wide impact on government, business, and university leaders in many nations. His best-selling books *Future Shock* (Bantam Books, 1971) and *The Third Wave* (William Morrow, 1980) have been published in some 30 languages.

MICHAEL T. TUCKER is an associate professor of finance at Fairfield University in Fairfield, Connecticut, the personal finance editor at *Black Elegance* magazine, and a business consultant. His current publishing and research interests are in the area of international finance and global ecology, and he has published many scholarly articles in finance and business.

MICHAEL A. VERESPEJ is a writer for *Industry Week*.

RICHARD WASSERSTROM is a professor of philosophy at the University of California, Santa Cruz, and the chair of the California Council for the Humanities. He has published in the areas of moral philosophy, social philosophy, law, and race relations, and he is the author of *Today's Moral Problems*, 2d ed. (Macmillan, 1979) and *Philosophy and Social Issues: Five Studies* (University of Notre Dame Press, 1980).

INDEX